DUBAI

To my beloved Dubai, from a loyal but critical friend

CHRISTOPHER M. DAVIDSON

Dubai

The Vulnerability of Success

Columbia University Press
New York

Columbia University Press
Publishers Since 1893
New York

Library of Congress Cataloging-in-Publication Data

Davidson, Christopher M.
  Dubai : the vulnerability of success / Christopher M. Davidson.
     p. cm.
  ISBN 978-0-231-70034-4 (cloth : alk. paper)
  1. Dubayy (United Arab Emirates : Emirate)—History 2. Dubayy
(United Arab Emirates : Emirate)—Economic conditions.
  3. United Arab Emirates—Foreign relations. I. Title.

  DS247.D78D28 2008
  953.57—dc22

                                        2008007558

∞
Columbia University Press books are printed on permanent and durable acid-free paper.
This book is printed on paper with recycled content.
Printed in India

c 10 9 8 7 6 5 4 3 2 1

CONTENTS

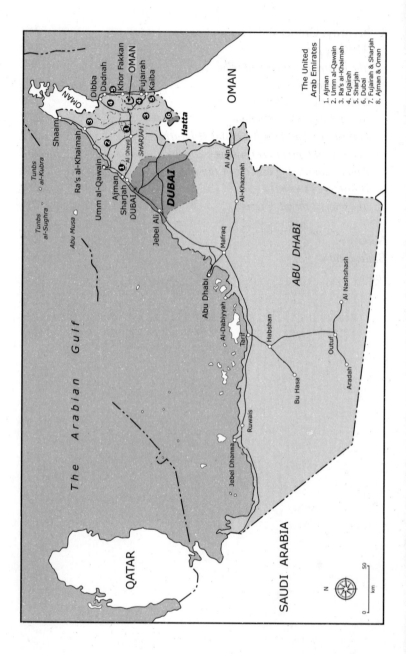

The United
Arab Emirates

1. Ajman
2. Umm al-Qawain
3. Ra's al-Khaimah
4. Fujairah
5. Sharjah
6. Dubai
7. Fujairah & Sharjah
8. Ajman & Oman

INTRODUCTION

Dubai is a remarkable success story. From its origins as a small fishing and pearling community in the early nineteenth century, the emirate's eponymous city has gone from strength to strength, having established itself as the premier trading entrepôt of the Persian Gulf by the beginning of the twentieth century and, in recent years, having boomed into a massive metropolis of more than two million people, most of whom are expatriates working in an increasingly multi-sector economy. Although oil wealth was the initial catalyst, allowing Dubai to gamble on investing in the infrastructure that facilitated the rapid socio-economic development of the 1970s and 1980s, it is really the emirate's pioneering model for post-oil development that has been most noteworthy. Indeed, faced with dwindling hydrocarbon reserves, since the mid-1990s Dubai has effectively diversified to the extent that non-oil related GDP contributions are now well over 90%.[1] This diversification has relied upon a balance of components including the ongoing expansion of Dubai's commercial infrastructure, the encouragement of light, import-substitution industrialisation, the introduction of a variety of specialist 'free zones', the aggressive promotion of a luxury tourist sector, and, in just the last few years, the groundbreaking launch of a freehold real estate market. Combined, these strategies have achieved much: the emirate has attracted the highest per capita levels of foreign direct investment of any Arab market,[2] the critics have been silenced, and Dubai is seemingly on track to join Hong Kong and Singapore as another

1

'global city' that will soon serve as a major command point in the organisation of the world economy.[3]

Crucially, this development has taken place against a backdrop of near complete political stability—a rarity in the region and undoubtedly a vital ingredient of Dubai's ongoing accomplishments. Reputable business intelligence publications now consistently rank Dubai very high against other global markets for 'short term political stability',[4] and have often placed the emirate in first or second place among Middle Eastern countries for its 'stable macroeconomic environment and institutional structures'.[5] Moreover, till recently Dubai's political history has always been celebrated for its careful management of regional and international relations, directed by an astute and flexible ruling dynasty. Although a constituent member of the United Arab Emirates since 1971, along with neighbouring Abu Dhabi and Sharjah, and the less populous emirates of Ra's al-Khaimah, Fujairah, Ajman, and Umm al-Qawain, Dubai has always managed to remain somewhat autonomous, preferring a loose confederation to a true federation. Indeed, the emirate has ensured that it retains a distinct national identity, controls its own natural resources, and maintains command of its largely independent development path. Thus, now more than ever before, Dubai warrants individual attention.

This book is not a storm warning, nor does it seek to detract from any of Dubai's extraordinary achievements. Instead my aim is to highlight several key problems that lie beneath the emirate's glittering façade. While some of the pathologies I describe are widely recognised, both domestically and internationally, many are most certainly not, and require much greater examination. Hence I hope that *Dubai: The Vulnerability of Success* will promote a greater awareness of the past and present of the emirate and help to offset the current literary imbalance resulting from the preponderance of Dubai-related hagiographies, conventional narratives, and other state-sanctioned materials.[6] Indeed, for the emirate to survive and to prosper as a truly modern entity, as a sophisticated twenty-first century city, and as a genuine player in the global economy, the time has come to subject it to a more detailed level of scrutiny and independent analysis

Structure of the book

The first chapter provides an historical overview of Dubai, describing its origins as a breakaway sheikhdom from the larger entity of Abu Dhabi, and accounting for its survival as a small state sandwiched between competing regional powers and the distant authority of the British Empire. Particular emphasis is placed on the political and economic structures of the nineteenth and early twentieth centuries, especially those that served as important antecedents to more contemporary structures, namely the long history of pre-oil 'rentier' wealth and Britain's careful management of client elites. The chapter also details the considerable indigenous resistance to these British-protected rulers, including the early attempts to initiate autonomous development outside of British networks and the efforts to reduce the powers of the monarchy.

The second chapter explores the catalytic role played by nationalism and the need for collective security in the years preceding Britain's withdrawal from the Gulf. The lower Gulf is not normally associated with fervent Arab nationalism, yet ideologies combined with local misgivings were sufficient to support an increasingly critical and violent 'National Front'. Left unchecked, such an organisation would have likely broken the British client system and destabilised the region. The various short-term containment strategies employed by the British and the rulers are considered, before an examination of the more durable solution of integrating Dubai into a regional federation of emirates capable of withstanding external interference and encroachment.

The third chapter considers Dubai's early economic development, emphasising the sheikhdom's emergence as the primary trading hub of the lower Gulf at the turn of the twentieth century, its rulers' historical preference for laissez-faire strategies, and their farsighted recognition of the need for investing in physical and commercial infrastructure. Connected to these successes, the chapter demonstrates how Dubai soon became the most attractive business environment in the region and subsequently benefited from a stream of skilled immigrant businessmen from the unstable Persian coast, from its less progressive neighbours, Sharjah and Abu Dhabi, and eventually from further afield. Indeed, it is shown that the emirate's remarkable entrepreneurial prominence is far from a recent phenomenon, and owes much to its fostering of an international merchant population long before the first oil exports.

The fourth chapter examines Dubai's economic development since the 1970s, beginning with an overview of its oil industry, and followed by a discussion of the emirate's growing realisation of the need to diversify its economic base and break free from some of the more harmful aspects of its dependency. Dubai has channelled much of its oil wealth into further improving infrastructure, thereby allowing it to pursue its commercial ambitions well into the next century, while also facilitating the launch of a new development model centred around other, non-oil related economic sectors including light manufacturing, foreign direct investment free zones, tourism, and, most notably, real estate.

The fifth chapter explains the remarkable durability of Dubai's essentially traditional polity and, crucially, its ongoing political stability — a key precondition for the emirate's ambitious economic reforms. Emphasis is placed on Dubai's particular brand of the non-democratic 'ruling bargain', and the specific components that make up this carefully balanced legitimacy formula are highlighted. These include personal resources and the resilience of the ruling Al-Maktum family; the patrimonial and neo-patrimonial resources employed by the state; the ideological, religious, and cultural resources utilised by the rulers; and above all the material component of this bargain in which oil rent and, with diversification, new forms of rentier activity are able to guarantee political acquiescence.

The sixth chapter considers the more damaging pathologies associated with this ruling bargain and the new development model. In particular, it assesses the negative effects of the rentier component of the legitimacy formula on Dubai's development, namely the persistence of an unproductive mentality and the over-reliance on distributive rather than extractive government functions. Moreover, the chapter focuses on the weaknesses of some of the new economic sectors, including their failure to alleviate Dubai's dependency on foreign economies, while also assessing the paradoxical impact of the required economic reforms on the emirate's non-material legitimacy resources. In addition, the chapter considers the effects of the much larger and seemingly less culturally compatible expatriate populations being drawn to Dubai's diverse sectors, and the long-term implications for the emirate's labour nationalisation strategies. Finally, an examination is made of the weakened state of civil society in the emirate and its interplay with both the ruling bargain and the newly liberalised economy.

The seventh chapter places Dubai's development and political stability within the wider context of the UAE federation, with a special focus on the long-running contest between emirate-level and central powers, and with an appreciation of Dubai's new found role as something of a post-modern city state with fewer needs for collective security and federal support. Subsequently, the chapter details various complications and instabilities in Dubai's closest neighbours, including financial scandals, decision-making blunders, and historical rulership contests in Abu Dhabi, Sharjah, and Ra's al-Khaimah. Most worryingly, it is shown that certain aspects of these power struggles remain unresolved today, and future flare-ups could undermine the foreign direct investment-reliant components of Dubai's development model.

The eighth chapter examines the external and internal threats faced by Dubai. An assessment is made of the emirate's defensive capabilities, within the context of the Abu Dhabi-led UAE Armed Forces, followed by a discussion of the numerous regional disputes and conflicts that continue to involve both directly and indirectly Dubai and its federal partners. Furthermore, the chapter revisits the ideological component of the ruling bargain by assessing the advantages and disadvantages of relying upon a western military umbrella. Finally, the internal threat is considered by investigating both the emirate's historical and contemporary role as a hub for criminal organisations and, perhaps most worryingly, its volatile relationship with various terrorist groups and its strategies for containing such menaces.

The chapters all seek to illustrate the increasing complexity of evaluating Dubai theoretically, especially given that in some senses it still cannot be considered a nation state. Specifically, they demonstrate that the emirate's persisting 'peripheral' economic structures continue to rely on neo-imperial core economies (initially Britain, and now most of Western Europe, the USA, and Japan), and therefore Dubai remains dependent on these 'metropoles' for its economic livelihood, albeit now from foreign direct investment and luxury tourism rather than the more straightforward hydrocarbon exports of the recent past. Further connected to such classical dependency theory,[7] sections of these chapters also highlight the deepening dependency of the client elite; a historical process that began over 170 years ago and which, at least according to some observers, is now increasingly being associated with the super-exploitation of the broader national population. Indeed, there remain many indigent Dubai nationals despite the distributive rentier wealth components of the implicit ruling bargain, and there now exists a growing concern among more outspoken nationals that entire districts of the city and their emirate are effectively 'out of bounds': they have become exclusive enclaves for foreign rent-seekers and tourists, and were clearly never created with nationals in mind. Confusingly, however, it is shown that Dubai can no longer completely fit into such orthodox dependency modelling given that other metropoles have now emerged alongside the traditional core. Although it is clear that most of the elite's strength and security arrangements are still drawn from western external sources, the latter chapters demonstrate that in recent years the emirate has also been subjected to much pressure from other powerful forces, including the international criminal fraternity and, by association, the international terror network. This predicament being partly due to the elite's conflicting ideological, cultural, and religious legitimacy resources, and partly due to the emirate's somewhat unfortunate geographic location—although widely marketed as being an ideal 'bridge between east and west', Dubai is between a rock and a hard place, surrounded by extremely unstable neighbours and the elements within them. These must be appeased. And while most of the development successes described in the earlier chapters can be directly attributed to the emirate's openness and the laissez-faire attitudes of its government over the last century, the hidden cost of this enormous freedom is the city's ongoing attractiveness as a logistical hub for these other, potentially more dangerous power blocs. Essentially, Dubai has to respond in two directions, and now walks a tightrope of dual-core dependency from which it cannot step down— or at least not until a sounder strategy has been prepared.

1
THE BIRTH OF A SHEIKHDOM

In the nineteenth and early twentieth centuries the tiny settlement of Dubai metamorphosed from little more than a fishing
and pearl diving base into a fully fledged sheikhdom with political
stability, an established ruling dynasty, and a key role to play in
a strategically significant region. This chapter charts a remarkable path, beginning with Dubai's humble origins as a vulnerable
breakaway state surrounded by more powerful neighbours, before
turning to the ruling family's early relationship with Britain and
its increasing reliance on imperial support for security guarantees
and, eventually, its economic well being. On several occasions the
ruling family faced significant internal opposition, firstly from
merchants attempting to initiate autonomous development and
reduce dependency on imperial networks, and then more seriously from reformers intent on limiting monarchical power and
destabilising what was increasingly perceived to be a British-
sponsored regime. Finally, it will be demonstrated how Britain
managed to steer Dubai through this troubled period, supporting
and strengthening her preferred clients whenever necessary.

The early struggle

Since the mid-eighteenth century a small village had existed at
the mouth of the most prominent natural water inlet in the lower
Persian Gulf. By the early nineteenth century, little had really

changed, with only a few palm frond *barasti* huts lining the shores of this creek. While the original name of the settlement has now become something of a mystery, it seems likely that it was named either after a type of locust, the *daba*, which frequently infested the area;[1] after a snake-eating mastigure lizard referred to locally as a *dhub*; or after a combination of the Hindi word *doh* (two) and the Arabic word *bayt* (house) in reference to two white houses which supposedly stood side by side close to the estuary's mouth.[2]

At this time, what little there was of Dubai fell loosely under the sovereignty of the Bani Yas, a powerful tribal conglomeration whose influence stretched along the coast as far west as the Qatari peninsula and deep into the hinterland. Dominated by the Al-Bu Falah clan and, by the 1790s, ruled by Sheikh Shakhbut bin Dhiyab of the clan's constituent Al-Nahyan family,[3] the Bani Yas had shifted their capital from the interior village of Al-Mariyah near the chain of Liwa oases to an island rich in brown gazelles or *dhabi*, and with its own freshwater source.[4] Shakhbut's sheikhdom, eventually known as Abu Dhabi, together with its Omani allies had become locked into a struggle for supremacy over the littoral of the lower Gulf with another major power group led by the Qawasim or Al-Qasimi clan of Ra's al-Khaimah in the north. The Qawasim's influence extended into the Musandam peninsula and even across to possessions on the Persian coastline, including the ports of Lingah and Al-Muhammarah, and the agricultural town of Disghgan in the province of Fars.[5] Crucially, Qawasim power also reached as far south as Sharjah, a larger settlement just a few miles away from Dubai, and there are accounts of the Qawasim occasionally seizing Dubai before being driven back again by the Bani Yas.[6] Thus, Dubai's earliest history was essentially one of subordination to either one or the other of these two blocs.

Within just a few years, however, the region's balance of power was transformed irrevocably following a conflagration between so-called Qawasim 'pirates' and the English East India Company.[7] Since the 1750s the Company had succeeded in closing most of

France's trading posts in India,[8] had become a tax and army-raising territorial power after it took over governments in Bengal, Bihar, and Orissa,[9] and had effectively established a monopoly over all overseas trade routes to the subcontinent, including the highly profitable sea lanes between Bombay and Basra.[10] Controversially, by 1760 the Qawasim had set up a trading post at Basidu on the strategic island of Qishm, close to the entrance of the Gulf, and had begun to ply the lucrative Indian trade route. Persia, the Company's erstwhile ally in the region,[11] was unable to intervene as its sphere of influence was declining due to security distractions along its northern frontiers,[12] thereby allowing this new Qawasim base to survive and prosper. With intimate knowledge of the local waters and winds these Arab traders were renowned for undercutting and outperforming the Company's shipping. Faced with declining trade receipts,[13] the Company began to accumulate evidence of Arab 'pirate depredations' with the intention of requesting Royal Navy assistance in suppressing their Qawasim rivals. Over time, hundreds of letters were despatched from Bombay to London, most of which held the Qawasim responsible for almost every incidence of damaged or missing British Indian trade vessels.[14] So successful was the campaign that by the turn of the nineteenth century the lower Gulf was referred to throughout the Empire as the 'Pirate Coast', regardless of the validity of the Company's claims.[15]

Following two token coastal bombardments of Qawasim installations in 1809 and 1816,[16] the Royal Navy finally came to the Company's assistance in 1820, chiefly in response to Britain's increasing fear that the so-called pirates had formed an alliance with the powerful religious-military Wahhabi movement.[17] The concern was that the Wahhabis, by extending their influence from the hinterland into the coastal towns, were aiming to rid the Gulf of 'anti-Muslim influences', including, most worryingly for the British, the Sultan of Muscat[18] — their key ally in the region.[19] A large task force of over 7,000 Omani soldiers and British officers landed on the beaches of Ra's al-Khaimah while the Royal Navy shelled the walls of the forts,[20] and after several hours of hand-to-hand combat the Qawasim sheikhs capitulated and entered into peace treaty negotiations. Simultaneous attacks had also been launched on other suspect pirate bases, including nearby Zaya and the port of Lingah (the latter having been attacked in error, it would seem, given that Britain later compensated the rulers of Lingah for damages),[21] before the task force swept down the coast attacking bases in Umm al-Qawain, Ajman, and finally Sharjah.[22] Crucially, British attacks went no further, and Dubai was spared any damage. Indeed, when members of the task force explored beyond Sharjah, they reportedly met peacefully with the Bani Yas governor of Dubai, Sheikh Muhammad bin Hazza Al-Nahyan, and promptly signed a peace treaty with his uncle, Sheikh Zayed bin Saif Al-Nahyan. Thus, in Dubai's case at least, the arrival of British power in the lower Gulf was a positive development: Dubai began a constructive relationship with the new external power and was immediately relieved from further Qawasim pressure and incursions, as Ra's al-Khaimah was forced to struggle for its own survival.

A breakaway state

When the Political Resident (Britain's most senior representative in the Gulf) made his first visit to the lower Gulf in the late 1820s, he confirmed in his reports the official tributary status of Dubai to Abu Dhabi (and in turn Abu Dhabi's acknowledgement of Omani supremacy).[23] He also remarked that as a town, Dubai already appeared to be fairly autonomous, with the dwellings of its 1,200 or so residents entirely surrounding the governor's small fort, and with three independently-controlled watchtowers complete with old Portuguese cannons guarding the main routes into the town.[24] Within just a few more years this apparent autonomy became something very real following a violent quarrel amongst

Abu Dhabi's leaders and a subsequent schism within the greater Bani Yas.

Although still alive, Sheikh Shakhbut bin Dhiyab Al-Nahyan had long since transferred power to his eldest sons, first Sheikh Muhammad bin Shakhbut Al-Nahyan, and then the more popular and charismatic Sheikh Tahnun bin Shakhbut Al-Nahyan.[25] In early 1833, Tahnun was assassinated by two of his younger half-brothers, Sheikh Khalifa bin Shakhbut Al-Nahyan and Sheikh Sultan bin Shakhbut Al-Nahyan, both of whom had returned from a period of exile after an earlier attempt to question Tahnun's authority.[26] Although Khalifa did eventually receive the support of his father and, more pertinently, recognition from the Sultan of Muscat, his position remained precarious given the population's admiration for the deceased Tahnun. Indeed, within months of his accession, Khalifa was forced to suppress two attempted coups, the first of these being a fairly straightforward filial challenge from two of Tahnun's full brothers,[27] but the second being far more complex, involving a number of cousins, merchants, and other powerful Bani Yas men,[28] including a certain Maktum bin Buti.[29] The revenge wreaked by Khalifa on the many conspirators may have consolidated his position as ruler of Abu Dhabi in the short term, but the general discontent arising from the violence and subjugation prompted the secession of nearly 1,000 tribesmen from Abu Dhabi in the summer of that year, perhaps representing one fifth of the sheikhdom's population.[30] Most were from the Qubaysat and Rumaithi sections of the Bani Yas,[31] but with the most prominent rebels being drawn from Maktum bin Buti's parent Al-Bu Falasah section—a clan originating from the Al-Sa'rah oasis in Buraimi and from the islands of Bateen and Tarut.[32] Maktum, together with his uncle, Ubaid bin Said Al-Falasi, led their band of exiles up the coast and settled in Dubai, thereby doubling the town's population. The two men assumed joint rulership of Dubai until 1836, when Ubaid died and Maktum became sole leader, thereby establishing the Al-Maktum dynasty.[33] In a daring

13

move, Maktum attempted to formalise Dubai's independence as
a sheikhdom by sending Khalifa a forged letter using the elderly
Shakhbut's seal (in this case a ring) which claimed that Shakhbut,
and by extension Oman, had authorised Maktum's sovereignty
over Dubai. An infuriated Khalifa sought to re-capture Dubai
and remove Maktum from power but was thwarted by the personal intervention of the Qawasim ruler, Shaikh Sultan bin Saqr
Al-Qasimi. Although weakened by the British, the Qawasim
were still prepared to head off challenges from Abu Dhabi, and
much preferred to have an autonomous Dubai serving as a border
zone buffer state.[34] As such, those who had historically been ag-
gressors towards Dubai became the protectors of its newly won
independence. Maktum seized upon this window of opportunity
and immediately set about upgrading Dubai's defences, should
the status quo shift: new town walls were constructed and, as recent archaeological excavations have confirmed, new guard towers
were constructed around the entrance to the creek.[35]

Safeguarding neutrality

The new Al-Maktum sheikhs soon proved themselves to be
shrewd negotiators and masters of regional alliances, managing
to consolidate their position further and fend off major attacks
by continuing to balance their opponents against each other. By
the late-1830s the Qawasim-Abu Dhabi tension had erupted
into a tribal war, with Dubai caught in the middle, yet still able
to capitalise upon its neutrality. Indeed, with neither of the two
main powers emerging victorious, one of the Qawasim's conditions upon agreeing to a cease fire was that Sheikh Khalifa bin
Shakhbut Al-Nahyan had to make the 'bitter concession' of formally recognising Dubai's secession from Abu Dhabi.[36] Although
Khalifa quickly reneged, by attacking Dubai again in 1838,[37] and
in 1839 attempting to gain British support for the reassertion of
his authority over Dubai,[38] both actions were unsuccessful in the
face of Qawasim opposition.[39]

Perhaps most dramatically, when in 1840 it became apparent that Abu Dhabi and the Qawasim had settled some of their differences and were plotting to overthrow the Al-Maktum family and partition Dubai[40] (with Bur Dubai on the western side of the creek to be absorbed by Abu Dhabi and with Deira on the eastern side of the creek to fall under Qawasim control),[41] Sheikh Maktum bin Buti pursued a range of counter-strategies. Firstly, he encouraged the Qawasim governor or *wali* of nearby Sharjah (Sheikh Saqr bin Sultan Al-Qasimi, the son of the overall Qawasim ruler) to cede from Ra's al-Khaimah.[42] Although the plan soon unravelled, with Saqr being killed, Maktum's attempts to bring the ruler of Umm al-Qawain (another semi-autonomous town, further up the coast and deeper into Qawasim territory) into an alliance were more successful, with Sheikh Abdullah bin Rashid Al-Mu'alla sending a large contingent to help Dubai resist any hostilities.[43] In the event, no attack came, perhaps in part due to an unpleasant outbreak of small pox that had made Dubai a particularly unattractive acquisition,[44] but certainly also as a result of this skilful political manoeuvring and Maktum's swift mobilisation of a coalition deterrent force.

With the threat of partition subsiding, Dubai was again presented with a breathing space, a period that Sheikh Maktum exploited by seeking improved relations with Abu Dhabi. Such an objective would remain distant as long as Sheikh Khalifa remained in power, so Maktum began to garner support for the seemingly competent Sheikh Said bin Tahnun Al-Nahyan, the second eldest son of the assassinated former ruler.[45] In 1845 Khalifa was eliminated and Said seized control, beginning a powerful Abu Dhabi-Dubai alliance that would have been unthinkable only a few years earlier. When Maktum died in 1852, the strong relationship with Abu Dhabi was further reinforced, as his successor and youngest brother, Sheikh Said bin Buti Al-Maktum,[46] recognised that Said bin Tahnun's star was fading and Dubai needed to back his most promising rival, Sheikh Zayed bin Khalifa Al-Nahyan, the

15

deposed Khalifa's only son. Indeed, in 1855 Said bin Buti offered Zayed refuge and armed guards in Dubai, and after an incident took place in Abu Dhabi that forced Said bin Tahnun into exile,[47] Zayed was installed as ruler and then supported by Dubai during an attempted return to power by Said bin Tahnun in 1856.[48]

Following Sheikh Said bin Buti's death in 1859, Sheikh Maktum's eldest son, Sheikh Hasher bin Maktum Al-Maktum, who had been deemed too young to rule in 1852, became Dubai's third independent ruler. In the same way as his two predecessors, Hasher succeeded in strengthening Dubai's position by maintaining and enhancing existing alliances. He kept agreements with several major tribes, including the historically problematic Duru, paying them subsidies when necessary, not only to guarantee Dubai's safety, but also so he could raise a large number of armed men when necessary.[49] Perhaps the greatest legacy of his long reign was his construction of several fortifications in Dubai's hinterland during the 1880s, most notably the three watchtowers that still overlook the mountain enclave of Hatta.[50]

By the 1890s good relations with Abu Dhabi had again become a source of security for Dubai, as both sheikhdoms were facing the shared threat of renewed Wahhabi incursions, especially in the area surrounding the Buraimi oasis—a key hub for overland trade routes. Sheikh Hasher's successor and younger brother, Sheikh Rashid bin Maktum Al-Maktum,[51] pledged over three hundred men to assist Abu Dhabi's defence—a significantly large force for this period.[52] Similarly, in the early 1920s when the newly installed ruler of Abu Dhabi, Sheikh Sultan bin Zayed Al-Nahyan, was opposed by a large rival faction comprising members of the Awamir, Bani Qitab, and Duru, the sixth ruler of Dubai, Sheikh Said bin Maktum Al-Maktum, recognised the shared nature of the threat and sent a force to attack a Bani Qitab settlement in Al-Falayah, before fighting alongside Sultan against the Duru. This was a calculated risk on Dubai's part, as it involved breaking his grandfather's described agreements with the Duru. In the event, the Duru were so badly weakened by the joint Abu Dhabi-Dubai actions that their counterattacks on Dubai amounted to little more than the stealing of property.[53] Throughout the rest of his reign, Said remained instrumental in forging alliances designed at deterring such threats. Notably, in 1925 he sent two members of his own family to Oman on Abu Dhabi's behalf,[54] with the aim of securing greater Omani assistance should Wahhabi attacks resume. Perhaps most significantly of all, in 1939 he married his eldest son and the man destined to become Dubai's most celebrated ruler, Sheikh Rashid bin Said Al-Maktum, to Sheikha Latifa bint Hamdan Al-Nahyan,[55] the daughter of one of Abu Dhabi's most respected former rulers, Sheikh Hamdan bin Zayed Al-Nahyan. Highly symbolic to most of the lower Gulf's population, the wedding cemented a long history of mutual assistance between the two major Bani Yas communities, and underscored Dubai's rapid maturation into a secure and contiguous sheikhdom in its own right.

Political dependency on Britain

In parallel to Dubai's successful management of regional relations, the Al-Maktum family itself became an internal pillar of strength for the sheikhdom during this period, providing the domestic political stability needed for the town to continue to grow. Much of this stability was due to the ruling family's early relationship with Britain. The Royal Navy's intervention on behalf of the English East India Company and its suppression of the Qawasim had reluctantly brought the vast British Empire to yet another territory, one which many in London deemed to be unworthy of colonial administration and expensive troop deployments. As such, it was decided to set up a 'cut-price' imperial system of indirect control that would require the local rulers to sign anti-piracy peace treaties[56] and to accept the authority of small British residencies and, in many cases, locally recruited British agents.[57] These truces were self-enforcing as the simple act of signing them elevated the ruling families above other members of the local elite and ensured them British 'trucial' protection in the event of domestic insurgency. Thus, in many ways the centuries-old ebb and flow of tribal power had been frozen in time, as Britain signed treaties with whichever family happened to hold the reigns of power at that time, and required the rulers to sign not only on behalf of themselves, but also on behalf of their 'future sons'. This effectively created a system of robust and British-dependent dynasties presiding over 'Trucial states', of which Dubai's Al-Maktum family soon became a prime example;[58] and some aspects of which Britain attempted to replicate in other parts of its empire later in the century, most notably with Zanzibar's branch of the Al-Said family.[59]

Although the first layer of this British protection and dependency did not specifically include Dubai, given that the initial treaties were signed in 1820, before Dubai existed as a separate entity, the ground was nevertheless prepared for a second layer of treaties introduced in 1835 which replicated most parts of the original agreements, with the only additional clause being that the various rulers would agree to abstain from any maritime conflict against each other.[60] By this stage, Dubai was of course independent and in a position to sign. Indeed, it is likely that these new treaties were introduced expressly so that Britain could recognise the new sheikhdoms of Dubai and Ajman (another settlement which, like Umm al-Qawain, had succeeded in gaining autonomy from the Qawasim).[61] Unsurprisingly the Qawasim and Abu Dhabi rulers were the least enthusiastic about the addition of these new signatories, given that it formalised the loss of their former territories in British eyes.[62] Undeniably, it was in Britain's interests to maintain as many regional divisions as possible, with the aim of reducing Qawasim power and preventing the emergence of any one indigenous power bloc that might challenge their cut price system. Tellingly, the British authorities at this time claimed that '...the immediate advantage of Dubai's split with Abu Dhabi as far as local politics is concerned, is the separation of the territories of Sheikh Khalifa [bin Shakhbut Al-Nahyan] and Sheikh Saqr [bin Sultan Al-Qasimi], the governor of Sharjah, by that of an independent power. This is expected to reduce the constant collision between the two chiefs.'[63]

Given the mutual benefits of the system, the 1835 treaties were renewed annually until 1853, when a general 'Perpetual Treaty' was signed by all of the rulers,[64] which was to remain in place for over a century. In 1892 a second layer of treaties was added to this continuous agreement in order that Britain could directly control all aspects of the rulers' foreign affairs. Three clauses were drawn up forbidding the rulers from entering into agreements with non-British parties, from allowing non-British parties to visit their territory, and forbidden from selling or mortgaging any part of the territory, unless it was to British agents.[65] By signing these documents, the Trucial rulers relinquished external sovereignty and were 'upgraded', at least in British terms, from being merely 'independent Arab sheikhs in special relations with His Majesty's Government'[66] to being full-blown protectorates, albeit without any transfer of territorial sovereignty or application of English law.[67]

Although seemingly in contradiction to the early desire to keep British involvement in the lower Gulf to an absolute minimum, the Empire's declining power and the encroachment of other powers into the Middle East forced Britain to add these more repressive elements of political dependency to their relationship with the Al-Maktum family and the other Trucial sheikhs. Britain could not afford to allow its client rulers to be courted by foreign governments. Indeed, France had already been gaining influence in Oman, the Ottomans were extending their empire deep into Arabia, the Germans had begun to construct the Baghdad railway and, most worryingly, Tsarist Russia was believed to be planning the construction of a port on the Persian coast of the Gulf. In 1903 the Foreign Secretary[68] reiterated this view by stating that 'Russia must have an outlet in the Southern Sea... I believe that if we allow any power to come down into the Persian Gulf they will inflict a great injury on India and enable that power to strike British India in the flank.'[69]

Accordingly, the powers of the British agent in the lower Gulf (initially an Arab, and then later a British diplomat)[70] were increased so as to keep the rulers under closer control. While the agent's original remit was simply to look after British Indian subjects dwelling in Dubai and the other sheikhdoms,[71] this later expanded to include the ability to fine wayward rulers on behalf of the Bahrain-based Political Resident. Moreover, the agents were also responsible for deciding which of the sheikhs should be given symbolic gifts of friendship from the British and, conversely, which sheikhs should no longer receive anything, thereby lowering their status in the eyes of the local population.[72] A good example of the latter category was a Trucial ruler who, in 1911, was the subject of the Political Resident's instructions to the agent:

'With reference to your letter... regarding the behaviour of the Sheikh in connection with the presents forwarded to him... the Sheikh will not be considered for any future presents until he writes in a written apology asking that his discourtesy may be overlooked and that it will not occur again.'[73]

This dependent political hierarchy remained more or less unaltered well into the twentieth century, with agents rarely tolerating local complaints made about British subjects (no matter how widely known their incompetence or villainy), with agents regularly calling meetings with the sheikhs and then dismissing them after long periods of waiting,[74] and, perhaps most significantly, with agents always receiving a greater public gun salute than the rulers, regardless of how well respected the sheikh was. Indeed, even the esteemed Sheikh Rashid bin Said Al-Maktum only ever received a five gun salute in the 1960s, compared to seven guns for the agent, and a protracted seventeen guns whenever the Political Resident was visiting Dubai.[75]

In return for such acquiescence and interference in their affairs of state, the ruling families were rewarded with unfailing support for their regimes given that Britain's official policy was to 'uphold the independence of Trucial sheikhdoms against their enemies for the sake of maritime tranquillity'.[76] When the Viceroy of India[77] visited the lower Gulf in 1903 and sought to reassure the sheikhs of the mutual benefits derived from the 1892 agreements, he also managed to work into his speech a statement regarding internal disputes: '...if they occurred, the sheikhs would always find a friend in the British Resident, who would use his influence as he had frequently done in the past, to prevent these dissensions from coming to a head, and to maintain the status quo.'[78] Similarly, in the late 1920s, following a series of fratricides in the region,[79] the Political Resident reconfirmed such support for the rulers and impressed upon London the need for an even stronger British position, claiming that 'Unless and until the Government of India is prepared to interfere much more than they have done in the past, and are prepared, if necessary, to bolster up a weak sheikh, however much they might regret it, the only other course will be to continue shaking hands with successful murderers.'[80]

A good example of such early interference on behalf of beleaguered rulers would be Britain's enduring support for Umm al-Qawain's Al-Mu'alla dynasty which, as demonstrated, had historically served as a key ally of the Al-Maktum family. From about 1915 and onwards, Abu Dhabi had repeatedly tried to gain influence in the dynasty's sheikhdom, supporting the assassination of Sheikh Abdulla bin Rashid Al-Mu'alla in 1923 by his cousin Sheikh Hamad bin Ibrahim Al-Mu'alla. By 1929, with support from Sharjah, it would seem that Britain chose to restore the original ruling line and maintained Umm al-Qawain's independence by engineering Hamad's downfall and installing Abdulla's younger brother, Sheikh Ahmad bin Rashid Al-Mu'alla, on the throne.[81] In much the same way, when Abu Dhabi was faced with the Qatari-supported secession of one its major tribes, Britain

21

again intervened in order to protect the integrity of the Trucial states system. A section of the Qubaysat had for decades been attempting to emigrate from Abu Dhabi and set up a new, independent settlement at Khor al-Udaid, close to the border with Qatar. When they finally succeeded in breaking away, Abu Dhabi wished to launch a naval expedition against Khor al-Udaid, which would have involved breaking the maritime peace established by the original 1835 treaties. Significantly, Britain chose to make an exception and allowed Abu Dhabi to use force to return the Qubaysat to the fold, on the condition that Abu Dhabi would in future guarantee the peace along the coastline leading up to the Qatari peninsula.[82] The Political Resident even stated that if the Al-Nahyan family was unable to regain control over the area by itself, then the British would step in and assist.[83] As such, the entire littoral was soon consolidated, with Abu Dhabi eventually able to build a police outpost at Khor al-Udaid.[84]

Economic dependency on Britain

While the lower Gulf was home to various economic activities during the nineteenth century, including fishing, animal husbandry, basic re-export trading, and some limited agriculture, these were primarily at the subsistence-level and rarely generated enough of a surplus to allow for any meaningful growth or development. Dubai's pearling industry and its associated trades (including boat building and rope manufacture)[85] were notable exceptions. The shallowness of the seas combined with an abundance of the largest pearls in the world enabled the sheikhdom's merchants to fuel massive demand for such luxuries in Bombay, Victorian Britain, and other wealthy markets. Indeed, writing in the latter part of the century, the author of Britain's *Gazetteer of the Gulf*,[86] sought to illustrate the scale of this boom. Using estimates based on trade receipts and interactions with the merchant community, he recorded that Dubai was exporting over ten *lakhs* worth of pearls [87] per annum in the 1870s, rising to an enormous 100 lakhs or one *crore* per annum by the late 1890s.[88]

Inevitably, such a lucrative activity attracted foreign entrepreneurs, many of whom sought to introduce new technologies that would have undoubtedly boosted productivity and perhaps even secured a long-term future for pearling. However, given the fears of foreign involvement in the region and the resulting 1892 treaties, Britain had little choice but to intervene in economic as well as political matters, so as to maintain the Gulf as a 'British lake' and bar the door to all outsiders. As the descendant of a prominent pearling merchant describes, following British restrictions placed on the size of pearling boats (so that they could only carry six or seven men),[89] in the late nineteenth century Britain also felt compelled to block the importation of pearling equipment (relating to bleaching and drilling) already being employed in the Mediterranean and the Far East, 'partly because of wanting the industry to remain in Arab hands, and partly from self-interest'.[90] By the turn of the century, the Political Resident had formalised this Anglo-Arab monopoly claiming that any use of modern technology would endanger a 'traditional economy',[91] and stating that: 'Within the three mile limit, and in any other water which might justly be considered territorial, the tribes of the Arabian Coast are entitled to the exclusive use of the traditional pearl fisheries. As regards pearl banks outside territorial waters it is held that, as a matter of international law, such banks are capable of being the property of the tribes to the exclusion of all nations.'[92]

As late as the 1920s little had changed, with British reports revealing that many European merchants (including individuals who had previously helped improve pearling techniques) were being prevented from returning to Dubai.[93] Moreover, the reports indicate that by this stage the prohibition on technology imports had been extended far beyond just pearling equipment to include many other goods, with the only exceptions being an automobile for the ruler of Ra's al-Khaimah, and a motor boat for the ruler of Dubai. The ban included even British-manufactured radio sets, lest the population listen to potentially subversive foreign broadcasts.[94] Even more draconian, there is evidence to suggest that Britain considered blocking or 'immobilising' entire pearling fleets and denying access to markets in the event of disputes,[95] with the Political Resident stating that:

'We can, if we wish, make ourselves extremely unpleasant to the Trucial Sheikhs and their subjects; indeed, by cutting off supplies and the seizure of pearling dhows we can kill all these small principalities, but by proceeding to extremes we certainly run a risk of antagonising world opinion, which appears to be on the look-out for any stick which is offered for beating the British empire with.'[96]

As with the earlier maritime truces, there were important political benefits associated with this increasingly dependent situation, especially for the ruling families. By this stage Dubai and the other Trucial states were beginning to claim a much higher strategic value, given the possibility of oil reserves and their potentially suitable locations as aircraft refuelling depots. As such, Britain sought to exploit another low-cost yet equally effective means of preserving the status quo. It was thought that if large sums of 'locational' rent could be channelled directly to the local rulers, then this would reinforce their client status with Britain. Such strategic subsidies would prolong the self-enforcement of the original treaties, while concurrently reducing the rulers' reliance on taxation from their merchant elites (which had previously been their primary source of revenue),[97] and thereby further reducing the likelihood of internal opposition or meaningful autonomous development outside of British control. Tellingly, in 1939 the British Political Resident remarked that '...a key reason for the goodwill between the British and the rulers was that negotiations over air and oil gave the rulers a square deal which carried a money bag rather than a big stick'.[98] Indeed, as an important historical antecedent of more contemporary structures, it is significant to note how much of the rulers' pre-oil 'money bag' was derived from this economic rent and its associated 'rentier structures.'[99]

Upon closer inspection, it would appear that the region has experienced a long history of such rentier wealth, with many of the traditional activities such as the booty from *bedouin* raids and the issuing of fishing licences,[100] together with examples of income from guano collecting concessions and red oxide mining authorisations all providing early indications of rent-gathering.[101] With the generous air landing fees of the late 1920s and onwards, this rentier wealth was raised to a new level. More extensive facilities were required for larger military aircraft en route from Basra to Bombay and from Cairo to Karachi,[102] and given that the Persian coast was no longer a viable option,[103] Britain sought to add to its existing Omani airbases in Salalah and on the island of Masirah.[104] In particular, Ra's al-Khaimah, Sharjah (by this stage an independent sheikhdom), and Dubai were deemed to be excellent alternative refuelling points.[105] Although the ruler of Ra's al-Khaimah, Sheikh Sultan bin Salim Al-Qasimi, proved to be uncooperative, even after being threatened with 'punitive action', agreements were easily signed with the other rulers.[106] In the case of Sharjah it was dictated that Sheikh Sultan bin Saqr Al-Qasimi would host a British airbase and provide 37 armed guards, and in return would receive a personal income of 500 rupees per month 'for the responsibilities he had accepted', and a further five rupees for every aircraft that landed in Sharjah.[107] In 1932 another agreement was reached in which Sharjah would provide similar landing facilities for Imperial Airways civilian passenger aircraft en route from Croydon to Bombay,[108] also in exchange for generous remuneration.[109] Parallel agreements were signed in 1937 with the ruler of Dubai,[110] allowing Imperial Airways to land flying boats in between buoys on the Dubai creek.[111] In the first year alone, this deal was reportedly worth more than 5,000 rupees in fees for Sheikh Said bin Maktum Al-Maktum.[112] These air agreements not only provided money, but, as the India Office reported, also provided 'greater protection for the chiefs of tribes who were willing to cooperate... and to protect them from any danger that they might face as a result of their cooperation.'[113] Indeed, on the occasions when demand for seats was very low on the outbound aircraft from Dubai, there is evidence that Said bought out all the empty seats with his own funds as he was anxious that the air companies should not change their minds and that the Al-Maktum family should not lose out on such a beneficial agreement.[114]

Oil, or rather oil exploration concessions added another layer to this rentier dependency. In 1922, in a further example of increasing British control over the lower Gulf's economic networks, the Trucial states undertook not to consider any oil concessions that were not supported by the British government. In other words the rulers were made to refuse any offers from the rival American oil companies that had already begun prospecting elsewhere in the Arabian peninsula.[115] At this early stage there was no firm proof of oil in the lower Gulf, but given that Britain had already imposed similar agreements on the rulers of Kuwait and Bahrain, it seemed practical to lock the entire Gulf into the same system. As such, in 1935 the London-based and British Government-backed Iraqi Petroleum Company (IPC)[116] formed a wholly owned subsidiary, Petroleum Concessions Ltd., which was to be the sole operator of concessions in the lower Gulf.[117] Unsurprisingly the Political Resident soon issued an ultimatum binding the local rulers to deal only through the British agent (by this stage a British national[118]), who in turn would only deal with Petroleum Concessions.[119] These accords, in much the same way as the 1922 agreement, should not necessarily be seen as reflections of British interest in the discovery of oil deposits in the region (given that Britain already had an abundant supply at that time), but instead as expressions of the continuing British desire to exclude other foreign parties from the region's affairs and, as one historian has noted, thereby 'symbolizing the considerable degree of isolation that British protection imposed on the Trucial states'.[120] These concessions also provided another high stream of income for the rulers, which, in some cases, even dwarfed the generous air landing fees. The twenty-five year Dubai concession (signed in 1937) provides such an example, as in exchange for leasing the IPC a part of the Hamriyyah district of the town and allowing for the construction of a jetty, Sheikh Said was to be given 60,000 rupees on signing; a substantial annual income of 30,000 rupees, and then the oil company would pay 200,000 rupees upon the discovery of any oil, with three rupees paid for every barrel extracted during the prospecting process.[121] By 1945, Sheikh Said's son and crown prince, Sheikh Rashid bin Said Al-Maktum, was able to renegotiate this concession far ahead of time, gaining even more favourable terms (achieving an unprecedented equal split in profits between the IPC and the Al-Maktum family).[122] IPC's generosity was almost certainly prompted by renewed American attempts to gain a foothold in Dubai's oil exploration: it would seem that in 1939 the Superior Oil Company had made unauthorised aerial surveys of Dubai and had offered Said a substantial five million rupees; and in 1944 had tried again, arguing that Dubai was receiving a poor deal from Britain.[123]

Significantly, by the mid-twentieth century, every single sheikhdom was in receipt of at least one form of rentier payment, with even Ajman (which was benefiting neither from oil concessions nor air landing agreements) being purposely selected to host a military land base, in order that its somewhat indigent ruler, Sheikh Rashid bin Humayd Al-Nu'aymi, could begin to collect an annual rent of 10,000 rupees.[124] In some cases, where there were certain semi-autonomous regions of existing sheikhdoms that could attract substantial rental activity in their own right, Britain even sought to create independent sheikhdoms and establish new client dynasties, thereby supporting the original system of maintained regional divisions and thwarting foreign interference. The best example of this strategy was the province of Fujairah on the Indian Ocean coastline which, although nominally falling under

Qawasim control, had been identified by American oil companies in 1951 as being effectively outside of the British rentier network. Indeed the American and Saudi oil giant, ARAMCO, had already begun to approach prominent members of Fujairah's dominant Sharqiyin tribe. While they were offering to pay rent for oil concessions, it is likely that ARAMCO never really expected to prospect for oil in the area, but instead sought to gain a foothold in the lower Gulf.[125] Given that the IPC was only able to deal with official Trucial rulers, it was unable to compete, prompting Britain to act fast: in 1952 Sheikh Muhammad bin Hamad Al-Sharqi was upgraded to the status of the other 1835 peace treaty holders, and Fujairah was declared to be a distinct Trucial sheikhdom. However, even after its British recognition, the rulers of Fujairah maintained particularly close links with American diplomats, perhaps with the intention of playing off different oil companies should oil ever be discovered. Local postage stamps issued by the Fujairah government in the 1950s regularly featured American presidents, astronauts, and other celebrities.[126]

Another sheikhdom had been created some years earlier on the same stretch of coastline, again with the intention of providing a new client ruler with rental income. The town and area surrounding the natural harbour of Kalba[127] was the most southerly town of the Trucial states before the border with Oman. Ever since 1903, its Qawasim governors had effectively ceded from the overlordship of Sharjah and Ra's al-Khaimah, but it was not until late 1936 that it finally gained formal independence and was recognised as a Trucial sheikhdom by the British.[128] This belated recognition was directly connected to Britain's need for another airbase, this time on the eastern littoral. With the air landing agreements in Sharjah already enriching the core of the Qawasim clan, Britain opted to provide another section of the family with a separate stream of rent so as to preserve better the regional status quo. To this end the Kalba branch of the Qawasim were offered 1835 treaties and, as British clients anticipating great wealth,[129] thus effectively elevated above Kalba's largest resident tribes, the Naqbiyin and the Sharqiyin.[130] In contrast to Fujairah's survival, Kalba's independent status lasted for only fifteen years, during which time the plans for an eastern airbase were shelved due to increasing British retrenchment and the greater fuel capacity of aircraft travelling between the Middle East and India. With the need for rent-seeking clients suddenly removed, Britain chose to renege on its treaty relations. Thus, when an opportunity arose in 1951 following the double murder of the second ruler of Kalba, Sheikh Hamad bin Said Al-Qasimi, and his secretary, Bin Hazeem, the orchestrators of the plot, Sheikh Saqr bin Sultan bin Salim Al-Qasimi (the son of Ra's al-Khaimah's former ruler[131]) and Hamad's cousin, Sheikh Ali bin Amir Al-Qasimi,[132] were arrested by the British and exiled to Saudi Arabia, while Sharjah was allowed to re-establish its control.[133] This was largely achieved by the ruler of Sharjah deciding to marry one of Hamad's daughters,[134] and appointing one of his uncles as the new wali of Kalba.[135] In much the same way, all other towns that were deemed to be strategically worthless by Britain were systematically denied any form of rent payments or prospects of independence. While Sheikh Abdulla bin Salim Al-Ka'abi, the Bani Ka'ab chief and tax collector of Mahadha, repeatedly presented his case to the British in the late 1950s, and even provided the British agent with many soldiers in an effort to improve relations, this was to no avail, as Britain allowed Mahadha to be absorbed into Oman.[136] And in the early 1960s Sheikh Ahmad bin Saif Al-Nu'aymi, the chief of the Na'im tribe in the town of Hamasa near to Jebel Hafit, hoped to gain autonomy from Oman and requested a treaty from the British, but was pointedly refused.[137]

Poverty and resistance

Although soon reaching enormous proportions, rentier payments continued to accrue directly to the rulers, with the bulk of the population remaining uninvolved in the wealth creation proc-

ess. Indeed, Sheikh Said bin Maktum Al-Maktoum and Sheikh
Rashid bin Said Al-Maktum believed, as did other neighbouring
rulers receiving such vast incomes from concessions and agreements, that these guaranteed annual rents were to be their personal revenues.[138] Thus when the non-rent related components
of Dubai's economy began to suffer due to regional and global
recessions in the 1930s and 1940s, many of those outside of the
ruling family thought that this external wealth should be distributed more evenly—to improve infrastructure and revitalize the
floundering local economy.

British-imposed controls over the markets and technologies
of the pearling industry had rendered previously profitable pearling operations vulnerable to competition, especially from Japan,
where the farming of 'cultured pearls' was driving down international prices and, so it would seem, producing larger and better looking specimens.[139] To make matters worse, this Japanese
competition came at the same time as depression was spreading
from the core economies of the United States and the European
empires. Despite its vast global realm, Britain was also suffering,
and with this recession the demand for luxury items such as Gulf
pearls fell rapidly. Moreover, with most of the great powers and
their colonies beginning to focus on self-survival in the build-up
to the Second World War, the markets remained closed and the
pearling industry never recovered.

The situation was so bad that during some pearling seasons in
the early 1930s, pearl diving crews often returned to Dubai to find
no merchants waiting to greet them, and, if there were, only to
be offered 'shockingly low prices'.[140] Crews found it increasingly
difficult to finance expeditions, with sometimes more than sixty
boats being tied up due to lack of advance payments.[141] Many of
the non-Muslim Indian brokers, who were able to practise usury,
attempted to take advantage of the situation, sometimes charg-
ing over 35 per cent in interest,[142] but when some merchants and
captains fell into six figure debt,[143] it became increasingly clear

that the industry had collapsed. The British agent estimated that by 1946 the pearl trade in Dubai was worth a mere £250,000 per annum, compared to over £3 million in the 1920s.[144] Thus, the enduring nature of this decline rendered Dubai poverty stricken right up until the first oil exports of the 1960s. Thus the lower Gulf was left to languish as one of Britain's poorest and least developed protectorates: little meaningful diversification had taken place, and hardly any groundwork for future regional development had been established.

Occasionally resentment caused by these worsening conditions was so strong that it flared into open resistance against the Al-Maktum family, with a series of insurgencies finally prompting the British to warn Sheikh Said that he not only had to protect himself from his enemies, but also that '…if British people in Dubai were put at risk then Britain would punish all those responsible'.[145] Perhaps the first example of such opposition occurred soon after the beginning of the economic downswing, when in 1929 a section of Said's inner council of notables allied with two disaffected members of the ruling family, Sheikh Said bin Rashid Al-Maktum and Sheikh Buti bin Rashid Al-Maktum, both of whom had previously been exiled to Sharjah.[146] Together they demanded that the ruler sever Dubai's damaging relationship with Britain and, in 1931, publicly supported Buti's son, Sheikh Said bin Buti Al-Maktum, after he had deliberately collided one of his boats with a British vessel and ordered his men to attack the crew.[147] More constructively, these opponents had also begun to call for the formation of a proper judicial body outside of British control, and later that year established a committee to carry out sentences on convicted criminals. Indeed, in one case committee members decided that an expatriate Arab who had been charged with theft should face a punishment of mutilation. Normally the ruler would have commuted such a sentence, but in this instance his powers were overturned, as the new authority wished to display its strength. The British agent was understandably concerned and pressed Said bin Maktum to restrain the committee.[148] By 1934 the situation had deteriorated even further, with the agent receiving frequent reports that members of the ruler's court had 'bad intentions' towards Said's family. In a rare act of gunboat diplomacy, a Royal Navy vessel was despatched to Dubai,[149] where she sat just off the coast and remained in full view of the local population. Said was invited on board where he received promises from the ship's captain that the British would if necessary supply him with rifles and ammunition.[150] After returning to the shore, Said immediately called a *majlis* or forum of prominent citizens and demanded their loyalty, while calling on some of his old bedouin allies to provide assistance. By that evening some 800 armed tribesmen had arrived on the outskirts of the town. Significantly, the British weapons were delivered by motor launch in open wooden boxes during the busiest part of the day and, in a further show of strength, RAF fighter planes that happened to be refuelling at the Sharjah airbase flew low over Dubai in an effort to subdue any remaining antagonists.[151]

The Dubai reform movement

The most serious crisis, however, erupted just a few years later, when in 1938 a much larger group of opponents, [152] some 400 in number, tried to reverse Dubai's economic marginalisation by imposing reforms on Sheikh Said bin Maktum al-Maktum and assuming control over all state finances. Led by the Al-Ghurair, Bin Dalmuk, and Bin Thani families,[153] and supported by both the exiled Easa bin Huraiz[154] and the ruler's influential second cousin, Sheikh Mani bin Rashid Al-Maktoum,[155] these men were emboldened by similar recent manoeuvres in Kuwait and by demonstrations in Bahrain.[156] A request was made to the ruler to grant 'freedom to the inhabitants in trade' by sharing the rentier wealth and allowing much more of it to be managed by the community in the interests of improving social conditions and boosting economic activity.[157] Unlike most previous Gulf rulership contests, Dubai's notables did not necessarily intend to depose Said. Instead, these merchants and other disgruntled individuals established a new consultative majlis in which the ruler would be recognized as the president of a fifteen member chamber, but in exchange would have to share 85 per cent of Dubai's total revenue.[158] The shared proceeds were to be spent in the name of the state and only with the prior approval of the new majlis.[159] As the Political Resident admitted in his report, it was a 'democratic wave that aimed at putting more power in the hands of the people', and in many ways this was far more unsettling than 'one sheikh taking over from another'.[160]

Although this merchants' majlis operated for only a very brief period, the correspondence and minutes of its meetings reveal how its members succeeded in establishing several important institutions, including a municipal council, in addition to implementing a social security system for the elderly,[161] and electing new customs officials to be employed by the state rather than the ruler.[162] Moreover, the movement made a considerable contribution to the education system and strove to re-open Dubai's schools. The merchants established an education department, appointed Sheikh Mani as Dubai's first Director of Schools, and, as noted in the majlis' documents, their representatives recruited the majority of teachers from the local population (many of whom were older Dubai men who had been educated when schools had flourished during the pearling boom).[163] Thus, in light of these efforts and their many other innovations and recommendations the majlis believed that its presence was welcomed by all of Dubai, and also felt that '...its mandate carried a responsibility towards all groups and communities within the state, and that to reform certain aspects of government improved the lot of the common man and was therefore a national duty.'[164]

Sheikh Said and those loyal to his regime were, however, far from defeated, and when in 1939 the majlis decided to add even more limitations to his income by allowing him to retain just 10,000 rupees of the state's revenue for 'personal use', he was obliged to consider resorting to force . Fearing attack, the majlis responded by blocking all access to the Deira shore of the creek from the ruler's supporters in Bur Dubai. Tensions between the two camps eased somewhat when Said's brother, Sheikh Juma bin Maktum Al-Maktum, was sent to talk with the notables and offered them access to certain trading activities that had previously been monopolized by the Al-Maktum family, including the operation of ferries and cars. Many of the Deira inhabitants were pleased with this olive branch and removed their guards from their towers.[165] However, some remained distrustful of the ruler's intentions, and soon after a more hard line faction of opponents including Sheikh Mani (backed by the ruler of Ra's al-Khaimah, Sheikh Sultan bin Salim Al-Qasimi), forced Said and Juma to withdraw their offer as they were concerned that any further destabilisation of the status quo would draw the British even deeper into Dubai's internal affairs.[166] Remarkably, the matter was only solved when, in another apparent peace-offering, Said's son Sheikh Rashid bin Said Al-Maktum proposed to hold the wedding feast for his aforementioned marriage to Sheikha Latifa bint Hamdan Al-Nahyan at a location in Deira, close to the house of his bride's Dubai-dwelling relatives.[167] When the day arrived, the merchants made the mistake of relaxing their vigilance to allow hundreds of bedouin loyal to Rashid to cross the creek, ostensibly to participate in the celebrations.[168] Throughout the afternoon, these men took up sandbagged positions on the rooftops of Dubai's highest houses,[169] and at a pre-arranged time in the early evening opened fire on Said's opponents while other teams of bedouin overcame the Dubai customs house and other majlis strongholds.[170] Later that evening Rashid arrived in Deira for the final ceremony, and announced that the city of Dubai was unified once more.[171]

Several newspapers across the Arab world reported that the entire membership of the merchants' majlis had been killed during this encounter, with their journalists hinting that Britain had encouraged the plotters in order to suppress a 'liberal modernist movement'.[172] In fact there were only about ten fatalities during the disturbances, including a key majlis member, Sheikh Hasher bin Rashid Al-Maktum, and one of his sons.[173] Of those who were taken prisoner, many were blinded in one eye by 'fire water' and allowed to 'buy' their remaining eye upon payment of a large fine.[174] Those who escaped remained in exile, unable to find refuge in any of the other sheikhdoms, before re-emerging from the desert in 1940 with a small force of armed bedouin. After unsuccessfully ambushing one of Sheikh Rashid's hunting expeditions, they fortified themselves inside a small redoubt close to the Sharjah-Dubai border. Sheikh Said had little choice but to despatch Rashid and Sheikh Juma to the scene with a large contingent of bodyguards. Following failed negotiations, the confrontation deteriorated into a protracted and somewhat farcical fire fight: ammunition was in such short supply that combatents had to run and collect the fallen bullets fired by their enemies before being able to reload. Eventually, following the personal intervention of Ra's al-Khaimah's Sheikh Sultan, a deal was brokered that allowed the exiles to receive compensation for their confiscated property in Dubai before agreeing to move away.[175]

The collapse and dispersal of the majlis would, in any event, have been inevitable given Britain's continuing support for the Al-Maktum family's client status.[176] Indeed, as a prominent Dubai national has described, the British

'had fears about what they saw as the emergence of progressive tendencies demonstrated by the separatists… and the establishment of an assembly which was actually representative of the community… it would be easier to keep dealing with traditional tribal structures than the more diffuse, less predictable activities of popular assemblies.'[177]

Although the British publicly viewed the merchants' majlis and their reform attempts with indifference, London's misgivings over the movement were nevertheless clearly in evidence. Most notably, in a revealing effort to bolster indigenous support for the beleaguered ruler following the dispersal of his opponents, the Political Resident's office speciously claimed that the majlis had collapsed due to mismanagement and a lack of popular support by stating that

'Recently there has been democratic movement in the State of Dubai which is in special treaty relations with His Majesty's Government. This was an internal matter and HMG however advised the Sheikh to associate his people with himself in his government according to immemorial Arab custom by formation of a Council. The Sheikh did not take this advice and a Council was forced on him by the people which owing to maladministration later grew unpopular. At the end of March Sheikh Said with his supporters dissolved the Council.'[178]

Even today certain state-sanctioned histories of Dubai gloss over this period, affording the movement scant recognition and, in some cases, describing its members as being 'self-interested politicians' and dismissing its reforms as ineffectual.[179]

Finally, despite the movement's collapse, it must be noted how many of its actions and suggestions were not without some long-term benefit for Dubai's inhabitants, with many of them forming the blueprints for later initiatives undertaken by the rulers themselves. In the late 1940s Sheikh Said and his new *Majlis al-tujjar* attempted to rejuvenate many of the merchants' planned improvements in an effort to boost the emirate's commercial prosperity.[180] Furthermore, upon his eventual succession in 1958, one of Sheikh Rashid's very first acts was to re-establish the Dubai Municipal Council, despite championing his father's cause against it twenty years previously. The new Municipal Council, when founded, appointed councillors to represent different sections of the community for periods of two years and was empowered to administer Dubai's first official development plans, all of which were commissioned by the ruler and prepared by British experts.[181] The key difference between this council and the merchants' original version was that all its decisions had to been confirmed by the ruler, while its financial support came from the ruler's office too. Thus Rashid chose to reform only when he had the approval of British advisers, and when the previously powerful merchant elites had seemingly lost their ability to challenge the dependency relationship.

2
FROM ARAB NATIONALISM TO COLLECTIVE SECURITY

The 1940s and 1950s witnessed a distinct progression from the earlier, primarily ruler-merchant, struggles to a more full blown version of Arab nationalism in Dubai. Flooded with propaganda and infiltrated by expatriate sympathisers to the Arab cause, Dubai had become the focal point of opposition to British rule in the lower Gulf. An indigenous 'National Front' emerged, and on several occasions the ruling family's position was severely compromised. A number of short term strategies were employed to contain the threat before economic conditions began to improve, allowing the rulers to placate more easily their opponents. Finally, by the late 1960s Britain had succeeded in engineering a federal agreement in which Dubai and its neighbours would come together independently of Arab nationalist support, and would enjoy at least some measure of collective security following Britain's eventual withdrawal from the region.

Evidence of imported Arab nationalism

As a former supporter of the Arab nationalist cause claims, the early incidents of opposition in Dubai, including the reform movement described in chapter one[1] had transformed the sheikhdom into a particularly fertile breeding ground for even more explicit anti-British activity by 'contributing to the sense of grievance which

39

many people began to feel about what was effectively a colonial presence in our land... their [British] readiness to intervene, in pursuit of their own ends, in the management of our society... was greatly resented.'[2] With similar, but much more powerful and more organised movements beginning to gain momentum in Egypt and the mandated territories at this time, it was therefore inevitable that linkages would be made with Dubai. Indeed, although the later examples of resistance to British control and the Al-Maktum family always remained somewhat familial and tribal in nature, there is nevertheless much evidence that most of the agitators were heavily influenced by imported ideologies, foreign newspapers, and in some cases even *agents provocateurs*.

By the time of the 1939 counter-coup, certain foreign Arab newspapers were already having some influence in Dubai, or at the very least were offering an accessible anti-British perspective on events in the lower Gulf. When the Political Resident drew up his annual report at the end of that year, specific warnings were included concerning the growing resentment elsewhere in the Arab world and the likelihood that such newspapers would increase their criticism of Britain's perceived exploitation of the Gulf sheikhdoms, and would seek to expose the dependent nature of the various ruling families.[3] To some extent, these fears were realized when, in 1945, two prominent Lebanese newspapers (*Al-Shara* and *Al-Nahara*) proposed an 'Arab federation of the Gulf' in which Britain would play no role and in which the city of Manama in Bahrain would serve as the capital, directing a common foreign policy, abolishing all passport restrictions, and forming a High Council for all of the constituent emirates. Most controversially, it was intended that this High Council would be a member of the recently formed Arab League, thereby shifting the Gulf from British influence to Egyptian.[4] Less constructively, several Egyptian newspapers (including *Al-Hilal* and *Al-Risala*) began to publish regular pictures of the British agent holding friendly conversations with Dubai's crown prince, Sheikh Rashid bin Said Al-Maktum,[5] claiming that the two met each other on a daily basis.[6] Perhaps most amusingly, certain Egyptian radio stations (notably Cairo Radio and Sawt Al-Arab) regularly announced that the commander of the British base in Sharjah had been killed. In one year the same announcement was made three times,[7] prompting the very much alive commander in question to solemnly lower the Union Jack to half mast when he held his troop parade.[8]

In many cases this heightened media activity was exacerbated by the many expatriate Arab schoolteachers that had flooded into Dubai as the sheikhdom expanded its schools to accommodate its growing infant population, including Al-Ahmadia in Deira, Al-Maktum in Jumeirah, and Al-Shaab in Bur Dubai.[9] Given that the number of indigenous educated people remained small during this period, Dubai relied heavily on graduates from Egypt, Iraq, Syria, Lebanon, and Yemen, many of whom held Arab nationalist views. Although like many expatriates today, these men were quite self-restrained, given their gratefulness for employment in Dubai, there are numerous examples of such teachers inciting students and raising their awareness of Nasserism, the Palestinian question and other Arab movements that were contesting British or French influence. Moreover, following the establishment of an Egyptian Educational Mission, it has been claimed that Egyptian intelligence officers were infiltrated amongst incoming schoolteachers in order to coordinate such activities.[10]

Perhaps the first instance of organized secular nationalism was when a student group was set up in the early 1950s in the predominantly Iraqi-staffed Al-Falah School in Dubai. As eyewitnesses have described, these schoolteachers encouraged many of their pupils to '…parade through the narrow streets of the town, carrying flags and chanting Arab nationalist songs, applauded by their parents and citizens.'[11] It is possible that many of these impressionable young students may have joined the Front for the

Liberation of Occupied Eastern Arabia (FLOEA)—a loosely organized, teacher-led underground nationalist group that advocated violence to 'end British colonialism and overthrow the ruling oligarchy.'[12] A group of students were caught trying to set fire to the British base in Sharjah as an act of protest,[13] and these may well have been FLOEA members. Later, in 1953, tensions again flared in Dubai's schools: as an interviewee revealed, many young boys were encouraged by senior students and expatriate staff to demonstrate in the streets while carrying banners and photos of Jamal Abdul Nasser. Most worryingly, Sheikh Rashid's guards had to be called in to disperse the students, as it seemed that they were heading towards the only school in Dubai that was not participating in the agitation.[14] By 1959 Dubai's schools had become so openly Arab nationalist that the British agent described pictures of Nasser being hung on the walls[15] and young boys (under the tutelage of Syrians) shouting out to him 'Down with colonisation and long live Jamal!'.[16] Similarly in 1960, while attending a school art exhibition he noticed Dubai and Egyptian flags everywhere, but no Union flags.[17] Moreover, almost all of the art projects were heavily influenced by nationalism, with one particularly memorable exhibit portraying a flag-wielding Arab trying to enter Palestine. The following year, at what was supposed to be a school sports day, the agent remarked that very few children were actually participating in any sports, with most concentrating on making Nasserite speeches.[18] Most dramatically, at another school event in 1961 many of the teachers had decided to hold celebrations in honour of the United Arab Republic. Ibrahim Al-Midfa, Sharjah's 'prime minister', chose to walk out, while an embarrassed Rashid was left sitting next to the British delegation. The Al-Maktum family and the other Trucial sheikhs were no longer able to control their teachers, prompting the agent to decide that 'In the rulers' interests we must try and curb them... maybe we will be able to devise such ways and means.'[19]

Indigenous Arab nationalism and the Dubai National Front

In the wake of the Suez Canal crisis and the subsequent confrontation between Anglo-French influence and Nasserite Egypt in the mid-1950s, the internationalized politics of Arab nationalism at last seemed to have influenced a critical mass of disgruntled Dubai nationals in powerful positions, not just Dubai's impressionable Arab expatriate-educated youth. Suez, along with a series of other Arab nationalist 'successes', had raised hopes that smaller Arab states could realistically survive possible Saudi or Iranian encroachment without British protection as their more powerful Arab brothers would guarantee their security.[20] By this stage secret British reports were fully reflecting this heightened level of Arab nationalist esteem, explaining that the threat to British clients and stability in the Gulf was no longer just from '...the teachers employed by the sheikhdoms, but also from the general psychological impact of Egyptian prestige... a particularly virulent kind of Arab nationalism emanating from Egypt which will be difficult to insulate against.'[21] During this most turbulent period in Dubai's history, local resistance to Britain and the Al-Maktum family, spurred on by developments elsewhere in the Arab world, had begun to evolve into more of an organized underground movement, complete with its own propaganda machine and a manifesto of action.

In 1953 the Dubai National Front was established. This was an alliance of Dubai citizens that, as most sources describe, opposed the influence of non-Arabs (primarily Indian and Persian merchants) and sought greater protection for local businessmen.[22] However, the Front's objectives were more far-reaching, with many of its members seeking to reduce the power of the ruling family and British interference in domestic matters. As the Political Resident's annual report described, the Front was a '...loose association of men opposed to the British agent, the ruler, and his crown prince... while on the surface the opposition was directed

43

at Rashid's support of the non-Arab merchants, the other motive was to rearrange government power away from client autocrats.'[23] Similarly, other British documents from the time depict the National Front as being '...yet another party demanding Arabia for the Arabs',[24] and explain that the movement was '...not really a party, but used as a term to collectively describe those who criticized Britain and Rashid.'[25]

The main voices and the permanent 'backbone' of the Dubai National Front in its early years were the Al-Futtaim and Al-Ghurair families, supported by Sheikh Rashid bin Said Al-Maktum's aforementioned uncle, Sheikh Juma bin Maktum Al-Maktum, who remained extremely influential (being accorded a one gun salute by the British, even though not a Trucial ruler),[26] and who by this stage was becoming increasingly frustrated with the status quo. Although Rashid chose to exile Hamad bin Majid Al-Futtaim along with Juma (and his six sons) to Dammam in 1955,[27] there were by this time enough well-known personalities capable of championing the nascent movement's cause.[28] Notable among these was Ahmad bin Sultan bin Sulaim, who may have been the Front's first official president. Bin Sulaim had been exiled to India during the Second World War after Rashid had accused him of inciting demonstrations against the Al-Maktum family and the British.[29] Also of prominence was Murshid Al-Usaimi, a merchant of Kuwaiti origin who had supported Dubai's stance during a period of tribal wars during the late 1940s[30] and distributed much of Kuwait's educational aid to Dubai.[31] He later benefited from customs exemptions which, given the shortages at that time, allowed him to grow rich from food imports to the lower Gulf. His great wealth and status elevated him to becoming one of Rashid's advisers and he was even granted a monopoly concession for a Kuwaiti-funded public electricity project in Dubai. But after a reorganisation of the customs system in the early 1950s, Al-Usaimi lost his lucrative exemptions and, following disputes with Rashid, the Al-Maktum family stopped buying construction materials from Al-Usaimi and blocked the Kuwaiti electricity project. In tandem with the new customs system, Rashid also introduced new courts that effectively stopped powerful notables such as Al-Usaimi and Bin Sulaim from holding private tribunals in their own houses.[32] Even today a story is still told of how these disgruntled citizens invited one of Rashid's newly empowered judges to dinner at their house and then served him one of his own camels.[33]

Other significant members of the Dubai National Front included Thani bin Abdulla who was previously one of Sheikh Rashid's chief advisors and therefore represented a major defection to the cause.[34] Indeed, the British believed that Bin Abdulla was one of Rashid's most dangerous opponents given his ability to steer debates in the ruler's majlis in favour of the Front's interests.[35] From the Al-Ghurair family itself, Hamed bin Majid Al-Ghurair was closely aligned with Al-Usaimi, backing many of his views and becoming involved in the Kuwaiti electricity project. It is also thought that he was a strong proponent of an independent Arabia, vocally supporting the Saudi cause and, according to British documents, perhaps serving as a Saudi agent in Dubai. His eldest son, Saif bin Hamed Al-Ghurair had similarly strong links to Saudi Arabia given his close relationship with the Saudi Ambassador to India—a relationship formed in Bombay as a result of Saif's lucrative gold smuggling trade to India on behalf of Kuwaiti merchants. It is also believed that Saif was a strong supporter of Nasser, and although he failed to win an audience with Nasser during his visits to Egypt, he nevertheless donated around 40,000 rupees to the Egyptian Arms Fund. Saif's younger brothers, Abdulla bin Hamed Al-Ghurair and Majid bin Hamed Al-Ghurair, were also recognized as being virulently anti-British and were believed to be regular visitors to Egypt. Abdulla was frequently involved in legal disputes, and during the height of the Front's influence was heavily fined for interfering with Rashid's customs department and the Dubai postal service.[36] Remarkably, when the first PO boxes were set up in Dubai, Abdulla had ensured that the Al-Ghurair family was assigned box number 1—a privilege most would have expected to go to the ruler.[37] Also worthy of mention are those members of the Front who fell just outside of this core leadership: the British estimated that there were 500 or so other supporters, with an average age of twenty-five, many of whom were from merchant families, were customs officials, or employees of the British Bank of the Middle East.[38] Of these, most were Sunni Muslims, thereby providing the Front with a natural hook for external Arab nationalist influences and for contacts within the Sunni-dominated Arab League.

Little could really be done to stop these men: apart from the occasional deportation or threats to crush uprisings by using loyal bedouin, Sheikh Rashid had no effective way of dealing with the subtle yet highly damaging opposition presented by the Dubai National Front. Over a critical two year period, between 1955 and 1956, the British privately admitted that Rashid was extremely weak and perhaps could not be propped up indefinitely. During 1955 anti-British slogans were being daubed on walls all over Dubai, communist newspapers were being smuggled into the city from Lebanon, and verbal attacks on Persian, Indian, and other foreign merchants were increasing in number and intensity. That summer, following Rashid's decision to pursue an alternative to the Kuwaiti electricity project (involving British, Persian, and other non-Arab investors), the Front made an unsuccessful attempt to sabotage the scheme, leading to its temporary closure.[39] And following the return of the exiled Hamad Al-Futtaim from Dammam later that year, the Front enjoyed something of a resurgence, as Al-Futtaim was thought to be distributing Saudi-supplied arms and money and also passing on intelligence to the Saudis regarding British forces and their deployments near the disputed Buraimi territory.[40] Indeed, following Britain's eventual reoccupation of the Buraimi oasis villages by the end of 1955, documents were discovered in the houses of Saudi supporters that implicated Al-Futtaim and provided enough evidence for Rashid to expel him for a longer period. In many ways this latest period of exile proved counter productive for Rashid as many pamphlets and graffiti in support of Al-Futtaim appeared, thereby giving the Front a much-needed figurehead.[41]

1956 was equally problematic for Sheikh Rashid and the British. The Dubai National Front's propaganda was becoming increasingly professional in its production, and it is likely that the leaflets were being printed in either Saudi Arabia or Pakistan, perhaps being supplied by Al-Futtaim's nephew, Majid bin Muhammad Al-Futtaim, who was thought to be regularly crossing the border.[42] While some of the printed messages were rather superficial, often criticising Rashid for spending too much time and money on hunting expeditions,[43] many made serious accusations, including claims that the British were controlling all internal affairs through their conduits in the British Bank of the Middle East or in the shipping company Gray Mackenzie.[44] The leaflets also argued that any new police force should be staffed by local men, not by foreigners, and most worryingly accused Rashid's men in the customs department of allowing shipments of narcotics to pass through Dubai. Indeed, there is evidence from the summer of 1956 of such a struggle over drugs following the seizure of a large quantity of narcotics by customs officials. The officials were not supported in their actions by their director, and when they complained Rashid chose to dismiss them, ratherthan him. The remaining officials in the department went on strike to protest against this manoeuvre, inspired by speeches delivered by the aforementioned Bin Abdulla and Al-Usaimi, while the dismissed employees were hired by leading members of the Front at a higher hourly rate, and in some cases were helped in finding jobs in neighbouring sheikhdoms.[45]

Following the Suez crisis, the latter months of 1956 saw the Dubai National Front's activities becoming more violent. A riot in Dubai led to part of the British agent's house being burned down; an attempt was made to destroy the transmitters near to Britain's airbase in Sharjah; and the car belonging to the Chief Officer of the Trucial Oman Levies was attacked.[46] During a trip to Ra's al-Khaimah the agent's car was followed and attacked, with youths reportedly shouting abuse at the passengers and daubing anti-British and pro-Nasser slogans on the sides of the vehicle.[47] Although the ruler of Ra's al-Khaimah, Sheikh Saqr bin Muhammad Al-Qasimi, was pressured into offering a 500 rupee reward for information relating to this incident,[48] none was forthcoming, and the British began to suspect that Saqr was effectively under the control of Hamed bin Majid bin Ghurair, who had by that stage gained something of a monopoly over fishing rights in Ra's al-Khaimah.[49] By 1958 the situation had deteriorated even further. During the summer a Pakistani doctor working for the British was fired upon[50] and a Union flag was stolen from the British agency headquarters and thrown into the creek, before being discovered the following morning.[51] In the autumn months an arson attack was made on the customs house, prompting the new Director of Customs, the Bahraini-born Mahdi Tajir, to request bodyguards from the British.[52] Even more disquietingly, an assassination attempt took place on Sheikh Saqr bin Sultan Al-Qasimi, the ruler of Sharjah, by a Baluchi servant, possibly in the employ of a Front sympathiser.[53] The Baluchi had been brought before Saqr on suspicion of adultery, but then pulled out a pistol before being seized from behind by one of Saqr's deputies.[54]

By this stage the Dubai National Front was encouraging many of its younger members to seek training and support overseas, away from British scrutiny, before bringing their ideas and skills back to Dubai. In early 1959 the British agent received multiple reports of certain families financing men to travel to Saudi Arabia.[55] Similarly, many of those who sought work in the relatively more prosperous Bahrain were urged to join the infamous 'Bahrain Club' on Muharraq island: as a hotbed of Arab nationalism, the Club had organised several anti-British protests before being closed down, with its leaders exiled to the island of St Helena in the South Atlantic. When the latter were released in the early 1960s, they sought refuge with fellow sympathisers in Dubai.[56] Perhaps most notably, a racket had been set up in which the Front arranged for some of its members to travel to Egypt via a circuitous route. After flying to Bombay, an innocent destination as far as the British were concerned, these men would be met by employees of the Egyptian consulate and provided with travel documents allowing them to visit Cairo for 'instructional courses'. After they finished they would fly back to Bombay, and then finally home to Dubai.[57]

Equally worrying for Sheikh Rashid were the Dubai National Front's attempts to broaden its base of support: by turning full circle with regard to Dubai's Persian population, the Front attempted to ally with prominent Persians against the Al-Maktum family, thereby temporarily dropping the more xenophobic elements of its campaign.[58] To extend its influence further amongst Dubai's citizens, the Front also backed the launch of the Dubai Cultural Club, a de facto platform for controversial speakers. Although the Club's first speaker restricted himself to making fairly innocuous comments about Arabs cooperating to solve social problems, it was the second guest, an Egyptian judge, who really alarmed the British with his bold pronouncements regarding Arab unification. Indeed, the British were so suspicious of him that they forced Rashid to dismiss the judge from office. Although, according to the British agent, his replacement was equally Arab nationalist, 'his words were fortunately lost on most of his listeners, since few of them understood his high, classical Arabic.'[59]

Predictably, therefore, the Dubai National Front's propaganda leaflets by late 1959 not only included repeated references to 'nation' and 'citizen' along with explicit mention of the Suez crisis, but also expressed this need to bring Persians onside. The following four excerpts were intercepted and translated by the Political Residency that very December:

"The Free nation of Dubai: All the Arab governments have begun to struggle beside their great sister, Egypt. All the Arab nations have contributed in the struggle and in the fight for turning out the colonial power and the cleanliness of the motherland from colonialism's foulness. The Agency and the Bank have started printing leaflets against Egypt and her brave leader. For what? Because they have supported Egypt and her nationalizing of the Suez Canal. O Free nation, be cautious of these leaflets and the British false colonialism. Wake up you free nation and get back your rights, respect, and your freedom and be as a nation"[60]

"Dear Dubai nation—to all citizens of Dubai... I am calling you all the Arabs, Persians and other Muslims to come together... We all have one religion and one home. We should follow as our brothers followed the path of unity. Unity is the basis of success and power on the earth. You cannot do anything against a nation unless you are united. Unity is the remedy for aggrieved nations. Brothers, do publish the voice of unity among your brothers and other citizens... We are attacked by three enemies; poverty, sickness, and ignorance... Is it not sufficient for you to suffer from imperialism, their supporters, and the galavyeen [sic: *qalveyen*] traitors?"[61]

"A Call to every brother citizen... We and you share one object; we all feel and suffer from Imperialism which is driving us under not only every day but every second. Start your movements for freedom from now on! Do not think that Imperialism cannot be resisted in your country in these days and do not listen to anyone who tells you to think first before resisting Imperialism. Your country is part of the Arab World. Get up from your sleep and contact all your relatives from Dhofar to Qatar... Rest assured that you are not an ignorant country and that you belong to the progressive Arab world. Join hands and listen to President Jamal Abdul Nasser who has said in the Egyptian constitution that Egypt is a part of the Arab world and a progressive country."[62]

"Oh free Arabs. Your feeling towards your Arab nationality must force you to go on a general strike... to show to the world that all Arabs are one nation and one people. That they are one heart. We request from all our free worker brothers to be ready to accept this invitation and to go on strike against the cruel colonialists. Let it be known to the West that today's Arab nation is not the same as it was in the past. Kindly keep this paper safe. Let others read it."[63]

Short term solutions: the Sudan connection

While reluctant to commit more energy and resources to main-taining stability in Dubai, and clearly preferring to prolong the inexpensive nineteenth-century system of self-enforcing treaties, the events of the late 1950s nevertheless forced Britain into as-suming a more proactive role in order to shore up their belea-guered clients. Indeed, given that Britain's oil concessions in the sheikhdom were beginning to warrant much greater attention in London, a continuation of such violent disturbances into the 1960s could not be tolerated. As the Political Resident described Dubai's population at this time, it was becoming 'partially hostile to Britain and capable of jeopardising the oil operations.'[64] He added that Britain could not afford a hostile regime to take root, especially one that would 'nationalise the oil industries... or seek the degeneration of administration in the hands of an irrespon-sible ruling family of the kind prevailing in Saudi Arabia'.[65] Thus from the early 1960s the British agent began to work closely with the ruling family on a number of strategies aimed at containing the Arab nationalist threat. In addition to greater public displays of British endorsement for Sheikh Rashid bin Said Al-Maktum, it was jointly decided to strengthen the local security forces, to reorganise Dubai's courts, and to introduce structural changes to the educational sector.

Since Sheikh Rashid's succession in 1958 (when HMS *Loch Insh* arrived in Dubai to deliver a formal letter of recognition and friendship), British warships had begun to call much more frequently than before, each time delivering Rashid's five gun salute with their powerful cannons. Given the awe-inspiring sight and sound of these vessels there is no doubt that such gun-boat diplomacy remained just as effective at subduing the local population as it had been earlier in the century.[66] Security on the ground was improved by assigning a former British officer from the Sudan Defence Force[67] to reorganise Rashid's Emiri guard

51

and, in cooperation with Rashid's cousin, Sheikh Muhammad bin Hasher Al-Maktum, the existing police force of loyal bedouin was reorganised and staffed by Pakistani expatriates.[68] This new force set up mobile police units to patrol the ruler's palace and the British agent's compound[69]—before the unrest such measures would never have been necessary. Similarly effective was Britain's strengthening of Rashid's control over the local courts following the arrival of a British-backed team of lawyers and judges from Bahrain, and the appointment of an openly anglophile Syrian *qadi*.[70]

Perhaps most significantly, Britain tried to destroy the main powerbase of the Arab nationalists in Dubai by removing some of the more troublesome expatriate teachers from the schools, and by appointing Banaga Al-Amin, a Sudanese acquaintance of the British agent, to be the new Director of Education. Al-Amin was given a brief to provide a 'sound, politics-free education', to restrict all student clubs to 'innocent activities' such as playing cards, and to ensure that politically sensitive magazines and books did not appear in schools.[71] He was aided in his task by the appointments of several other pro-British Sudanese and Zanzibaris elsewhere in Dubai's administration,[72] and by an injection of British funds into the education system.[73] Up until this point Britain had shied away from developing Dubai's schools further given that certain members of the ruling family were afraid that improved formal education might lead to demands for reform of the traditional political system. Indeed, in the 1950s the Political Resident had stated Britain's similar concern that '…it is inevitable that with a spread of education there will in due course be demands of modification in the existing patriarchal forms of the government. There may even be some anti-British agitation.'[74] Thus by the early 1960s, Britain had been forced to choose the lesser of two evils and to invest finally in local education. Sheikh Rashid faced strong opposition to this reorganisation, especially from the aforementioned Murshid Al-Usaimi, and Egypt was so incensed by Al-Amin's appointment that they flew in a delegation to complain to Rashid.[75] Although Al-Amin's tenure was short, Arab nationalist influence over Dubai's schools had nevertheless been greatly reduced and all such Egyptian delegations were denied entry (with their aircraft being instructed to turn away).[76] In order to curb any further influx of Arab nationalist sympathisers, Britain had begun to refuse certain Arab airlines, most notably Egypt Air, from landing anywhere in the lower Gulf.[77]

Although these strategies were distinctly short-term in their objectives, and would have probably been unable to quell any further serious unrest, they were nevertheless sufficient for the moment, as significant changes to the levels of rent from the oil concessions soon allowed Sheikh Rashid to go one step further than his father ever could and free his population from all forms of taxation. Indeed, as commercial quantities of oil exports finally began to flow out of Dubai (some twenty years later than the first Kuwaiti oil exports[78]), most Dubai nationals were elevated above any kind of extractive state, and found themselves able to import goods on an unprecedented scale. A frenzy of consumerism began, and the previously belligerent merchant families that had backed the Dubai National Front lost much of their power base. Young men had money in their pockets and businesses to run, and busied themselves with keeping pace with the region's oil boom rather than concentrating on political reform. Moreover, the most powerful notables were handsomely placated as the ruler awarded them received exclusive import and construction licences. Many of these are still in place today, and grant certain families the sole right to run certain franchises (e.g. for the import of Rolex, to distribute Mercedes-Benz cars or to run European supermarket chains). Indeed, it is no coincidence that some of Dubai's biggest and wealthiest family trading empires today received their licences in the 1960s, and most tellingly featured prominently among the proponents of the National Front in the 1950s. Thus by the time of the 1967 Arab-Israeli War and the region-wide discrediting of the Arab nationalist states' military prowess that is normally considered a key landmark in the decline of Arab nationalism, in Dubai the nationalist impulse was already waning due to altered domestic circumstances.

Long term solutions: the road to federation

Nevertheless, the Arab nationalist threat remained in the background throughout the 1960s, and as successive Labour and Conservative governments retrenched the imperial presence and the withdrawal of British forces and administrations from remaining outposts 'east of Aden' continued to gather pace, it was feared that unless Britain established even stronger states in Dubai and the other Trucial territories, then any future British exfiltration from the lower Gulf would render these sheikhdoms (and by association Britain's valuable oil concessions) highly vulnerable to external interference. Indeed, many Dubai nationals still were sympathetic to Nasser's cause, with locally produced postage stamps featuring his portrait,[79] and with several ardent supporters in the Dubai Municipal Council even attempting to erect a statue following his death in late 1970.[80] Moreover, some of the 'financially appeased' merchants regretted that oil revenues came so fast and permanently froze what they considered to have been a process that was reaching an inevitable and beneficial conclusion. A decade after the height of unrest there remained a sense of nostalgia for the period of struggle (and this remains the case today with some of the older members of Dubai's merchant families).

In addition to the fear of resurgent nationalism, Britain was also faced with growing regional security concerns, all of which would have left Dubai and its neighbours exposed should British protection have been reduced. Most immediately, in nearby Oman the Dhofar Liberation Front's leader, Mussalim bin Nafl, had declared that, should he succeed in wresting power away from Sultan Said bin Taimur of Muscat, then his campaign would be extended to the lower Gulf, destroying those sheikhdoms that were 'founded on principles that served British interests as well as western oil interests in the region'. As will be demonstrated later in this volume, the Liberation Front's supporters had already been carrying out clandestine attacks in British zones of influence, especially in Dubai,[81] and had later established a National Democratic Movement for the Liberation of the Arab Gulf—a more organised, and certainly more violent version of the earlier FLOEA.[82] More broadly, it was believed that the lower Gulf and western oil interests would also be targeted by the Soviet Union should Britain weaken its grip. Indeed, at a time of heightened Cold War tensions, Britain was so alarmed by the prospect of Soviet encroachment that it had begun to share Gulf-related intelligence with its erstwhile oil-prospecting rival, the United States.[83] These fears seemed to be well founded when in 1968 the Kremlin issued its first ever statement regarding the Gulf, emphasising that it sought 'regional defence alliances in order to protect its southern boundaries'.[84]

The solution was thought to be improved collective security, an idea that had already been circulated by the Political Resident in the 1930s.[85] It was felt that if Britain could encourage the rulers to build upon some of the fledgling Trucial-wide institutions that had been set up in the 1950s and early 1960s, then some form of federation of sheikhdoms might become possible. It was of course crucial that Britain remained at the helm of such a process, for if she were unable to bring the Trucial states together on her own terms, then there was a real risk that the Arab League would try to become the architect of such a union in the lower Gulf. As British Foreign Office reports warned '...if the rulers were prepared to admit the League to their territories it would be difficult, if not impossible, for the British to oppose an Arab organisation, accepted throughout the world as representing the Arab states collectively, from taking over many of the functions which she had reserved for herself.'[86] Moreover, it was stated that 'a failure to keep the Arab League out of the Trucial States would be a turning point in the history of the Gulf and our [the British] position here... leaving a chaotic situation behind.'[87]

Indeed, as early as 1945 Cairo had already proposed such a federation, and in 1964 Sayed Nofal, the Deputy Secretary General of the Arab League, had resurrected the scheme and presented his plans to Sheikh Rashid bin Said Al-Maktum, and to the rulers of Abu Dhabi and Sharjah, Sheikh Shakhbut bin Sultan Al-Nahyan and Sheikh Saqr bin Sultan Al-Qasimi. Nofal's intention was that the old 1835 peace treaties with Britain should be broken and that a new, independent Arab federation would be supported by generous League development aid that would be administered from a federal capital in Sharjah. Most worryingly for the British, when the League's Secretary General, Abdul Khalek Hassouna, managed to visit Sharjah later in the year, he was reportedly carried shoulder-high through the streets, and it was alleged that 20 million Egyptian pounds had already been deposited in a Sharjah bank account to serve as seed money for the project.[88]

Britain and her clients were therefore placed under great pressure to upgrade and augment what few cooperative institutions already existed in the lower Gulf, fearing that their influence and status would be lost if they delayed much longer. Fortunately, there was already a functioning Trucial council, a Trucial army, and a Trucial fund, and these were to serve as building blocks for the development of the federation. In 1952 the Political Resident had set up the Trucial States Council, partly in response to the Egyptian revolution and partly as an early British recognition of the need to give local rulers at least some involvement in the management of their own affairs.[89] Although it was initially chaired by the British agent, attended by British oil company representatives and their interpreters,[90] and had no formal constitution,[91] it nevertheless did engender some degree of 'corporate sense' between the previously disparate sheikhdoms,[92] and by the mid-1960s Britain had begun to relax her control so as to allow the chairmanship to be rotated between the Trucial rulers, assisted by a deliberative committee comprising two delegates from each sheikhdom.[93] Moreover, in an effort to provide the rulers with some experience of foreign relations Britain also began to allow the Council's members to develop contacts and make visits outside of the British network, thereby ending the 1892 treaties of exclusivity. Most notably, Sheikh Rashid was authorised to visit a number of regional capitals including Kuwait City, Doha, Damascus, Cairo, and Tehran; and remarkably was permitted to tour the Conoco, Inc. headquarters[94] when visiting the United States in 1963—a rival to the described British Iraqi Petroleum Company.[95]

Responsible for administering British-designed five year development plans, the Trucial States Council managed to achieve several region-wide objectives, including the provision of scholarships for talented subjects of the Trucial states, the appointment of a touring doctor for remote areas, and the establishment of agricultural trials stations.[96] By far the Council's greatest success was the creation of the Trucial Oman Scouts in 1956, a small but well-trained army for the Trucial states born out of the Trucial Oman Levies that had existed to protect British oil exploration teams from raiders. Made up of local bedouin (including Dhofaris) and Jordanians, the Scouts were officered by British soldiers and commanded by a British colonel or *qaid*.[97] Their tasks included supporting the various guards and police forces controlled by the individual rulers, most notably the Dubai police force, in addition to securing British installations such as the airbase in Sharjah, and containing some of the more troublesome hinterland tribes, most notably the Awamir.[98] To pay for all of these new services and this improved security force, Britain had set up a Trucial States Development Fund to support the Council. Although, as an act of appeasement, the British agent had initially agreed to appoint an Arab League supplied director to the fund, this decision was soon overturned and a British administrator was installed until the experienced Dubai banker, Easa Saleh Al-Gurg, was in a position to assume the directorship, with Sheikh Saqr bin Mohammad Al-Qasimi of Ra's al-Khaimah serving as the nominal chairman. Other nationals joined the fund's office, many of whom, includ-

ing Abdullah bin Humayd Al-Mazroui,[99] had earlier been sent by
the British to Baghdad for specialised training.[100] While the bulk
of the fund's budget was supplied by London, with smaller contributions of around four per cent from both Sheikh Rashid and
Sheikh Shakhbut, by the mid-1960s over £1 million had begun to
come from Abu Dhabi and Dubai's former adversaries in Saudi
Arabia, following the British embassy in Jeddah's brokering of a
deal with King Faisal bin Abdul-Aziz Al-Saud which recognised
the shared threat of Arab League encroachment in the Gulf.[101]
Most significantly, by the late 1960s, with Abu Dhabi's oil revenues beginning to flow, Shakhbut's successor and more capable
younger brother, Sheikh Zayed bin Sultan Al-Nahyan, was in
a position to contribute over 80 per cent of the budget, thereby
making the Council financially self-sufficient.[102]

The United Arab Emirates

Despite a statement made by the Foreign Secretary in early 1967[103]
that claimed 'Britain would most certainly continue to honour its
military commitments in the Gulf,'[104] by the end of the year a
Westminster white paper called for a full British withdrawal,[105]
and had set a time frame of just four years. While not unexpected,
many of the Truial sheikhs and the British administrators had
hoped for a longer period of transition, but by this stage deteriorating economic conditions in Britain,[106] combined with a feeling
that an ongoing footprint in the Gulf was unsustainable, were
enough to justify the removal of Britain's presence and the cutting
of its annual £300 million expenditure on maintaining Middle
Eastern bases.[107] Indeed, as a special report conducted by a former
Political Resident argued, [108] any continued British military protection would be 'self defeating as it would lead to even stronger
local opposition and have undesirable consequences on British
[oil concession] interests.' Certainly it was felt that a proper withdrawal and a replacement of the 1835 treaties with more relaxed
'treaties of friendship' would 'signal to the people of the Gulf an

end to imperialism and reduce the pressure of Arab nationalism on the rulers.'[109]

What Britain really needed was for collective security-building to continue and accelerate more rapidly, so that the Trucial institutions would be even better placed to become independent federal institutions within just a few more years. As such, from the time of the announcement there began furious efforts to bring together the rulers as frequently as possible, with the aim of ironing out their parochial differences and establishing greater common ground. What Britain did not want was to create something too heavy and unwieldy: the Political Resident was well aware that the Trucial states (along with Qatar) were relatively 'primitive and needed to be kept under a more colonial character',[110] and therefore recommended a much looser system that still retained monarchical sheikhdom-level powers and respected local institutions. Indeed, Britain sought to avoid the mistakes that had been made during Zanzibar's troubled de-colonisation in 1963 and the violent overthrow of its ruling sultan the following year,[111] while also learning from the troubles she had experienced when withdrawing from south-western Arabia in 1967. Over-centralisation had soon led to tensions emerging between the five sheikhdoms and one sultanate that made up the former Aden protectorates, eventually exposing this 'Federation of Yemeni Emirates of the Arab South' to external influences and an unstable Arab nationalist movement.[112]

The first few meetings during this critical period of federal negotiations were led by Dubai, as the British had already identified Sheikh Rashid bin Said Al-Maktum as the man most capable of holding such a union together. As early as 1960, the British Lord Privy Seal[113] had asked Rashid at a meeting in London whether he would prefer Britain to draw up a plan or for the local rulers to find their own solution.[114] Preferring a British plan, Rashid confirmed within a year to the Foreign Office that he was confident of leading such a union, but admitted that Dubai would only really be able to serve as a capital for the sheikhdoms to the North and East, given Abu Dhabi's much higher potential for oil exports.[115] Nevertheless by 1967 most of the federal meetings had been held in Rashid's house[116] (having been brokered by the aforementioned Mahdi Tajir[117]) and by the end of the year Rashid met with Abu Dhabi's new ruler, Sheikh Zayed bin Sultan Al-Nahyan, at the Za'abeel palace in Dubai to discuss an 'equal union' between the two sheikhdoms. By February 1968 the two rulers met again, this time at a specially constructed campsite at Ghantoot, close to their shared border, and agreed to a 'document of union' that called for common immigration, defence, foreign, and security polices, along with a Dubai-Abu Dhabi flag of unity. Remarkably, some Arab states recognised this early two-member federation as an independent entity from the moment the document was ratified.[118]

By this stage, Sheikh Rashid's early predictions about Abu Dhabi's economic prospects had been confirmed, and, given Abu Dhabi's ability to make massive contributions to the Trucial States Development Fund, Rashid graciously informed Sheikh Zayed that he should become the first president of the federation.[119] The Foreign Office soon acknowledged this shift, with their special envoy[120] reporting that Dubai would be unable to lead any federation as eventually people would gravitate to Abu Dhabi as employment prospects increased there, and that Dubai would have insufficient oil revenues to support a federation that did not include Abu Dhabi.[121] Thus Zayed assumed chairmanship of the next meeting, an important occasion given that Abu Dhabi and Dubai hoped to bring on board the other Trucial sheikhdoms, along with Britain's other Gulf protectorates of Bahrain and Qatar. Their proposal was to amalgamate the five smallest sheikhdoms into one mini-union, the United Arab Coastal Emirates, thereby allowing these poorer territories to have one combined voice alongside Abu Dhabi, Dubai, Bahrain, and Qatar.[122] By May of 1968 this plan had fallen through, not least because these 'coastal emirates' felt that their proud individual histories would be sidelined by such a merger.

Towards the end of the summer, a milestone was reached when the nine delegations met together in Qatar to hold the first session of the Supreme Council of Rulers. Based on a Kuwaiti-devised draft constitution, this council comprised of Sheikh Zayed, Sheikh Maktum bin Rashid Al-Maktum (the first formal involvement in federal politics for Sheikh Rashid's eldest son), Sheikh Khalifa bin Hamad Al-Thani (the Crown Prince of Qatar), Sheikh Easa bin Salman Al-Khalifa of Bahrain, Sheikh Khalid bin Muhammad Al-Qasimi of Sharjah, Sheikh Saqr bin Muhammad Al-Qasimi of Ra's al-Khaimah, Sheikh Rashid bin Humayd Al-Nu'aymi of Ajman, Sheikh Ahmad bin Rashid Al-Mu'alla of Umm al-Qawain, and Sheikh Hamad bin Muhammad Al-Sharqi of Fujairah.[123] In a notable development the Supreme Council discussed the creation of various commissions that would consider certain federal issues and be based in specific emirates. In particular, the commissions for labour, real estate, and health care were to be based in Qatar; the commission for foreign policy was to be based in Bahrain; the commission for communications was to be based in Abu Dhabi; and the commission for commerce was to be based in Dubai.[124]

But by the end of the year the Supreme Council of Rulers' work appeared stillborn, as significant divides were beginning to emerge between the nine members. Bahrain believed that the proposed commissions gave too much power to Qatar, and insisted that two of Qatar's three designated commissions should be shifted to the smaller sheikhdoms. Most worryingly, by the spring of 1969 Bahrain had begun to boycott all federal meetings held in Qatar, and Sheikh Easa's representatives were informing foreign journalists that Bahrain was preparing to become an independent state.[125] Concerned that a federation would not survive without Bahrain, Sheikh Rashid intervened and attempted to bring Bahrain back to the table. The latter was also insisting on a system of proportional representation should any future *Majlis Watani al-Ittihad* or Federal National Council be established. Given that Bahrain had by far the largest population of nationals (over 200,000), Dubai had difficultly persuading the less populous sheikhdoms to accept such a condition.[126] Nevertheless, in late 1969 Sheikh Rashid succeeded in staging another session of the Supreme Council, with Bahrain agreeing to ease its demands,[127] with Sheikh Zayed being elected as President, with Rashid assuming the Vice Presidency, and with Sheikh Khalifa of Qatar becoming Prime Minister. Moreover, it was decided on the first day of the conference that Abu Dhabi should serve as the federation's temporary capital until a new city could be built along the border of Abu Dhabi and Dubai.[128]

Unfortunately, on the last day of the meetings, the promising federation of nine dramatically fell apart, leaving just seven members. Inaccurate rumours had reached the Political Resident that the session was about to collapse, prompting him to despatch a message to the rulers stating that 'Britain would be extremely disappointed if the difficulties were not overcome.' Seemingly outraged by such a blatant act of imperial interference, the delegations from Bahrain and Qatar walked out; although in all probability their respective sheikhs must have used the event to disguise their more serious misgivings over federal involvement.[129] Certainly, Bahrain and Qatar had never wanted to be too close to Abu Dhabi, given that Saudi Arabia continued to claim large portions of Abu Dhabian territory. Bahrain meanwhile was anxious to improve relations with Iran, especially given that Tehran had already claimed the sheikhdom as the country's fourteenth province: closer relations with Sharjah and Ra's al-Khaimah would therefore be problematic given their comparable territorial disputes with Iran.[130] Similarly, Qatar was apprehensive about joining an Abu Dhabi-dominated union given a long-running quarrel over the island of Halul (on which Abu Dhabi had recently established a police presence),[131] and, more seriously, given its prophetic fear that Abu Dhabi's oil wealth would eventually lock all of the other sheikhdoms into a subordinate role.[132]

Predictably therefore, Bahrain signed individual peace agreements with Iran and Saudi Arabia, and in August 1971 declared itself an independent state.[133] The next month Qatar followed suit, leaving Abu Dhabi, Dubai, and the other Trucial sheikhdoms with just three months before the British deadline. The departing Political Resident had earlier met with Sheikh Rashid and discovered he had serious doubts that a federation could now succeed—a view shared by Britain's special envoy, who was frustrated that the nine member federation was now an impossibility.[134] Indicative of their desperation, and in what would appear to be the clearest recorded confirmation of Britain's dependent client system, during Britain's final year of protection both Rashid and Sheikh Zayed made concerted efforts to persuade London to prolong its military presence in the lower Gulf, and even offered to meet the costs from their own state coffers. Indeed, in a somewhat unguarded interview with a British newspaper, Rashid chose to dismiss pan-Arabism, stating that 'Abu Dhabi, Dubai, and in fact the whole coast, people and rulers, would all support the retaining of British forces in the Gulf even though… they may not give a direct answer out of a respect for the general Arab view.'[135] As an earlier report to the British cabinet stated of Zayed, '[He] would be happy to contribute the funds himself from his oil revenues to secure the continuance of the benefits he and his fellow rulers derived from the British presence in the Gulf. His neighbour, Sheikh Rashid of Dubai, made a like proposal a fortnight later. The oil producing sheikhdoms under British protection… would be perfectly willing… to meet in proportion to their respective means, the annual cost of retaining the British forces in the Gulf.'[136]

Such pleas fell on deaf ears, especially following a House of Commons debate that cautioned against British involvement along such lines for fear of British soldiers being branded as 'mercenaries.'[137] By December 1971 Sheikh Rashid and Sheikh

Zayed were left with little choice but to sign a hastily constructed and British-crafted provisional federal constitution with their neighbours.[138] To make matters worse, due to several changing circumstances described later in this volume,[139] Ra's al-Khaimah took a last minute decision to withdraw, leaving just six members in place. At a press conference following the official ceremony at Rashid's guest house in Al-Dhiyafah, a statement was made that the new federation remained 'keen to welcome other countries to join the United Arab Emirates, and especially brother emirates who have signed the Agreement of the Union of Arab Emirates in Dubai on 28th February 1968.'[140] This betrayed the uncertainties of the signatories about such a small federation while keeping the door open for Qatar, Bahrain, and Ra's al-Khaimah to join at a later date.

For Dubai and the five other newly united 'emirates', the federation managed to hold together in the months following its inception, despite many pessimistic predictions from prominent international diplomats and observers,[141] and thereby provided at least some of the necessary collective security envisaged by the withdrawing Political Residency. Although, as will be discussed more fully in the final chapter, Iran pressed certain territorial claims on Sharjah,[142] claiming that the UAE was a British plot and that '...there is no doubt that the colonialists' and the imperialists' policies cannot rest for a moment without trying to exercise their hateful role through rear guard actions... the UAE is no more than an obedient instrument for the ambitions of the imperialists and the colonialist';[143] the situation was quickly diffused, and due to fast-moving external developments Ra's al-Khaimah applied to join the federation by the end of the year.[144] Thus, with its immediate security guaranteed, the UAE had been able to define its territories, and was soon recognised by the United Nations, the Arab League, France, and Germany. Moreover, while the USSR initially refused to acknowledge the UAE, asserting that it was 'part of an extended Imperial plan'; when Britain fi-

nally removed its naval covering force and its remaining personnel from the Sharjah airbase in 1972,[145] recognition was eventually forthcoming.[146] A new Federal National Council was created
to sit underneath the Supreme Council of Rulers and the new
twelve member federal cabinet, and these were to be supported
by other rapidly established federal institutions and ministries,
most of which were upgraded versions of the old Trucial offices.
As will be described in the analysis in later chapters of Dubai's
neo-patrimonial government, these were just enough to provide
a veneer of modern governance for the fledgling state.[147] Furthermore, most of these structures remained loose and de-centralised,
and—as the British had hoped—did not assume control over all
emirate-level resources or powers. Finally, and most symbolically,
within another year the seven emirates were also able to agree on
a new federal flag, a set of new federal postage stamps,[148] a new
currency—the UAE Dirham,[149] and, perhaps most challengingly,
the requirement for all of the emirates to drive on the right in
order to avoid inter-emirate accidents.

3

THE FOUNDATIONS OF A FREE PORT

Although times were often austere for Dubai's economy, exacerbated by the aforementioned British controls on technology imports and market access, there were nevertheless periods of prosperity, not least following the pearling boom at the turn of the twentieth century. Moreover, Dubai was rapidly becoming an attractive environment for re-export trading—a simple activity that required no technology injections or problematic foreign assistance, and thereby escaped British scrutiny. Indeed, the political stability afforded by the client protection system, combined with the Al-Maktum family's shrewd lowering of most taxes and duties, were enough to position Dubai as the safest and most profitable free port of the lower Gulf. When political and economic problems arose in India, Iran and its Arab neighbours, Dubai was well placed to benefit from influxes of skilled and experienced merchants who sought to relocate their operations to a new trade hub. Dubai welcomed such valuable immigrants, and by mid-century, even if resources were at times low, its rulers invested in whatever physical infrastructure was deemed necessary to maintain such commercial pre-eminence and the loyalty of a cosmopolitan trading population.

Flourishing free trade

Following Dubai's secession from Abu Dhabi and its balancing of regional powers, the relative tranquillity of the town facilitated merchant activity as early as the 1840s. The sheikhdom's first in-dependent ruler, Sheikh Maktum bin Buti, remarked that soon after his arrival in Dubai there were over 40 shops and 100 trad-ers in the *souq*, compared to just a handful of outlets dating from earlier times.[1] By the 1880s, under the guidance of Maktum's eldest sons, Sheikh Hasher bin Maktum Al-Maktum and Sheikh Rashid bin Maktum Al-Maktum, Dubai's merchant community had grown even further, with foreign visitors to the town observ-ing that '…although Abu Dhabi had emerged as the strongest and most influential military and political power of the Trucial sheikhdoms, Dubai had become the principal commercial port on the Gulf coast.'[2] It was, however, in the late 1890s and early 1900s that Dubai changed beyond recognition, following Sheikh Mak-tum bin Hasher Al-Maktum's removal of as many trade barriers as possible, including customs fees and licences for vessels. A five per cent tax on trade was abolished, and over 200 Dubai-registered boats and 3,000 merchants were exempted from further tariffs.[3]

A free port was born, and within a few years the number of boats berthed in Dubai had risen to 400, eclipsing the historically larger fleets of Abu Dhabi and Sharjah. Moreover, Dubai's new standing was attracting far more British-registered boats, with the number of such visiting vessels increasing from only three or four per annum to over thirty-five by 1900.[4] In a notable devel-opment, in 1904 the British India Steam Navigation Company, that hitherto had been operating the route between Basra and Bombay, began using Dubai as a calling point. This brought five additional large vessels to Dubai every year, dramatically boosting the revenues of the town's *souq*, and thereby confirming Dubai's position as the main distribution centre for goods along the whole littoral from Qatar to Ra's al-Khaimah.[5] So significant were these steam ships that a major new building in the Dubai textile market was named in honour of the largest—the *Sardhana*.[6] By the 1950s Dubai's status as the new business capital of the Trucial coast was again consolidated following Britain's decision to shift her agency headquarters from Sharjah to Dubai, given that most British trade was now connected to Dubai,[7] and from 1961 onwards the Political Resident[8] began to visit Dubai ahead of all the other sheikhdoms when touring the lower Gulf.[9] By the mid-1960s Dubai's population had grown to over 100,000,[10] by far the largest conurbation in the region, and could claim a fleet of over 4,000 dhows[11]—an astonishing contrast with Sheikh Maktum bin Buti's original settlement.

Textiles, gold, and electronics

Most of the goods passing through Dubai's free port were products 'informally' shipped out from the Indian subcontinent and the Far East. This merchandise was often destined to be re-exported back to Asia in such a way as to avoid local restrictions, or, as the expatriate population grew, to be distributed to customers in Dubai itself. Although, as will be demonstrated later in this volume,[12] this re-export trade was at times indistinguishable from a large-scale smuggling racket, the Dubai mindset remained firmly one of supply and demand, with the city's merchants carving out a niche for themselves.

Perhaps the strongest example of such successful free trade was Dubai's cornering of the South Asian textiles market following India's independence from Britain and the attempts of its first prime minister, Jawaharlal Nehru, to replicate the Soviet miracle by using the state to plan and protect the economy. These restrictive practices effectively meant that India-based merchants could not meet the demand for their products and nor could many customers purchase the quantities of fabric that they desired, thereby allowing Dubai the opportunity to become an intermediary. In particular, cotton voiles from the Khatau, Sriram, and Srinivas mills were heavily in demand, especially in Iran where such material was found to be the most comfortable to wear. Most of the offers and purchases from India were communicated to Dubai using the British Cable and Wireless Company, which had two offices—one on each side of the creek. Although it sometimes took many months for the products to arrive (with the textiles often left in warehouses in Bombay for long periods until a steamship was scheduled to sail past Dubai), the system nevertheless proved reliable and encouraged the Dubai traders to source goods from even further afield. Sasooni cotton from the Nichibo mills in Japan was in great demand along with cotton latha from the Nishinbo Three Peaches and Toyobo Flying Dragon mills. These broad cloths were extremely popular in the Gulf, especially during the *haj* season. Dubai again played the role of re-exporter, with its merchants carefully ordering the necessary materials well in advance so as to overcome the lengthy five month shipping time from Japan. Similarly profitable was Dubai's trade in sourcing specialist western textiles for wealthy Indians and Pakistanis resident in both Dubai and Bombay. Specifically, a number of fashionable sari and wedding dress manufacturers had begun to favour American manufactured 'bamboo sharkskin,'[13] and by the late 1960s various brands of polyester were being sought from the United States (Dacron), Britain (Terylene), Japan (Tetron), and Germany (Tergal).[14]

Similarly lucrative were Dubai's gold re-exports following Nehru's decision to levy duties on precious metals,[15] which led to India's losing its position as Asia's primary gold market. A huge amount of gold had to be shipped into India every year, notably to satisfy dowry payments,[16] and by 1966 it is believed that over four million ounces were being transported annually between Dubai and London. This was second only to France's gold trade with Britain, and represented over ten per cent of all the gold mined in the non-communist countries at that time.[17] Also benefiting from high Indian demand and Indian restrictions was Dubai's electronics trade, which by the late 1960s and early 1970s saw over two million electrical appliances being re-exported through Dubai.[18] Most of this early business was centred on the supply of European transistor radios and tape recorders (especially those manufactured by Grundig and Telefunken), as more advanced products were still considered expensive. However, as piped water and electricity became more commonplace in India, an increasing number of white goods and air conditioning units from North America were also arriving in Dubai. By the late 1970s Japanese goods entered the market, with Dubai re-exporting millions of Hitachi personal stereos to the subcontinent,[19] and by 1982 demand for televisions (to enable households to watch the Asian games being held that year) was so high that the Indian government was forced to allow legal imports of sets, an opportunity that Dubai's traders made sure they did not miss.[20]

Persian Immigration

Since the very beginning of Dubai's free port strategy, the sheikhdom benefited from a huge influx of Persian merchants. As conditions worsened in Qajari Persia and then later in the Shah's Iran, experienced traders required a new base for their activities, and Dubai was keen to embrace and absorb into its own national population these influential Gulf businessmen. Most of these early immigrants were from settlements on the southern coastline of Persia, which had formerly been possessions of the Ra's al-Khaimah-based Qawasim clan.[21] Indeed, since the 1720s the Qawasim sheikhs had established control over the aforementioned port of Lingah[22] in addition to the towns of Junj and Luft, and by the 1730s their settlers had begun to settle a number of nearby islands, including Qishm.[23] Moreover, by 1812 a number of other tribes from the lower Gulf (led by Sheikh Khaz'al of the Al-Ka'ab) had staked their claims in Persia, establishing another port at Al-Muhammarah and setting up a hinterland agricultural community at Disghgan in the province of Fars.[24] It is noteworthy that these towns were ethnically Arab, with most of the population wearing Omani-style *qraiat* turbans[25] and with written records from the nineteenth century demonstrating that Arabic rather than Farsi had always been the primary language, although the accent was

71

considerably softer than the *khaleeji* Arabic spoken elsewhere in the Gulf.[26]

Lingah proved to be particularly prosperous, with Britain choosing to install an agency there in the 1820s, much like it had done in the Sharjah-Dubai area. Furthermore, the town was short-listed as a possible site for the first Political Residency in the Gulf, before a town further up the coast was eventually chosen.[27] Much of the port's success was due to its close proximity to lucrative pearl beds and its very relaxed taxation system—the Qawasim rulers preferred low tariffs, and although the right to levy customs duties on trade through Lingah had been sold to a Belgian 'tax farming' company, these foreign tax collectors had little real impact on the local economy.[28] Thus, throughout the nineteenth century Lingah and its satellite settlements continued to grow. However, during the mid-1880s Nasser Al-Din Shah Qajar's government in Tehran,[29] which had previously been unable to project its power as far south as the Anglo-Arab sphere of influence, began to receive Russian backing[30] and felt sufficiently emboldened to encourage the Persian Imperial Customs Company to impose taxes on Lingah and Qishm.[31] To make matters worse, new Persian laws were imposed on these Arab townsmen, refusing them permission to bury their dead on the islands (as had been their custom) and preventing merchants from registering new boats unless their wives agreed to stop covering their faces.[32]

At first, the Qawasim attempted to resist, with the ruler of Lingah, Sheikh Qadhib bin Rashid Al-Qasimi, declaring in 1887 that his city was an 'emirate under Ottoman protection' (even though there had been a British agent in place for over sixty years[33]). Given that he was deported to Tehran just a few months later,[34] and that his family home on the island of Sirri was seized by the Persians, this was probably an act of desperation as formal Ottoman support was never likely to materialise.[35] It therefore became clear that those who opposed the Persian taxes and social reforms had little option but to emigrate, with many returning to the Qawasim homelands of Ra's al-Khaimah and Sharjah. However, a significant number of the most successful merchants (in addition to most of Lingah's resident Indian financiers and moneylenders)[36] were aware of the more attractive trading conditions in Dubai, and in the early 1890s opted to move their businesses there. These *ajami* Arabian-Persians were led by Muhammad Hajji Badri, Abdul Wahid Fikree, Sheikh Mustafa Abdullatif, and Ghulam Abbas, the latter of whom had brought about half of the Al-Ansari family with him.[37] Recognising the wealth such men could bring to Dubai, Sheikh Rashid bin Maktum Al-Maktum offered these immigrant merchants personal protection and provided them with prime plots of land close to the creek, in order for them to build houses and settle their families.[38] Indeed, parts of these buildings survive today in the old Bastakiyah quarter of Bur Dubai (named after Bastak—a small town in Persia), and boast some of the best examples of the wind tower architecture that was originally native to Lingah.[39] Equally welcoming to the ajami community was Rashid's nephew, Sheikh Maktum bin Hasher Al-Maktum, who, following his succession in 1894, sought to bring as many of the newcomers to his majlis as possible, hoping to learn what they needed from Dubai in order for their businesses to flourish.[40]

By the turn of the century, the ajamis had already begun to make their mark on Dubai's economy, having brought with them considerable shipping experience and access to hitherto untapped Asian and African markets. As a contemporary businessman noted of this period '…this drain of expertise from Lingah was to be the foundation for Dubai's strong growth after 1902… Persia's loss was Dubai's gain.'[41] And when a prominent European geographer[42] visited Dubai in 1903 he recorded that a larger number of families had recently arrived from Persia 'after escaping the arbitrary rule in their own country' and appeared to be prospering in their new home.[43] Indeed, by that stage it was clear that Lingah had declined into obscurity,[44] especially following the British

India Steam Navigation Company's addition of Dubai as a port of call—this decision was effectively at Persia's expense given that Lingah had formerly been the steam line's primary port in the lower Gulf, and had served as the main conduit for Indian goods for the previous forty years. As has been noted, '...without these regular steamer visits, the city of Lingah, a bustling trading centre, quickly declined.'[45]

Persian immigration to Dubai continued throughout the following decades, as notwithstanding Dubai's economic slowdown, prompted by international recession and the decline of pearling, it still offered a better business environment than anywhere else in the Gulf. In particular, by the mid-1920s Reza Shah had sought to increase Tehran's control over his southern coastal towns even further, raising taxes yet again, and, in the same way as his predecessors, attempting to modernise and secularise the population by changing dress codes and requiring local schools to teach in standardised Farsi rather than in Arabic.[46] As before, such encroachment was deemed unacceptable by merchant communities, prompting a second wave to transfer their assets to Dubai and thereby follow many of their relatives who had left in the 1890s. By the outbreak of the Second World War, conditions had deteriorated once more following British fears that Reza would ally Persia (which had been renamed 'Iran' in 1936 in respect of the state's new modern identity) with Nazi Germany. Britain and the Soviet Union were left with little choice but to occupy the northern part of Iran and install Reza's son, Muhammad Reza Shah, on the throne. However, many Iranians refused to accept such external interference and refused to support their new ruler, with some openly praising the Nazis. Fearing further unrest Britain chose to blockade all of Iran's ports, including those on the southern coast, thereby crippling what remained of the local merchant economies. Although Dubai also suffered from this British embargo, given that Iran had always been one of its greatest trading partners, in the long term it gained, as a third contingent of disgruntled ajami businessmen arrived. Moreover, given that Britain had been rationing the quantity of foodstuffs entering the Gulf during these war years, this sudden population influx to Dubai allowed Sheikh Said bin Maktum Al-Maktum to strike a new deal with the British, increasing Dubai's quota of food to such an extent that many Dubai-based merchants, including the aforementioned Murshid Al-Usaimi,[47] soon enjoyed surpluses that they could then sell on for a profit to their less fortunate Trucial neighbours.[48]

The large ajami merchant community's presence was not always appreciated in Dubai, especially as many of the original Bani Yas families were resentful that people whom they still considered to be Persians rather than Arabs were rapidly becoming part of the national population. There was a deep concern that such 'foreigners' would always have divided loyalties and might at some future time support Persia against the interests of Dubai. In 1928 there was a serious backlash against these immigrants following the British interception of a Dubai-registered vessel crewed by ajamis en route to Persia. The boat was found to contain some kidnapped women and children and was believed to be depositing these captives in Lingah, where they would have their valuables confiscated and sold, before being imprisoned. Furious Dubai nationals attacked houses in the Bastakiyah quarter and mobs assaulted prominent ajamis as they went about their business.[49] There is some evidence that even the British agent in the Trucial states (at that time an Iraqi)[50] supported this hostile reaction by discriminating against 'non-Arabs' such as the ajamis.[51] The matter was only resolved following the arrival of a British gunboat off the coast of Dubai and the placing of considerable British pressure on the Persian administration to investigate the problem and to guarantee the repatriation of the prisoners. The British chose to compensate the families of the missing people, indicating Britain's recognition of the need to calm fears and ensure that the economically vital ajami section of Dubai's population maintained its confidence in the sheikhdom's security and stability.[52]

Regrettably, some tension between the communities remained and problems resurfaced, especially during the Dubai National Front agitation of the 1950s and, most worryingly, during the 1960s following the Shah's de facto recognition of the state of Israel. Incensed Arab nationalists daubed the property of prominent Dubai ajamis with graffiti, and in some cases broke into their homes and smeared excreta on the walls.[53]

Nevertheless, the Al-Maktum family and most of Dubai's merchants continued to value and respect their ajami residents and colleagues, and in time relations with the majority of Dubai's other citizens improved. An Iranian hospital was established in Dubai by Abu Torab Mehra in the late 1960s,[54] and in 1971, following the formation of the United Arab Emirates and the immediate seizure of certain UAE islands by Iran (see later),[55] Sheikh Rashid bin Said Al-Maktum's third eldest son and the head of Dubai's security services, Sheikh Muhammad bin Rashid Al-Maktum, sought to prevent any further backlashes by deploying forces to protect various ajami properties.[56] In the event such protection was not necessary, and by 1979 relations were further enhanced, as the Islamic revolution and the eventual formation of Ayatollah Khomeini's Islamic republic in Iran prompted a fourth wave of merchant migration to Dubai—one that continues unabated up to the present day, with many Iranians that are disaffected with the Ahmadinejad administration relocating their businesses, assets, and families to Dubai. Indeed, there are now over 40,000 Dubai nationals who are of ajami origin—perhaps half of the emirate's 'indigenous' population[57]—most of whom are successful entrepreneurs or government employees, and they have been complemented by a growing number of permanently resident Iranian nationals prospering in Dubai.

Abu Dhabi immigration

As more of a land power, Abu Dhabi had little of the commercial history of Lingah, but by the turn of the century the sheikhdom had a small but flourishing merchant community that had been enriched by the pearl trade and had then sought to diversify its interests by engaging in re-export. Unfortunately, political instability and the rulers' unwillingness to foster economic development soon rendered Abu Dhabi inhospitable to those with any commercial ambition, obliging many families to follow the ajamis' lead and transfer their operations to the more business-friendly Dubai. Indeed, following a time of high profile fratricides within the Al-Nahyan family during the 1920s,[58] concurrent with a period in which Abu Dhabi suffered some of the highest taxes in the lower Gulf, there is evidence that a great many merchants left. Even when one of these short-lived rulers, Sheikh Hamdan bin Zayed Al-Nahyan, visited Dubai to try to persuade his former merchants to return, very few did.[59]

By the early 1950s conditions had improved little, with even more families having emigrated from Abu Dhabi during the Second World War.[60] Although stability had been achieved under Sheikh Shakhbut bin Sultan Al-Nahyan, his introverted and overly cautious leadership failed to recognise the need to improve socio-economic conditions and invest in the necessary infrastructure for his shrinking population to survive and prosper. When Britain introduced its aforementioned five-year development plans for the region, few of the funds were earmarked for Abu Dhabi, with the British preferring to channel their limited resources into the seemingly more worthwhile projects taking place in Dubai and Sharjah.[61] Moreover, even when offered external assistance, Shakhbut often refused, favouring minimal interference in his sheikhdom's affairs. Most worryingly, years after the first schools had opened elsewhere in the Trucial states, Abu Dhabi still had no formal education system by the mid-1950s. When Shakhbut was approached for advice in 1954 by Sheikh Saqr bin Sultan Al-Qasimi of Sharjah, who was struggling with the dilemma of whether or not to permit the sons of an exiled man to remain in a Sharjah school, Shakhbut proudly informed him that

77

such a matter would never even be an issue in Abu Dhabi because there was not even a single school.[62] Shakhbut had declined the same Kuwaiti and other Arab aid to build and develop schools that his neighbours had accepted,[63] and even though such aid led to political complications in Dubai,[64] this was still a great blow for Abu Dhabi as it effectively delayed the emergence of a skilled and educated population. Unsurprisingly therefore, when in 1961 Shakhbut finally succumbed to pressure and reluctantly agreed to build schools in Al-Bateen and Al-Falahia,[65] he claimed that he wanted all of the teachers to be local men and for them only to discuss matters relating to Abu Dhabi—no international geography or history were to be taught as they were deemed to be irrelevant.[66] Similarly disgraceful was Shakhbut's lack of interest in developing healthcare: when a team of surgeons from a mission hospital in India arrived in Abu Dhabi in 1956 to explore the possibility of opening a hospital in the town, their efforts came to nothing,[67] yet when they visited Shakhbut's younger brother and the wali of the sheikhdom's second largest town of Al-Ayn, Sheikh Zayed bin Sultan Al-Nahyan, they were much more successful. This created a bizarre scenario in which the capital city lagged some six years behind a hinterland town in the building of a modern hospital.[68] Even when the construction materials required for Abu Dhabi's hospital were delivered by the British in 1962, they remained untouched in their packing crates on the beach for several months.[69]

In contrast to the Al-Maktum family's preference for free trade, Sheikh Shakhbut exacerbated Abu Dhabi's existing problems by constructing trade barriers wherever possible, preferring protectionism and short term gains from tax revenue. In particular, all foreign firms seeking to set up business interests in Abu Dhabi were charged an 'entrance fee,' and were made well aware of Shakhbut's dislike for non-Abu Dhabi merchants. Indeed, only one or two Dubai merchants per year were allowed to open branches in Abu Dhabi,[70] and even well-known Bahraini and

Qatari merchants were often kept out. When Muhammad Kanoo of Manama visited the Trucial states in 1958, Sheikh Rashid bin Said Al-Maktum immediately came to a mutually beneficial arrangement with the Kanoo Group, whereas Shakhbut chose to keep Kanoo waiting, and eventually pressed for an enormous 20 per cent share of all profits.[71] Significantly, even indigenous merchants found life increasingly difficult, as at this time Shakhbut had imposed a ban on any new construction in Abu Dhabi, and any new business venture had to obtain written permission from the ruler's office, which was often unforthcoming.[72] This development may have been precipitated by Shakhbut having caught one of his leading merchant families corresponding with Rashid and a group of Dubai merchants[73]—an incident that would have played upon his fears that Dubai was planning to make inroads into Abu Dhabi's economy.

Similarly problematic for Abu Dhabi merchants was Sheikh Shakhbut's mistrust of banks and modern accounting. Much like the delays in establishing hospitals and schools, Abu Dhabi was some years behind Dubai, which had set up banks much earlier. Even when a Dubai-based team from the British Bank of the Middle East was finally granted permission to visit Abu Dhabi in 1958, Shakhbut reportedly refused to sign any of the contracts that had been drawn up and 'exasperated all concerned'.[74] Although, after a year of negotiations and considerable persuasion, a branch was finally opened in Abu Dhabi, it soon became clear that its methods were not understood or appreciated by Shakhbut. The latter had on one occasion ordered a large consignment of rifles and an electricity generator, and had taken out the necessary loan. When bank officials delivered these to Abu Dhabi they quickly realised that Shakhbut had no intention of actually paying off his debts, having misunderstood the concept of a loan and fully expecting the goods to be given to him as a gift in recognition of his position as ruler. In the subsequent quarrel Shakhbut accused the bank of stealing money from him and tried to blame and fire his British-approved financial advisor,[75] prompting the British agent to intervene and persuade Shakhbut to at least pay for the generator, if not the rifles. It was felt that unless such a compromise was reached then Shakhbut would have definitely expelled all bank officials from Abu Dhabi.[76] Equally worrying for the bank was Shakhbut's similar reaction to their attempts to help set up a proper municipality office in Abu Dhabi. When in 1959 one of their most prominent Dubai employees[77] was asked by the British to help Shakhbut's youngest son, Sheikh Sultan bin Shakhbut Al-Nahyan, to establish something similar to what already existed in Dubai and Sharjah, Shakhbut visited the site of this much-needed development and became so distrustful of all the written records he saw that he ordered the two men to purchase kerosene from the souq and to burn everything and disband the project.[78]

Under Sheikh Shakhbut, relations with the British agent also deteriorated, prompting even more Abu Dhabi merchants, many of whom believed business would become increasingly difficult if their sheikhdom fell from favour with the British, to settle in 'more favoured' Trucial states such as Dubai. By 1953 Shakhbut had openly begun to negotiate with the Iraqi Petroleum Company's American rival, Superior Oil Company,[79] and by the late 1950s he was proving uncooperative towards Britain's attempts to foster collective security through meetings of the Trucial States Council. Indeed, it was noted that Shakhbut rarely attended the Council's scheduled meetings, and often preferred to send an (unprepared) deputy in his place. Moreover, from the minutes of those meetings where Shakhbut did make an appearance, it seems that he spoke against the federation and came across as unpredictable to his peers.[80] By 1961 the agent had admitted that 'with Shakhbut present in meetings it is impossible to get many progressive ideas debated as he continually says that things are alright as they are now.'[81] The Foreign Office duly noted that it was unlikely that Abu Dhabi in its present situation could play any meaningful role in the further activities of the Council or the economic development of the Trucial states.[82] Over the next few years, little changed, with Abu Dhabi continuing to block all suggested joint ventures. A proposal to join a Trucial-wide postal system was vetoed by Shakhbut, even though it offered greater efficiency and was favoured by all of the other rulers,[83] and in 1966, following the marriage of Sheikh Rashid's daughter, Sheikha Mariam bint Rashid Al-Maktum, to the ruler of Qatar, Sheikh Ahmad bin Ali Al-Thani, an attempt to set up a joint currency between Qatar, Dubai, and Abu Dhabi was similarly scuppered, as Shakhbut mistrusted Qatar's motives and preferred to side with Bahrain and Oman, even though neither of these could offer Abu Dhabi any tangible benefits for its cooperation.[84] The latter's merchants were consequently disadvantaged and further isolated, as the Qatari-Dubai riyal went ahead without their inclusion.[85]

Even in political matters, the British began to mistrust Shakhbut's stance, believing him, if anything, to be too strongly and too openly opposed to Arab nationalism. Although Arab nationalism represented a serious threat to the stability of Dubai,[86] it was nevertheless felt that Shakhbut should at least acknowledge that such sentiments might exist among his people, otherwise the sheikhdom was likely to become even more of powder keg, primed for revolution or readjustment of power, than was Dubai or Sharjah. A number of Abu Dhabi merchants and notables were disgusted by their ruler's total lack of respect for the Arab cause, with many feeling that in Dubai there was at least some meaningful political activity taking place. As the Political Resident reported to the Foreign Office at the time of the Suez Crisis in 1956, the 'rulers of Abu Dhabi clearly welcomed Britain's intervention in Egypt, and hoped that Nasser would be taught a lesson and removed completely.' Even the usually more diplomatic Sheikh Zayed remarked to the British agent that 'Britain should do to Cairo what the Russians have done to Budapest.'[87] Although this strong reaction could probably be partly explained by the Al-Nahyan's

81

erroneous belief that Abu Dhabi's traditional enemies in Saudi Arabia had strong links with Cairo, and although Sheikh Rashid and the rest of the Al-Maktum family probably also wished (albeit secretly) for the demise of the Jamal Abdul Nasser administration, the British agreed that the rulers of Abu Dhabi should not be quite so brazen about the matter.[88]

Perhaps most remarkably, even by the mid-1960s, when large revenues from oil exports had begun to accrue, Abu Dhabi remained grossly underdeveloped, with Sheikh Shakhbut continuing to distrust drastic change of any kind. Indeed, the British believed the greatest irony at this time was that Shakhbut's aforementioned four per cent contribution to the Trucial States Development Fund,[89] which was to fund Trucial-wide projects, was actually much greater than the amount he was spending on improving infrastructure in his own sheikhdom. As such, some of the smaller, non-oil producing sheikhdoms began to see the benefits of Abu Dhabi's oil long before Abu Dhabi's own population did.[90] Certainly, the British agent had already remarked to his assistant after visiting Abu Dhabi that: '...it could hardly seem stranger that this potentially oil-rich town now consists of barasti huts, a broken down market, a picture of Nasser in a coffee shop, and just a few buildings put up by the oil company.'[91] Moreover, slightly later British reports described Abu Dhabi as being a 'complete scandal'.[92] Similarly damning were the observations of the Political Resident's wife[93] who, when touring Abu Dhabi in 1963, noted that: 'tarmac roads have been made in odd stretches, but Shakhbut refuses to pay for their upkeep... the road from the Agency is a sea of mud and the beach is still used as a public lavatory',[94] before concluding that: '...at the moment everything remains at a standstill; and all those involved in trying to get a move on are being slightly driven around the bend... with Shakhbut's view that modern development may destroy all that is good in the simple structure of tribal society.'[95]

Given the bans on construction and restrictions on new businesses, Abu Dhabi's merchants were unable to cash in on any of the new oil-related opportunities. As a prominent businessman recalls, this was incredibly frustrating, especially when those arriving in Abu Dhabi had to source their goods from elsewhere:

'...the people of Abu Dhabi could see them importing cars, trucks, materials and equipment but since nothing was being bought here, there was no benefit to the local economy. The local merchants could not provide the needed products and services nor could they accommodate the increasing number of oil workers because they lacked capital and were forbidden from building anything.'[96]

Most embarrassingly, the bulk of oil company supplies were purchased in Dubai and then transported to Abu Dhabi or its outlying oil-rich islands such as Das.[97] And to the consternation of many Abu Dhabi nationals, the oil company had little choice but to award the contract for the construction of Abu Dhabi's first desalination plant to a newly created Dubai-based company.[98]

In 1966 Sheikh Shakhbut was finally deposed after it had become clear to the majority of the Al-Nahyan family that the situation could not continue any longer. Shakhbut's far more astute and forward-thinking brother, Sheikh Zayed, was the natural choice to succeed, having accrued considerable administrative experience as the wali and de facto ruler of Al-Ayn, and having gained the support of Shakhbut's youngest son and heir apparent, Sheikh Sultan.[99] Moreover, given that Shakhbut's eldest son, Sheikh Said bin Shakhbut Al-Nahyan, who had earlier been implicated in a serious shooting incident, had been spending time in Europe receiving medical treatment and was therefore also beyond consideration, the British agent had no objection to sending a small number of military policemen to Abu Dhabi to safeguard the succession of Zayed, as he too believed him be the most capable.[100] In the event, the transfer of power was peaceful, with Shakhbut briefly remonstrating but then eventually accepting the need for abdication, and then agreeing to be flown out of Abu Dhabi.[101]

However, even with this long overdue change of leadership, the consensus was that the damage had already been done: although Abu Dhabi's oil wealth soon allowed the infinitely more energetic Zayed to take the lead in federal affairs and position Abu Dhabi as the UAE's capital,[102] considerable merchant emigration had irrecoverably weakened Abu Dhabi's business community, while boosting that of neighbouring Dubai. When new companies were finally set up in Abu Dhabi in the late 1960s and early 1970s, most had to rely heavily on Arab expatriate managers; whereas comparable companies in Dubai were almost always led by experienced local merchants—some of whom were originally from Abu Dhabi.

Sharjah immigration

With a larger population than Dubai, with a comparable natural water inlet, as the second town of the veteran Qawasim traders, and as the first site of the British agency following the 1835 peace treaties, Sharjah had served as the commercial capital of the Trucial states for much of the nineteenth century and the first few decades of the twentieth. However, much like Abu Dhabi's merchants, many members of Sharjah's business community transferred their operations to Dubai following a series of questionable leadership decisions and resulting economic problems in their home sheikhdom. The first identifiable wave came in the mid-1930s when the Al-Bu Shamis family, which controlled the semi-independent coastal area of Hamriyyah (an enclave sandwiched between Ajman and Umm al-Qawain), wished to allow the British to develop the beach area so as to facilitate the unloading of vessels. This prompted a quarrel between the family's leader, Sheikh Hadif Al-Shamsi, and the ruler of Sharjah, Sheikh Sultan bin Saqr Al-Qasimi, who remained opposed to such development. Moreover, at about the same time the Al-Bu Shamis had suffered a serious raid by members of the aforementioned Awamir: although Hadif's men pursued the thieves and eventually recovered the stolen booty,[103] it was nevertheless felt that Sultan should have done more to protect his citizens.[104] This combination of disappointments prompted many members of the Al-Bu Shamis to leave Sharjah, with many settling in Dubai, where, as with the earlier Lingah immigrants, they were welcomed and offered a prime plot of land near to the creek—this they chose to rename Hamriyyah in memory of their original homeland. Indeed, this prominent and prosperous family remain in Dubai today, while ironically the disputed beach area in the original Hamriyyah is now a major Sharjah export processing zone.[105]

In the late 1930s Dubai became home to even more Sharjah families following another dispute, this time over the Al-Ghusais district (close to the present day Dubai International Airport). It is thought that the inhabitants of Al-Ghusais, much like the Al-Bu Shamis before them, were hoping to transfer their allegiance to the seemingly more progressive Al-Maktum family. A brief battle for secession ensued, with the pro-Dubai faction managing to overcome the Sharjah loyalists courtesy of a female spy within the Qawasim's ranks, and with Al-Ghusais subsequently being recognised as part of Dubai and as the new border between the two sheikhdoms.[106] Similarly, between 1938 and 1940 around 400 other disgruntled individuals, many of them wealthy merchants, left the Hira district of Sharjah for Dubai. Led by Ali bin Abdullah Al-Awais and Rahman bin Abdullah, they saw greater opportunities for expanding their businesses if they moved to the much more trade-friendly Dubai.[107] In a series of desperate moves, Sheikh Sultan sought to stem this flow of emigrants from Sharjah, realising that Dubai was poised to overtake his sheikhdom as the effective capital of the lower Gulf. In particular, he requested that the British re-route their steamer service and their postal deliveries from Dubai to Sharjah.[108] Although the British agent refused, it is interesting to note that during the Second World War Sultan repeated his demands, using the increased wartime importance of the Sharjah airbase as extra leverage. While the agent did temporarily agree to the re-routing,[109] this was not enough to offset Sharjah's commercial decline, with a 1948 report by the Imperial Bank of Iran (the forerunner to the British Bank of the Middle East) claiming that almost all merchant activity along the Trucial coast was taking place in Dubai,[110] and that Dubai's population was around four times greater than that of Sharjah.[111]

The final blow for Sharjah came in the 1950s as a result of Sheikh Saqr bin Sultan Al-Qasimi's indecisiveness regarding the dredging of his town's harbour. Since the end of the war both the Sharjah lagoon and the Dubai creek had begun to silt up with mud, preventing larger boats from reaching their unloading points. In some places the situation was so bad that the water was only two feet deep,[112] and in Dubai's case the silt was so heavy that the mouth of the creek would shrink by over 600 yards in the winter months,[113] with the heaviest area of these build-ups eventually becoming the inhabited district of Shindagha.[114] Given that such water inlets were the vital arteries of trade in the Trucial states, it was essential that the silt be cleared as soon as possible so that business could resume. Sheikh Rashid bin Said Al-Maktum soon recognised this need and swiftly set about raising the necessary revenue to recover Dubai's creek. He initially gambled by floating a 'creek bond' with the idea of encouraging his merchant population to contribute to Dubai's infrastructural improvements. The bond was believed to be successful, although in any event Rashid would have prevailed, as he managed to persuade the oil-rich Kuwaiti government to step in and buy out the bond after just a year and a half.[115] With the Kuwaiti investors onboard and with the necessary funding in place, Rashid approached the British agent to ask him to search for suitable consultants. Thus, between 1958 and 1960 Dubai's creek was dredged by Overseas Ast. of Austria, in cooperation with Britain's Sir William Halcrow and Partners.[116] Moreover, the area of the town bordering the creek was planned out by John Harris and Partners, another British firm, which allowed for ships of up to 800 tonnes to enter Dubai, rather than just the dhows of the past.[117] In stark contrast Saqr was wary of allowing any more British interference in Sharjah than he had to, and, as will be shown later in this volume,[118] was at this time communicating with the Arab League's representatives rather than with the agent. Britain had offered to develop Sharjah's lagoon in the same way as Dubai's creek, but it is thought that Saqr was holding out for some kind of funding from Cairo to conduct the work.[119] In the meantime all he had done was to have a small canal dug close to the water's edge, which ended up flooding part of the area.[120] Any Arab League assistance was either unforthcoming or was simply too slow to materialise, and by 1960 the Sharjah lagoon had to be closed to all shipping for several months,[121] with ships arriving at other times of the year having to rely on tug boats. As a series of British reports stated, by the late 1950s Dubai was receiving 110 boats per quarter compared to just 31 for Sharjah, and by the end of 1960 Dubai had received 79 boats, with none calling at Sharjah, and with all cargo bound for Sharjah having to be relayed through Dubai.[122] Throughout this period yet another wave of merchants gave up on Sharjah and moved to Dubai—clearly Sharjah did not prioritise business in the same way that Dubai did. As a prominent Dubai national recalls of this troubled time for Sharjah: '...the experience of Sharjah which, prior to the silting up of its creek, had every advantage and might well have become the commercial centre of the southern Gulf, had shown how important it was to have unimpeded access to a port whose facilities allowed the direct unloading of merchandise without having to be dependent always on the use of tenders.'[123]

Other Arab immigration

In addition to immigrants arriving from Abu Dhabi and Sharjah, Dubai also welcomed merchants from other sheikhdoms, and indeed other areas of the Gulf and the Arab world. In only rare and isolated cases have merchant families actually left Dubai, and even then, as was the case with the Bin Lutah family's move to

Ajman, the exodus was usually only temporary.[124] Petty traders from further up the coast in Ajman, Umm al-Qawain, and Ra's al-Khaimah often moved their primary offices to Dubai, and less obviously, many of the hinterland bedouin (who had previously visited Dubai to sell tins of well water or tins of collected rain-water[125]) chose Dubai as their preferred dwelling place when they finally opted for a more settled lifestyle and a more permanent form of business.[126] In time, these Trucial Arabs were joined by Muscatis from the Indian Ocean coastline, and by would-be merchants from Bahrain (notably a group of Shia businessmen led by Mirza Al-Rahma), Iraq (primarily from the Zubair province and led by Saleh Al-Usaimi), and Qatar.[127] All were united by a desire for free trade and a respect for Dubai's laissez-faire policies.

Much like the more recent Iranian influxes, Dubai has continued to benefit from Arab immigrants, especially from areas that have suffered war or serious instability. Most notably, the number of Iraqis moving their businesses to Dubai increased dramatically after Abdul Salam Arif's 1958 Arab nationalist revolution in Baghdad[128]—an influx that remained high following the worsening conditions during the Iran-Iraq war of the 1980s, and the 2003 Anglo-American invasion of Iraq and subsequent civil war. Similarly, throughout the latter quarter of the century Dubai became home to many Lebanese and Kuwaiti merchants, as a result of the protracted Lebanese civil war and the 1990 Iraqi invasion of Kuwait. Although there were previously far more prosperous Arab trading centres than Dubai, the ports of Beirut, Jounieh, Tripoli, and Kuwait City soon became far less attractive, with many choosing to make a permanent move. Indeed, it can be argued that Dubai directly benefited from such conflicts given that its merchant community absorbed such experienced families and existing businesses, and, as will be described below,[129] its rulers then played a key role in rebuilding these shattered war-torn Arab economies.[130]

South Asian immigration

From further afield, Dubai's emerging status as the premier port of the lower Gulf was successful in attracting not only Persians and Arabs, but also an increasing number of merchants from the Indian subcontinent. Although many Indians and Ceylonese had worked in Dubai during the nineteenth and early twentieth centuries in order to take advantage of pearling opportunities, most were only temporary visitors, and were present only during certain seasons of the year, with their main bases always remaining in Bombay or Karachi. Nevertheless there were around fifty such resident families in Dubai in 1900 (and around seventy-five in Sharjah), many of whom had lived there since the 1860s when they had first arrived as the representatives of British companies in India.[131] Among the most prominent were those of Askerandas Wabhi, Dhamanmal Isardas, and Keshavdas Tarachand.[132] However, during the decline of the pearling industry, from the late 1920s and onwards many of these original subcontinental merchant families left the Trucial states and closed down their offices in Dubai. Crucially though, from the 1950s and onwards when the Nehru's protectionist policies began to take effect, and with the consequent wealth of re-export opportunities opening up, it made sense for many South Asian merchants to return to Dubai and avail themselves of its free port status.

As a prominent Dubai-based Indian businessman recalls of this period, Indian merchants '...saw the opportunity and adopted a frontiersman philosophy of getting in on the ground floor.'[133] Some 150 Indian Muslims, led by Jaji Jaffer Ali of Hyderabad, were among the first to arrive in this wave, and were soon followed by other prominent textile and gold merchants including Gordhan Adnani, Narainda Lakhiani, and Vashdev Bhatia.[134] While the Al-Maktum family could no longer keep welcoming such immigrant merchants by donating prime land as it had done in the past with the ajami incomers, many of these Indians were nevertheless the beneficiaries of exclusive and brand-specific trade licences issued by the ruler. These became especially lucrative when the electronics boom took hold and the various multinational companies were looking for Gulf-based agents to serve as their local re-exporters and retailers. Although as described earlier some of these electronics licences were granted to powerful indigenous merchant families so as to placate Arab nationalist sympathisers within their ranks[135] (most notably the Al-Futtaim family's authorisation to run the Oman National Electronics chain of shops), the vast majority were allocated to newly arrived but highly experienced Indians.[136] In particular, Gordhan Bhatia became the importer for Sony and was so successful that the Sony brand became known locally as 'Gordhan Sony'. Later, by the 1970s Sony products were imported by another high profile Indian businessman, Manu Chabria, who had set up the thriving Jumbo Electronics retail outlets. Similarly the Gajaria Brothers brought JVC to Dubai,[137] while Akil Arjoumand introduced Sanyo products, Muhammad Sahrif Bukhash imported NEC goods, and the Indian Jashanmal family, who came originally from Sind, traded in almost every other product available.[138] Thus, by the latter quarter of the century, a huge number of Indian businessmen were living and prospering in Dubai. Represented by the well-subscribed Indian National Association,[139] they had emerged as an equally vital component in Dubai's continuing commercial success, coexisting most profitably with the large communities of other immigrant merchants.

Also significant, although not adding to Dubai's commercial expertise as such, was the great influx of less skilled South Asians at this time, many of whom came to seek opportunities in the booming construction, retail, and various service sectors that had begun to flourish on the back of the free port's success. Indeed, by the early 1960s there were over 100 Pakistani families in Dubai who had come to work as shopkeepers, tailors, and barbers.[140] Moreover, after 1958, when Oman sold its Makran protectorate in Baluchistan to Pakistan,[141] hundreds of Baluchis had arrived to work as *hamals* or luggage porters, and a large number also came to help staff Sheikh Muhammad bin Hasher Al-Maktum's aforementioned new police force.[142] Labourers were hired from both India and Pakistan to help build the new offices for many of these businesses, with many indigenous merchants also hiring their services given their knowledge of the Hindi and Urdu languages from the pearling era.[143] In addition, many had also come from the subcontinent to work for the oil companies during their ongoing exploration work, with some British reports claiming that by the late 1950s over a third of the oil labour force was from India alone.[144] Certainly, by the late 1960s and early 1970s the number of such working class immigrants was enormous, with it being estimated that over 1,000 South Asians per week were landing on the Indian Ocean coastline, most of whom were destined for Dubai. It has even been claimed that some of the earliest motorcars imported into Dubai were purchased for the express purpose of bringing Pakistanis across the mountains from Fujairah so that they could work in Dubai without the need for visas or time- consuming paperwork.[145] When some of Sheikh Rashid bin Said al-Maktum's advisors questioned him on the subject of these illegal residents he simply replied 'What is the problem, so long as they are paying rent in Dubai?'.[146]

Gambling on infrastructure

While free trade policies and some degree of political stability had been enough to attract foreign merchants to Dubai during the first half of the twentieth century, the necessity for the extensive creek dredging operation during the 1950s had reinforced the view, already held by the ruling family and many of Dubai's notables, that there was a need for even greater physical infrastructural improvements, especially with regards to transport and communications. For if Dubai was to continue thriving as a free port then it would have to maintain its position as the most trade-friendly environment in the lower Gulf. Crucially, given the sheikhdom's limited resources in the years preceding significant oil revenues, this could only really be achieved by taking something of a gamble on such costly projects. Moreover, alongside such massive new construction it was also recognised that as an increasingly large and complex business community began to diversify into new areas of trade that involved ever-increasing amounts of capital, Dubai would have to establish a far more advanced financial and regulatory infrastructure if it was to maintain the confidence of its merchants.

As with its willingness to seek external Kuwaiti assistance over the creek improvements, Dubai was prepared to court foreign investment and loans to finance its infrastructural improvements. It was believed that any interest or costs that accrued would easily be paid out of the dividends such projects were likely to generate for the sheikhdom's commercial sector. As such, by 1959 Dubai was borrowing heavily from the affluent Qatari ruling family in order to conduct drilling operations to provide the city with new fresh water sources.[147] Eventually water was found in Al-Awir, just south of Dubai, and further projects modernised existing bedouin wells within the vicinity.[148] Similarly, in 1962 Qatari financing was sought to build the first proper bridge across the creek,[149] finally connecting Bur Dubai with Deira and reducing the need for using *abra* water taxis to ferry goods from one side to another. In a symbolic gesture, when the aforementioned marriage between the ruler of Qatar and Sheikha Mariam bint Rashid Al-Maktum took place a few years later, the palace in their honour was constructed adjacent to this new Qatari-funded 'Al-Maktum Bridge.' During the mid-1960s more infrastructure was completed, including a Saudi-financed tarmac-surfaced road between Dubai and Ra's al-Khaimah, street lighting, and other small sections of road.[150] In 1965 Sheikh Rashid bin Said Al-Maktum again approached Sir William Halcrow and Partners and asked them to draw up plans for constructing a deep water port in Shindagah. By 1967 a blueprint was complete, although with only provision for four berths, given the company's projections for Dubai's future trade. Rashid demanded that the plans be changed so that the port would accommodate sixteen berths, despite the cautious recommendations of his British advisers. As a testament to Rashid's vision during this critical period, when the new Port Rashid was finally opened in 1971 with sixteen berths it was immediately oversubscribed, and in 1976 it was expanded again to accommodate an additional twenty berths. Moreover, to enhance this port project further a tunnel was constructed in 1972 close to the entrance of Shindagha, so as to provide easier access for Deira traffic to the port, and in 1975 the Hamriyyah area alongside the creek was upgraded to provide more efficient unloading facilities for the many traditional boats that still visited Dubai.[151]

In parallel to these important maritime transport improvements, Sheikh Rashid was also determined to create a proper airport in Dubai. By the end of the 1950s Dubai still had no air infrastructure in place, as its air agreements signed in the late 1930s only applied to flying boats landing on the creek.[152] Most commercial flights to the lower Gulf continued to land at the relatively well equipped Sharjah airbase, at which the British had laid a proper surfaced strip in 1939,[153] while the RAF's military needs were being serviced by new airfields constructed on Bani Yas island and in the hinterland of Abu Dhabi.[154] Rashid was painfully aware that all visitors and prospective immigrants had to fly to Bahrain and then, unless they attempted an uncomfortable boat journey, often had to wait days before catching a connecting flight to Sharjah, before finally crossing overland to Dubai. Also, although the new Gulf Aviation airline stopped at Sharjah and the Indian Kalinga airline began to call there en route to Nigeria, seats were often limited and flights were far from frequent.[155] As a result of Sheikh Sultan bin Saqr's attempts to reinforce Sharjah's status during the Second World War, the British had agreed to a quota system in which aircraft landing at Sharjah (which were usuallly 22 seaters) would have most of the seats allocated to oil workers, four allocated to 'guests of the ruler of Sharjah' while only two seats would be available for visitors to Dubai.[156]

Thus, in 1959, with the creek dredging well underway, full attention was given to remedying this situation, with Sheikh Rashid stating to his majlis that '...an airport is necessary as it will bring us within hours of places which it has taken us days or weeks to reach... we have already lost one opportunity to Sharjah.'[157] Given his acute awareness of the opposition that had been generated by his father's majlis during the negotiations for earlier British landing rights,[158] he was also keen to stress that British assistance would be sought not as part of some opaque rental arrangement but as part of an effort to extend Dubai's laissez-faire commercial tradition into an 'open skies' policy.[159] With this in mind Rashid confessed to the British agent that he was embarrassed that Dubai still had no airport and claimed that he was '...under pressure from the merchant community to build an airport, even if it meant that these facilities could only be afforded by passing a higher cost on to them... also Dubai must have an airport if it is to enhance its own name.'[160] Predictably the project was opposed by Sheikh Saqr bin Sultan of Sharjah who lobbied the British with claims that there was simply no need for a Dubai airport given that Sharjah could continue to serve all of the Trucial sheikhdoms.[161] Indeed, it would seem that the British initially shared this view, with a similar proposal from Sheikh Shakhbut bin Sultan Al-Nahyan for an Abu Dhabi airport being flatly refused, and with a British expert in Dubai reporting that the city did not have a suitable plot of land with a hard surface, despite Rashid's efforts to clear the Al-Rashidya area close to Deira.[162] Worryingly for Dubai it seemed that the closest they could get to British permission at this time was for there to be some form of joint Dubai-Sharjah airport which would have an auxiliary airstrip far out of town and nearer to Jebel Ali.[163]

Later in the year momentum began to build as Sheikh Rashid realised he needed to persuade the British that Dubai would be prepared to bear the full cost of building its own airport and that Britain therefore stood to lose nothing. To this end, he encouraged the British agent to write a memorandum to the Political Resident stating that Britain had no right to prevent Dubai from embarking on such a project,[164] and, perhaps more importantly, he persuaded a well known British pilot, Freddie Bosworth, who had already been heavily involved in Dubai's gold trade (and who later became one of the directors of Gulf Aviation) to travel to Bahrain and approach the Political Resident with this message. On hearing Dubai's suggestion and Rashid's willingness to seek his own financing, it is reported that the Political Resident immediately agreed, claiming that '...on those terms Rashid could build ten airports if he wished.'[165]

In early 1960 work began on a large plot of land that stretched from Al-Ghusais across to the Al-Rashidya area. By the end of the year the new development boasted a modest-sized terminal building and an air tower (managed by International Airadio Limited), and was officially named Dubai International Airport.[166] Again, with commercial activity at the very forefront of Dubai's ambitious strategy, the airport was the first in the Gulf to have a duty free shop. As a prominent Indian businessman remembers '...the carpark for the airport shop was built to accommodate 500 cars—there were not even this number of cars in the entire city, but within just a couple of years the carpark had to be expanded.'[167] Most importantly, and as a great validation of Sheikh Rashid, within a year both Gulf Aviation and Kuwait Airways had begun to land in Dubai, and although Imperial Airways (by this time renamed the British Overseas Aviation Company – BOAC) had initially refused to fly there, claiming that it was unprofitable, Rashid solved this problem by copying his father's 1930s strategy[168] of buying out seats on aircraft by ensuring that advanced bookings were made on BOAC aircraft by all British

expatriate staff working in Dubai, before then personally guaranteeing all of the remaining seats, up to the 60 per cent threshold
required by BOAC to operate its flights.[169]

With regards to a regulatory infrastructure, in the late 1950s
there were still no trade licences or trade receipts being issued in
the Trucial sheikhdoms, nor were there any opportunities to raise
mortgages or cede property for commercial purposes. Thus, with
increasingly complicated and valuable transactions taking place,
demand was rising from the merchant community for a much
more sophisticated framework to be put into place. Once again,
Dubai was the pioneer, with Sheikh Rashid recognising the need
for 'sheikhly decrees' to set up limited liability companies. With
assistance from the British agent and the business-savvy Easa
Saleh Al-Gurg, Rashid appointed a Bahrain-based British lawyer
to draw up the necessary articles, and by 1958 such decrees began
to be issued. The first company to be incorporated as a Dubai-
based limited liability company was International Traders Limited, which had earlier opened a branch of its Kenyan operation
in Dubai with the purpose of selling off its surplus stock from
Africa and Singapore, and this was soon followed by the newly
established Dubai Electricity Company.[170] In 1965 the licensing
system, together with a number of other new commercial decrees
were further regulated following the establishment of the Dubai
Chamber of Commerce and Industry—the first such institution
in the lower Gulf. [171]

The storage and lending of money used by Dubai's businesses
was similarly formalised at this time by the arrival of several foreign
banks and the incorporation of a number of local ones. Previously,
most merchants had traded with their own money, which they
looked after themselves, and with most preferring to stock goods
according to capacity rather than running the risks of overstock-
ing. Moreover, those that did have surplus cash normally chose to
place it with Indian businessmen, who they felt were reliable and
could be called upon 24 hours a day. Or, if they wished to transfer

money to other merchants then they would do it by using the informal *hawala* system, which, as will be shown later, has its roots in the South Asian expatriate community's preference for sending remittances back to the subcontinent in a manner that avoided the high costs associated with using legitimate Indian banks.[172]

Although a branch of Eastern Bank had existed in Sharjah for some time, with its representatives sometimes travelling into Dubai to do business,[173] the first real bank to exist in Dubai was the Imperial Bank of Iran, which set up an office in 1948 and which later became known as the British Bank of Iran, before then being renamed the British Bank of the Middle East after the British Government acquired the majority of the bank's shares in 1952.[174] Crucially, the British Bank was the first institution to really extend credit to merchants in the Trucial states, thereby again reinforcing Dubai's commercial pre-eminence in the region and attracting many foreign companies seeking such banking facilities.[175] Satisfied with the bank's performance and its key role in Dubai's economy, Sheikh Rashid signed a monopoly agreement with its directors which was to last for twenty years (rather than the twenty-five years requested by the bank), and which provided a clause requiring the bank to employ Dubai nationals wherever possible. For a short period the monopoly did hold, as the Arab Bank of Doha had attempted to open a branch in Dubai before being promptly shut down,[176] but due to an incidence of violence inside the British Bank's offices, a disgruntled Indian merchant was able to lobby enough support for an alternative in Dubai, and duly a branch of Eastern Bank was opened.[177]

Seeking greater direct involvement in the banking sector, in 1962 Sheikh Rashid's majlis began discussing the creation of a National Bank of Dubai,[178] and the following year a team of British advisors helped to establish the new entity in cooperation with a local director (Ali Al-Owais) and Rashid's important ally and future son-in-law, the ruler of Qatar. Given that the British Bank's headquarters were located in the Shindagha area of Bur

Dubai it was decided that the National Bank should be based in Deira,[179] and by 1970 a fantastic convex-shaped new building had been completed close to the creek.[180] In 1969 the National Bank was joined by the new Commercial Bank of Dubai (co-owned by Commerzbank, Chase Manhattan, and the Commercial Bank of Kuwait),[181] and by 1971 five other foreign banks had opened up in Dubai, including First National City Bank of New York.[182] Of these newcomers, some did become a source of concern, including the Lebanese-run Intra Bank (one of the original backers of the National Bank of Dubai), which fell into a category of Dubai-based banks described as being '…immediately recognisable by the lavishness of their presentation, the elegance of their offices and generally the well-concealed scarcity of their reserves.'[183] Moreover, in the early 1970s a number of other dubious local banks had emerged, often set up as prestige projects by members of indigenous merchant families. Most notably, the Union Bank of the Middle East, the Dubai Bank, the Gulf Bank, and the Middle East Bank all reached the point of bankruptcy. Nevertheless, with Dubai's reputation and commercial prowess once again at stake, these were all effectively rescued by Sheikh Rashid's eldest son and crown prince, Sheikh Maktum bin Rashid Al-Maktum, who together with Easa Saleh Al-Gurg formed the new Emirates Bank International from the remnants of these failed ventures.[184]

4
THE DIVERSIFICATION
OF THE ECONOMY

With considerable oil revenues beginning to accumulate by the time of British withdrawal, the level of rent-derived or 'rentier' wealth accruing to the ruling family and the newly independent emirate of Dubai increased massively, far surpassing the earlier exploration and air landing rents, and allowed for hitherto unfeasible development policies to be pursued. While some of these new oil-related strategies met with success, including energy dependent industrialisation and selective overseas investments, it was nevertheless recognised that such strategies, coupled with any continuing reliance on oil exports, would soon render Dubai's economy vulnerable to the vagaries of the international economy and other uncontrollable external events. Moreover, given the emirate's relatively modest long-term hydrocarbon reserves, there was never an expectation of sustaining such an economy in quite the same way as some of the other Gulf emirates, most notably oil rich Abu Dhabi. Hence the Al-Maktum family's planners sought to reinvigorate Dubai's historically successful commercial sector by using what oil wealth they possessed to build even more infrastructure, and, by the 1990s, it was hoped that further non-oil related sectors could be added to the emirate's portfolio. In particular, with the aims of maintaining a balance of trade and attracting foreign direct investment, these were to include a light manufacturing base, several export processing 'free zones,' a luxury tourist industry, and the launch of a real estate market geared to foreign investors. Superficially, such diversification would appear to have worked, as although there have been some concerns, especially with real estate, Dubai has nonetheless managed to almost free itself of oil dependency, with many of the emirate's post-hydrocarbon development strategies now seemingly admired and emulated elsewhere in the region.

Oil strategies

Although Sheikh Said bin Maktum Al-Maktum had signed oil exploration concessions in the late 1930s,[1] the first major drilling did not take place until 1952, when the 'Bab One' area in Jebel Ali was first surveyed,[2] but it was not until the early 1960s and after three more failed tests that oil was finally discovered in Dubai.[3] Nevertheless, despite such a slow start, the development of the sheikdom's oil industry soon gathered pace, with further reports of commercial quantities of oil in 1965 being enough to spark an anticipatory construction boom in Dubai,[4] and with a breakthrough finding having been made at the *Fateh* or Fortune oilfield fifteen miles offshore in late 1966. By 1969 production at Fateh was underway, and within four years two additional oil fields at Faleh and southwest Fateh had begun to export.[5] Although these first exports were more than thirty years later than those of Kuwait and Saudi Arabia, they were still earlier than those in most of the other federated emirates, with Sharjah commencing pumping in 1972 from its Mubarak oilfield, and with Ra's al-Khaimah not beginning until 1984 from its Saleh reserves.[6]

With the original concessions held by the London-based Iraqi Petroleum Company expiring in the late 1960s,[7] Sheikh Rashid bin Said Al-Maktum created the new Dubai Petroleum Company (DPC) to manage all of Dubai's onshore oilfields and some of its offshore possessions, and later set up the Dubai Marine Areas Company to manage the remainder of Dubai's offshore oil. Crucially, as with the original exploration concessions, these new arrangements still involved British oil companies. However, in a complete contradiction of the described 1922 treaties,[8] and as a clear indicator of both Britain's greater flexibility towards the Trucial rulers during this time of federation-building and London's associated desire to foster favourable post-independence relations with Dubai, there was also an opportunity for Rashid to involve several other foreign oil companies. Rashid and his majlis favoured this approach, as it was thought it would always ensure that Dubai had access to the latest technologies, and, perhaps more importantly, it would also return Dubai to its historically successful strategy of balancing foreign relations by creating numerous allies in different countries, all of whom would have a vested interest in the prosperity of the sheikhdom. Indeed, it would appear that upon its launch the DPC had no less than seven different non-British partners, including Total and Campagnie Francaises des Petroles from France, Repsol and Hispanoil from Spain, RWE-DEA and Wintersall from Germany, and even Britain's major rival—the American Continental Company (Conoco).[9]

By the early 1980s the DPC's volume of oil exports had increased greatly, following discoveries at the Margham onshore field close to Hatta, and at the new Rashid offshore field. In 1991 Dubai reached a production peak of about 420,000 barrels per day, with proven reserves of over four billion barrels, thus representing around $1.5 million per capita value of oil reserves for Dubai nationals.[10] With such abundant resources Dubai was able to harness its comparative advantage of cheap energy and had already begun to set up heavy industries capable of producing metals, plastics, gases, and other hydrocarbon-dependent goods that could be profitably exported. Most notably, in 1979 Dubai Aluminium (DUBAL) was opened, quickly becoming the centrepiece of Dubai's industrialisation programme. By 1980 a liquid natural gas plant (DUGAS) was established so that gas could be captured from oil drills, and by the following year the Dubai Cabling Company (DUCAB) had also

101

begun exporting.[11] All have been successful, with DUBAL at one point accounting for over 60 per cent of Dubai's non-oil exports,[12] and since then a number of other energy-reliant companies have been established, including Arabian Liquid Chemicals, the Gulf Metal Foundry, Gulf Engineering Industry, and Foseco Minsep (producing chemicals and waterproofing compounds).[13]

In tandem with this strategy, much of the wealth generated by oil and these related activities has been placed overseas, so that interest payments on such investments can be used as something of a buffer should Dubai's domestic economy falter. Indeed, while many of the Trucial rulers, including Sheikh Said, had often held considerable personal assets abroad (especially in India),[14] the oil booms made possible substantial purchases of property and stock in western Europe, north America and other 'safe' locations. Most of these investments have been handled by the Dubai Holdings group and its various subsidiaries, most prominently Dubai International Capital, the Dubai Investment Group, and Jumeirah International. Currently chaired by one of Sheikh Muhammad bin Rashid Al-Maktum's closest lieutenants, Muhammad Abdullah Al-Gergawi, Dubai Holdings together with these smaller government parastatals are now thought to control over $15 billion of overseas assets[15] and are believed to be capable of generating around $2 billion in revenue per annum.[16] Over the next three years they intend to triple the value of their assets.[17] Significantly, while many of the group's investments have been in short term instruments such as US Treasury bills and in reliable foreign companies such as DaimlerChrysler,[18] EADS (the Airbus parent company),[19] and the Doncasters Group,[20] in recent years many of its overseas acquisitions have also been connected to hotels, sports facilities, and often glamorous or prestigious projects. Examples would include the Travelodge chain, the Carlton Tower and Lowndes hotels in central London, a fashionable art deco hotel in Manhattan,[21] a share in the Arsenal Football Club's new stadium in Holloway, and, most conspicuously, the London Eye and the Madame Tussauds waxworks centre.[22] In late 2006 Dubai International Capital even attempted to purchase the Liverpool Football Club, only to be defeated by a massive bid from an American consortium,[23] and in 2007 Manchester United football club became the main target. As will be shown later in this chapter, this strategy is now not only being used to provide a reliable source of revenue, but is also helping to promote the name and reputation of Dubai to the most desirable audiences, thereby supporting a number of the emirate's newer and more diverse economic sectors.

Oil limitations and the shadow of Abu Dhabi

Despite such promising returns, it was nevertheless accepted some time ago that such oil-backed strategies would never be enough on their own to allow Dubai to maintain its status as the lower Gulf's economic capital. Moreover, while it was acknowledged that heavy industries and overseas investments should certainly remain an important component of Dubai's economic plan, it was recognised that they would never provide the emirate with a future of oil-financed self-sustainability. Also, with Abu Dhabi just a few hours drive away, there has always been a keen awareness of Dubai's limitations, given the massive oil reserves and the much greater potential for oil-related development enjoyed by its more resource-rich neighbour. Indeed, with sizeable exports from Das island commencing in the early 1960s,[24] Abu Dhabi soon began to command around ten per cent of the world's proven hydrocarbon deposits and now accounts for over 90 per cent of the United Arab Emirates' oil exports, pumping around 2.5 million barrels per day—a figure that could rise to nearly three million per day by 2010.[25] Abu Dhabi's per capita value of oil reserves per national may now stand at about $17 million: more than eleven times greater than Dubai's value.

Thus, as many Dubai nationals comprehend, Abu Dhabi has always dwarfed the capabilities of the DPC and Dubai Holdings. Its overseas investments now outrank those of even the much longer established Kuwaiti Investment Authority (KIA): in the mid-1990s it was estimated that Abu Dhabi held somewhere between $60 and $100 billion overseas,[26] but now this figure could be over $360 billion—substantially higher than KIA.[27] Of these investments, it would seem that the ruling family hold around $50 billion,[28] with private Abu Dhabi investors holding about $150 billion, and with the Al-Nahyan-chaired Abu Dhabi Investments Authority (ADIA) managing over $160 billion.[29] Interestingly, much like Dubai Holdings, but on a considerably larger scale, ADIA houses teams of foreign experts and scours the globe for a variety of investment opportunities, currently favouring a mixture of 60 per cent 'guaranteed bets' in the developed world (such as the recent acquisition of a five percent stake in the Fiat-controlled Ferrari),[30] with around 35 per cent being placed in the emerging markets of Southeast Asia,[31] and with a few 'wild cards' in areas identified for substantial future growth (including Libya's tourist infrastructure).[32] Symbolically, ADIA now occupies the tallest building in Abu Dhabi,[33] thus underscoring the centrality of the institution's role in Abu Dhabi's development strategy. Similarly enormous are Abu Dhabi's oil-associated heavy industries, many of which are now sufficiently competitive so as to undercut German and Japanese rivals. Prominent examples would include the Abu Dhabi Polymers Company (also known as Borouge), the Abu Dhabi National Oil Company's partner chemicals firm, Borealis,[34] and the Abu Dhabi Shipbuilding Company which provides materials for and builds an increasing number of military and commercial vessels.[35] Such a commitment to heavy industries has now been reaffirmed by Abu Dhabi's recently announced plans to pump more than $8 billion into the sector over the next few years,[36] much of which will be corralled into the new Khalifa Port and Industrial Zone,[37] and can be further illustrated by considering the distribution of manufacturing establishments in the UAE: given that Abu Dhabi accounts for well over half of the federation's overall manufacturing output, it is highly indicative that the emirate hosts only about 300 plants, a mere ten per cent of the total number in the UAE, compared to the 1600 or so much lighter plants in Dubai.[38]

Clearly unable to compete over the long term with its regional rivals as an oil focused emirate, Dubai's planners also felt that pursuing such externally oriented strategies would eventually place the emirate's economy at greater risk from 'dependent circumstances.'[39] Indeed, following a series of oil price slumps in the 1980s,[40] and a number of oil industry security scares during the Iran-Iraq War and the invasion of Kuwait,[41] it became increasingly apparent that Dubai's economy was extremely fragile. Secondly, it was felt that even with the DPC's very balanced multinational concessions, Dubai's economy still remained in the hands of a select group of foreign companies and oil-consuming nations. Such companies were believed to be the greatest beneficiaries from Dubai's oil given their insistence on purchasing only crude products, thereby preventing any refinement or value addition to the commodity in Dubai.[42] Indeed, it has been estimated that at one point the foreign companies were making more than four times as much revenue from each barrel as the DPC, further promoting the view that the emirate had become dependent and that, in the words of a veteran Dubai national '...the western powers had left the region through the front door, but were coming back in again through the window.'[43] Thirdly, it was feared that having such a narrow economic base would eventually expose Dubai to the dual threats of unemployment due to a lack of meaningful job opportunities outside of the oil and public sectors, and that of an increased money supply and possible hyperinflation given that the economy would not be able to absorb any surplus liquidity generated by the oil revenues.[44] By the early 1990s, oil-related strategies again came into question following changing energy consumption patterns in the consuming nations. Dubai's oil exports began to decline to around 300,000 barrels per day,[45] and this was partly blamed on a combination of stronger antipollution legislation in the West and new oil-producing regions in Central Asia and Latin America beginning to come onstream.[46]

Diversification—more commercial infrastructure

In the mid-1980s, following a particularly bad month of interruptions to oil exports during the ongoing Gulf conflict, Dubai's crown prince, Sheikh Maktum bin Rashid Al-Maktum, together with his two eldest brothers, Sheikh Hamdan bin Rashid Al-Maktum and Sheikh Muhammad bin Rashid Al-Maktum, met to discuss the emirate's future direction. At a time when other governments in the Gulf were reacting to the war by increasing their overseas investments in the West, the Al-Maktum family decided the best solution was to buck the trend by making a commitment to invest in their own domestic infrastructure so that Dubai would be able to support and enhance its existing re-export oriented commercial sector while also facilitating broader diversification away from oil in the future.[47]

Even during the height of the oil boom in the 1970s Dubai had continued to build trade-related infrastructure, therefore providing the emirate with strong foundations for such non-oil strategies. In 1972 Sheikh Rashid bin Said Al-Maktum had decided to complement the aforementioned Port Rashid project with a second and even larger deep water port. Although, as before, Rashid faced some opposition from his advisors over the viability of such a port, a site was nevertheless chosen to the west of Dubai, and by 1979 the development opened with a massive 66 berths,[48] making the new Port Jebel Ali nearly twice the size of Port Rashid and one of the largest ports in the world. Soon after, and equally controversially at the time, Rashid opened Dubai's new dry docks compound. As Dubai's most expensive project, many believed it to be a mistake, especially given that Bahrain was also building a dry dock and therefore would provide strong regional competition. However, again having faith in Dubai's potential, Rashid had correctly predicted the subsequent increase in Gulf traffic, and the resulting rise in demand for ship repair facilities ensured that the dry docks were soon fully booked.[49] Perhaps most symbolically, throughout this period Dubai's merchants had also been lobbying Rashid to construct some kind of new trade headquarters to serve as the emirate's centre for commercial administration. In 1974 the plan had been to construct a low-lying World Trade Village complete with office compounds and open-air spaces to allow for international music and art festivals to take place.[50] While clearly a portent for many of Dubai's future projects, this design was, however, soon superseded by a much grander ambition to create a forty-storey tower block that would become the Middle East's tallest building.[51] Thus in 1979 the Dubai World Trade Centre was completed and ceremonially opened by Queen Elizabeth II.[52] Although the Centre was soon overtaken by even greater build-ings, its trade-related title, distinctive architecture, and prominent location close to Dubai's arterial highway succeeded in conveying a message to visitors that Dubai was not just about oil.

Over the following two decades investment in such physical infrastructure continued unabated with at times an estimated 25 per cent of GDP being spent on building and improving Dubai's network of seaports and roads.[53] Of particular note was a joint project with Abu Dhabi in the 1990s to connect the two emirates with a 150 mile long paved road along the coast, where there had previously only been a dirt track. Now referred to as Sheikh Zayed Road (when in Dubai) and Sheikh Maktum Road (when in Abu Dhabi), the highway has continually been widened and is now one of the longest roads on the Arabian peninsula.[54] Shortly after, a parallel trunk road was constructed so as to provide a separate and more peripheral route for heavy goods vehicles.[55] More recently, in an effort to improve transport within the city and to remedy Dubai's infamous traffic problems, at an enormous cost a number of new bridges have been constructed across the creek, including a floating road, in addition to large road tunnels underneath sec-tions of the airport's runways. Connecting the two shores of the creek, a new water bus service has begun operating, providing a more salubrious alternative to the existing abra water taxis.[56] And a major project has been undertaken with the assistance of Japanese and Canadian firms to set up a four line subterranean metro system linking the airport and the seaports with the more distant suburbs of the rapidly expanding city. While many residents are disgruntled due to the excavations these projects entailed, this is likely to be a short term problem with Dubai poised to emerge in 2010 with the most advanced mass transit system in the developing world. Although Dubai's maritime facilities have not developed quite so dramatically as this inland infrastructure, they have nevertheless recently benefited from substantial reorganisation under a streamlined new state-owned parastatal managed by the renowned Dubai businessman, Sultan Ahmad bin Sulayman. Indeed, with the recent merger of Dubai Ports Authority and Dubai Ports International, the Dubai Ports World Company has assumed responsibility for both Port Rashid and Port Jebel Ali, and, in an apparent dovetailing with the aforementioned overseas investments strategies, it has begun to acquire operations in other countries. Certainly, Dubai Ports World Company is now the fourth biggest ports operator in the world, controlling 15 complexes across the Middle East, Asia, Europe, Latin America, and Australasia. In particular, it has made major investments in Jeddah, Djibouti, Gwadar in Pakistan, Constantza in Romania, and in the Indian port of Visakhapatnam. Moreover, although it spectacularly failed to assume control over the Peninsula and Oriental Steam Company's (P&O) American operations in early 2006 due to an outpouring of xenophobia and anti-Arab sentiment in the US Congress, Dubai Ports World Company nevertheless uncontroversially acquired both P&O's British facilities and the US-based CSX International, bringing its total worth to some $8 billion.[57]

Equally remarkable has been Dubai's commitment to building up its air infrastructure. By 1960 Sheikh Rashid had already provided Dubai International Airport (DXB) with a terminal building and the region's first duty free shop,[58] and Dubai had overtaken Sharjah as the lower Gulf's main air hub, with the the airport attracting numerous international airlines including BOAC and Lufthansa. Moreover, by 1974 DXB was also serving a large number of aircraft belonging to the new Gulf Air (an airline jointly formed from the remnants of Gulf Aviation and backed by the governments of Abu Dhabi, Qatar, Bahrain, and Oman).[59] Realising that Dubai needed to go even further and to create a truly international airport so that its 'open skies' policy could really attract airlines and businessmen from far flung destinations, Rashid appointed his third son, Sheikh Muhammad, to head a new steering committee.[60] Millions of dollars were invested in expanding the airport and by the mid-1980s the gamble on infrastructure once again appeared to have paid off with over forty airlines visiting DXB at least once a week.[61]

A serious obstacle did however present itself when Gulf Air, which by this stage had become the main operator using DXB, voiced its dissatisfaction with the Al-Maktum family's laissez-faire approach. Although respectful of Dubai's free port strategies that had served the emirate so well in the past, it was argued by Gulf Air's board of directors that other airports in the region were willing to offer subsidies and preferential landing rights for the airline, thereby making DXB an increasingly less attractive base. Given that the main protagonist seemed to be Dubai's fellow UAE partner, Abu Dhabi, the issue was particularly sensitive, and reached a crisis point in 1984 when Gulf Air attempted to push Sheikh Muhammad into a decision by drastically cutting its scheduled flights into DXB from 84 per week to just 39.[62] Understandably alarmed, Muhammad called on foreign experts, most notably Maurice Flanagan, to draw up a list of options for Dubai. While most of the options presented to Muhammad recommended some kind of accommodation with Gulf Air, the final and most drastic option on the list was for Dubai to break free of its dependency on Gulf Air by setting up its own independent airline.[63] Although not an entirely novel idea, given that Sheikh Rashid's majlis had already discussed the idea back in 1961,[64] most of the advisors believed this latter course of action was impossible given the strong regional competition such an infant airline would face from both Gulf Air and Kuwait Airways. Nevertheless, in defiance of his critics and in emulation of his father's boldness, in late 1985 Muhammad provided Flanagan with over $10 million in seed money to lease a number of Pakistan International Airlines Boeing 737s[65] and appointed his uncle, Sheikh Ahmad bin Said Al-Maktum, to launch 'Emirates'—a completely new, Dubai-based, airline.

Sheikh Ahmad's new team recommended that in order for Emirates to survive, Sheikh Rashid's open skies policy would have to be dropped or at least curtailed, with some small degree of protection permitted. Sheikh Muhammad intervened and rejected the proposal on the grounds that it was against everything that Dubai stood for, and demanded that the airline should post profits from the very beginning so as to prove that it did not receive subsidies. Remarkably the airline soon lived up to these great expectations, and has since turned a profit in every year, even in the troubled 2001.[66] Moreover, Emirates has been able to expand continuously its fleet, and by 2010 it is expected to be flying over 100 aircraft to over 100 destinations. Of these planes, a large number will be Boeing 787 Dreamliners that are capable of flying direct to Sydney, New York, Houston, and even Los Angeles. These purchases are thought to underscore Emirates' commitment to long haul routes and its intention to position Dubai as a global hub, in much the same way as the Dubai Ports World Company's described international reach. In addition, the 787s will be joined by a number of the new A380 Super Jumbos—the largest aircraft in history—of which Dubai has been Airbus' biggest and most loyal customer.[67] Moreover, several milestones have been reached by Emirates, and these have yet to be matched by other Middle Eastern airlines, including a promise never to fly aircraft more than five years old, and a commitment as early as 1992 that all aircraft should have personal video displays, even in the economy class cabin.[68]

Much of Emirates' success can also be attributed to the extensive upgrades and additions to DXB, encouraging the airline to accommodate more passengers and, in 1999, allowing the airport to overtake the Mecca-servicing King Abdulaziz Airport in Jeddah to become the busiest hub in the region. Most notably, in 1998 the new Sheikh Rashid Terminal was opened, with the original terminal being renamed Terminal 2, and more recently a third and even larger terminal has been built following an enormous excavation in Al-Rashidya. In the near future Dubai's air infrastructure will expand even further to include a second airport on the western side of the city, close to Jebel Ali. Although construction is yet to begin, it is estimated that upon its completion in 2017 the new 'Dubai World Central Airport' (JXB) will be the fourth largest airport in the world: boasting six runways and three terminals it will be able to handle in excess of 120 million passengers per annum.[69]

Also of note, in terms of commercial infrastructure, has been the massive growth in the number and size of Dubai's shopping malls since the late 1990s. Many of the largest of these are either run by major government-backed parastatals, most notably the forthcoming Dubai Mall,[70] or are owned by the most powerful of the old merchant families. Indeed, the giant Mall of the Emirates is an asset of the aforementioned Al-Futtaim family, while both the Burjuman Centre and Dubai's first mall, the Al-Ghurair Centre were built by the Al-Ghurair family. With the recently opened Ibn Battuta Mall and Reef Mall, Dubai's tally of such centres now stands at over thirty-five. With protectionism seemingly prohibited, competition is fierce but healthy, and now requires newer and less established malls to offer novelties such as giant aquariums, ice rinks, and snowy ski slopes in order to attract customers. Dubai has actively encouraged these megaprojects by making it much easier for individuals or investors to buy adjacent plots of land to house their

111

malls. Tellingly, in Abu Dhabi, where such governmental backing has been absent until very recently,[71] there is a considerable contrast given that only three malls currently exist,[72] and only very powerful businessmen who are part of or are closely connected to the ruling family can really attempt such projects—the best example being Sheikh Surur bin Muhammad Al-Nahyan, a candidate for crown prince during the 1970s and the proprietor of the Abu Dhabi Mall and Trade Centre.

Alongside these physical improvements,[73] Dubai has boosted its commercial sector by building up the emirate's non-physical supporting infrastructure. In 1989 a Department of Commerce Marketing was established in order to 'contribute to economic diversification by promoting non-oil development; and creating new opportunities for the Dubai business community by attracting trade and investment.'[74] In practice, the Department has therefore complemented the existing Dubai Chamber of Commerce and Industry and has promoted more aggressively the emirate's reputation as a trade entrepôt to overseas delegations. Furthermore, it has also set up offices in several regional and international capitals including London and Paris. With regard to financial and regulatory infrastructure, since 1980 the Dubai business community has benefited from the establishment of a UAE Central Bank (originally the UAE Currency Board): although this new institution did introduce certain protectionist measures (notably the limiting of foreign banks to having just one main branch in each emirate), and, as will be discussed later in this book,[75] has at times been unable to intervene in particularly serious disputes, it has nevertheless contributed to growing confidence in the sector.[76] Also supportive, especially for Dubai's entrepreneurs, has been the Emirates Industrial Bank (EIB). Since its launch in 1982 this semi-government-backed[77] bank has provided low-interest 'soft loans' in excess of $350 million to various new business projects, especially those unrelated to the oil sector.[78] In parallel to these state run developments Dubai has continued to attract more foreign banks and offers a conducive environment for more locally-chartered banks. By 2006 there were believed to be more than 150 branches of 50 different banks operating in Dubai. These have included prominent regional banks such as Bank Melli and Bank Saderat of Iran, Habib Bank of Pakistan, Baroda Bank of India, and Arab-African International Bank; but more significantly have also included highly reputed international banks such as HSBC, Barclays, BNP Paribas, Lloyds, Citibank, and Standard Chartered.[79]

Diversification—light manufacturing and agriculture

With the triple aims of complementing the commercial sector, providing additional non-oil related activities, and reducing the value of imports into the emirate, since issuing an industrial law in 1979 Dubai has also built up both its light manufacturing and agricultural processing sectors. Indeed, drawing from the first article of this law which stated that 'the government must prepare a productive base capable of allowing manufacturing industries to thrive and thereby reduce the reliance on oil,'[80] Dubai has focussed on relatively simple manufacturing plants that have rarely required expensive foreign technology and have not been dependent on cheap energy to offer a competitive advantage in the same way as the heavier, oil-dependent, industries. In the 1980s several such plants, most of which produced construction materials such as cement and piping that would have been costly and inefficient to import, were established and by the 1990s these were joined by many more low cost 'import substitution industries' manufacturing goods such as plastic water bottles, ice cream, and workers' uniforms. At one stage Dubai's cost of imports was held in check,[81] and much of this brief success has been attributed directly to this sector.[82]

Similarly, Dubai's agricultural sector enjoyed modest growth during this period of early diversification, with attempts to increase both the productivity and total cultivatable area of land meeting with some success. Substantial government investment in rural infrastructure, farming equipment, and the development of new, desert-hardy crop strains has allowed many farms and agricultural businesses to flourish. Moreover, the improved conditions in Dubai's hinterland have also attracted former bedouin to a more settled existence, thereby boosting the emirate's national population. Output has increased, with vegetable production tripling during the 1990s, with dairy production rising a hundredfold over a twenty year period,[83] and with the emirate now enjoying one of the highest per capita agricultural productivity rates in the Gulf.[84] With regard to available farming land, results have been equally promising, with an afforestation programme (although nothing in comparison to Abu Dhabi's ambitious afforestation strategy) having facilitated an increase of cultivatable hectares in Dubai from 3,400 in 1987 to around 6,500 in 2007.[85] Perhaps the most important outcome has been the improvement in food security, with Dubai now being over 80 per cent self-sufficient in several foodstuffs.[86]

Diversification—free zones

Considerably more complex has been Dubai's strategy of attracting foreign, non-oil related investment by setting up export processing zones specifically for foreign companies. Unlike the relatively straightforward commercial, manufacturing, and agricultural sectors, for this form of diversification significant and at times controversial reforms were needed to overcome existing legislation. Indeed, since the mid-1980s federal directives emanating from Abu Dhabi, most notably the 1984 'Commercial Companies Law', had required all of the UAE's constituent emirates to adhere to a local sponsorship or *kafil* system that required all registered companies to be at least 51 per cent owned by a UAE national.[87] While there may have been some evidence of an informal precedent for such an arrangement in Abu Dhabi, at a time when many foreign merchants were not permanently resident in the Trucial states and required an indigenous partner, and while some in Dubai viewed the system as a necessary price to pay for the collective security benefits of federal integration, these protectionist rules were nevertheless viewed as inappropriate given that they impeded further investment and diversification while also undermining the emirate's reputation as a *laissez-faire* free port.

As will be discussed later in this book,[88] given that Sheikh Rashid bin Said Al-Maktum was keenly aware of the need to avoid federal confrontations, his planners decided that the best course of action was for Dubai to circumvent federal law by creating special authorities to manage zones within the emirate that would technically fall outside of UAE jurisdiction. It was decided that Rashid's pioneering 'free zone' project would be set up alongside the new port at Jebel Ali so as to allow foreign companies easy access to unloading facilities and also to keep the new authority on the periphery of the city and as something of an 'enclave'. Launched in 1985 by the Dubai Department of Industry, the Jebel Ali Free Zone Authority was initially administered by the aforementioned Sultan Ahmad bin Sulayman, who had just returned to Dubai after receiving an American education and been handpicked for the task by Rashid.[89] In addition to guaranteeing 100 per cent foreign ownership, among Sulayman's other objectives was a need to 'supply the zone with all the necessary administration, engineering, and utility services required by its clients.'[90] In practice this meant that foreign companies could expect to move into ready-made 'lease office buildings', would benefit from streamlined visa processing for their employees, and would enjoy cheap energy and good transport infrastructure. In many ways the timing was perfect as many merchants disadvantaged by the Iran-Iraq War and the Lebanese civil war, and who had previously been wary of investing in Dubai due to the 1984 kafil system (referred to as the 'golden dirham' system by the Lebanese) and their reluctance to take on a local 'sleeping partner,' now found that they had a suitable alternative. Indeed, the zone enjoyed rapid growth, and was soon home to around 300 very diverse companies including textiles manufacturers, chocolate factories, and farm machinery exporters. By 2002 the zone had expanded to accommodate over 2000 companies, and today it employs over 40,000 workers and has generated over $6 billion in investments.[91] About a quarter of these companies are Middle Eastern, while over 30 percent are Asian, and about 45 percent are either Western European or North American.[92] Jebel Ali has proved particularly popular with multinationals hoping to establish a Middle Eastern headquarters, and in some cases has even begun to host companies intent on total relocation. Of this latter category the most high profile recent entrant has been Halliburton, which in 2007 chose to shift its base from Texas to Jebel Ali given its more 'conducive business environment' and of course given Dubai's prime location close to the oil fields in Iraq and Halliburton's opportunities in Kazakhstan and other parts of Central Asia.[93]

So successful was this first free zone that many of Dubai's neighbours began to introduce Jebel Ali-style enabling legislation and have proceeded to set up their own authorities. Ra's al-Khaimah established its RAK Free Trade Zone, Sharjah launched its Hamriyyah Free Zone in the aforementioned coastal enclave between Ajman and Umm al-Qawain,[94] and sections of the new Khalifa Port and Industrial Zone in Abu Dhabi will also be operated under a free zone authority.[95] Pushing the boundaries even further, Dubai has since created many other, more specialised, free zones to attract and accommodate new sectors that have specific infrastructural requirements. As crown prince, Sheikh Muhammad bin Rashid Al-Maktum announced in 1999 that Dubai would be creating two new 'cities': one for internet companies and one for media companies. He believed he had identified a number of niches in the Arab world, and that Dubai ought to position itself at the forefront of such industries. Within a year his eldest brother, in his capacity as ruler, had issued emirate-level enabling legislation that built upon the experience of Jebel Ali and added new articles in support of such new foreign firms. Indeed, the 'Dubai Technology, Electronic Commerce, and Media Free Zone Law' promised that establishments would be excluded from any restrictions placed on the repatriation and transfer of capital for fifty years, would never be nationalised, and would be free to choose employees of any nationality (except Israelis).[96] Set up by Muhammad Abdullah Al-Gergawi in partnership with Sun, Cisco, and Siemens, by late 2000 Dubai Internet City was ready to open its doors, providing IT infrastructure (including a dedicated submarine Internet cable) to over 100 companies that had been waiting to move in. Incredibly, by 2007 the City had expanded to house nearly 850 companies employing some 10,000 workers, and now boasts the Middle Eastern headquarters of leading technology firms including Microsoft, Hewlett-Packard, Dell, and Canon. In the near future it is also likely that the City will house some form of IT university that will provide on-site internships in partnership with some of these businesses,[97] and that the City's management will advise on other, similar projects elsewhere in the developing world, including India's 'Smart City'—a vast IT-related free zone in Kerala.[98] In parallel, and situated on an adjacent site, Dubai Media City was launched at the same time and operated by a new Media Free Zone Authority. Much like the Internet City, the Media City also has around 800 companies, and these include many leading regional and international brands including LBC from Lebanon, the Saudi-owned MBC's new Al-Arabiya service, Al-Jazeera from Qatar, in addition to CNN, the BBC, and Reuters. Soon the City's facilities will be expanded further to include a village of studios to facilitate onsite production and to encourage a greater Dubai-based TV industry. Perhaps the strongest indicator of the project's success to date is that since 2006 almost all international news service reports that are filed in the Middle East are prefaced with 'Dubai', indicating their Dubai Media City location. Also flattering for Media City have been Ra's al-Khaimah and Fujairah's attempts to create alternatives—hop-

117

ing that accelerating costs in Dubai will force many companies to relocate, in late 2006 these emirates established respectively the Media and Film Free Zone, and the Creative City.

More recently, several other zones have been established around Dubai, so many in fact that perhaps one third of the city's land area is now controlled by free zone authorities. These have included the Dubai Airport Free Zone, located close to Terminal 2 of Dubai International Airport and providing facilities geared towards international cargo companies such as Federal Express and DHL. Also notable is Dubai Silicon Oasis, which aims to foster a semi-conductor production industry; Dubai Flower City, which will provide the necessary infrastructure for the re-exporting of garden products; Dubai Healthcare City, which will serve as a base for foreign medical companies and services, including the Harvard Medical School;[99] and Dubai Knowledge Village, which, since its launch in 2003, now houses branches of several international universities. Although most of the universities involved are distinctly second or third tier western or Australian institutions, most have still generated considerable revenue from their Knowledge Village operations given the many young professionals who now live in Dubai or are willing to travel there in order to gain western-accredited MSc or MBA degrees. Indeed, with many new campuses setting up, including those of Britain's Middlesex and Heriot-Watt Universities, Dubai hopes to attract 150,000 students within the next decade.

Finally, and perhaps most significantly among these newer free zones has been the Dubai International Financial Centre (DIFC) and its constituent Dubai International Financial Exchange (DIFX). This zone was conceived not only to advance further and complement the commercial sector's existing financial infrastructure, but also to provide a means of absorbing surplus liquidity often generated by oil economies. Indeed, even though Dubai itself was diversifying from oil, it was felt that the DIFX would be well positioned to benefit from such liquidity in its hydrocarbon rich neighbours, most notably Abu Dhabi, Kuwait, and Qatar.

Sheikh Muhammad's planners hoped to create a zone unencumbered by local legislation and, in an effort to boost investor confidence, created a dollar-denominated environment and based the DIFC's regulatory framework on English law,[100] not least because most Dubai nationals and expatriates in the Gulf with a financial background have been trained in the City of London. In a similar fashion to the Dubai Internet City, Muhammad enlisted foreign experts (from Standard Chartered and Julius Bär) to assist with the project, and in 2004 the Dubai Financial Services Authority was set up to administer the DIFC, chaired by Anis Al-Jallaf—a veteran Dubai banker and chairman of Emirates Bank International.[101] An impressive Arc de Triomphe-style headquarters building was constructed close to Sheikh Zayed Road, and within months this 'gateway' complex was home to international financial institutions including KPMG, Swiss Private, Swiss International Legal, Merrill Lynch, and Credit Suisse.[102] Within the next few years, more banks, including Mirabaud and Volaw, are likely to open branches, with many citing the DIFC's impressive infrastructure, its solid reputation, and its potential to serve as an alternative location to the City of London for Islamic banking products. Indeed, the DIFC's location close to emerging markets in Muslim-dominated Pakistan and East Africa is thought to be ideal, as is its proximity and historic linkages to Mumbai (Bombay)—a market which is likely to become enormous when the rupee becomes fully convertible and as India continues to liberalise its economy. Moreover, although suffering a shaky start in 2005, the DIFX has also gained momentum, with many international firms believing that it will soon serve as an important bridge between the time zones of the much higher volume stock exchanges in Europe and Asia.[103]

Diversification—tourism and leisure

Also attracting non-oil related foreign investment and boosting the domestic economy has been Dubai's commitment to building up a luxury international tourist industry since the 1990s.

119

Capitalising on winter sun, long stretches of sandy beaches, and shallow seas, Dubai soon emerged as a credible alternative to the Mediterranean and Florida, and more recently has also become a major regional destination for healthcare and education tourism. Furthermore, with new festivals, exhibitions, and sporting events, together with the reputation-building overseas acquisitions and the notable success of the Emirates airline brand, Dubai's tourist potential has continued to grow, with several million visitors per annum expected by 2010, and with the industry's GDP contributions looking set to rise even further.

Perhaps most remarkable has been the speed of the sector's growth, especially given that Dubai had no hotels at all in the 1950s, with business guests having to stay with colleagues, and with any visiting dignitaries being put up at the British agent's house. Indeed, the only hotel in the lower Gulf was in Sharjah, opened shortly after the construction of the Sharjah airbase in the 1930s. This was the first building to have air-conditioning, as Imperial Airways had insisted that its crews needed to be able to sleep properly. Commonly referred to as the Sharjah Fort Hotel and managed by International Airadio Limited,[104] it remained the only alternative to Bahrain's more luxurious Gulf Hotel until 1960 when the 35 room Airlines Hotel opened in Al-Rashidya in support of the newly opened Dubai International Airport (now the site of Le Meridien Village Dubai). By the late 1960s two larger hotels had opened, with the 85 room Carlton Towers in Deira also servicing the airport, and with the much grander 45 room Ambassador Hotel in Bur Dubai being used to host banquets and receive Dubai's most distinguished guests.[105] Over the next decade foreign chains began to move in, with both the Sheraton and Intercontinental groups choosing to build large five star hotels on the Deira side of the creek.

By 1990 some 600,000 visitors per annum were staying in Dubai's seventy or so hotels, with most utilising the 25 four and five star business hotels.[106] From 1992 onwards the sector mushroomed, with a newly established Dubai Tourism Promotion Board (later integrated into the Dubai Department of Commerce Marketing) concentrating on international promotions and positioning Dubai as not just a commercial hub, but also as a resort destination. Under the direction of Khalid Ahmad bin Sulayman and with offices set up in Britain, France, the USA, India, and South Africa,[107] the new 'Destination Dubai' initiative[108] was judged to be highly successful, especially given that by 1995 the number of visitors had doubled to over 1.3 million per annum, with the majority being sun-seeking tourists staying in Dubai's forty-five new resort hotels.[109]

In the late 1990s Dubai entered the international high-end tourist market by investing in some of the world's most luxurious hotel projects. With Sheikh Muhammad bin Rashid Al-Maktum establishing the Jumeirah International group, work began on the iconic Jumeirah Beach Hotel to the west of Dubai. With nearly 600 rooms and suites housed in a unique wave-shaped design, the hotel opened in 1997 and remained the emirate's prime hotspot until the completion of the group's even bigger project just two years later. Built on a small manmade island close to the Jumeirah Beach Hotel, the sail-shaped Burj Al-Arab became the world's first seven star hotel in 1999. Although it required massive investment and almost certainly continues to make considerable losses, this has been seen as a small price to pay for the enormous television coverage of Dubai that it has generated. Moreover, even though the hotel became the subject of much controversy following the Christian architect's revelations that its superstructure was built in the shape of a crucifix (only noticeable when viewed from the sea), its picture was quietly removed from Dubai's car number plates, and it continues to be widely admired and recognised as Dubai's most famous landmark. Importantly, alongside these beachfront properties, at this time Jumeirah International also committed to managing the Emirates Towers Hotel, housed in the second of two new 300 metre towers that had been constructed in downtown Dubai. These constructions have become highly symbolic of Dubai's strategy—while Abu Dhabi's tallest building is oil-related, Dubai's two skyscrapers house hotel bedrooms and commercial offices.

By 2000 3.4 million tourists were coming to Dubai each year,[110] a testimony to these pioneering developments, and in recent years Jumeirah International has added to its portfolio by converting the Al-Maktum family's former winter camping ground into the Al-Maha Desert Resort, by building the new Fairmont Hotel close to Sheikh Zayed Road, and by redeveloping the beachfront to the west of the Burj Al-Arab in order to accommodate two large hotels (Al-Qasr and Mina As-Salam) and an adjoining shopping mall, the Madinat Jumeirah, which has been built in the traditional fashion complete with replica Lingah-style wind towers. In mid-2007 another Dubai entity even purchased the Cunard line's most famous cruise ship, the QE2, which is now destined to be moored off the coast of the emirate and will serve as a luxurious floating hotel.[111] It is estimated that at one point over 10 per cent of Dubai's GDP was invested in these Jumeirah and other government-backed tourism projects.[112] Similarly ambitious have been the foreign chains, with both the Sheraton and Hilton groups expanding their number of properties, and with many other leading companies choosing to build flagship hotels in Dubai. Most notably the Thai Dusit and the Chinese Shangri-La chains have constructed large tower block hotels on Sheikh Zayed Road, while the Hyatt group now has two sizeable complexes on either side of the creek, and Le Meridien has several hotels and furnished apartment towers all around the city. Other chains from India and elsewhere in the Middle East have also been keen to participate in the industry, with the joint-Abu Dhabi, joint Lebanese-managed Rotana group and the Indian Ramee International both operating countless properties in Dubai. Together, it is thought that these predominately luxury hotels, most of which enjoy much higher occupancy rates than the lower class hotels, now account for nearly two thirds of all tourists to Dubai, which as of 2007 may be as high as 6.5 million per annum.[113]

Dubai's tourist industry has not relied on hotels and beaches alone, as planners have been keenly aware that Dubai must always provide additional incentives to draw people to the emirate and to fend off competition from other destinations. With this purpose in mind, several leisure and recreation-oriented initiatives have been launched to make Dubai not only the region's commercial capital, but also its entertainment hub. Again, much like the rapid rise in the number of hotels, this sector has also grown beyond recognition over the last few decades. Indeed, in the 1960s there were few identifiable entertainment outlets in Dubai, with only a handful of restaurants (including an Indian-run Chinese restaurant) and two cinemas that played Hindi movies. Interestingly though, especially given the fairly conservative and Islamic nature of society in the lower Gulf, there was a casino in Ra's al-Khaimah that often remained open throughout the night. Guests of Dubai businessmen were normally taken to dinner in Dubai or Sharjah in the evening and then driven up to the casino afterwards.[114] Since then several western-style cinemas and hundreds of restaurants have opened in Dubai, and, with the increasing number of hotels (which are licensed to serve alcohol) many bars and nightclubs offer both tourists and residents a vibrant nightlife. Companies offering trips into the desert (most notably Arabian Adventures) have proved particularly popular, and within a few years Dubai will have opened the enormous 'Dubailand': as one of the world's largest theme parks it will include dozens of hotels and restaurants alongside replicas of the Eiffel Tower and the Great Pyramids, and will even have a large 'Jurassic Park' with moving dinosaurs.

Also successful in attracting tourists (and further complementing the commercial sector) has been Dubai's investment in promoting and running an annual shopping festival. Although Sharjah had been the original tourist hub of the UAE and had run a Ramadan shopping festival along Al-Wadha Street for many

123

years (attracting Russian tourists intent on importing designer goods and consumer durables into the Soviet Union),[115] since the mid-1980s, when alcohol was banned in the emirate due to complications described later in this book,[116] Sharjah effectively relinquished its position and by the mid-1990s Dubai began planning its own version of the shopping festival. First staged in 1996, the ubiquitous Muhammad Abdullah Al-Gergawi ensured that the new Dubai Shopping Festival was the largest event ever to take place in the UAE: with promotions in hundreds of hotels, restaurants, and shops, and with dozens of street entertainment events it was estimated that over $1 billion was generated by the festival in its first year.[117] It has been a perennial success, including in 2002 (in the wake of the September 11th attacks), and has only had to be cancelled on one occasion, following the unexpected death of Sheikh Maktum bin Rashid Al-Maktum in early 2006. To support the festival, and to provide similar activities during other seasons, Dubai also created a giant 'Global Village' that houses mini, country-specific, compounds selling goods and performing traditional dances. In the late 1990s the village regularly hosted compounds constructed by Ba'athist Iraq (complete with pictures of Saddam Hussein above every stall) and even the Taleban-controlled 'Islamic Emirate of Afghanistan'. In 2001 the Dubai Summer Surprises festival was launched to promote regional tourism in the traditionally slow summer months, and within a few years the giant Dubai Festival City is due to open—located on a massive site on the Deira side of the creek, the new complex will provide a permanent home for the Global Village and serve as the focal point for future festivals.

Further in support of tourism has been Dubai's commitment to live music and the performing arts, with a recently opened theatre in Madinat Jumeirah now hosting several major touring companies each year, and with the Dubai International Film Festival showcasing new releases and attracting many leading Hollywood names to the emirate, including Johnny Depp and Orlando Bloom.

Similarly successful have been the well attended annual Dubai International Jazz Festival staged in Media City and the Dubai Desert Rock festival, the latter of which has persuaded established acts such as Aerosmith and Iron Maiden to headline. Moreover, since 2001 other large venues such as the Dubai Aviation Club, the Dubai Country Club, and the Nad Al-Sheba racetrack have brought other stadium-filling artists to the city, including Elton John, Robbie Williams, Blue, Jennifer Lopez, and Julio Iglesias. Most of these events have brought thousands of tourists to Dubai from across the region and many parts of Asia, just so they could see their favourite performers.

Exhibition tourism has also been extremely profitable for Dubai, with many business hotels being filled to capacity during off peak periods due to an increasing number of professional and industrial exhibitions. In particular, Dubai's annual GITEX event, staged in an annex of the World Trade Centre, has grown to become the third largest IT-related international event since its launch in 1998, and now brings in around 130,000 visitors from over 3,000 companies. Similarly well attended are Dubai's Arabian Travel Market exhibition which now hosts delegations from over 100 of the Middle East's tourist companies and attracts about 25,000 visitors, and the bi-annual Dubai Air Show which, since its launch in 1989 has expanded to feature nearly 100 aircraft marketed by over 500 companies.[118] During the 2005 show over 30,000 tourists flocked to the airport to see one of the first of the new A380 Super Jumbos take off and fly low over the city.[119]

Finally, and perhaps most distinctively, Dubai has boosted tourism and continued to promote itself internationally by hosting several world class sporting events. Central to this strategy has been Dubai's relationship with the international horseracing industry. Following the opening of two small racetracks in Al-Ghusais and Za'abeel 1969 by Sheikh Maktum and Sheikh Muhammad,[120] Sheikh Rashid's sons' love of racing continued to grow, especially following their visits to British racecourses in the early 1970s. Significantly, in 1976 Muhammad purchased three horses in Britain for himself and Maktum, and within a few years both were enjoying victories with *Hatta* and *Shaab*.[121] By 1980 their middle brother, Sheikh Hamdan bin Rashid Al-Maktum, had also got involved, and tasted his first victory in Britain with *Mushref.* Incredibly, just two years later the three brothers had won thirty-sx victories between them, and with Maktum's *Touching Wood* winning the St. Leger they had scored their first classics success.[122] Throughout the 1980s and 1990s the family continued to triumph in major international races with Muhammad's *Pebbles* famously winning the Breeder's Cup in America. By the late 1980s the Al-Maktum family translated their success on the track into profitable overseas investments in the form of British-based stabling and stud operations. Hamdan set up his Shadwell Farm operation, with Maktum establishing the Harwood stud, and Muhammad the Darley group—named after one of the three founding sires of modern thoroughbred racing.[123]

In parallel to this international success, the brothers continued to build up Dubai's horseracing infrastructure. In 1981 the first proper horserace meeting was staged at the Dubai camel track, and another course was built near to the Metropolitan Hotel on Sheikh Zayed Road.[124] By 1988 work had finished on the lavish new circuit at Nad Al-Sheba and within a year it was hosting several meetings each year. In 1992 it was chosen to host the new Emirates Racing Association, and in late 1993 it became the primary home of the Godolphin organisation. Named after Godolphin Barb, another of the three founding sires, this new organisation was an amalgamation of the three brothers' horseracing operations and also included the horseracing interests of their younger half-brother Sheikh Ahmad bin Rashid Al-Maktum, who had earlier set up a racecourse in Jebel Ali.[125] By 1995 the industry enjoyed a major fillip following a European Union decision to remove the UAE from its horse quarantine blacklist. This finally allowed European horses to visit Dubai freely, and the Emirates Racing

Association duly sought classification for nine of its annual races from the International Cataloguing Standards Committee. Able to host accredited races, the brothers immediately announced that the emirate would stage the world's richest horserace: the Dubai World Cup. In 1996 the World Cup was attached to a bill of other high profile races and boasted an impressive $4 million in prize money. Given that Sheikh Muhammad had already experimented with sponsoring British races in the 1980s (including the Dubai Champion Stakes at Newmarket[126]) he was conscious that such prize money was a very small price to pay for international exposure, and in this case would definitely bring the wealthiest and most glamorous members of the international racing circus to Dubai. Indeed, first won by *Cigar*, the World Cup has since attracted some of the world's greatest horses including the American *Captain Steve* and, most memorably, Muhammad's own strategically named *Dubai Millennium*. Within the next few years even more lucrative races are likely to be added to Dubai's calendar and even more horseracing enthusiasts are expected to attend, as Dubai is constructing an even bigger racecourse at Maydan, adjacent to Nad Al-Sheba. Currently scheduled for completion in 2009, it will be built in two stages and will be surrounded by an entire 'Horseracing City,' which in true Dubai style will feature hotels, restaurants, and horse-related leisure facilities.

Alongside horseracing, Dubai has diversified its sports industry to include a European PGA golf tournament—the Dubai Desert Classic—and for many years has staged both the Dubai Rugby Sevens competition and an annual ATP tennis tournament. All of these have brought sports celebrities to Dubai (although often as a result of huge appearance fees), including Tiger Woods, Andre Agassi, and Roger Federer; and all have been responsible for sustaining high hotel occupancies. Moreover, although Dubai's adventures in motor racing have been much less successful despite the completion of a new autodrome and the hosting of A1 races since 2005, it is likely that Dubai's hotels will greatly benefit from the Abu Dhabi Formula One Grand Prix (which will begin in 2009) in the same way that they already accommodate the majority of tourists attending the Bahrain Formula One Grand Prix. Dubai is also in the final stages of constructing a 'Sports City' which will include Manchester United's first Middle East-based soccer school, and which will feature both indoor and outdoor stadia, a 'Golf City,' and a cricket stadium. Indeed, although Dubai has now controversially become the home of the International Cricket Council following its move from Lords in London, until this new stadium is built, the only world class cricket facilities in the UAE are those in Sharjah. Most ambitiously, it is hoped that Sports City, which is after all the largest planned leisure complex in the developing world, will serve as the launch pad for Dubai's 2016 Olympic bid.

Diversification—real estate

Encouraging greater foreign and expatriate investment from individuals, and closely associated with the tourist sector and its associated 'entertainment infrastructure' has been Dubai's more recent diversification into freehold real estate. With the multiple aims of converting impressionable tourists into holiday home or buy-to-let purchasers and, perhaps more realistically, persuading nationals of less stable or less prosperous parts of the developing world to make a safe investment and create a new residence for their family; the real estate sector has managed to circumvent and modify existing restrictive legislation much like the free zone developments, and now accounts for another sizeable slice of Dubai's non-oil related GDP. Indeed, on paper at least the sector has enjoyed enormous growth; with a staggering number of projects close to completion or in the final planning stages, with demand consistently outstripping supply, with a massive support and marketing industry booming in parallel, and with a frenzied speculation market emerging for those seeking to trade in their mortgage deposits for a quick premium.

As late as the mid-1990s there was no property market in Dubai, with most of the developed land around the city having been donated by the ruling family to other national families so as to build new homes for themselves or to build residential and commercial blocks to lease out to expatriates and businesses. In 1997, however, this began to change following an announcement that the new $200 million 'Emirates Hills' residential complex near to the Emirates Golf Club would offer luxury villas to all GCC nationals and, notably, 'to other foreigners.'[127] This project was managed by Emaar Properties, a company that had been set up in the early 1990s by Muhammad Ali Al-Abbar, the first director of Dubai's Department of Economic Development. Up until the launch of Emirates Hills, Emaar had confined itself to building fairly nondescript condominiums on land provided by Sheikh Muhammad bin Rashid Al-Maktum, with the intention of offering the same sort of short term leases as were common everywhere else in the Gulf. However, following work experience in Singapore, where he had recognised the potential of a vibrant real estate sector, Al-Abbar returned to Dubai and encouraged Muhammad to press ahead with reforms that would enable the emirate to create such a sector.

In much the same way that the pioneering Jebel Ali Free Zone actually broke the described federal laws regarding foreign business ownership during the 1980s, the marketing of Emirates Hills villas to foreigners was also technically illegal, as only UAE nationals were permitted to own property in the UAE. Indeed, although Sheikh Muhammad and Al-Abbar sought to work around the federal law by offering 99 year leases to foreigners with the promise of renewal following a nominal payment of just $1, there is no doubt that in the early days of Dubai's real estate market, Emaar had entered a legal minefield. Certainly, the federal government could in theory revoke all ownership rights from investors,[128] thereby rendering the sector reliant on an unwritten

129

promise from Muhammad that there would be future enabling legislation.[129]

Nevertheless, such an assurance and the open backing of the Al-Maktum family were enough to kick start the largest property boom in the Middle East, with Emaar selling out all of its available plots within days of the official launch, and with several other projects receiving equally enthusiastic receptions. Most notably, the Westside Marina development (later renamed Dubai Marina) proposed to cut a manmade canal inland from the sea and construct a number of high specification residential towers with marina and coastal views; the 'Greens' complex close to Sheikh Zayed Road began to advertise quiet poolside three storey blocks complete with integrated amenities such as supermarkets, gyms, and social clubs; and the Emaar Towers located close to Al-Maktum Bridge offered city centre living in large apartments with balconies overlooking the creek. In addition, several large villa complexes (The Springs, The Meadows, and Arabian Ranches) were launched in the hinterland, most of which are now complete. Following in Emaar's footsteps has been Dubai Properties, a group with close links to Dubai Holdings, which began work on the enormous 36 tower Jumeirah Beach Residence on the beachfront of Emaar's new marina. Believed to be the largest single phase residential project in the world, it has cost over $1.6 billion and is expected to house over 25,000 residents upon completion. Perhaps even more significant among Emaar's stable mates has been Nakheel. Chaired by Sultan Ahmad bin Sulayman, Nakheel is a property company dating back to 1990, but which following the success of Emirates Hills sought backing from the government together with a personal commitment from Sheikh Muhammad, and embarked on several of Dubai's most remarkable real estate developments. Most famously, Nakheel has constructed two separate 'Palm Islands' off the coast of Jumeirah and Jebel Ali, both of which will feature villas, apartments and, in cooperation with the Trump Organisation and the Taj group, several five star hotels. As giant patches of reclaimed land they will expand Dubai's waterfront from about 70 km to over 500 km given that each 'palm' will have several fronds and a number of additional, more exclusive mini islands in the shape of Arabic lettering to represent one of Muhammad's best known poems, and in the shape of dolphins (for his private beach residences).[130] In 2004, with both palms being sold out, Sheikh Muhammad instructed Nakheel to launch a third palm off the coast of Deira,[131] and a further archipelago of islands further out at sea. While the Deira development has seemingly stalled, the archipelago project, currently entitled 'The World', has attracted enormous international media attention given that its 300 or so islands will each represent a separate country, and given that several high profile investors have already committed to purchasing various islands (or more likely have received them as donations for publicity purposes). Specifically, it is believed that David Beckham and Rod Stewart have acquired 'England' and 'Scotland' respectively, while Shah Rukh Khan has bought 'India,' and Michael Schumacher has signed up for 'Germany'.

By early 2006, with several such projects now completed, the three big developers were thought to have already provided in excess of 30,000 new homes, most of which were sold to expatriates. As the newly installed ruler of Dubai and vice president of the federation following his eldest brother's death, Sheikh Muhammad felt in a strong enough position to press ahead with more comprehensive Dubai-specific legislation to safeguard the real estate sector. By this stage, with Dubai claiming over $50 billion in committed property-related projects,[132] the federal government was presented with something of a *fait accompli*, and indeed there is evidence that for quite some time before, Abu Dhabi had come to terms with Dubai's strategy.[133] By the spring of that year Muhammad unilaterally announced the Dubai Property Law. This included articles stipulating that foreigners were entitled to own real estate in 'some parts of Dubai, as designated by the ruler', and would be entitled to receive residency visas from the Dubai government (previously residency visas were only issued to foreigners subject to proof of employment). Moreover, to settle investors' minds further, the law called for the establishment of a Lands Department that would provide a centralised land registry capable of issuing deeds upon purchase.[134]

With this new legislation in place, demand for Dubai's more recently announced projects soared, and additional developments were soon launched. In some cases, demand was so high that prospective customers for these new off-plan villas and apartments were advised to arrive at sales centres on the morning of the launch in order to queue for a lottery-like ticket that would entitle them to make a purchase. In particular, Emaar, which became a 67 per cent publicly owned company following its flotation on the aforementioned DIFX,[135] has pressed ahead with its magnificent Burj Dubai: a mixed residential, commercial, and hotel complex that will total some 165 or more storeys and is being built with a dynamic design to ensure that upon its completion in 2008 it will be the world's tallest structure. Complimenting the Burj will be the 'Old Town' district that features more traditional architecture and will form a boulevard at the skyscraper's base. Next door to the Burj, Dubai Properties has been constructing an enormous Venetian-style downtown area of smaller skyscrapers that will be connected by small canals fed from a larger waterway that will extend all the way into the creek. This 'Business Bay' project is thought to be employing nearly 10 per cent of the world's cranes[136] and is likely to transform Dubai's skyline into something of a Middle Eastern version of Manhattan Island. Similarly ambitious, and also incredibly popular with investors has been Nakheel's latest scheme: envisaging a coastal city larger than downtown Beirut, the $13 billion Dubai Waterfront will stretch out far beyond Palm Jebel Ali and will feature the confusingly titled Al-Burj, likely to become Dubai's second tallest building, as its centrepiece. Also noteworthy have been the attempts of some developers to provide investment opportunities for lower and middle income households, especially the large middle class South Asian community. Indeed, Nakheel's oddly titled 'Jumeirah Village', sandwiched between the two main arterial highways, and its equally strangely named 'International City', located on the periphery of the desert, have now been joined by other mid-range developments from new property companies, including Sama's rather bizarre looking 'The Lagoons.' Together, they have enjoyed some success, albeit not on a par with the high-end projects—the deeds of which continue to be sold and re-sold for significant profits.

It would now appear that several of the other emirates are seeking to replicate Dubai's real estate success, with Ra's al-Khaimah being the first to jump on Sheikh Muhammad's bandwagon. In much as the same way as the 2006 Dubai Property Law, the elderly Sheikh Saqr bin Muhammad Al-Qasimi has formulated his own enabling legislation. Although this originally required expatriate property buyers to also invest in Ra's al-Khaimah's free zone, this clause has now been dropped and the emirate's government has invested over $6 billion in constructing some 5,000 residential units targeted at foreigners.[137] Most notably, through its Ra's al-Khaimah Properties and Khoie Group parastatals, a number of Emaar-like projects have been announced, including Mina al-Arab, Khor Qarm, and Marjan Island. Positioning Ra's al-Khaimah as a more tranquil and picturesque alternative to the big city feel of Dubai, these would seem to have enjoyed modest success, although few investors are likely to believe the developers' claims that Ra's al-Khaimah is just a '45 minute drive from Dubai.' Similarly popular have been Umm al-Qawain's Al-Salam City and Ajman's numerous developments, including Al-Ameera Village and the Pearl Residence, all of which have benefited from the conurbation effect from nearby Dubai. Despite also passing a foreign ownership law, Sharjah has been more cautious than its northern neighbours, preferring to keep such foreign investment more discreet, although these concerns have now been balanced as efforts are underway to develop the more secluded Nujoom

Islands to the east of the city. Demand for Dubai-style property is high elsewhere in the region too, with Emaar's new International Development section currently involved in joint ventures with other Middle Eastern property companies,[138] while also advising on projects in India and Pakistan.

Abu Dhabi now also has several real estate companies, some of which, like Emaar, have opened themselves up to public ownership. Prominent among these is crown prince Sheikh Muhammad bin Zayed Al-Nahyan's Al-Dar group, which has been responsible for the vast Al-Raha Beach complex, the exclusive Al-Gurum Resort, and Yas Island; Sorouh has been developing Al-Reem island by building Shams city and its showpiece 80 storey 'Sky Tower'; and the ruler's eldest son, Sheikh Sultan bin Khalifa Al-Nahyan, has been constructing villas on the seaward side of the Marina Mall. Abu Dhabi's apparent diversification is not quite the same as Dubai's given that the development of the real estate sector is not primarily geared to attracting foreign direct investment. While some foreigners are purchasing property in Abu Dhabi, most buyers are primarily GCC nationals or other Arabs, with the lion's share of marketing being aimed at a 'culturally compatible' Arab and Muslim audience. Abu Dhabi property billboards normally feature family scenes with covered women, whereas Emaar and Nakheel's giant adverts normally depict Caucasians on the beach or Levantine women drinking alcohol in outdoor cafes. Moreover, the pricing of Abu Dhabi's properties is much higher than in Dubai, with no real attempt to supply the lower end of the market. Indeed, given its vast oil reserves and the ongoing success of oil-related strategies, Abu Dhabi does not need to open up so fast or to share any of the Dubai-associated risks that are explored later in this book, preferring instead to add this new sector with the primary aim of providing more luxurious homes and more varied employment opportunities for an increasingly educated and skilled national population that previously could be accommodated only by oil companies or the public sector.

Superficial success

Taken as a whole, these diversification strategies would seem to have greatly reduced Dubai's reliance on oil exports and oil-related strategies such as energy dependent heavy industries and oil-financed overseas investments. By the mid-1990s Dubai's non-oil sectors were already contributing 82 per cent of the emirate's GDP,[139] and in 2006 the figure may have been as high as 95 per cent.[140] In comparison, the UAE's total non-oil GDP contributions are only 63 per cent,[141] and it is believed that Dubai is responsible for the vast bulk of the UAE's total foreign direct investment inflows of about $3 billion per annum (compared to $2.1 billion in 2003 and $0.5 billion in 1995).[142] It is thought that Sharjah and Ajman bring in more foreign direct investment than Abu Dhabi, which ranks only fourth in the UAE[143] and therefore indicates its preference for more oil-focused activities. This figure of $3 billion has now placed Dubai and the UAE far ahead of Gulf peers such as Kuwait (which manages only $0.5 billion per annum[144]), and among the top Middle Eastern countries for such investment, despite a much smaller population. Recent international reports published by the United Nations Conference on Trade and Development (UNCTAD) have begun to compare Dubai's foreign direct investment potential with that of Geneva, New Delhi, Tokyo, and even New York; and have ranked the emirate 17th out of over 100 surveyed countries with respect to foreign investment attractiveness.[145] Thus, on paper at least, Dubai would appear to have escaped from its former dependency and certainly gives the impression that it has succeeded in creating a self-sustaining, multi-component economy capable of generating vast wealth independently of the old oil industry, which is now most often described as 'simply ticking over.'

5

POLITICAL STABILITY AND
THE RULING BARGAIN

Dubai's impressive economic development would never have been possible without a bedrock of political stability. Its relative tranquility has always been highly attractive to immigrant merchants from more troubled regions, and now, with rapidly accelerating levels of foreign direct investment remaining central to the success of Dubai's diversification strategies, such constancy is arguably more crucial than ever before. Yet Dubai is still an autocracy, where real evidence of an opening for true democracy proves hard to find, and where far less political reform has occurred than in neighbouring Gulf states, including even Saudi Arabia.[1] Indeed, international NGOs regularly rank Dubai and the umbrella federal government of the United Arab Emirates as being among the least free political systems in the world.[2] This is especially significant given that many of the distinguished mid-twentieth century 'modernisation theorists' predicted that all such traditional polities would eventually fail: most especially those monarchies that were on the cusp of great socio-economic growth afforded by massive oil revenues.[3] How, then, has Dubai managed to overcome this 'sheikh's dilemma' of pursuing economic reform without succumbing to meaningful political reform?[4] While part of the answer is to be found in the Al-Maktum family's impressive internal strength, much can also be attributed to an unwritten 'ruling bargain' that exists between the rulers and the national population. With distributed oil wealth serving as the cornerstone of this pact, in much the same way as earlier generations of rulers placated their restless merchants with other material benefits,[5] the bargain also includes several other components, including the development of a patrimonial and technocratic network, the provision of a veneer of modern, 'neo-patrimonial' government institutions, and the careful exploitation of a range of ideological, religious, and cultural resources.

Strengthening a dynasty

After successfully leading an Abu Dhabi breakaway state in the early nineteenth century, Sheikh Maktum bin Buti and his descendents steered their infant sheikhdom through a series of regional conflicts, gaining independence for Dubai from its larger neighbours and establishing mutually beneficial relations with Britain. A dynasty was founded, and a series of status-building peace treaties combined with subsidies and, in some cases, military intervention, ensured that the Al-Maktum rulers survived several insurgencies and attempted reforms during their years of British protection. Since 1971, without such direct powerful backing, or at least not in terms of domestic support, the ruling family has developed new mechanisms for ensuring its internal stability. As with the other UAE dynasties, it was soon realised that the old divisions, palace coups, and fratricides within the ruling families must come to an end, at least publicly, otherwise they would be exposing themselves to both external inference and heavy criticism from their indigenous populations. Moreover, with no desire to open up the decision-making process or to provide for political participation, it was further recognised that the rulers would have to become much more than the great warriors or charismatic leaders that their forefathers were. Instead, the newer generations of the Al-Maktum family would also have to possess much stronger personal resources: they would have to position themselves as savvy politicians, shrewd businessmen, and patrons of the arts.

Following the death of Sheikh Said bin Maktum Al-Maktum in 1958, the succession was clear cut, given that his eldest son, Sheikh Rashid bin Said Al-Maktum, had been the de facto ruler of Dubai since the 1930s. Rashid had already proven himself an effective statesman during his successful resolution of the merchants' reform movement and his careful containment of the Arab nationalist threat,[6] and was therefore firmly in control of the family and its resources at the time of Britain's departure and the onset of oil revenues. As the architect of many of Dubai's ambitious infrastructural projects, and credited with much of the enormous socio-economic transformation of the emirate during the '70s and '80s, Rashid was rightly regarded as the 'Father of Dubai' and enjoyed widespread popular support and respect by the end of his reign. Indeed, although never on the scale of the state-sponsored hero-worshipping that continues to take place in Abu Dhabi in honour of Sheikh Zayed bin Sultan Al-Nahyan, it was not uncommon for large unofficial posters of Rashid to be erected around Dubai or for spontaneous car rallies to take place waving flags depicting Rashid's face. As a further testament to the genuine affection that many held for him, during his car journeys around the city after recovering from a bout of ill health in 1982, the roads were regularly lined by both nationals and expatriates cheering his name.[7] In the aftermath of his death in the summer of 1990, a forty day mourning period was held across the UAE, despite the escalating Kuwaiti crisis in the northern Gulf. His obituaries featured in several leading international newspapers, with many describing him as being the first 'modern' ruler of Dubai and hinting that he had already succeeded in developing Dubai into an entrepôt that would soon be comparable to Singapore and Hong Kong.[8]

Leaving behind three mature sons to Sheikha Latifa bint Hamdan Al-Nahyan and a younger son to a second wife, Sheikh

Rashid had ensured the longevity of the dynasty, especially given that his three eldest had all taken an active role in the economic planning of the 1980s and, between them, had already accumulated much experience in the emirate-level government, in the federal government, and in the military. With carefully balanced positions and responsibilities something of a deal was struck, with all of the brothers placated and with most of their cousins and other prominent members of the family also able to contribute to Dubai's ongoing success. Most notably, the 49 year old Sheikh Maktum bin Rashid Al-Maktum succeeded his father to become a figurehead ruler of Dubai and a 'chairman' to preside over his siblings. In addition to his seniority and crown prince status, which he had held since 1964,[9] he was believed to be particularly well suited for the role given his bilingual abilities courtesy of a British education,[10] and his regular deputising for his father since his twenties. There is evidence that Maktum made regular visits to the other Trucial sheikhdoms during the late 1960s to boost Rashid's attempts to create a federation, in addition to serving as director of his father's Lands Department[11] and playing a key role in reducing the influence of Arab nationalist teachers in Dubai.[12] Following the formation of the UAE, Maktum became the federal prime minister at the age of only 30 (making him the youngest prime minister in history), remaining in that position until 1979, when, following a federal dispute discussed later in this volume,[13] Maktum stepped down to become deputy prime minister underneath his father. Throughout the 1980s, as Rashid's health declined, Maktum took back many of the prime minister's responsibilities before regaining the title officially in 1990 following his succession.

Just three years younger, Sheikh Rashid's next eldest son, Sheikh Hamdan bin Rashid Al-Maktum, was the natural choice to become the deputy ruler of Dubai underneath Sheikh Maktum. Named after his maternal grandfather, a former ruler of Abu Dhabi, Hamdan was also educated in Britain,[14] and had gained much experience of both the federal and Dubai economies since his appointment as UAE Minister of Finance and Industry in 1973 (a position that he still holds today). Indeed, during the early 1980s, when worldwide recession had had a serious impact on the Gulf economies, Hamdan was credited with having reduced the UAE's $2 billion federal budget deficit and having achieved a more favourable balance of payments. Moreover, Hamdan has also headed the Dubai Municipality since 1974, along with Dubai's Departments of Information and Health Services, and one of Dubai's major petroleum products companies, EPPCO.[15] Perhaps most significantly, Hamdan has also chaired the successful DUBAL, DUGAS, and DUCAB, which, as described in the previous chapter, have all played a central role in Dubai's heavy oil-oriented industrialisation programme.[16]

Aged 42 upon Sheikh Maktum's succession, Sheikh Muhammad bin Rashid Al-Maktum was at least the equal to his older brothers, having held a series of powerful roles and having been accorded with key responsibilities since his youth. As a bilingual graduate of the same language institute as Sheikh Hamdan, Muhammad then went on to train at the Mons Officer Cadet school (a subsection of the Royal Military Academy, Sandhurst), allowing him to take over the Dubai police force from Sheikh Muhammad bin Hasher Al-Maktum when he returned from Britain in 1968. His military training also persuaded his father's majlis to confer on him the task of setting up the Dubai Defence Force (the DDF) during Britain's withdrawal, a position that also facilitated his appointment as the UAE's Minister for Defence in 1976, at the age of just 28.[17] Throughout the 1970s his military expertise was put to the test, with Muhammad involved in a series of hostage negotiations and conflict resolutions. In particular, as will be discussed later in this study, he communicated personally with a number of aircraft hijack teams, and on several occasions ensured the peaceful release of passengers.[18] By the 1980s, with his involvement in the development of Dubai International Airport

141

and the establishment of the new Emirates airline,[19] in addition to his assumption of chairmanship duties at the Dubai Petroleum Company and several other private companies,[20] Muhammad had also proven himself to be a highly capable businessman with a good feel for Dubai's development needs and a clear vision of the emirate's future strategies.

Although only in his 30s at the time of his father's death, and although only a half-brother to his older siblings, Sheikh Ahmad bin Rashid Al-Maktum was also well placed to take part in Dubai's senior administration, eventually being assigned the deputy directorship of Dubai's police and public security services. Much like Sheikh Muhammad, he had received rigorous officer training and served in the DDF before becoming commander of the Dubai branch of the UAE Armed Forces following the amalgamation of emirate-level militaries in the 1990s.[21] Confusingly, in 1990 another commander in the DDF, also named Sheikh Ahmad, had emerged as a powerful figure within the Al-Maktum family. As the youngest brother of Sheikh Rashid, and the offspring of a late remarriage by Sheikh Said bin Maktum Al-Maktum,[22] Sheikh Ahmad bin Said Al-Maktum is actually younger than all of Rashid's four sons.[23] Most prominently, of course, Ahmad had been appointed chairman of his nephew Muhammad's Emirates airline in 1985,[24] so was particularly well suited to become Dubai's new director of civil aviation in addition to supervising the activities of the Dubai Tourism Promotion Board.[25] Also significant were the sons of Rashid's middle brother, Sheikh Khalifa bin Said Al-Maktum, who between them held an array of top posts and served as strong supporters of the newly installed Sheikh Maktum. In particular, the eldest son, Sheikh Muhammad bin Khalifa Al-Maktum, became the director of Dubai's Lands Department, while the second eldest son, Sheikh Mani bin Khalifa Al-Maktum, was selected to be the new director of the ruler's office,[26] and one of his younger brothers, Sheikh Rashid bin Khalifa Al-Maktum, was appointed head of Dubai's traffic section.[27]

With most of the major players accommodated within the power structure, Sheikh Rashid's death did not lead to the unravelling of the dynasty; however, one of Sheikh Maktum's first major challenges was the greater incorporation of a distaff branch of the family that had remained outside of the inner circle for several decades. It was felt that the Al-Maktum family would be considerably strengthened if the 'Juma faction' could be better integrated than it had been under Rashid. As Sheikh Said's younger brother, Sheikh Juma bin Maktum Al-Maktum had never become ruler of Dubai, but had remained highly influential, as attested by the fact of his being accorded a gun salute by the British—a privilege normally reserved for rulers.[28] By the 1950s he had emerged as an opponent to Sheikh Said and Rashid, playing a key role in the Dubai National Front before being exiled with his sons to Saudi Arabia.[29] Eventually returning to Dubai, his sons were unable to compete with Rashid or his sons, but by the 1980s many of his grandsons had emerged as capable military officers and administrators. From 1990 and onwards, Maktum ensured that these grandsons of Juma were promoted and made part of the establishment. In particular Sheikh Muhammad bin Ubayd Al-Maktum, the youngest son of Juma's eldest son became Sheikh Muhammad bin Rashid's undersecretary in the UAE Ministry of Defence,[30] while Sheikh Hasher bin Maktum Al-Maktum, the eldest son of Juma's second son, served as the UAE's ambassador to Iran and then took over the directorship of Dubai's Department of Information (following on from Sheikh Hamdan bin Rashid) along with the editorship of one of Dubai's most popular daily newspapers, *Al-Bayan*,[31] and, as will be discussed, now also sits on Dubai's highest executive council. Among Hasher's younger brothers, Sheikh Ahmad bin Maktum Al-Maktum became the Deputy Commander of Operations and Training in Sheikh Ahmad bin Rashid's Dubai Central Military Command;[32] Sheikh Marwan bin Maktum Al-Maktum was installed as head of the First Maktum Brigade of the Dubai Emiri bodyguard;[33] Sheikh Buti bin Maktum Al-Maktum was appointed Deputy Commander of Logistics and Administration in the military command; and the youngest, Sheikh Al-Mur bin Maktum Al-Maktum, joined Marwan to serve in the Emiri bodyguard.[34] Interestingly, the Juma faction remains loyal and powerful today, with some of Juma's great-grandsons now taking on senior roles—it is also noteworthy that Sheikh Muhammad bin Hasher Al-Maktum was chosen to head Dubai's Department of Courts in the 1990s.[35]

Sheikh Muhammad's succession

Although Sheikh Maktum bin Rashid Al-Maktum and his father had smoothed the 1990 succession and provided sufficient consolation prizes for all others involved, Maktum was not in a position to appoint a new crown prince from among his own sons, given their young age and the relative power of his younger brothers. As such, it became increasingly unlikely that the Al-Maktum family would be able to follow the customs of primogeniture as it more or less had done for the previous century. As a temporary solution, no crown prince appointment was made, there existing an unspoken understanding that Sheikh Hamdan bin Rashid Al-Maktum as deputy ruler and the next eldest brother would succeed in the event of Maktum's death. However, by the mid-1990s Sheikh Muhammad bin Rashid Al-Maktum's personal resources were continuing to increase, with his earlier business and administrative successes being complemented by his efforts in setting up many of Dubai's new diversification projects. Moreover, his military background, combined with his well-known sporting prowess (the winner of several international endurance horse races) and, after previously preferring to publish anonymously, his emerging status as a respected *nabati* poet in his own right[36] were all raising his profile within Dubai and across the UAE. Muhammad was becoming regarded as a dynamic and multi-talented ruler-in-waiting, and was consequently beginning to enjoy tremendous popular support from both younger and older generations of Dubai nationals. Given his arranged marriage to Sheikha Hind bint Maktum Al-Maktum, the daughter of Sheikh Juma bin Maktum Al-Maktum's second son, he was also seen as the man most likely to preserve the family's unity and to cement further the two main branches.[37]

Five years after his succession, Sheikh Maktum issued a decree in early 1995 that Sheikh Muhammad would become his crown prince.[38] Officially, Maktum remained ruler, but Muhammad was effectively the premier, much as his father had been to his grandfather. His new 'Executive Office of the Crown Prince', eventually located on the top floor of the taller of the two Emirates Towers, duly became the main centre of power in Dubai. Ironically, therefore, Maktum had really been more of a ruler when his father was still alive than after his succession. As such, when Maktum died during a vacation to Australia in early 2006, there was little real transition of power in Dubai, with Muhammad simply assuming the new title of ruler and taking over his brother's role as federal prime minister. As the tenth Al-Maktum ruler of Dubai, Muhammad's position was probably stronger than any of his nine predecessors, but this did not slow his accumulation of additional personal resources, with his sporting career continuing until 2003 (with participation in the European Open Endurance Championship), with his publication of a book entitled *My Vision: Challenges in the Race for Excellence*, and perhaps most notably, with his wedding in 2004 to a 'junior' wife, the Jordanian Princess Haya bint Al-Hussein. With Princess Haya being the half-sister to King Abdullah, this represented a marriage between the Al-Maktum dynasty and the highly esteemed lineage of the royal Hashemite family.

Sheikh Muhammad has not yet turned his attention to succession arrangements, with recent communications stating simply that 'the matter is in hand'.[39] Although this is certainly not an immediate cause for concern given that Muhammad is still in his fifties and the Al-Maktum family seems to present a united front, there is nevertheless still some unease over the future, especially

145

on the part of foreign investors who have relied heavily upon Muhammad's support. In particular there is a concern that there is no confirmed candidate for crown prince and that Dubai's polity has not yet reached the level of sophistication as have some of its Gulf neighbours in which institutional strength has been sufficient to remove unsuitable successors from power (in the case of Kuwait),[40] or has allowed for a clearly defined 'succession decision' to be made following the ruler's death (in the case of Oman).[41] As it stands, Muhammad's older surviving brother, Sheikh Hamdan, is most likely to succeed, perhaps as some kind of regent, given that he has been deputy ruler of Dubai for over seventeen years. However, within the next few months, as the younger generation of the Al-Maktum family gains greater experience, the crown prince is more likely to be one of Sheikh Rashid bin Said Al-Maktum's grandsons. Given that Sheikh Maktum's youngest son, Sheikh Rashid bin Maktum Al-Maktum, died tragically in a car accident in 2002 and his eldest son, Sheikh Said bin Maktum Al-Maktum, has since married into a non-Bani Yas family,[42] it is increasingly likely that the next ruler will be one of Muhammad's seven sons. For several personal reasons, Sheikh Rashid bin Muhammad Al-Maktum, the eldest of these sons and an Asian Games gold medal winner,[43] has been excluded from powerful positions, but the second eldest son, Sheikh Hamdan bin Muhammad Al-Maktum is rapidly emerging as a suitable candidate. As the chairman of his father's executive council, he is now gaining administrative experience, but, perhaps more importantly, his love of poetry has already gained him much support among younger Dubai nationals. Indeed, he is nicknamed '*fazza*', referring to his high ethics and poetic nature, and his handsome face has already begun to appear on large posters around the city and on a dedicated website that is advertised outside major shopping malls.[44] Much like his father, his poems are regularly featured in songs by famous local singers (and even rappers), and in early 2007 he staged a mass poetry reading at the World Trade Centre. Attended by over 700 enthusiasts, he was introduced on stage by Muhammad, and then began reciting his work, interspersed with comments of praise for his father's work. By the end of the session the predominantly Dubai national audience was interacting with him, calling out their own poetry in response to his. Thus, with much popularity, and with greater responsibilities and more significant positions in the Dubai administration likely to be conferred upon him in the near future, Hamdan should soon be installed as crown prince, definitely supported by his popular younger brothers: accomplished horseman Sheikh Ahmad bin Muhammad Al-Maktum[45] and the Sandhurst-trained Sheikh Maktum bin Muhammad Al-Maktum. The dynasty will therefore soon have another generation of rulers capable of drawing on significant personal resources.

Distributed wealth

Throughout Dubai's history, rulers have always ensured that a portion of the sheikhdom's wealth was distributed to the national population, often as a means of buying loyalty and preventing political opposition. Even during the lean years following the decline of the pearling industry a number of rent-generating activities (including air landing rights and oil exploration fees) ensured that the Al-Maktum family could always accumulate at least some wealth.[46] During this period Sheikh Said bin Maktum Al-Maktum would regularly receive visitors to his majlis who were seeking financial assistance. Normally he would listen to their story and then instruct his clerk to hand out six rupees, a sum sufficient to feed a family for several months.[47] On one occasion Said mistakenly issued an enormous 60 rupee payment to a particularly indigent national. Although his clerk noticed and reported the error, Said decided that the amount should remain at 60 as it was his fault and he did not want to disappoint one of his townsmen.[48] Following his succession, Sheikh Rashid bin Said Al-Maktum continued this practice throughout the 1960s, albeit with less emphasis on handouts and with more attention being

147

given to helping his needy visitors find jobs (especially by writing references for them so that they could work for the British) or by donating them land on which to build houses or set up businesses.[49] Although the British approved of such wealth allocations and subsidies as an important political tool, they warned Rashid not to give land away too freely, as it was a valuable asset in a poor state, and could generate significant revenue for his family if it were auctioned instead.[50]

By the early 1970s, with income flowing from the Fateh and Faleh oilfields, Sheikh Rashid extended further his disbursements. With much higher levels of rent flowing to the Dubai government via the DPC, it finally became possible to offer free housing to poorer nationals, and even to provide accommodation for those bedouin hoping to live a more settled existence. Several large, low-cost housing projects were undertaken during this period, including the construction of four-storey tenements in Karama, Satwa, and Al-Ghusais. Free housing continues today, with members of the Al-Maktum family regularly handing out keys to less fortunate families. Although the Dubai properties are not comparable with those of the Zayed Housing Programme in Abu Dhabi, which has an annual budget of over $170 million[51] and has constructed entire new communities in the desert such as Khalifa City, Muhammad City, and Al-Shahama, they are nevertheless well appointed villas in quiet areas such as Al-Barsha and Al-Twar. They give nationals, with a combined household income of less than $2,700 per month, the opportunity to live in accommodation that would otherwise be far beyond their means.[52]

In parallel to such projects, the government also allocated a share of its rentier wealth to other aspects of its citizens' lives. In particular, free education and healthcare began to be offered in the 1970s, and continue to be provided today, with most nationals still not expected to pay medical costs or school and university fees. Moreover, those nationals who graduated with degrees or other qualifications were normally found jobs within the government or its various parastatals. Although this practice only really extended up until the mid-1990s when public sector departments became too bloated, for many years it was entirely possible for a young national to be promoted to the level of deputy director within just a few years of graduation, and given that he would often be supported by an expatriate Arab or South Asian assistant, his job would effectively be 'disguised employment,' with no real need to work a full day or to handle all responsibilities. Similarly, those nationals who preferred non public sector work were encouraged to set up businesses by being given free office space and low interest or interest free loans by semi government-backed banks such as the Emirates Industrial Bank.[53] Indeed, due to its history as a free port Dubai has always shied away from protective measures for nationals including the much maligned *kafil* sponsorship system that ensured 51% ownership for nationals and has been prevalent elsewhere in the UAE and the Gulf;[54] therefore a system of such 'soft' loans aimed at encouraging entrepreneurship was thought to offer the perfect balance of economic and political solutions. Another important example of such business-related largesse would include the government's provision of free farming equipment and farm workers' subsidies in an effort to build good relations with hinterland communities and to improve the growth of the agricultural sector,[55] which was seen as an important component of the diversification strategy.[56] Moreover, all nationals continue to receive smaller but no less significant benefits from the state: they do not have to pay for local telephone calls and are exempt from the annual community charge normally placed on all houses and apartments. Although only minor perks, these are a constant reminder that the government is a distributor rather than an extractor of wealth.

With the slow down of Dubai's oil industry and the greater emphasis being placed on developing non-petroleum related sectors in the 1990s, there was concern that falling government oil revenues would jeopardise the state's allocative capabilities. In particular it was feared that if free housing, soft loans and other wealth transfers could not be sustained, then the Al-Maktum family would no longer be able to rely on the same level of political acquiescence from the population as it had enjoyed in the past. Moreover it was felt that if the government attempted to reverse the flow of wealth and began to tax nationals, then there would be a backlash that might even resurrect the old, pre-oil, demands for political reform. Fortunately, with successful diversification the problem has solved itself, as Dubai emerges as a post-oil rentier state, with many of its nationals remaining above the wealth creation process courtesy of the land and property they own.

With the introduction of free zones, the relaxation of property laws, and subsequent influx of foreign investment, land that had previously been worthless could suddenly be rented or sold for considerable profits. Many of Dubai's new business parks, resorts, hotels, and apartment blocks have been built on plots of land that were previously just patches of sand. The families who were given this land by the ruling family in previous years were transformed into 'mini-rentiers' in their own right. Indeed, while nationals had been renting out property ever since the occupants of the original low-cost government housing began building their own villas and leasing their former apartments to expatriates, and while many nationals illegally sublet government-provided villas of the 1980s and 1990s to foreigners and have moved in to smaller apartments,[57] the new real estate sector and Dubai's fast growing population have provided rich pickings for landlords, as rents have soared. Although the government sometimes listens to the concerns of rent-paying expatriates and as a token gesture occasionally imposes rent-rise ceilings, given that the landlords are predominantly nationals the government is in reality more than happy to allow for substantial rent increases. Thus, the rentier political system can be sustained without the need for specific state subsidies, and those unable to meet higher rents are expected to move to outlying areas or nearby 'dormitory' emirates such as Sharjah or Ajman, and then commute to work in Dubai.

Preserving the rentier elite

The extensive rent-financed wealth distributions of the past, and the more recent creation of a landlord elite have only been possible because of the very small size of the indigenous population of Dubai, which is still probably less than 80,000.[58] Ever since the growth of the pearling industry and the introduction of laissez-faire policies in the late nineteenth century, Dubai has been home to a large expatriate population,[59] and, as the following chapter discusses, with the oil booms and launch of new non-oil sectors, the number of foreigners moving to the emirate has continued to mushroom and to dwarf the number of 'local' families.[60] Although this highly unusual demographic structure is beginning to cause many problems for Dubai, the huge imbalance is actually favoured by the government, at least in terms of political stability. If the national population had grown in tandem with the expatriate population or, more likely, if it had become larger due to dilution through mixed marriages, then the benefits provided by the allocative state would not have been at such a high level. Indeed, emirates such as Sharjah, Ra's al-Khaimah, and Fujairah, all of which have much larger national populations[61] and fewer state resources have struggled to maintain an allocative system, and have had to rely heavily on backing from Abu Dhabi.[62] More broadly, given that the fantastically oil-rich Saudi Arabia has a huge national population of over 22 million,[63] it has therefore had to spread its rentier wealth much more thinly. Thus, in many ways Dubai and its richer but more populous neighbour, Abu Dhabi, can be regarded as two of the purest examples of rentier states. Tellingly, if one accepts that Dubai's GDP per capita is probably around $50,000 across its total population of some 2.2 million,[64] then the GDP per capita of the relatively small number that are *bona fide* Dubai nationals is likely to be over $120,000.[65]

151

As such, it has been a priority of the ruling family to preserve and foster this small 'rentier elite,' which it has achieved in part by offering benefits to those who keep their families 'pure' from foreign blood, and in some cases by penalising those that flout these norms. In some ways these preservation strategies have much in common with the rules drawn up in Zanzibar in the 1930s to safeguard the 'Arabness' of its small ruling elite.[66] Most famously, in 2002 the UAE's federal government announced a package of subsidies entitled the 'Sheikh Zayed Marriage Fund', and set up an office within the Ministry of Labour and Social Affairs to administer the aid across federation.[67] Ostensibly this fund was to provide a one-off payment of about $11,000 in order defray some of the escalating dowry costs faced by young men hoping to marry.[68] However, more subtly the payment satisfied the twin aims of providing a means of wealth distribution by the state while also giving men a financial incentive to choose a national bride—significantly the marriage fund cannot be accessed if the man intends marrying an expatriate. More restrictively, those national women who choose to marry an expatriate man effectively have to give up their nationality, as their children will not be entitled to a UAE passport and therefore neither they nor her husband will be entitled to the benefits of the welfare state. In addition, other measures are in place to discourage such relationships, with all internet dating websites blocked in the UAE for fear of encouraging mixed marriages,[69] with all state-run educational establishments for national females (most notably the female only Zayed University and the female only branches of the Higher Colleges of Technology) remaining distanced from society, and with separate leisure and beach clubs available exclusively for national women. And if one of the latter marries a non-national man she would effectively be ostracised from both her family and broader society, even if her fiancé is a fellow Muslim. This is a relatively recent and state-induced mentality and is connected neither to religion nor local culture, given that in the pre-oil era it was not uncommon for women from Dubai to marry other 'culturally compatible' Muslim Arabs. Lastly, and perhaps most significantly, the dress code for the national population has become stricter: local men will invariably wear a white *dishdasha* while local women will almost always wear a black *abaya* and *shaila*. Once again this is a relatively new oil era phenomenon, with little connection to either religion or culture: such clothes immediately distinguish Dubai and other Gulf nationals from expatriate Arabs and thereby serve as a national uniform of privilege for citizens of rentier states. In the past, the dress code was far more varied and individualistic.

The patrimonial network

Very closely connected to the allocative state's need to preserve the national population has been the ruling family's preference for relying on certain trusted families to staff the emirate's administration. This has led to the development of a 'patrimonial network' drawn from the most steadfast members of the rentier elite. Although not on quite the same scale as in Abu Dhabi, where entire families or sub-tribes commonly fill whole 'lines' of employment in certain government departments and ministries,[70] in Dubai there are nevertheless clearly identifiable vertical lines of communication extending in a pyramid fashion from the ruler and his closest associates down through loyal intermediaries before reaching members of 'lesser' national families. Conversely, this pyramid can also work in reverse on those occasions when highly placed individuals abuse their powers or oppose the ruling family: in addition to being stripped of their position, their extended family's name is tarnished, thereby frustrating the employment prospects of all other members of that family.

In particular, the Al-Maktum family works closely with several prominent families from Sheikh Maktum bin Buti's parent clan: the Al-Bu Falasah section of the Bani Yas tribe. As well as those with the family name Al-Falasi, these have included the Al-Tayir family, which is closely related by marriage to the Al-Maktum family. Most notably, Humayd Al-Tayir used to be the UAE's Minister of State for Financial and Industrial Affairs and therefore the effective deputy to Sheikh Hamdan bin Rashid Al-Maktum, the Minister of Finance and Industry. He has also represented Dubai on the board of directors of the UAE Central Bank, chaired the Emirates Industrial Bank, and has assisted Dubai's delegations to the International Monetary Fund. Other members of the Al-Tayir family have held influential posts in the Dubai Chamber of Commerce and Industry, in the Jebel Ali Free Zone Authority, and in the Dubai Ports World Company.[71] Similarly connected to the Al-Bu Falasah has been the Al-Habtur family, which has also held positions in the Chamber in addition to providing many of Dubai's representatives to federal institutions.[72] The Bani Sulayman, as another Al-Bu Falasah family, have continued to be rewarded with key responsibilities, with its members having served in both the Chamber and the Jebel Ali Authority; with Khalid Ahmad bin Sulayman having taken a leading role in running the Dubai Department of Tourism and Commerce Marketing; with the aforementioned Sultan Ahmad bin Sulayman now chairing two of the government's most important new parastatals: Nakheel and the Dubai Ports World Company;[73] and with Omar Ahmad bin Sulyaman having been appointed the new governor of the Dubai International Financial Centre. Other favoured families drawn from the Al-Bu Falasah would include the Al-Bawardi, many of whom were prominent in Sheikh Maktum bin Rashid Al-Maktum's office,[74] and several smaller families such as the Harib,[75] which have staffed the Sheikh Hamdan-chaired EPPCO and DUBAL.

Outside of the Al-Bu Falasah section, few other Bani Yas clans are prominent within Dubai's patrimonial network, as most of these, including the Mazari, have normally been excluded from very sensitive or high profile positions, as they have historically been regarded as having their primary allegiances to their sub tribe's home sheikhdom—either Abu Dhabi, Ajman, or Umm al-Qawain.[76] A notable exception is the Qubaysat clan, which although originally from Abu Dhabi, had many members that had supported the Al-Bu Falasah in the 1830s. Consequently, many serve in the Dubai Municipality today.[77] Moreover, those Bani Yas families that have proven themselves as capable merchants have often been rewarded with important posts in the administration. In particular, the previously antagonistic Al-Ghurair family which, as described, had successfully moved into the retail sector,[78] has since had appointments in the Dubai Chamber of Commerce and Industry, the Dubai Municipality, and the Dubai Water and Electricity Authority (DEWA). Similarly, the Al-Futtaim family, which had also been heavily involved in Arab nationalist activities in the 1950s,[79] had later diversified successfully into automobile distribution and supermarket chains,[80] and many of its members now work in the Chamber and DEWA.[81]

Beyond the Bani Yas tribe, the ruling family has been keen to co-opt into its administration many members of Dubai's naturalised immigrant Arab tribes and merchant families—especially the descendants of longstanding residents that moved to Dubai before the early twentieth century. In particular, members of the breakaway Al-Bu Shamis tribe from Sharjah have been employed in both the Dubai Chamber of Commerce and Industry and the Dubai police,[82] while members of the Ajman-based Al-Matrushi tribe now also serve in the Chamber and in civil defence. Similarly, many of those families from the Umm al-Qawain-based Al-Ali tribe who chose to move to Dubai now have relatives working for Sheikh Muhammad bin Rashid Al-Maktum's office and have represented Dubai in various international organisations such as UNIDO, in addition to serving on the telecom provider Etisalat's board of directors. Indeed, through the Al-Owais family, the Dubai-based contingent of the Al-'Ali have even provided a former federal Minister for Water and Electricity[83] and the current Minister for Culture, Youth, and Community Development.[84] Many members of the Manasir tribe who reside in Dubai have also been incorporated, despite the Manasir's alliance with Abu Dhabi during various tribal disputes in the 1940s.[85] Some now work in the police while others are employed in Muhammad's office. From the Sudan (Al-Suwaidi) tribe, which also has many Dubai residents, a few families (including the Bani Tamim section) also work in the police,[86] while others (including the Belhul family of the Bani Tamim) have been involved in both Dubai's healthcare administration and the Dubai Ports World Company.

Of those families that had arrived in Dubai from Baluchistan following the handover of Makran from Oman to Pakistan,[87] many became naturalised Dubai nationals and were eventually offered greater administrative responsibilities following their successful careers in the Dubai police force. Most notably, the Al-Belushi and Bin Lutah families have represented Dubai in federal institutions while the Al-Nabudah family's Said bin Juma Al-Nabudah was the longstanding chairman of the Dubai Chamber of Commerce and Industry. Also of significance among the Baluchi population has been the Al-Majid family, especially through Juma Al-Majid, who quickly emerged as one of Dubai's most prominent businessman and has served on the boards of many of the emirate's banks, in addition to establishing his own cultural foundation.[88] Similarly, from the highly respected ajami merchant community from Lingah, many families were also soon brought into the administration, with the Darwish, Al-Tajir, Al-Fardin, Al-Sayegh, Galadiri, Al-Mulla,[89] and Al-Ansari families now occupying many positions in the Dubai Municipality, in DEWA, in Etisalat, and in the National Bank of Dubai.[90] Most conspicuously of course, the ajami Al-Gurg family has provided the UAE with its long serving ambassador to Britain, the aforementioned Easa bin Saleh Al-Gurg, while a member of the Gargash family now holds the new position of federal Minister of State for Federal National Council Affairs.[91]

Lastly, it is noteworthy how Sheikh Muhammad has maintained the patrimonial network of Al-Bu Falasah clans and loyal non-Bani Yas groups built up by his father and elder brother while also bringing in many highly capable young professionals from less well established families. Indeed, since succeeding as crown prince and embarking on Dubai's many diversification projects, Muhammad has sought to 'hand pick' the most able employees from his various organisations and groom them for higher responsibilities. This strategy has led to an expanding contingent of 'technocrats' within Dubai's administration, and many of these relatively young men have now reached the directorial level, and, in some cases, been appointed to high government office. To date such a mixed social structure does not exist elsewhere in the UAE, although there are a few notable exceptions in Abu Dhabi, namely Khaldun bin Khalifa Al-Mubarak, the young American-educated director of Sheikh Muhammad bin Zayed Al-Nahyan's development-focused Mubadala Corporation.[92] Particularly strong examples of Dubai technocrats would include Muhammad Ali Al-Abbar, who rose to become director of Dubai's Department of Economic Development and the chairman of Emaar,[93] and who now also serves as vice chairman of both the Dubai World Trade Centre and DUBAL, in addition to representing Dubai in the World Economic Forum. Equally prominent among these technocrats has been Muhammad Abdullah Al-Gergawi, who set up the Dubai Shopping Festival before being appointed chairman of Dubai Holdings and launching the Dubai Internet City.[94] Al-Gergawi has now risen to ministerial level, having recently been appointed Minister of State for Cabinet Affairs, and therefore effectively Sheikh Muhammad's deputy in the federal cabinet. Similarly powerful has been Dubai's other technocrat minister, Muhammad Khalfan bin Kharbash, who for many years has balanced his chairmanship of several of Dubai's banks and development-related institutions with his role as Humayd Al-Tayir's replacement as Minister of State for Financial and Industrial Affairs.

A hybrid government

To lend greater legitimacy to this patrimonial network, which after all is still little more than an extended system of patronage grafted onto a traditional polity, the ruling family has made great efforts to support an outside layer of more modern 'neo-patrimonial' governmental institutions. Indeed, while the main power clearly rests with established families and prominent individuals, the ruling family has voluntarily transformed the polity[95] by building up various emirate-level councils and departments, most of which are run along seemingly legal-rational lines with codified regulations and procedures. Moreover, in cooperation with the other hereditary monarchs in the UAE, the federal institutions that were established following British withdrawal in 1971 have been maintained and in some cases upgraded. When pro-democratic sentiments have occasionally arisen in spite of the allocative state, very limited political reforms have been introduced in an effort to extend the government's legitimacy and preserve its usefulness in furnishing the polity with democratic 'window dressing.'

Providing Dubai with an ostensibly modern government has been the Dubai Executive Council. Presided over by Sheikh Muhammad bin Rashid Al-Maktum, the council is now chaired by his aforementioned second eldest son and likely crown prince, Sheikh Hamdan bin Muhammad Al-Maktum, with Muhammad's uncle Sheikh Ahmad bin Said Al-Maktum serving as deputy chairman, and Muhammad Abdullah Al-Gergawi acting as secretary general. Of the twelve other members who sit on the council, these include no less than three members of the Bani Sulayman (two brothers and their nephew),[96] a member of another Al-Bu Falasah family, the Harib,[97] and a representative from the Al-Suwaidi's Bani Tamim section.[98] Also present are Sheikh Hasher bin Maktum Al-Maktum of the Juma branch and

Muhammad Ali Al-Abbar. Effectively in control of the emirate's day-to-day affairs, this distinctly neo-patrimonial council also acts as an umbrella organisation, with several smaller councils operating under its jurisdiction (including, up until 2006, the Ahmad Abdullah bin Bayat-chaired Dubai Education Council), and with representatives being fielded from the emirate's various public and private sectors. Significantly, it is regarded as dynamic and flexible, with its relatively small core of members often meeting in relaxed settings such as the conference suite of the Emirates Towers Hotel. Unlike its counterpart emirate-specific councils in Abu Dhabi and Sharjah, the Dubai Executive Council does not have to respond to any form of organised consultative council or *majlis as-shura*—it simply answers directly to the ruler. This is certainly a testament to Dubai's particularly strong version of the 'ruling bargain' and its more business-focused national population that to some extent views the government as a board of directors rather than as a forum for political participation. Indeed, at present, public opinion across the emirate is still canvassed through fairly traditional regional *majaalis,* which can then report their conclusions to the ruler's court or *diwan*. With the Abu Dhabi National Consultative Council beginning to take on greater responsibilities in recent years, it is likely that Dubai will soon have to create a more formal consultative body. In 2003 there was some discussion regarding the setting up of such a regulated *majlis*,[99] but no action has yet been taken.

Working underneath the Dubai Executive Council are more than twenty-five different government departments and offices,[100] all of which have clearly defined responsibilities and a seemingly transparent structure. Almost every one of these is headed by a key member of the fairly small patrimonial network, and in some cases the larger departments even have directors with overlapping responsibilities in both the Executive Council and other departments. Moreover, the secondary layer of deputy directors in most of these institutions most often comprises close relatives of the

159

senior administrators. In particular, Muhammad Ali Al-Abbar has multiple roles as director of the Department of Economic Development in addition to membership of the Executive Council and the chairmanship of Emaar, while Khalid Ahmad bin Sulayman presides over the Department of Tourism and Commerce Marketing while also sitting on the Executive Council. Similarly, the Dubai Municipality is currently headed by Hussain Nasser bin Lutah of the Baluchi family, while the Dubai Lands Department is directed by Sheikh Muhammad bin Khalifa Al-Maktum of the Juma branch of the ruling family, and the Department of Civil Defence is directed by Rashid bin Thani Al-Matrushi of the notable Ajmani immigrant family.

At the federal level, the UAE's government is run along much the same neo-patrimonial lines, with the various ruling families and their emirate-specific patrimonial networks contributing a certain quota of representatives to what may at first appear to be modern institutions, but which are in reality the arms of a 'monarchical presidency.' Most notably, the UAE's highest authority is the Supreme Council of Rulers (SCR), which has the power to initiate policy and to reject laws that have previously been passed. In much the same way as the old British-designed Trucial States Council of the 1950s and 1960s, the SCR is simply a meeting of the seven hereditary rulers and, on occasion, their crown princes and closest advisors. While the old Trucial States Council did at least allow for elections and a rotating chair, the presidency and main powers of the SCR now always rests with Abu Dhabi, given its vast oil wealth and immense contributions to the federal budget,[101] and the vice presidency of the SCR always rests with Dubai, given its secondary role in federal contributions. Indeed, although the original federal constitution being considered during the negotiations between 1968 and 1971 gave each SCR member an equal vote,[102] the hastily introduced British provisional constitution on the eve of independence endowed Abu Dhabi and Dubai with veto powers over the five 'lesser' members. Moreover, while the provisional constitution did call for an SCR presidential election every five years,[103] there has only been one such formal occasion following the end of Sheikh Zayed bin Sultan Al-Nahyan's thirty-three year presidency in late 2004, and the constitution has since become permanent without such a clause. Although Sheikh Maktum bin Rashid Al-Maktum automatically became acting president given his position as vice president, within a few days he announced that the SCR members had unanimously decided to install Zayed's eldest son and the new ruler of Abu Dhabi, Sheikh Khalifa bin Zayed Al-Nahyan, as the UAE's president. Even if Khalifa were to pass away, the presidency would again be conferred upon Abu Dhabi's crown prince, Sheikh Muhammad bin Zayed Al-Nahyan, as Abu Dhabi's financial support for the poorer member emirates of the federation would greatly outweigh the renowned dynamism and leadership skills of the new vice president, Sheikh Muhammad bin Rashid Al-Maktum.

Subordinate to the Supreme Council of Rulers is the federal Council of Ministers (COM), but given that the SCR meets infrequently and often only informally, the COM and its various ministries formulate the bulk of the UAE's policies and it is responsible for much of the day-to-day running of the federation. As with the emirate-level Dubai Executive Council, the COM is dominated by traditional elites and members of patrimonial networks, and, like the SCR, is structured in favour of the wealthiest emirates. Originally, the portfolios in the COM were distributed in such a way that Abu Dhabi controlled six important positions, with Dubai controlling the premiership and three other important positions, with Sharjah controlling three less important positions, with Ra's al-Khaimah and Fujairah each controlling two positions, and with Ajman and Umm al-Qawain having just one position. In practice Abu Dhabi has always controlled more than six positions given that many of the Ministers of State (the deputies of the official ministers) have been members of the Al-Nahyan family, and have been effectively in control of their respective ministries. For many years a token (Abu Dhabi-based) Ajmani was the Minister for Foreign Affairs,[104] while Sheikh Hamdan bin Zayed Al-Nahyan served as Minister of State for Foreign Affairs. Now, with Hamdan's younger brother, Sheikh Abdullah bin Zayed Al-Nahyan, installed as the minister, the Al-Nahyan family controls seven positions in the cabinet, with de facto control over other positions given that Sheikh Nahyan bin Mubarak Al-Nahyan is essentially Minister for both Education and Higher Education. This is because his deputy, Hanif Hassan Al-Qassimi,[105] is now Minister for Education; and given that Dubai's control over the Ministry of Defence is purely nominal, with Abu Dhabi controlling the amalgamated military, and with the Supreme Commander, Deputy Supreme Commander, and Chief of Staff of the UAE Armed Forces all being from Abu Dhabi.[106] In total, including these Al-Nahyan ministers, there are now eleven members of ruling families sitting on the COM, the highest number there has ever been since its inception in 1971, and the remainder are all either identifiable as members of established families or are powerful technocrats with close links to the rulers of their respective emirates. In Dubai's case these are Sheikh Hamdan bin Rashid Al-Maktum, the long serving Minister for Finance and Industry; Muhammad Abdullah Al-Gergawi, the Minister of State for Cabinet Affairs; Anwar Muhammad Gargash, the Minister of State for Federal National Council Affairs; Abdul Rahman Muhammad Al-Owais of the Al-Ali tribe, the Minister of Culture, Youth, and Community Development; and of course Sheikh Muhammad himself, who now serves as both Prime Minister and Minister of Defence. Moreover, even though the new Minister for Economy and Planning, Sheikha Lubna bint Khalid Al-Qasimi, is a member of the Sharjah ruling family and the niece of Sheikh Sultan bin Muhammad Al-Qasimi, she can nevertheless be considered another member of the Dubai COM contingent given her close relations with the Al-Maktum family and her previous professional experience with both the

Dubai Ports Authority and the Dubai Chamber of Commerce and Industry.

The federal legislature, or more accurately the UAE's consultative chamber, is another institution that emerged from the negotiations of the late 1960s. Originally comprising forty delegates autocratically appointed by SCR members, including an internally elected speaker and two deputies, this *majlis al-watani al-ittihad* or Federal National Council (FNC) sits for sessions of two years at a time. Once again, this is an institution that is weighted heavily in favour of Abu Dhabi and Dubai, with these emirates being eligible to supply eight members each, compared to six members from Sharjah and Ra's al-Khaimah (despite these emirates having higher populations of nationals than Dubai), and just four members each from the three smallest emirates.[107] With a broader social profile, the FNC was intended to serve as a forum for debate for members of other established families not represented on the COM, alongside distinguished professionals from less notable backgrounds. Indeed, Dubai's contingent has often been made up members of the aforementioned Al-Habtur, Belhul, Bin Lutah, and Al-Ghurair families,[108] in addition to prominent lawyers and academics such as Muhammad Al-Roken.[109]

Controlled political reform

In recent years the Federal National Council's role has been called into question, with many arguing that it is little more than a civilised talking shop and that it has rarely questioned the decisions of the Council of Ministers or the Supreme Council of Rulers. Indeed, although there are examples of debates in which the FNC has participated in decision-making by presenting its suggestions to the SCR, these have normally been over concerns that were already shared by the COM, such as the need to tighten anti-drugs legislation and to further modify the UAE's property laws.[110] In cases where the FNC's views were likely to diverge from the relevant minister's, such as over the price of petrol or the cultural

163

content of terrestrial television,[111] the FNC has repeatedly failed to convert its formal recommendations into policy. Remarkably there have been examples of the FNC's letters to ministers having remained unanswered for several months, and occasions when the FNC has been unable to persuade ministers to attend their sessions and answer basic questions on their policies.[112]

These complaints have been compounded by growing discontent with the old system of 'direct democracy' in which citizens could voice their grievances to their tribal sheikh who would in turn attend the *majlis* of a member of the ruling family, normally after Friday prayers, and then raise these issues on behalf of his tribesmen. Many have felt that with a rapidly growing national population and with greater urbanisation and a consequent breakdown of tribal identities, such a traditional method of governance cannot be sustained and should be replaced by a stronger and more regulated FNC that can better represent its constituents. Aware of this concern, for some years the rulers have attempted to circumvent the need for drastic reform by introducing short term measures aimed at easing some of this pressure. In particular, many of the sheikhs who hold a majlis have appointed intermediaries to act as agents, and have thereby increased the number of grievances that they can hear and which they can attend to. Furthermore, there continues to exist a school of thought even at the highest levels of government that if details of potentially controversial policies can be gently 'leaked' and allowed to filter through the old patrimonial networks, then any possible public backlash can be determined in advance of promulgation.[113] Both the federal government and the emirate-level governments have invested heavily in e-governance in recent years, with almost all ministries and departments having developed sophisticated websites that not only allow citizens to access government services online, but also permit them to record their problems and receive an answer within a few days. Dubai has been pioneering in this regard, with most of its prominent sheikhs having interactive websites, including Sheikh Muhammad bin Rashid Al-Maktum,[114] and with its various government offices now all providing electronic forums for discussion and feedback. Most of these appear to work well, with strict quality control and guaranteed response times. Certainly they are far in advance of e-government services in western democracies.

Nevertheless, despite the increased number of intermediaries and provision of 'internet democracy,' by late 2005 it was acknowledged that the allocative state and its neo-patrimonial structures would need to be complemented by at least some political reform. Given the fast pace of reforms to consultative chambers in Bahrain, Qatar, and Oman, coupled with Dubai and the UAE's increasingly diverse and foreign investment focused economy's joining of several international economic organisations that required at least a nominal roadmap towards 'good governance',[115] there emerged an understanding that the hereditary rulers would have to make some concessions, otherwise the federation and its constituent emirates would be branded as being backward not only by the international community but also by the nationals of its closest neighbours. As such, in early 2006 the aforementioned Anwar Muhammad Gargash was entrusted with the newly created position of Minister of State for Federal National Council Affairs, and was given a brief to investigate methods of increasing the FNC's powers and its role in political participation.[116] Within months, plans were drawn up to stage limited elections, and in late 2006 the UAE's first ballots were held across the federation. Regrettably these elections, which should have been viewed as historic and symbolic, were widely regarded as farcical given that only twenty of the forty positions were to be elected, and, more worryingly, given that only specific 'electoral colleges' that had been nominated by the various rulers could vote on these 'open' positions. Thus, the reforms were seen to be incomplete as all of the FNC members would still be chosen by the SCR, albeit a little more indirectly than before. The

165

rules applied to membership of these electoral colleges attracted caustic criticism, and for good reason: of the 350,000 or so UAE nationals who were above the age of 18 and therefore eligible to participate, only 7,000 were selected, with many of these drawn from a small number of families, with some voters being under the age of 16, and with some even being dead.[117] When pressed to comment on the unexpectedly low voter turnout (of around 60 per cent), a prominent member of the government stated '...this is particularly disappointing given that all of the candidates and participants were from very good families, and were all personally approved by the UAE's rulers.'[118]

Although the 2006 reforms were perhaps overly cautious and the planners had misjudged the level of political consciousness in the UAE at that time, they still played an important role in readying a population previously unaccustomed to such formal participation for more extensive reforms in the years ahead. As Gargash has already explained, the next round of FNC elections in 2010 will almost certainly involve all forty positions and the electoral colleges will be greatly expanded.[119] Moreover, as Sheikh Khalifa bin Zayed Al-Nahyan has announced, the FNC will be considerably strengthened before then, as he intends it to become a more powerful 'bridge between population and government.'[120] And in mid-2007 the FNC began to experiment with a new system of opening its doors to members of the public, in an effort to allow other interested parties to visit and participate in certain debates. Most notably, the FNC held a widely publicised session on the subject of the UAE's education policies which was well attended by teachers, academics, students, and the Minister for Education, Hanif Hassan Al-Qassimi.[121] As such, the newly reinvigorated FNC may still be capable of playing an important role in shoring up neo-patrimonial structures and the government's legitimacy over the next few years, and the very gradual process of reform undertaken so far may prevent the

UAE from being exposed to problems that could develop in the more rapidly reforming polities elsewhere in the Gulf.

Ideological, cultural, and religious resources

Closely linked to the strategies of strengthening the dynasty, maintaining the distribution of wealth, and managing a neo-patrimonial government, have been the attempts to boost the monarchy's ideological, religious, and cultural legitimacy. If certain public stances, charitable donations, and support for particular events and causes can enhance the reputation of the Al-Maktum sheikhs and the other hereditary ruling families by emphasising their generosity, piety, and commitment to Arab brotherhood, then Dubai and other UAE nationals will be far more accepting of the autocratic ruling bargain, safe in the knowledge that their guardians are at least well intentioned and benevolent. Moreover, given the described historical reliance of these dynasties on British support, their strong resistance to the waves of Arab nationalism in the mid-twentieth century,[122] and, as will be demonstrated in later chapters, the UAE's current problematic dependency on the western military umbrella,[123] such devices may also serve as a useful diversionary tactic.

It is no coincidence that over the past thirty years the federal government (and sometimes Dubai unilaterally) has intervened in every single regional conflict, either by hosting peace negotiations or by offering some kind of political support. Ostensibly this has been billed as a realistic foreign policy for a small state surrounded by larger powers, and a continuation of the lower Gulf's long tradition of balanced relations and neutrality.[124] However, such a policy has also been a display of the UAE's efforts to create some public distance from the West and to be seen as superficially co-operating with Arab nationalist or fellow Sunni Muslim-dominated states. The UAE has received a great deal of positive press coverage across the Arab world for its actions. Its partial participation in the Organisation of Petroleum Exporting Countries' (OPEC) price fixing and supply restrictions of the 1970s and 1980s[125] was regarded as being the most effective way for the militarily weak infant state to assist Egypt, Syria, and Iraq in their struggle against Israel. Moreover, during the early 1980s, even when the US was initially supporting Iran, the federal government attempted to side with Iraq,[126] believing that, on the international stage at least, it was important that the UAE should stand shoulder-to-shoulder with an Arab state. Again, in early 1991 the UAE tried to save Iraq by brokering a last-minute deal with the Al-Sabah family of Kuwait.[127] Only when that failed did the Supreme Council of Rulers take the bold step of making the UAE the first Arab state to join the US-led coalition against Iraq, believing that the Ba'ath Party had reached the point of collapse and that the need to support openly another traditional Arab monarchy had finally begun to outweigh the risks of antagonising the most powerful Arab state. The UAE also tried to head off the 2003 Anglo-American invasion of Iraq by offering Saddam Hussein and his family sanctuary in Abu Dhabi on condition that he respected George W. Bush's ultimatum and left Iraq.[128] Although it would appear that Saddam actually accepted this proposal, only for the Arab League to later force the UAE to withdraw it on the grounds that it represented interference in a fellow member's internal affairs,[129] many of Saddam's closest aides have since relocated to the UAE. Muhammad Said Al-Sahhaf, Saddam's Minister of Information (who was dubbed 'Comical Ali' following his spirited press conferences during the bombing of Baghdad) now lives in Abu Dhabi with his relatives and sometimes even attends state-sponsored banquets, while Muhammad Al-Duri, Saddam's ambassador to the United Nations, now resides in Ajman, after spending the last few years in Dubai.[130] Izzat Al-Duri, his close relative and Saddam's principal advisor, does not however seem to have sought immunity in the UAE, and currently remains at large with a US-sponsored $10 million bounty placed on his head.[131]

The UAE has also maintained its peace-brokering momentum by positioning itself as the key intermediary in the looming Iranian nuclear crisis. Incredibly, in May 2007 the UAE hosted the Iranian President, Mahmoud Ahmadinejad, just two days after talks had been held with the visiting US Vice President, Dick Cheney,[132] and just hours after Cheney had stood on a US aircraft carrier[133] off the coast of Dubai and issued a strongly worded warning to Iran.[134] Given that this was the first ever visit of an Iranian head of state to the UAE, due to a long-running territorial dispute discussed in a later chapter,[135] it is likely that both Sheikh Khalifa bin Zayed Al-Nahyan and Sheikh Muhammad bin Rashid Al-Maktum were attempting to find some common ground for these seemingly polarised leaders. Perhaps the only instance of the federal government's failure to find a suitable middle ground and serve as an 'active neutral' has been over Afghanistan. Throughout the 1990s the UAE was one of only three states to recognise the legitimacy of the hard-line Taleban regime and its 'Islamic Emirate of Afghanistan,' hosting a Taleban embassy in a small villa in downtown Abu Dhabi, and a less formal consulate in Dubai.[136] Together with Saudi Arabia and Pakistan it was reasoned that Shia-dominated Iran needed to be contained by a 'Sunni box' in which a cooperative Afghanistan could play a major role.[137] Since 2001 and the onset of the 'War on Terror', the UAE is been keen to play down this former relationship,[138] but six years later it still remains tarnished by the association.

The UAE has also openly supported the Arab cause by providing substantial socio-economic aid, either dispensed through charities or by UAE personnel despatched as part of larger humanitarian task forces. During the 1973 Yom Kippur War Sheikh Rashid bin Said Al-Maktum informed both Anwar Sadat and Hafez Al-Assad that the UAE's resources were at their disposal. When the fighting entered its second week, Rashid backed up his promise by instructing Sheikh Muhammad to send medical teams to the battlefield,[139] and then issued a statement to the international media claiming that '…the UAE follows with great concern the news of the fighting that our brothers have launched in order to liberate our land and our nation's dignity. The UAE believes this war concerns the whole Arab nation, which should place all its means at the disposal of this effort.'[140] Following the Palestinian Liberation Organisation's revival in 1974 and its recognition by the Arab League as being the 'sole legitimate representative of the people of Palestine,'[141] Rashid oversaw the donation of millions of dollars to the PLO for the purpose of helping families who had lost members in the Occupied Territories. And in 1985, concerned that Palestine's leading university would close due to lack of funding, he encouraged Sheikh Maktum bin Rashid Al-Maktum to sponsor the construction of a new campus at Birzeit.[142] Today, through the Al-Maktum Foundation and the Muhammad bin Rashid Charitable and Humanitarian Establishment, Sheikh Muhammad and Sheikh Hamdan bin Rashid Al-Maktum continue to support many projects in Palestine, including new schools, clinics, and orphanages.[143] While their aid has now been dwarfed by the massive Abu Dhabi-funded $62 million Sheikh Zayed Residential City in Gaza,[144] and their charity is disbursed discreetly in Palestine, such generosity is well known in Dubai, and generates much goodwill for the ruling family.

In much the same way, Dubai and the UAE have also channelled considerable aid to Lebanon since the outbreak of civil war in the mid-1970s. Following Syria's creation in 1976 of an Arab Deterrent Force that aimed to defeat the Druze-led Lebanese National Movement and to discourage Israel from entering the war,[145] Sheikh Maktum pledged to pay 15 per cent of the costs incurred by any Arab state that contributed troops to Syria's coalition. Furthermore, within a year, Sheikh Muhammad committed UAE troops to serve in the Force—the first time its soldiers had faced active duty—and travelled to Beirut twice to supervise personally their deployment.[146] Similarly, during the second phase of the war, sparked by Israel's 'Peace for Galilee' invasion of southern Lebanon and its attempts to destroy the Palestinian 'terrorist camps,' the Al-Maktum family again provided assistance, with Muhammad co-ordinating transport planes to fly food, blankets, and tents into the worst hit areas within just a week of the first attacks.[147] It is thought that Muhammad (who by this stage was a trained pilot) may have flown one of the planes himself, but it is more likely that he was photographed inspecting one of the aircraft before take-off.[148] Throughout the remaining years of the conflict, Maktum administered over $5.5 million to charities that were managing refugee support in Lebanon,[149] and, following the closure of the Lebanese consulate in Dubai due to lack of funds, he personally financed its upkeep, a tradition which his estate continues even today.[150] During the summer 2006 Israeli bombings of Hezballah towns in southern Lebanon and the Bekaa Valley, in a very understandable act of public chest-beating the UAE's Ministry for Foreign Affairs denounced the United States for not condemning Israel's aggression, but, like all other Arab foreign ministries, was unable to offer the Lebanese any substantive assistance. Nevertheless, immediately following the ceasefire, UAE aid once again poured into Lebanon, from both ruling families and government organisations. Large and rather tasteless billboards were erected across the UAE to advertise this munificence and some were also set up in Lebanon by late 2006, but not in areas that had been bombed and received the aid—instead they were placed in prosperous Christian towns and suburbs such as Jounieh and Achrafieh: the areas of Lebanon most frequented by UAE nationals and other Gulf Arab tourists.[151] In the summer of 2007 the UAE resumed more practical support, having sent three aircraft laden with armaments to be used by the Lebanese Army in its suppression of violence in the Nahr El-Bared refugee camp north of Tripoli.[152]

The UAE was also heavily involved in Kuwait's reconstruction following its liberation in 1991, with Sheikh Muhammad despatching medical teams to Kuwait City and ordering supplies of mineral water to be delivered to those areas in which desalination plants had been destroyed by the retreating Iraqis.[153] By 1992, attention had been turned to troubled Muslim populations beyond the Middle East, with the UAE providing military engineers to the UN-endorsed US intervention force in war torn Somalia. While these units initially concentrated on clearing mines and repairing infrastructure, they also assisted in building local schools, orphanages,[154] and mosques, some of which are still named after the Al-Nahyan and Al-Maktum sheikhs that funded them.[155] In 1993 a second UAE detachment arrived in Somalia, and over the next few years similar contingents were sent to Rwanda, Uganda, and Mozambique.[156] Perhaps most notably, in 1995 the UAE also began actively to assist European Muslims caught up in the conflict in the Balkans, with Muhammad ordering airlifts of wounded Bosnians, many of whom were flown to hospitals in Dubai and then cared for by the UAE's branch of the Red Crescent.[157] Moreover, in 1999, when fighting erupted between Serbs and Albanians in Kosovo, and Serbia chose to intervene, the UAE was the only Arab country to participate in the NATO-led peacekeeping force. A mechanised battle group backed up by several Apache helicopters protected a Muslim refugee camp and assisted in setting up tents and a field hospital.[158] In addition to several million dollars of aid from the federal government and the Muhammad bin Rashid Charitable and Humanitarian Establishment, all of the UAE's terrestrial TV stations participated in a charity telethon. The event raised $15 million and then Muhammad doubled this sum, although not anonymously. The money was used to build over fifty new mosques in Kosovo in 2000.[159]

Today, it is thought that the Al-Maktum family and the Dubai government are more seriously committed than ever before to supporting such causes, with an estimated 3.5 per cent of the emirate's state revenue being assigned to foreign aid. This is more than three times the relative contributions of most western states.[160] For example, Dubai's funds for tsunami relief projects in South East Asia and earthquake relief in Iran have been enormous,[161] and in the summer of 2007 Sheikh Muhammad made what is believed to be the largest gift in history when he donated $10 billion to a new pan-Arab educational foundation.[162] While the foundation is intended to help create a more knowledge-based society in the Middle East and to reduce the region's perceived technology gap with Europe and Asia, it is significant that the endowment was very widely publicised across the UAE (even on Muhammad's own website) and carefully presented to international news agencies as a personal act of charity rather than as a necessary governmental investment.[163] The foundation has since been unimaginatively named the Sheikh Muhammad bin Rashid Al-Maktum Foundation for Education. Dubai's foreign aid for Arabs and Muslims has now also become much more organised, with many smaller charities (including Muhammad's daughter's Shaikha Latifa bint Muhammad Al-Maktum Charity Organisation) falling under the administrative umbrella of either the Muhammad bin Rashid Charitable and Humanitarian Establishment, or under the broader, UAE-wide, Red Crescent organisation, currently chaired by Sheikh Hamdan bin Zayed Al-Nahyan, one of the Council of Ministers' two deputy prime ministers. As with all of its other physical projects, Dubai has invested heavily in infrastructure for aid, having set up a free zone in 2003 specifically for humanitarian NGOs and built huge warehouses close to both ports for the exclusive use of offices based in this new 'Dubai Humanitarian City'.[164] Now in its fourth year, this zone currently houses branches of dozens of international aid organisations in addition to the headquarters of several regional groups. As such, Dubai has effectively become the charity capital of the Middle East.

With regard to boosting its religious legitimacy, the ruling family has been similarly proactive, with Sheikh Muhammad sponsoring several events relating to the promotion and awareness of Islam. Most famously, each year prisoners are released from Dubai's jails if they can recite the entire Koran in the presence

173

of judges, or their sentences may be reduced by up to five years if they can remember large sections of it.[165] Moreover, both Dubai and the federal government provide substantial funding and state endorsements for large Islamic conferences that attract scholars and clerics from across the Muslim world. In late 2004 a symposium was staged on the topic of the Prophet's Way of Dawa and Guidance—several hundred people attended, including various Arab ministers of justice and even Muhammad Said Tantawi, the Grand Imam of the Al-Azhar Mosque in Egypt. Such dignitaries were the personal guests of members of the ruling family, and Sheikh Khalifa used the conference as an opportunity to stress the UAE's 'support for efforts that help convey Islam's message of peace and brotherhood.'[166] Dubai has also made great efforts to support sharia-compliant Islamic banking. The emirate now stages the International Islamic Finance Forum, and, through Muhammad Abdullah Al-Gergawi's Dubai Investment Group,[167] Sheikh Muhammad has recently acquired a 40 per cent stake in the Malaysian-based Bank of Islam—a very strict institution that prohibits any financial activities that derive profits from alcohol, pork, or gambling.[168] While many have viewed such interests as contradictory to Dubai's described diversification strategies, especially its promotion of a real estate sector that relies heavily on western-style mortgages and speculative investments, and an international financial free zone in which companies do not have to adhere to federal law, it is nevertheless important that the polity continues to pay lip service to its Islamic roots.

Finally, alongside explicit support for Arab causes and the maintenance of religious resources, the Al-Maktum family has been keen to strengthen certain cultural components of the ruling bargain. By preserving memories of Dubai's history and the achievements of its most powerful dynasty, it is thought that the ruler's position at the head of a contemporary neo-patrimonial system will make more sense to the national population. As with the investment in aid-related infrastructure, this need has been taken extremely seriously by the government, with a veteran anthropologist in Dubai observing that '...cultural revival is growing so fast as to reach levels of national industry... with heritage revival appearing at this time juncture as an expanding national cultural industry.'[169] Dubai has opened a number of museums, having begun with the 1970s refurbishment of the Al-Fahidi Fort—Sheikh Maktum bin Buti's original residence. More recently, several traditional houses around the city have been restored and converted into art galleries, including Sheikh Said bin Maktum's house in Shindagha, which now features photographs of pre-oil Dubai. These fairly conventional museums have now been complemented by much larger open air complexes, each of which celebrate a particular aspect of Dubai's heritage and reinforce both tribal history and the role of the various Al-Maktum rulers. Good examples include the Pearling Village, which features replicas of Dubai's old fishing and pearling boats; and the newly constructed Hatta Heritage Village which boasts restored traditional forts and towers. All of these sites also host cultural activities such as singing, dancing, pottery making, basket-weaving, and cooking. These 'live' activities have served to create 'living memories' and 'imagined communities,'[170] not only for Dubai's increasing number of tourists and to compliment the foreign investment strategy, but also for the younger generations of nationals who would otherwise be ignorant of their past.

In an effort to reinforce further these memories, new activities which are contemporary reinventions of the past have also been established. Members of both the Al-Maktum and Al-Nahyan families have heavily sponsored camel racing in Dubai and Abu Dhabi and, in much the same way as their investments in horseracing, large camel circuits have been built. Although camel racing was never really a part of bedouin lifestyle, except at special occasions such as weddings,[171] this new multi-million dollar industry nevertheless provides another forum for the rulers to greet their nationals in an ostensibly traditional context. Indeed, the opening ceremonies of such race meetings often feature bedouin dances, poetry in honour of the attending sheikh, a large banquet of local delicacies, and an opportunity to wear traditional dress. And in another example of attempts to personalise his legitimacy, Sheikh Muhammad has lent his name to some of these cultural projects. In particular, his love of bedouin nabati poetry has served as a launch pad for sponsored poetry-reading competitions in colloquial Arabic, and, most conspicuously, since 1999 his eponymous Sheikh Muhammad bin Rashid Centre for Cultural Understanding has restorated many traditional houses in the old ajami Bastakiyah quarter, in addition to supervising cultural activities held at the Jumeirah mosque.

6

THE DUBAI PARADOX

Although Dubai's various economic strategies have succeeded in reducing the emirate's dependency on oil, and while the Al-Maktum family's carefully evolving non-democratic ruling bargain seems to have secured political stability for the near future, there are a number of deeper and interconnected problems associated with these advances that are beginning to materialise. These hidden costs are likely to have a serious impact on Dubai's long term prospects for further meaningful development. In particular, the persistence of rentier structures, even though now focused on new, non-oil related activities, continues to tie the government to burdensome distributive practices and breeds a certain unproductive mentality among the national population. Furthermore, it is becoming increasingly apparent that many of the new sectors, especially those geared towards attracting foreign investment, are making Dubai even more reliant on foreign economies than it was during the oil booms. The rapidly expanding expatriate population, which differs greatly from the predominantly Muslim immigrant communities of the past, coupled with the diversification process and all of its prerequisite reforms and relaxations, are also likely to weaken many of the ruler's described ideological, religious, and cultural legitimacy resources, in addition to undermining national identity, carefully constructed indigenous elite structures, and the government's attempts to nationalise or 'emiratise' at least some sections of the labour force. Finally, many segments of Dubai's civil society remain enfeebled, and in their present condition are unlikely to lend effective support to the emirate's development.

Rentier pathologies

The ruling family and the government of Dubai were able to circumvent demands for political participation from their people throughout the 1970s and 1980s. High oil revenues allowed the state to set up a system of distributed wealth in which all members of the national population, even recently urbanised bedouin, were provided with housing, jobs, education, and welfare. Even today, this allocative state remains, as although the government no longer receives substantial oil revenues, it now derives considerable rental income from many of the new economic sectors that have been established. Moreover, many nationals themselves have become rentiers in their own right, as the diversifying economy has provided them with opportunities to become landlords. The diversification process has transformed what were previously worthless tracts of desert into multi-million dollar real estate opportunities. While this continuity of rent has shored up the ruling bargain and thereby facilitated development by contributing greatly to political stability, the persistence of such rentier structures are nevertheless creating huge problems for Dubai, or at least for the indigenous population. Put bluntly, most young nationals are unfit for meaningful employment, and, as will be shown later in this chapter, with increasing numbers of skilled and educated foreigners flooding into the emirate, these nationals are unable to compete for jobs as the new economy's private sector expands at a much faster rate than the public sector.

Referring to the time when Dubai relied on oil exports, reports from the National Bank of Dubai warned that 'such revenue will actually be a hindrance to the creation of other wealth as it discourages technical training and hard work and produces an uncompetitive rentier mentality.'[1] By the mid-1990s members of the ruling families had begun to voice publicly their concern over their own people's inactivity and apathy. In 1995 Sheikh Zayed bin Sultan Al-Nahyan remarked of Abu Dhabi nationals that he 'could not understand how physically fit young men can sit idle and accept the humiliation of depending on others for their livelihood';[2] and the following year Sheikh Muhammad bin Rashid Al-Maktum complained of 'voluntary unemployment' in Dubai, stating that 'unemployment is a waste of natural resources and is wrong when the UAE is providing all its sons and daughters with opportunities that were unattainable a generation ago.'[3] Today the situation would seem no better, with a weekday visit to any of Dubai's major shopping malls revealing legions of able bodied young men drinking coffee and playing video games when one would expect most to be gainfully employed or attending a college or university. Incredibly, about 54 per cent of those nationals in receipt of social security benefits are believed to be of working age.[4] Alarmingly, an early morning tour of any government department or other institutions that predominantly employs nationals will reveal many empty desks, with a worryingly high number turning up for work very late or taking long unexplained absences. In early 2002 Muhammad began a campaign of personal spot checks, immediately firing anyone who had not turned up for work on time,[5] and many of these summary dismissals were at very senior levels. Most of these unprofessional employees are the products of this extreme nanny state in which every financial aspect of their life has been taken care of—jobs have therefore not been synonymous with economic livelihood. As one of Dubai's veteran merchants describes the situation today '…of Dubai's young nationals, probably only 20 per cent will be worthwhile, becoming academics and professionals, and businessmen. About 60 per cent can probably be written off, the consequences of the all-too-easy acceptance of the pleasures which will be handed out to them.'[6]

Connected to this unproductive lifestyle, rentierism has also created a generation of nationals that has no experience of an extractive state. Although Dubai has historically pursued *lais-*

179

sez-faire strategies aimed at the promotion of its status as a free port,[7] the complete abolition of all taxes and the introduction of the 'ruling bargain' subsidies from the 1970s and onwards has effectively created a population incapable of coming to terms with any form of future demands from the state. As Dubai continues to develop and the government is required to offer more costly public services, this is likely to become an even bigger problem, as even gentle forms of direct taxation such as limited income tax on very high earners cannot be contemplated. Thus far, the only solution has been the gradual implementation of a number of indirect government levies, most of which the population does not yet associate with extraction, and which have therefore become carefully managed 'hidden taxes'. These are not thought to be too offensive to the rentier mindset or too disruptive to the material component of the ruling bargain, although given that most are regressive, there is a concern that resentment may build among the less prosperous sections of the population if too many more are imposed.

Notable examples to date would include Dubai's introduction of a 5 per cent housing fee on all freehold properties,[8] the recent implementation of *salik* road tolls on some of the emirate's busiest highways, the government's entitlement to a share of all taxi fares (which has been passed on to the customer following substantial fare increases in 2006), and the widespread use of parking meters since 2001. Along with non-discriminatory hidden taxes, Dubai has also encouraged the use of taxes or charges specific to expatriates, or at least more likely to be paid by them than by more sensitive nationals. These have been connected to the residence visas that are now offered to foreigners who buy property in which to live. While most real estate advertisements promise such visas for expatriates, they do not specify that a substantial fee has to be paid to the relevant government department. At present this stands at about $1,600, and has to be renewed every three years.[9] Furthermore, even though Etisalat's telecommunications monopoly has been broken, the new entrant, Du, is effectively another parastatal of the federal government,[10] and it is no coincidence that both companies charge inexplicably high and remarkably similar rates for certain overseas calls. In particular, fairly short calls made to India, Pakistan, and other home countries for the emirate's large South Asian expatriate population normally cost several dollars, much more than calls to other parts of the world.[11] In the near future, extractive practices would seem set to continue along this indirect path, with Dubai already planning a small $3 tax to be paid whenever a resident makes a government-related transaction. This is likely to be called the 'Knowledge Dirham' and the government is promising that a portion of the fee will be used to support cultural activities.[12] In 2008 this may be joined by a small value-added tax (VAT) that will be imposed on most non-essential commodities. Indeed, the Gulf Cooperation Council has already agreed on a VAT band of between 3 and 5 per cent, and it would seem that each of the UAE's constituent emirates will be free to choose its own tax bracket. It has been estimated that if Dubai were to impose the full 5 per cent VAT, it would generate about 2 per cent of the emirate's present GDP.[13]

Compounded by the distributive system and the lack of extraction, a third rentier-induced problem is the national population's chronic over-consumption. Although the growth of the real estate sector and the launch of the Dubai International Financial Exchange have recently provided a few new avenues into which wealth may be channelled, shopping still remains the primary pastime of most men and women, and the resulting high level of consumer imports places a significant strain on the balance of payments. The emirate's surplus fell from over $11 billion in the early 1980s to just $0.5 billion by the mid-1990s. Today, the situation would seem little different, with Dubai estimated to have one of the lowest trade balances in the Gulf,[14] despite the successes of its manufacturing sector and import substitution strategies. The value of consumer imports has risen from about $2 billion in the mid-1970s to over \$23 billion today, at fixed prices, with over half of these imports being goods purchased in shopping malls. These imports now represent nearly three-quarters of the emirate's total non-oil related trade, with re-exporting firmly in second place, and exports a distant third.[15] As such, this particular pathology poses something of an insoluble conundrum, given that over-consumption is so deeply rooted in Dubai's economic and political structures. Indeed, as a prominent local academic has observed '...great emphasis has been put into encouraging the non-oil sector, and that share of the GDP has increased. However, such development has its shortcomings... a prevalence of high income and consumption sustained without recourse to local production and the existence of high levels of conspicuous investment.'[16]

Diversification pathologies

The growth of Dubai's non-oil related economic sectors has allowed the emirate to reduce greatly its reliance on oil exports and other oil-related strategies including overseas investments and heavy, energy-dependent industrialisation.[17] Yet it is becoming increasingly apparent that this diversification may not have actually reduced Dubai's dependency on foreign economies. If anything, the emirate may now be more vulnerable than ever before to uncontrollable external circumstances. With most of Dubai's GDP now accounted for by free zones, tourist resorts, real estate projects, and all of their associated construction, retail, and service industries,[18] there is little doubt that if foreign investment or foreign interest in Dubai were to decline, then the new and superficially successful post-oil economy would stumble. Indeed, as will be discussed later in this study, in the long term Dubai is unlikely to remain aloof indefinitely from the effects of regional conflict, organised crime and terrorism,[19] the close impact of which is likely to lead to a very rapid loss of confidence in these sectors.

Many of the multinationals with regional branches in Jebel Ali, Dubai Internet City, Dubai Media City, and other zones would most likely withdraw their personnel and close their operations in the event of a crisis, and would think carefully about return- ing afterwards. Given the success of Dubai's free zones, other re- gional ports, most notably Aqaba in Jordan,[20] have set up similar authorities, and these are soon likely to position themselves as serious alternatives. Problems in Dubai or elsewhere in the UAE would therefore lead to swift relocations for many companies that wished to maintain a Middle Eastern headquarters. Similarly, in- ternational luxury tourists would be unlikely to continue visiting Dubai should its reputation as a safe destination wane. Many of the European and North American tourists (who now comprise 38 per cent of all visitors[21]) who choose their holiday from high street travel agencies or the internet do not really consider Dubai to be part of the Middle East, but if there were to be negative publicity, this misconception would immediately change. In October 2001 most of Dubai's five star hotels were empty, with even the Burj Al-Arab having its power cut off temporarily due to zero occupancy. 2001 was the only year that the total number of visitors to Dubai did not increase, despite the sector's strong performance in the months prior to September 11th.[22] Given the much greater and more diverse population of tourists today, it is likely that demand would be even more elastic should there be a future problem that more directly concerns Dubai, especially as there are many alternative winter sun resorts, some of which offer arguably far superior cultural and historical sights and experiences than those of the lower Gulf. Similarly, should confidence in Du- bai's real estate sector be shaken by internal or external events, then a significant proportion of foreign investors would attempt to sell their deposits and undoubtedly cease further payments, preferring to cut their losses. Indeed, although members of west- ern governments have claimed that most of the veteran expatri- ates who choose to invest in Dubai are 'fairly robust' and would weather such storms,[23] it is more realistic to assume that many of the latest generation of investors would be far less resilient. These are after all predominantly private individuals who are responding to convincing Emaar or Nakheel advertisements in international property magazines or those attending Dubai-sponsored exhibitions in their home country. Moreover, in much the same way as Dubai faces competition from new free zones, other developing states are beginning to adopt elements of Dubai's real estate industry in an attempt to emulate its success,[24] and should the pioneer stumble these are likely to provide very attractive alternative venues for international property investors.

Closely linked to these renewed dependency concerns, certain aspects of Dubai's diversification would seem to be generating other economic problems, many of which may eventually inhibit growth or expose further weaknesses in the new sectors. With regard to the increasing free zone activity, most of which is aimed at attracting international investment, there is a fear that Dubai is now promoting the globalisation of its economy ahead of any real commitment to regional integration. Such unbalanced integration is thought to be undermining the primary need for building a safety net in the form of a strong Gulf economy.[25] Given the regional breakdown of companies operating in Jebel Ali, most are non-Middle Eastern, with very few being from Gulf states.[26] And there continues to exist a feeling among many Arab investors that such free zones are merely 'foreign enclaves' and are therefore not really tailored to their needs[27]—although part of this reluctance is probably rooted in their past experiences with the UAE's formerly restrictive practices such as the aforementioned *kafil* sponsorship system.[28] If one considers Dubai's major trading partners in 2000, following the launch of the numerous 'second generation' free zones, it is noticeable that the emirate's formerly significant regional trading partners were already falling well outside of the top twenty. Indeed, by 2001 Dubai was importing $1.6 billion worth of goods from Japan, and between $1.3 and $1.5 billion from each of the US, Britain, India, and China.[29] This compared with just $0.2 billion from Iran, Dubai's erstwhile primary supplier. Similarly, by this time Dubai was exporting between $82 and $135 million to the US, Britain, Japan, Korea, and Tawain, while exporting less than $27 million to Bahrain, Kuwait, and Yemen.[30] Today, it would seem the divide between global and regional trading partners has widened further, with Dubai now importing between $3.1 and $6.1 billion from Japan, the US, Britain, China, India, and Germany; with Turkey being the closest regional trade partner supplying $1.3 billion of imports;[31] and with no Arab economy featuring in the top thirty.[32]

Further problems associated with Dubai's increasing integration into the global economy include the complications resulting from the joining of various international organisations, in particular the World Trade Organisation (WTO), which the UAE acceded to in 1996. In addition to the pressure such memberships have placed on Dubai and the federal government to pursue good governance and to introduce limited political reforms,[33] there has also been an expectation that Dubai will begin to conform to certain international standards, some of which may impact severely on its current developmental model. Indeed, WTO membership is regarded as strengthening some aspects of the regional economy, most notably through the assistance being provided to the Arab Monetary Fund,[34] and through the improved copyright controls that have been implemented following the WTO-TRIPS agreement (Trade-Related Aspects of International Property Rights), which has provided better protection for indigenous software, media,[35] and pharmaceutical companies.[36] However, the WTO's involvement in breaking up the UAE's monopolies has been regarded as somewhat intrusive, with many arguing that such infant companies, especially those that represent key components of the federation's technological infrastructure, should not be exposed to foreign or private sector competition. Despite the high cost of international calls, many have credited Etisalat with having achieved for the UAE the highest level of teledensity in the Middle East and provided its population with some of the most sophisticated telecommunications products available.[37] It has been argued that because Dubai and the UAE already have very clear development strategies of their own in place, they cannot really benefit from any of the assistance in economic restructuring that the WTO normally provides to its newest members.[38] Also, as a further disincentive, given that Dubai has many long-standing bilateral treaties in place with its major trading partners,[39] there is thought to be little benefit in having joined the WTO's 'favoured nations list', especially when oil and gas-related products are still not included on the list of recognised reciprocal concessions.[40]

Similarly, the UAE's joining of the International Labour Organisation (ILO) in 1997 has been regarded as another double-edged sword for Dubai's future development. While it is certainly important that all workers are treated humanely and that the emirate conforms to international labour conditions, many of the new ILO conventions that the federal government rather hurriedly and perhaps unwisely agreed to in 2002,[41] following an ILO-sponsored symposium held in Dubai,[42] have led to the creation of several informal and worryingly confrontational workers' associations that the police do not yet seem to know how to control. Previously, federal law forbade workers from engaging in any form of collective bargaining, although the rather backlogged Ministry of Labour and Social Affairs was obliged to investigate all individual complaints.[43] For white collar professions, employee associations have been permitted, and for some years these have been allowed to raise collectively work-related issues and to file protests with the government.[44] Good examples would include the Emirates Bankers' Association, which was set up in 1982,[45] the UAE Teachers' Association which, on occasion, has defended the rights of individual teachers and has sued the Ministry of Education,[46] and the UAE Journalists' Association, which was founded in early 2004.[47] While this earlier system was clearly imperfect, and relied on the cooperation and goodwill of the relevant ministry, there was nevertheless always some room for manoeuvre, and labour conditions never felt particularly repressive given that most workers in Dubai are essentially opportunistic Indian and Pakistani expatriates—especially those undertaking the most menial and, in the ILO's eyes, the most vulnerable jobs. While such foreigners may have experienced poor working conditions in Dubai, their employment was entirely voluntary, was normally for a short term of two or three years, and was usually paying wages several times greater than could be expected in South Asia (about \$3,000 per annum).[48] Such workers rarely come to Dubai with unrealistic expectations of what their conditions will be, given that most often at least one of their relatives would have previously worked in the Gulf before returning to his home country much wealthier than hitherto.

In contrast, while some of the recently organised workers' disputes have been genuine attempts to redress unfair practices (including delays in paying salaries and lack of compensation for injured employees),[49] the new ILO-inspired relaxations have been responsible for a huge upsurge in serious and violent labour actions, many of which have delayed the completion of construction projects. In late 2005 a massive demonstration was held on Sheikh Zayed Road that involved over 1,000 workers drawn from several different camps.[50] Acutely aware that the world was watching, the Dubai authorities were unsure how to react, and the city ground to a halt. Emboldened by the outcome of this protest, in 2006 an even larger strike was staged at the construction site for the aforementioned Burj Dubai skyscraper. Incited to violence by a number of ringleaders, over 2,500 workers went on the rampage: security guards were attacked and several million dollars worth of damage was caused as vehicles were torched, computers destroyed and machinery broken.[51] By the end of the year nineteen other worker-related incidents had occurred.[52] In early 2007 a stoppage was held on a main road by over 300 workers who had initially complained that their living conditions were 'cramped' and that their salary was 'insufficient for their needs,' before eventually broadening their demands.[53] They effectively blocked traffic for several hours, with the police being reluctant to clear them from the road[54]—a remarkable development given that all of the workers were expatriates, and only a few years earlier would have been swiftly deported and replaced by a more pliable contingent.

In parallel to these serious dependency and international integration concerns, it is also important to consider some of the practical limitations of Dubai's new economic activities, especially those associated with real estate. Despite the legal workarounds and the introduction of the Dubai Property Law in 2006, many still regard the sector to be something of a legal minefield, and this may eventually reduce investor confidence. As of 2007 it was still only possible to re-sell property to buyers who had taken out mortgages with the same broker,[55] thereby severely complicating the resale process. According to one team of international lawyers, '...legally Dubai is still a total disaster. There is not only the law of ownership to worry about, but also Islamic inheritance law to consider.'[56] Indeed, most of the real estate projects that foreigners are buying into are not within the boundaries of free zones and are therefore still subjected to various aspects of *sharia* law, some of which are thought to be incompatible with the sector's needs. Equally worrying is the lack of residential associations, which, as will be discussed below, are normally a key feature of civil society. Investors in Dubai cannot be certain that a new highway or skyscraper will not be built close to their property, and given the current environment there is little manoeuvring space for effective collective protest. In the last few years there have been instances of significant alterations to original blueprints or unannounced new developments being undertaken alongside existing projects.[57] While in some of these cases the initial investors were offered compensation,[58] the system has nevertheless often left buyers very vulnerable.

Compounding these concerns, there is also a worry that with rapid expansion of the sector and with several dozen new projects being announced each year, the 'Dubai bubble' will eventually burst, as supply will at some point overtake demand. There still exists a mentality in Dubai that only brand new properties are acceptable, with many residents continuing to reject buildings that are only four or five years old. This unwillingness to be a second-time resident is likely to impede a future re-sale market, especially in the luxury sector. Also, the emirate only has a limited beachfront, with the Jumeirah Beach Residence already extending as far as the Jebel Ali Free Zone, and with the Sharjah border preventing any further coastal developments to the East. As such, any new real estate projects that will claim to feature natural beauty and uninterrupted sea views will be at least an hour away from the city. Similarly disquieting for the sector are the unknown long term consequences of the spiralling property speculation industry. Although many of the largest projects are now complete, worryingly few of the units actually appear to be inhabited. Ultimately, therefore, it will become apparent that certain developments have not become genuine residential communities, and the property prices will adjust accordingly. Indeed, as a visiting journalist recently remarked '...when the definitive history of Dubai comes to be written... the emirate will either be hailed as a stunning feat of engineering, or displayed as a warning of the perils of rampant property speculation.'[59]

The expanding expatriate population

Due to its status as the region's most attractive commercial entrepôt, the sheikhdom has been home to large immigrant communities since the late nineteenth century. Following the oil booms of the 1970s and, more markedly, since the development of new economic sectors geared to attracting foreign investment and integrating Dubai more fully into the international system, the number of expatriates working and living in the emirate has increased enormously. This explosion has not only resulted in an expansion of the foreign population in real terms, drastically reducing the proportion of indigenous nationals, but has also completely altered the makeup of Dubai's society. Many of the newcomers are now either non-Muslim or share very few of the historical and cultural linkages with Dubai that were enjoyed by the earlier immigrants from Persia, India, or other parts of the Arab world.[60] Moreover, the vast majority are young men, which has led to an incredibly skewed gender balance; and given that many of these are very short term residents, most aim to remit the bulk of their income to their home country and are therefore unwilling to integrate into a cosmopolitan society. Thus, while Dubai benefits greatly from the skills of such immigrants, and while in many ways the traditional polity prefers to have such an apolitical transient foreign population, these unusual demographics are nevertheless beginning to have a negative impact on some aspects of society and the labour force.

In 1968, just before Dubai's first oil exports, it was estimated that around 38 per cent of the sheikhdom's population were foreigners,[61] however, by 1976, seven years after the Fateh field had commenced production, it was thought that the expatriate contingent had swelled to over 60 per cent,[62] with over 100,000 work permits being issued each year. Over half of these were made out to Indian nationals, with about a third going to Pakistanis, and just over a tenth going to other Arabs.[63] Even at this early stage in Dubai's development, nearly 7,200 permits were being issued to Europeans. In stark contrast, of Abu Dhabi's 50,000 or so work permits issued at that time, almost all were being distributed to Arabs and Pakistanis.[64] Incredibly, just over twenty years later, following a household income survey carried out in 1998, it transpired that Dubai nationals represented just 17 per cent of the emirate's population, with nearly three-quarters being Asians (including a large Filipino contingent), Africans, Europeans, or other non-Arabs.[65] Today, it is likely that the 80,000 or so nationals[66] account for just four per cent of the total population. With official population estimates of 1.2 million in 2005 and 1.6

million in 2006,[67] it is probable that Dubai's population has now surpassed the two million mark, though such statistics have historically underestimated the number of expatriates. While such inaccuracies have often been blamed on political sensitivities, the problem has mostly been due to poorly conducted and infrequent surveys. Indeed, the first official census, held in 2005, was heavily criticised given that labour camps were excluded, and given that several households were double counted, while data from others was inaccurately recorded due to the lack of multilingual census staff or the reluctance of some expatriates to open their doors to uniformed officials. Conservative estimates are that over 350,000 residents were omitted from the survey.[68]

Although there is some anxiety felt by the indigenous community with regards to their shrinking minority status, and growing concern about increasingly organised expatriate-led labour unrest, the government still does not really fear an ever-expanding foreign population on the grounds of security, given that most immigrants are only granted residency status subject to an employment visa. The majority are required to leave Dubai promptly following the termination of their contract and, if necessary, can be deported back to their home country. Such a huge foreign population does not yet impact on the political participation or wealth distribution aspects of the ruling bargain, given that most immigrants are mercenaries attracted by relatively better salaries than in their home country and only intend to reside in Dubai temporarily. Although there are misgivings over rising daily costs and rent increases, most of today's immigrants are financially content, and, rather than seeking redress from the government are more likely to seek employment elsewhere should conditions become unacceptable. Indeed, while many are proud of their adopted home and most appear to be experiencing something of a 'boom time happiness', few expatriates would extend their loyalties to Dubai much further than this. And while there are a few rather vocal veteran expatriates of twenty or more years who hope to live their entire lives in Dubai and eventually retire there, only a small number actively seek citizenship and a voice in local government.

The cost of such an apathetic and mixed foreign population is that Dubai's social structure is becoming more and more fragmented as different communities emerge and then fail to integrate with each other, with most individuals uninterested in investing in society or befriending their neighbours, and with the majority content to treat their job as a stepping stone to another destination or as a temporary residence before eventually returning home. Although the slogan of the Dubai Shopping Festival is 'One World, One Family', and although a large sign on Sheikh Zayed Road welcomes visitors to the emirate with the phrase 'Our world is getting bigger and better', Dubai cannot be considered a cosmopolitan city. Despite the government's efforts to create centres for multicultural understanding,[69] and its displaying large billboard posters depicting happy Dubai national families interacting with westerners and other expatriates, most ethnic groups prefer to remain distinct, each with their own social networks, clubs, and community centres. As such, 'Dubai society' continues to feel somewhat disharmonious (and at times racist), and in its present state the emirate would seem unlikely to become a melting pot comparable with other major international metropolises.

Also contributing to a negative atmosphere has been the huge imbalance between male and female populations in Dubai, given the very unnatural, economy-driven structure of the expatriate community. Even as early as the mid-1980s men made up 67 per cent of the total population,[70] and today official reports indicate that over three quarters of Dubai's residents are male.[71] Moreover, it is likely that the real proportion is even higher given the described census inconsistencies and exclusion of countless illegal immigrants working in Dubai, the majority of whom are probably male.[72] Countless problems can be attributed to this unevenness, with different expatriate communities suffering from slightly different pathologies depending on their relative gender mix.

Amongst the Filipino community, most of whom are single females working in the retail and tourist sector, many are having to delay their marriage age until they have the opportunity to return home. Among other communities, serious psychological problems have been noted,[73] and in many of the villages in the supplier countries there is believed to be a discernable 'Dubai syndrome' when male heads of households leave behind large families for extended periods.[74] Most worryingly, among those communities in Dubai that are heavily male (given that most choose not to bring their wives in order to save more money, or given that they are earning below the threshold salary that would entitle them to bring their families with them[75]), there is a very high level of sexual frustration, with the emirate's prostitution industry and the incidences of HIV infection having increased correspondingly.[76] Indeed, as will be discussed elsewhere in this book, although Dubai has historically been a major centre for human trafficking[77]—an unfortunate side effect of being a successful free port— the racket has now reached such a scale that the city is becoming regarded as the region's centre for sex tourism. Thousands of girls arrive from Central Asia and the Far East every month, most of whom survive on constantly renewed tourist visas. While there have been some very recent attempts to curb street prostitution,[78] there still remain large zones of the city where hostesses operate from low class hotels and parking lots.[79] Very rarely do the police intervene.

Loss of identity and the erosion of the ruling bargain

This large and heterogeneous expatriate population, combined with the attempts to create a more foreign investor and tourist-friendly environment in Dubai, have also led to an erosion of some components of the non-democratic ruling bargain. In many ways this has been unavoidable and would seem to be the political price that Dubai has to pay for pressing ahead with its development model. An increasing number of nationals are beginning to voice their concerns, believing that in some cases the ruling family and the government have gone too far in their efforts to accommodate foreigners, and that the national identity of Dubai and the former non-material privileges of the indigenous elite are now under threat. While this disillusionment has not yet reached the stage of organised opposition, with most preferring to remain fairly discreet, there are nevertheless some veteran Dubai nationals who are beginning to publicise their fears, often by conducting frank interviews with western newspapers. Such actions are beyond the reach of any censors, and should their frequency increase the establishment will be placed in an increasingly difficult position. Most notably, in 2006 an intrepid former Dubai representative to the Federal National Council claimed to a major US daily that the city he lives in today is now unrecognisable and is not even Arab anymore. Moreover, he complained that when he visits one of the many malls, the vast majority of patrons are foreigners, and that he rarely hears Arabic. Most damningly the article recorded that despite religious prohibitions,

'...drinking is unabashed, and he fears public wine-tasting parties are on the way, with the beaches of his youth having been taken over by hotels and their occasionally topless sunbathers and other westerners whose dress is deemed inappropriate... he grimaces at women jogging in the streets, sometimes with their dogs, considered unclean under Islamic law, and the celebration of Islamic holidays and the country's national day pale before the more commercialised commemoration of Christmas.'

Interestingly, the former FNC member concluded that he and his family felt they were in 'internal exile' and in an effort to maintain their Arab and Muslim identities they had had to move away from the central area of the city to an outlying suburb.[80] Tellingly, this is not an isolated case, with there being many examples of national families moving out of Dubai completely, or at least building a new family home in another emirate so that their children would still be able to grow up in an Arab city.[81]

Little of the content of such interviews is exaggerated, with a spate of recent changes and concessions in the emirate being perceived as openly attacking the indigenous way of life. Even the ruling family is facing direct criticism for some of its most obvious attempts to become more accessible and acceptable to expatri- ates. In particular, there is a concern that the rulers are no longer honouring their supposed role as first among equals, especially given that some local newspapers have begun to refer to the Al-Maktum family as being 'royal', rather than as a *hakim* or ruling family. Also problematic has been the issue of foreign wives in the ruling family, with Sheikh Maktum bin Rashid Al-Maktum's second marriage to a young Moroccan, Bouchra bint Muhammad, in the 1990s having caused considerable controversy with more conservative elements of Dubai society, and having prompted his well respected first wife to call for the dissolution of the Moroccan marriage.[82] Similarly, Sheikh Muhammad bin Rashid Al-Maktum's marriage to a Jordanian princess in 2004 has also proved controversial. While this latter union has, as described, provided Dubai with something of a bloodline alliance with the royal Hashemite family of Jordan,[83] it has meant that Muhammad's esteemed Dubai national first wife, Sheikha Hind bint Maktum Al-Maktum, has faded from the spotlight, especially given that Princess Haya bint Al-Hussein chooses not to cover, and, like Bouchra, has been featured in western society magazines, in a not dissimilar fashion from other glamorous royals such as Queen Rania and the late Princess Diana.[84] *Hello Magazine* published glossy photographs of Haya's wedding and has since pictured her in western dress at horseracing and polo events.[85] Thus although the Al-Maktum family remains in an extremely powerful position given its internal strength, its careful succession arrangements, and its control over a close-knit patrimonial network,[86] such re- cent developments will undoubtedly have an adverse impact on its personal legitimacy.

Dubai is also becoming seen as increasingly indifferent to alcohol consumption. Till recently alcohol could only be purchased in hotel bars and restaurants or in specific and very discreet stores if a resident could prove their non-Muslim status to the police (often by acquiring the signature of a priest or vicar) and had been provided with a 'liquor consumption licence'. Now almost anybody can purchase alcohol, as licences are rarely checked and hotels are non-discriminatory. Moreover, in violation of the original Trucial States alcohol regulations that date back to the mid-1950s,[87] in the last few years it has become possible to consume alcohol during Ramadan and on Islamic holidays. Indeed, many hotels serve alcohol after 6pm during Ramadan, and bars no longer close on the eve of major holidays. Nor is there any real prohibition on the daytime consumption of food during Ramadan. It is now almost acceptable to walk down a busy street eating a takeaway meal, and indeed major fast food chains remain open for this purpose—in the recent past a policeman or offended national would have remonstrated at such a sacrilegious act, but now, with all year round tourism and an increasingly culturally insensitive expatriate population, this has become impossible. Also eroding the status of Islamic holidays has been the shopping mall-backed rise of the commercial and distinctly secular Christmas, as alluded to in the abovementioned newspaper interview. As late as the 1990s Christmas trees were rarely seen in public places in Dubai, but are now featured prominently in all retail outlets, hotels, bars, and restaurants. While in the past government-sponsored *Eid* and national day street lights and decorations were always dismantled shortly before Christmas, so as to avoid any confusion; they now remain in place throughout the Christmas period, especially if Ramadan is late and finishes in December. Perhaps most obviously, the Muslim sabbath day is now also under threat, given that in late 2006 the official public sector weekend changed from Thursday and Friday to Friday and Saturday. Ostensibly to bring Dubai and the UAE more in line with other Middle Eastern states,[88] the real reason was to provide government departments and companies in Dubai with an extra day of contact and trade with their internationally based counterparts and colleagues. There is now a real fear that Dubai will eventually follow the western weekend, especially given that many private sector employees are already following such a schedule.

While gambling remains a fragile taboo, with no lawful casinos in operation, Dubai has nevertheless legitimised such thrills by allowing lottery-style tickets at horseracing events and by recently introducing prize-carrying 'national bonds'. Incredibly, it must also be noted that as part of the emirate's aforementioned overseas investments strategy,[89] Dubai Holdings has now acquired a $5 billion, 9.5 percent stake in the Nevada-headquartered MGM Mirage corporation—the world's largest gaming group and the proprietor of the Monte Carlo, the Bellagio, Caesar's Palace, the Luxor, the Mirage, and several other extravagant casinos on the Las Vegas strip. It was also reported in the *Financial Times* that Dubai Holdings has bought a 50 per cent stake in the company's forthcoming $7 billion residential and leisure CityCenter project.[90] Thus, in alliance with MGM Mirage, Dubai has now become a major player in the US gambling industry and therefore a very real Arabian Las Vegas, albeit currently somewhat distanced from the activity itself.

Also regarded as undermining national values and customs has been the recent lack of respect for Islamic mourning periods. In late 2004, following the death of the UAE's president and the ruler of Abu Dhabi, Sheikh Zayed bin Sultan Al-Nahyan, a forty day period of mourning was declared across the whole federation, during which alcohol, live music, dancing and late openings were to be prohibited. While Abu Dhabi and the other emirates followed this practice diligently, in Dubai all hotels, bars, and restaurants were open as usual—even on the day of Zayed's funeral—and with the exception of a few posters of Zayed hung off the sides of skyscrapers in mid-construction, business was back to normal after just a few days. Similarly in early 2006, following the death of Sheikh Maktum, the only real concession to mourning was the cancellation of the Dubai marathon and the postponement of the Dubai Shopping Festival. This delay was initially opposed by sections of the establishment, given the negative impact it would have on Dubai's commercial and tourist sectors. Also alarming has been the noticeable decline in emphasis on Dubai's mosques. While mosques in Abu Dhabi and other Gulf states remain ubiquitous, and can be reached on foot from most residences, in Dubai they are becoming much scarcer, with most new property developments not even featuring them. Indeed, in some of the newer shopping malls there are either no mosques at all, or there are 'inter faith prayer rooms,'[91] much like those one would find in an airport in a secular state. Moreover, mosque broadcasts at prayer times have ceased in most malls, and in some suburbs of the city, in which there are predominantly non-Arab populations, an emirate-level decree has required that the volume on mosque loudspeakers should be reduced so as not to disturb residents.

Further threatening religious and moral standards has been the increasing acceptance of homosexuality in Dubai. Indeed, in much the same way as the tolerance of prostitution, this is quite remarkable given that the emirate purports to be a relatively conservative Muslim state that continues to draw great legitimacy from its religion. Significantly, the federal penal code of 1987 outlawed all homosexual activity across the UAE and called for judges to punish acts of sodomy with the death sentence. Although a little less severe, the more recent Dubai-specific penal code still calls for the punishment of 'public and private consensual homosexual acts' with ten years of imprisonment.[92] In late 2005 a mass arrest took place at a secluded resort hotel situated close to Ghantoot on the border between Abu Dhabi and Dubai.[93] Reportedly, a multiple 'gay wedding' was taking place between 22 national men, 11 of whom were dressed as women. The transvestites were ordered to receive male hormone injections in addition to their prison sentences[94] and within days mobile phone videos that had been recorded by arresting officers were circulating amongst the Dubai national community, thereby irrecoverably tarnishing the family names of those arrested. In most cases, however, these anti-homosexual laws are now flagrantly violated, with openly homosexual men walking around shopping malls, and with certain well known hotel bars and nightclubs serving as de facto 'gay clubs'. Police raids occasionally close down such clubs, but this appears to be little more than a gesture, as the community soon moves to another well-publicised venue.

Similarly confusing for the national population has been the Dubai government's shifting position on Israel. Support for oppressed Palestinians and the Lebanese has long been an integral component of the UAE's ideological resources,[95] and indeed ever since the formation of the federation in 1971 there has been a boycott of all relations with Israel enshrined in the constitution. According to the first two articles of federal law number 15, '…any natural or legal person shall be prohibited from directly or indirectly concluding an agreement with organisations or persons either resident in Israel, connected therewith by virtue of their nationality or working on its behalf…'[96] Thus, in theory it remains illegal to do business with Israelis and even to place a telephone call to Israel or to visit an Israeli website (with the suffix dot.il), and it is of course impossible to return to the UAE if there is an Israeli visa stamp in one's passport. Moreover, most maps in the UAE's schools and universities feature either a full Palestinian state or a black mark in the place of Israel. In recent years Abu Dhabi has sought to uphold this public anti-Semitic stance, recognising its continuing necessity in the Arab world. In 1999 the Zayed Centre for Coordination and Follow-Up (ZCCF), a think tank whose purpose was to invite high-profile academics and policymakers to lecture in Abu Dhabi, was established. The ZCCF hosted several anti-Semitic speakers and authors whose work had already been the subject of international condemnation. When Sheikh Zayed attempted to donate $2.5 million to Harvard University in the summer of 2003 in order to establish the Sheikh Zayed Chair for Islamic Religious Studies,[97] an on-campus petition was signed by hundreds of students and staff calling for the university to block the donation on the grounds that ZCCF's track record was wholly unacceptable.[98] Zayed's donation was duly rejected and later that year the ZCCF was closed in disgrace, having greatly damaged Zayed's international reputation during the last year of his reign. Given their need for warm relations with all of their investor and tourist supplying countries, Dubai has been understandably keen to distance itself from such strategies, with the Al-Maktum family unwilling to make the same mistakes as Abu Dhabi. Indeed, in mid-2007 the Dubai Knowledge Village free zone[99] suffered an embarrassing setback when a proposed campus for the University of Connecticut had to be cancelled following the refusal of the university's general assembly to sanction any relations with the UAE until it 'adopted a more pro-Zionist position regarding its dealings with Israel.'[100]

Thus, while the official boycott remains in place, the rules have been bent to allow at least some informal connection with Israel. Over the last few years there have been reports of Israeli businessmen operating in Dubai, especially as the emirate has tried to build upon its existing gold trade by moving into the international diamond trade.[101] And when, in an effort to position itself more centrally in the international economy, Dubai chose to host the 2003 annual meetings of the WTO, the IMF, and the World Bank, the government was required to accommodate delegations from all member states, including Israel.[102] Most Dubai nationals quickly became aware that a group of Israelis was staying in the World Trade Centre hotel—the first time Israelis had officially entered the emirate for thirty-two years. Furthermore, and even more publicly, when in early 2006 the Israeli Ministry for Tourism signed a deal with the new Arsenal stadium in London to provide billboard and scoreboard promotions of Israeli tourist destinations, the Dubai government offered no objection, even though it was the major sponsor and creator of the stadium[103] and the logo of Emirates airline is featured prominently on the inside and the outside of the building.[104] Dubai has had to concede ground on this particular ideological resource, although given the likely backlash from sections of the national population should such relaxations become more apparent, the cost to legitimacy will be very high.

The Dubai government's wavering attitude towards the declining use of Arabic may also have a negative impact, especially as the modern language is regarded by many as providing an important source of continuity with classical Arabic and with the high Quaranic culture of the past. While most nationals accept that it is impossible to slow the tide of globalising forces and the penetration of 'Internet English' into society, it is nevertheless thought that some effort can be made to safeguard the language in academia and to at least ensure that the city remains bilingual. Indeed, in recent years the neighbouring government of Sharjah has implemented schemes aimed at promoting the use of Arabic, including a requirement that all public sector institutions should use Arabic in their meetings and correspondence.[105] Similarly, the Sharjah-based Arabic Language Protection Association has attempted to correct missspelt Arabic shop signs and street names, has drawn up plans to introduce new and more interesting Arabic language lessons in schools, and has sought to increase the number of Arabic language tutors for expatriate workers. As the association's chairman, Abdullah Al-Midfa, has explained, such actions have been imperative in order to '...preserve the Arabic language from an awkward mix of foreign vocabularies and dialects, and to limit the negative influences of the multicultural environment on the UAE's official language.'[106]

In contrast, it would appear that Dubai has done absolutely nothing to support Arabic, and in some cases has actively discouraged its use. Most shop signs are in English, and there is no requirement to translate into Arabic. In the cases where Arabic translations do exist they are mostly awkward transliterations and are never inspected for their accuracy. Remarkably, many government-sponsored telephone services provide much better support in English than in Arabic,[107] and, as of 2006, taxi drivers in Dubai began to face $150 fines if they were found to be driving vehicles with Arabic rooftop signs rather than English ones.[108] Perhaps the greatest concern among nationals is that it is now impossible to receive a university education in Arabic within the emirate. Indeed, although Sharjah offers both English and Arabic language universities (the American University of Sharjah and Sharjah University respectively), the only tertiary sector institutions in Dubai are the Higher Colleges of Technology, the American University of Dubai, the plethora of foreign universities operating out of Knowledge Village,[109] and Zayed University. Only the latter claims to produce bilingual graduates, but at present the university is only for females, and even now it would seem that its Arabic language courses are being marginalised with the introduction of an all-English curriculum on integrated learning programmes, and with all final year 'capstone' projects normally being written and presented in English. A common complaint from instructors in Zayed University's Arabic department is that their students can barely punctuate a sentence in Arabic, and that it is definitely becoming their second language. However, very few Dubai nationals are totally fluent in English, so there is a growing feeling that a population of linguistically rootless people is being created. As Abdullah Al-Midfa states, '...a quick observation of the language used at present indicates a looming catastrophe. The new generations are becoming more and more distant from their native tongue... this has given rise to a new form of broken language that combines various accents emerging on the surface.'[110] While this broken language was originally referred to quite jokingly as 'Arabish', in Dubai the term has now entered everyday usage.

Further eroding national identity and abetting the deterioration of the patrimonial component of the ruling bargain has been the declining elite status of the national population, despite their material benefits.[111] In many ways this reduced status is an unavoidable consequence of the opening up of the emirate to wealthy foreign investors and tourists: whereas up until recently Dubai nationals rested at the top of the social hierarchy (with the exception of some western expatriates), and were always made to feel superior to all other Arabs and foreigners,[112] this is now beginning to change. Many nationals now contend that they feel unwelcome in certain parts of the city, and often complain that restaurant and hotel managers discriminate against national dress—their erstwhile symbol of privilege. Indeed, in most of the best resorts and outlets only western dress is permitted, and signs are placed outside entrances to this effect. While such moves are ostensibly to protect the licence holder from openly serving alcohol to Muslims, in practice they exist to filter out certain customers in order to make the venues more tourist-friendly. Understandably therefore, some nationals argue that they are missing out on the 'best of Dubai', as their city is being developed in such a way as to favour those who have bought expensive properties or are visiting on luxury holiday packages. Some even claim that the government's attempts to gentrify particular neighbourhoods for the benefit of foreigners are effectively herding nationals into ghetto suburbs, and that the community of nationals is being treated as a quaint curiosity that can add to the emirate's touristic appeal. In 2007 the Department of Tourism and Commerce Marketing began to install booths in shopping malls and staff them with young nationals so that tourists could have the opportunity to 'talk to a local'.[113]

Equally of concern has been the relatively recent rise in financial hardship among nationals, as it would appear that the government is no longer ensuring that all nationals receive their due benefits. Many of the latter are now falling into serious debt as they attempt to buy the same types of cars and housing that wealthy foreigners are purchasing. While the Municipality's official line remains one of 'no poverty in Dubai,'[114] and its employees have on occasion sought to discourage university research projects on the subject, there are now indisputably large slum areas in Al-Ghusais, Al-Rashidiya, and other parts of the city where many bona fide national families (who hold their 'family cards' and can produce valid national identity documentation) are living on just a few hundred dollars per month, with no apparent state support. While the problem is of course nothing compared to poorer emirates such as Fujairah and Ra's al-Khaimah, where there are many indigent families, it is nevertheless viewed as unacceptable that the relatively much more prosperous Dubai government is not fully addressing the issue. In just the last few years an appreciable number of Dubai nationals have been observed working as supermarket checkout assistants,[115] as janitors, and as truck drivers. Their salaries are likely to be lower than the unofficial minimum wage for nationals, which is thought to be $1100 per month for those with secondary education.[116] With foreigners becoming increasingly aware of this new phenomenon, the national population can no longer being held in the same high esteem as before.

Lastly, also associated with the decline of the indigenous elite has been the seemingly unstoppable dilution of the national population despite the marriage fund and all of the other aforementioned preservation strategies.[117] With an increasing foreign female population, many national men choose to take an expatriate wife—not only to avoid costly dowries, but also because they can circumvent arranged marriages and therefore avoid being answerable to another respected national family for their marital conduct. Indeed, in 2005 it was estimated that of the 1,300 or so registered marriages involving Dubai national men, over 300 were to foreign women.[118] For those who insist on marrying Muslim Arab women, liberal-minded Moroccan girls are thought to be the most desirable and large groups of them are flown over to Dubai to serve as hostesses at private parties. Interestingly, Eastern European and Russian women are a popular alternative, as most will indulge in pre-marital sex and readily convert to Islam, as becoming the wife of a Dubai national will provide them with financial security and the trappings of an elite status that they are unlikely to achieve elsewhere. Most often, such relationships begin in the city's many bars, through marriage brokers, or in Beirut's 'super nightclubs,'[119] where groups of national men on vacation are likely to meet such women. It is now common to find national men married to women from Thailand and China—some of whom have undoubtedly worked as prostitutes in Dubai, while others have been brought over following package tours to Bangkok. In some cases national men who have been studying abroad will also marry western women,[120] and there are small communities of British, American, and Canadian women living as Dubai nationals. Crucially, most foreign brides rarely speak or ever learn Arabic, some never convert to Islam, and most fail to integrate properly with the man's family. As such, the divorce rate is accelerating, believed to be 31 per cent for mixed marriages compared to 26 per cent for 'pure' national marriages.[121] Moreover, mixed-race children are increasingly growing up in broken homes and are being discriminated against by their 'pure' peers.

Conversely, and equally problematic has been the increase in Dubai national spinsters, given that fewer national men are available to marry and, as described, national women are strongly discouraged from marrying foreign men as they will face shame from their family, and their children will be denied state benefits.[122] Nevertheless, about fifty such marriages do take place every year in Dubai,[123] and there are believed to be over 14,000 such mixed couples across the UAE. The government refuses to recognise the legitimacy of these relationships, despite their legal and religious status, and cuts most social security benefits, free education, and healthcare to these families.[124] Indeed, in early 2006 a protest was held by some of these national women outside the Dubai branch of the Ministry for Labour and Social Affairs.[125] Similarly, in early 2007 a busload of national women from all over the UAE appeared at the premises of a newly-established human rights association: demands were made that their husbands and children be granted citizenship and be treated in the same way as the wives and children of national men who had married foreigners. It was also claimed that the government had issued their husbands with an ultimatum, compelling them to seek foreign passports or otherwise face deportation.[126] As most would agree, the government is now being placed in an impossible position, as it cannot expand the rentier elite, yet at the same time it cannot ignore this looming crisis.

The labour nationalisation conundrum

In addition to the pervasive rentier mentality, the sheer size of the foreign population is making it difficult for those Dubai nationals who do seek employment actually to find positions. While the national population remains small, it is nevertheless increasing in size, with one of the world's highest growth rates (about 4 per cent per annum), and it also has a very youthful demographic structure, with more than 45 per cent thought to be under the age of twenty-one.[127] Given that the number of 'protected' jobs in the public sector cannot keep up with this increase (with 800 nationals recently applying for eighty jobs in one particular government department[128]), most nationals find themselves competing for jobs in the private sector, where their employers are less likely to provide them with preferential treatment and, in some cases, may actually discriminate against them given both their history of privilege and their perceived higher salary demands. Of the 300,000 jobs that are created in Dubai each year, most are now in the private sector, and it is thought that only 1 per cent of this workforce is actually comprised of nationals.[129] Most worryingly, some 35,000 or so nationals across the UAE are now involuntarily unemployed,[130] and remain spectators on the periphery of their country's development.

Throughout the 1990s and early 2000s the federal government attempted to solve this problem by intervening and forcing certain private sector companies to employ a minimum quota of nationals and to provide them with financial incentives to ensure they remained in their positions. A labour law was introduced in 2002 so as to regulate the employment of nationals in the private sector, as part of which nationals were to benefit from a special pensions fund and to be 'guaranteed better rights as employees' including a maximum number of working hours per week and a guaranteed finishing time of four o'clock in the afternoon for women with children of school age.[131] The federal National Human Resource Development and Employment Authority (Tanmia) also earmarked specific categories of jobs for nationalisation, and required employers to appoint a certain percentage of nationals. In particular, banks were asked to increase their relatively small proportion of national employees[132] to 40 per cent, and to ensure a minimum 'emiratisation growth rate' of over 4 per cent per annum in order to meet their target.[133] Similarly, insurance-related companies were required to have an emiratisation rate of 5 per cent, and trade-related companies were to have a rate of 2 per cent. Those companies that hired disabled or special needs nationals would have their quotas cut in half.[134] In retrospect these draconian strategies largely failed, as they effectively priced nationals out of the market and made them even less attractive hiring prospects. Even in banks, nationals still only make up 25 per cent of the workforce, with many managers either massaging their employment statistics or using outsourcing to hire non-nationals and thereby disguise the true breakdown of their employee base.[135] It is thought that in most sectors expatriates are now willing to take a 135 per cent lower salary than similarly qualified nationals,[136] most of whom would normally expect a salary of around $30,000 in addition to an employer pension contribution of over 12 per cent.[137] Even when Dubai national entrepreneurs are quizzed on their hiring patterns, many will admit to an unwillingness to employ their compatriots due to relatively high expenses and 'unnecessary complications.' Most would prefer to take on hardworking and cost-effective South Asian expatriates,[138] most of whom can easily be dismissed should they prove unsuitable.

Today, the only long term solution to the problem is believed to be through the superior training of nationals for specific jobs so as to allow them to compete more effectively with experienced expatriates, without the need for such government intervention in their favour. For some time companies have offered incentives to provide summer schools and internships for nationals, although most of these, including the Al-Futtaim Group,[139] are so closely connected to the neo-patrimonial network that they hardly represent genuine private sector experiences. Universities and the Higher Colleges of Technology (HCT) have also had little visible impact on improving labour nationalisation, as for many years they have been underfunded and had difficulty in expanding. Indeed, it has been claimed that the tertiary sector's budget has not risen in real terms since 1996, and though some new campuses have been built in the last few years, there is a looming enrolment crisis as per student financial support has declined by over 20 per cent since 2000.[140] A federal government white paper estimated that the HCT institutions across the UAE may have had to turn away 3,000 students in 2007 in order to maintain the quality of their programs.[141] Most of these universities and colleges have been plagued by cronyism, in part due to the initial teams of expatriate advisors that were brought in having chosen to employ only their compatriots. For some years this has led to a very uncompetitive hiring process and has provided the UAE with a mediocre pool of academic staff. Although the Ministry of Higher Education and Scientific Research's short-lived Office of Higher Education Policy and Planning attempted to improve drastically the learning environment, increase the budget, and shake up the sector's management, the current strategy still seems to be one of papering over cracks by setting up new universities rather than first attempting to fix existing problems. In the late 1990s Zayed University was created at a time when the University of the UAE in Al-Ayn required much greater attention. This new, western-managed, university was seen as preferable to tackling the problems of more entrenched Egyptian expatriate management in Al-Ayn. Most recently, and perhaps most disturbingly, even more universities are being created, often beyond the Ministry's jurisdiction. In some cases they are clearly not fulfilling the nation's needs and will certainly be unable to contribute to labour nationalisation. In particular, the Sorbonne University in Abu Dhabi offers French language education and is therefore clearly not in tune with private sector demands—it seems to be more of a prestige project. Unsurprisingly the university has struggled to fill its places and has had to offer a large number of scholarships in its first year, as even Francophone Lebanese expatriates favour English language education.

Civil society and the media

It has been argued that for a nation's successful long term development there needs to be a fundamental shift in the state-society relationship[142] and the fostering of an intermediate network of institutions and associations that can operate in a public civic realm without fear of closure.[143] In particular it is thought that Dubai's remarkable development strategies will never reach their full potential unless such a civil society exists. The population, both national and expatriate, therefore needs to be provided with a better forum, not necessarily for any political discussion that might threaten the ruling bargain, but rather so that people can air their grievances and contribute ideas and suggestions that may improve the labour force's relationship with the state. Most importantly, society needs to have associational life, residential associations, a vibrant media, and an intellectual environment in which issues can be openly discussed.

Workers' associations have been considerably strengthened in recent years following the UAE's accession to the ILO, and correspondingly there have been efforts to protect nascent human rights organisations, following specific criticism from the US Department of State's Bureau of Democracy, Human Rights, and Labour.[144] Indeed, there now exists the quasi-independent Emirates Human Rights Association, which was set up in 2006, and which complements existing human rights departments in the various emirate-level police forces, most prominently Dubai's.[145] Ostensibly the association is based on the UN's Universal Declaration of Human Rights and draws from European and American conventions on human rights.[146] Moreover, given the efforts to attract charity and aid-related INGOs to Dubai,[147] there is a feeling that such supranational organisations are beginning to boost domestic associations given that they often employ nationals and are therefore providing blueprints for future indigenous organisations. Good examples would include Dubai's branch of the UNDP, which currently trains several dozen nationals, and Dubai's offices for the World Health Organisation and Médecins Sans Frontières.

Major obstacles remain to be overcome, as many other categories of civil society organisations are either non-existent or remain in a severely weakened state, for example the absence of proper residential associations. The root of the problem would seem to be the government's unwillingness to allow autonomous groups to emerge, perhaps due to fear of allowing venues for unmonitored political debate to take place. Indeed, various controls have been placed on associations, including a requirement that all have to seek a licence from the Ministry of Labour and Social Affairs, and to submit their membership lists and budget reports for annual review by Ministry staff. These restrictions were only formalised in 2001,[148] and contradict the original federal Social Welfare

Societies Law of 1974.[149] There have been occasions in recent years when meetings of unlicensed associations were raided and disbanded, as an article introduced by the 2001 amendments has given the Ministry the right to dissolve immediately all groups.[150] More subtly, it is important to note that even among those associations which do conform to the guidelines, the vast majority are either in receipt of government subsidies or are heavily patronised by a powerful individual. As such, few can be genuinely classified as civil society organisations, as most come under the umbrella of either a federal ministry, an emirate-level government department, or a prominent sheikh or dignitary.

Among the first of these categories, good examples would include the Emirates Association for the Revival of Folk Arts, the budget of which is allocated and administered by the Ministry of Finance and Industry,[151] and the Emirates Environmental Group, which is supported by the Ministry of Labour and Social Affairs.[152] Among the second category, the Sharjah government is a particularly good example, contributing more than $30 million to over 25 different local associations, including the Sharjah Arts and Theatre Association and the Marine Club for Arts and Tourism.[153] With regard to the latter category, in Dubai the much discussed Muhammad Ali Al-Abbar chairs the UAE Golf Association, while the ruler's eldest son, Sheikh Rashid bin Muhammad Al-Maktum presides over the Dubai Football Club. Similarly in Abu Dhabi, the Emirates Heritage Club is chaired by Sheikh Sultan bin Zayed Al-Nahyan, with the Environmental Research and Wildlife Development Agency (ERWDA) being directed by his younger brother Sheikh Hamdan bin Zayed Al-Nahyan, and with almost every women's association in the emirate being under the wing of Sheikha Fatima bint Mubarak Al-Qitbi.[154] Understandably therefore, almost all of these legitimate associations, groups, and societies pursue only sanitised objectives and tend to steer away from potentially controversial topics. As such, meaningful criticisms or suggested refinements to the government's development

211

plans are unlikely to emerge from this quarter. Interestingly, those associations specifically for expatriates that do not have patrons or government backing and are therefore outside of this 'network' often go to great lengths to stress their apolitical nature.[155]

Perhaps most contentious has been the role played by indigenous media and intellectual organisations, which are often regarded as being fundamental prerequisites for true civil society and successful development.[156] In recent years there have been some signs that the media community in Dubai and the UAE may be gaining strength, given the public assurances of many prominent sheikhs that freedom of speech needs to be protected across the country. In particular, in late 2004 the Minister for Higher Education and Scientific Research, Sheikh Nahyan bin Mubarak Al-Nahyan, stated at a book fair held in Abu Dhabi that '...the UAE now lives in an age in which people should be supplied with all kinds of information... all people have the right to choose and select information and are wise enough to make that choice. No information should be withheld from the public in this day and age.'[157] Similarly, the following month, Sheikh Muhammad bin Rashid Al-Maktum repeated his earlier freedom of speech statements made during the opening of Dubai Media city in 2000,[158] by urging media representatives to 'maintain objectivity in their pursuance of truth... and by promising to iron out difficulties hindering them as they carry out their duties,' before stating that 'all authorities must render all facilities and moral support to media corporations operating in Dubai... which must remain an oasis of responsible freedom and democracy of opinion and expression.'[159] Also promising has been the strengthening of the UAE Journalists' Association. Despite accepting a $130,000 donation from Sheikh Khalifa bin Zayed Al-Nahyan just three months after its establishment in 2004,[160] the Association does seem to have some independence, and has recently managed to intervene successfully on behalf of its members. Notably, in 2005 two *Gulf News* reporters who had been covering an episode of stabbings in Sharjah (and thereby harming the emirate's tourist industry) were arrested by Sharjah police, but following the Association's lobbying of the Ministry of Interior, they were eventually released.[161] Moreover, in 2006 the association steadily campaigned for a reduction in the penalties that could be imposed on journalists. In an interview that year the Chief Justice of the Federal Supreme Court, Abdul Wahab Abdul, appeared to agree with the Association's views, stating that '...jail and detention terms incurred by journalists for offences related to their profession should be scrapped... and should be replaced by fines and suspension from work for limited periods...'[162] And in 2007 the Association also staged the Emirates Media Freedom Conference in cooperation with Zayed University—with a healthy attendance the event at least helped to publicise the cause of journalists in the UAE. It must also be noted that in much the same way as the described 'blueprint' NGOs that are setting themselves up in Dubai, the increasing number of foreign media companies in Media City may also be having a 'demonstration effect' on domestic media associations, perhaps giving them a greater feeling of collective security and obliging the government to extend the same freedoms enjoyed in the free zones to the rest of the emirate. Indeed, there are already strong examples of linkages between foreign and domestic media in Dubai, with the BBC in cooperation with *Gulf News* having screened a series of half hour documentaries that were somewhat critical of Dubai,[163] and with an Arab media company in cooperation with a Ra's al-Khaimah TV company producing a series that dealt with controversial UAE-related issues, including the accountability of sheikhs, in a comic manner.[164]

Despite such glimmers of hope, true freedom of speech remains a distant prospect, with a mixture of formal and subtle controls still being exerted on those who choose to question or criticise the polity in any manner that is more than just superficial. Many would contend that too few outlets for independent expression exist given the financial dependency of most major media companies on governmental and semi-governmental organisations.[165] In particular, Dubai's Arabic daily newspaper *Al-Bayan*, together with two other UAE-based Arabic dailies, are owned by their respective emirate-level governments, while the three other Arabic papers, including Sharjah's *Al-Khaleej*, receive generous state subsidies.[166] Similarly, Dubai's two best-selling English dailies, *Gulf News* and *Khaleej Times*, also receive subsidies,[167] as does Sharjah's English language paper, *Gulf Today*.[168] Although there are now two seemingly self-sufficient new English papers in Dubai, *Emirates Today* and *Seven Days*, their relevance is questionable as both seem to have positioned themselves at a tabloid audience. With regard to domestic terrestrial TV companies the situation has been much the same, with most being owned by Emirates Media International (EMI)—a parastatal chaired by a powerful minister and a highly placed member of the Abu Dhabi ruling family,[169] and which has on occasion forbidden its employees from communicating with unapproved foreigners and representatives.[170] Interestingly, EMI also operates the national news agency, *Wikalat Anba' Al-Imarat*, publishes the *Al-Ittihad* Arabic daily, and has purchased the formerly independent Ajman TV company.[171]

More oppressively, Dubai and the UAE have suffered from a long history of censorship, examples of which continue up to the present. For many years, censorship controls were administered by the much maligned federal Ministry of Information and Culture (and its branch office in Dubai), headed by Sheikh Abdullah bin Zayed Al-Nahyan, before the anachronistic nature of the Ministry's work prompted its closure in 2006 and the division of its duties between several different ministries. While most associated the Ministry's work with the confiscation of videos and the crude black pen marks that blot out sensitive articles and pictures in imported newspapers and magazines (including, quite unnecessarily, photographs of classic nude paintings in esteemed international art magazines), its activities often extended much further, with it having sought the closure of publications, occasional media blackouts, and the arrest of outspoken critics. Indeed, throughout the 1970s and 1980s several newspapers had to be shut down, including the Sharjah-based *Al-Shuruq* that had described the Supreme Council of Rulers as being irresponsibly slow in setting up the UAE,[172] and then later the Dubai-based *Al-Azmina*, that was believed to be encouraging strikes and had been reporting on sensitive topics such as the human cost of Dubai's development.[173] When disasters have happened, most notably the catastrophic collapse of the dry dock gate in Port Rashid in 2002 that cost dozens of lives, all media representatives were denied access to the story.[174] Perhaps most disturbingly, journalists, professors, and other academics who have challenged the authorities have frequently been harassed. In the 1980s two lecturers from Dubai together with members of a prominent Sharjah family had begun to write somewhat leftist opinion pieces in newspapers. All were briefly jailed and temporarily banned from publishing.[175] Rather disappointingly, most of these erstwhile intellectual opponents of the regime seem to have appeased the establishment, with the Sharjah family having switched to a more moderate stance, and with both of the lecturers now writing wholly complimentary pieces on the successes of Dubai's development[176] and the ruler's 'futuristic vision for Dubai as an international hub that keeps a delicate balance between modernity and the city's Arab and Islamic identity... Dubai has always been a symbol of peaceful coexistence and interfaith tolerance and will remain so under the visionary leadership of Sheikh Muhammad.'[177] To illustrate the extent of this volte-face it should be noted that the PhD thesis written by one of these academics in the mid-1980s had decried the political dependency of the hereditary ruling families.[178] More recently, journalists have been arrested for supporting aggrieved employees of the aforementioned EMI[179] and for publishing satirical columns that have featured Gulf Arabs. In particular, in 2001 a Qatari reporter working for *Gulf News* was seized and, according to an international human rights report, subjected to sleep deprivation and physical abuse during a two week detention before being expelled to his home country. The Ministry attempted to sue *Gulf News*, and only agreed to drop the law suit following a front-page apology for publishing the pieces.[180] Similarly, in 2005 a prominent law professor and human rights activist was imprisoned without formal charge in Dubai and questioned for two separate periods of three days about the content of his lectures.[181] In previous years he had also been prohibited from teaching and writing newspaper articles.[182] The establishment has occasionally also sought to extend its control to western academics, albeit often unsuccessfully. Specifically, a UAE-related book by a British academic that was published in 2005 by a respected US press[183] did not receive ministerial permission to be distributed in UAE bookshops, yet bizarrely was ordered by libraries and is on reading lists in most UAE universities, given that it can be easily imported from online booksellers.[184] Furthermore, in early 2006 the Ministry's subsidiary Department of External Affairs attempted to block or amend a scholarly article on UAE succession patterns in a leading peer-reviewed US journal by the same writer.[185] More forcefully, in late 2006 a *bona fide* academic visitor on a prestigious US scholarship was interrogated and deported following his research on expatriate Asian communities in Dubai.

Another source of concern has been the Ministry's history of Internet censorship. A proxy server has been in place since the 1990s that prevents all users from directly accessing the Internet, which allows the authorities to block access to or even bowdlerise certain websites and Internet documents. While most of these prohibited sites can be justified on the grounds of protecting the UAE's cultural values (including the blocking of sites relating to alcohol, gambling, pornography, and magic), in reality the censorship goes much further with sites relating to human rights (most notably a website that records experiences from the UAE's prisons[186]), democratisation, and criticism of the ruling families also being blocked. In the summer of 2005 one of Dubai's most widely read blogs was temporarily blocked, and was only re-opened following outrage amongst the international blogging community and a petition sent to Etisalat.[187] Such restrictive practices are now regarded as completely unnecessary and inappropriate by both nationals and expatriates, especially given that a range of new Internet technologies that facilitate computer-to-computer connections (including 'bit torrents') now exist, and effectively allow users to bypass the Etisalat proxy. Moreover, in the free zones and some of the universities, there are direct internet lines that are also beyond Etisalat's control, as the government is aware that multinational companies and visiting academics would not tolerate such a system. Similarly undermining the role of censorship, a number of the new real estate projects that are targeted at high end foreign investors are also beyond the proxy.

Finally, as another unfortunate by-product of the distributed wealth and patrimonial network components of the ruling bargain, it must also be noted how censorship continues to exist in many other less controlled forms, as many journalists and academics choose to self-censor and most often prefer to tow the line rather than promote proper journalism and the full exploration of issues. Indeed, given the consequences for the extended families of outspoken nationals,[188] many Dubai and UAE nationals would think carefully before writing sensitive reports or opinion pieces that might ultimately jeopardise the jobs and positions of their relatives. Equally, most foreign journalists, especially those expatriate Arab and South Asian reporters working for the English daily newspapers, prefer to self-censor, even if sometimes they are not aware of it themselves. While not in receipt of explicit state handouts and thereby not part of the rentier elite as such, they are nevertheless receiving salaries and employment packages that would be much higher than in their home countries. In such situations, there is understandably little incentive to disrupt the lucrative status quo for the sake of a society that is not even one's own. Quite tellingly, articles by expatriate journalists will often be written in such a way as to report superficially on events while also avoiding direct criticism of any government body. Key examples in recent years would include the coverage of labour disputes, in which some journalists stated in their columns that reports should not be 'written in bad faith by twisting facts to portray the UAE in a poor light' and should recognise that '...the UAE, which opened the door of livelihood wide for millions of expatriate workers has got nothing to hide. There is no country in the world that welcomes foreign workers the way the UAE does.'[189] Moreover, while the aforementioned *Khaleej Times* might boast the triply suspect slogan 'The UAE's best English newspaper... fearless coverage... the truth must be told!', it is difficult to imagine how the newspaper's journalists, much like those working for the rival *Gulf News*, would ever feel any compulsion to tell sensitive truths given the likelihood of losing their jobs and being deported.[190]

7
THE STABILITY OF THE FEDERATION

Dubai's accession to the federation of United Arab Emirates provided the emirate with much needed collective security following Britain's withdrawal from the Gulf in 1971. Moreover, the loose, decentralised nature of the arrangement allowed Dubai and its neighbours to avoid any immediate unravelling and, at least for a few years, any resurgence of parochial, emirate-level interests. However, as with the diversification of the economy and the maintenance of the ruling bargain there have been certain hidden costs resulting from this history of federal flexibility. Notably, more than three decades later, many of the initial problems associated with the amalgamation still remain unsolved, and in some respects Dubai is now beginning to drift even further away from the federal model as it aspires to becoming a post-modern city state that is capable of addressing its own development needs. Moreover, instabilities and uncertainties in the other emirates persist, and given their geographic proximity to Dubai and the ramifications of these problems for federal security and prosperity, future problems in these close neighbours may have serious consequences for Dubai's reputation and therefore its efforts to attract foreign investment and international tourism.

Preserving flexibility

Ironically, Britain's attempts to bring the sheikhdoms together under the Trucial States Council in the 1950s and 1960s[1] were in many ways responsible for consolidating the independence of each sheikhdom, as they became more formally recognised within the region as separate entities with their own ruling families and agendas.[2] Following the formation of the United Arab Emirates the Supreme Council of Rulers agreed that Britain's flexible system of confederation should be continued, as it would be risky to attempt to centralise all key powers too early in the new relationship[3]—all were mindful of the failures of the Yemeni federal experiment.[4] As such, while the temporary capital of Abu Dhabi was made permanent and it was accepted that the federal ministries should assume responsibility for foreign policy, immigration, and other matters of 'supreme national interest,' it was also recognised that each emirate should maintain control over its own natural resources, and therefore its own economic development path. Consequently, Article 23 of the provisional constitution provided a loophole that allowed the individual emirates to manage independently their own hydrocarbon industries.[5]

While such clauses have been credited with maintaining the early integrity of the UAE and preventing 'opt-outs' during the first oil boom, by the late 1970s they had nevertheless become a source of much concern among those nationals who believed they served to separate the rich from the poor, and were therefore ultimately an impediment to long term collective security, political stability, and balanced economic development.[6] In 1976 a series of events triggered the first real crisis of confidence in the federation, prompting Sheikh Zayed bin Sultan Al-Nahyan to threaten his resignation and thereby dismantle the union. In particular, when the time came to draw up a more permanent version of the constitution, a committee of 28 prominent nationals from across the UAE was convened to consider the matter. Essentially the committee was divided between those who continued to regard themselves as representatives of their native emirate, and those who viewed the drawing up of a new constitution as being an opportunity to remove emirate-specific articles and press ahead with greater centralisation.[7] Crucially, these 'federalists' were supported by Zayed and argued that Article 23 was preventing efficient wealth distribution across the UAE, and claimed that certain emirates, most obviously Dubai, would need to make much greater contributions to the federal budget. It was thought that during the federal negotiations of the late 1960s, Sheikh Rashid bin Said Al-Maktum had insisted upon a secret unwritten condition that his government would never have to pay for anything other than for federal services specifically extended to Dubai.[8] Although the committee refrained from completely abolishing Article 23 it nevertheless recommended to the SCR that each emirate should in future only be able to retain control over 25 per cent of its hydrocarbon income.[9] Dubai and several other emirates regarded such an amendment as evidence of increasing federal encroachment and as being against the spirit of the 1971 compromises. Rashid refused to sign off on the recommendations and the SCR was left divided. Zayed viewed this lack of cooperation as being a direct challenge to his vision for the federation[10] and, according to a Bahraini newspaper report,[11] he offered to stand down as president of the UAE.[12] It is likely that this decision was also influenced by his equal disappointment over Dubai's failure to settle a minor territorial dispute with Sharjah at that time. Indeed, a quarrel over an area of about 150,000 square metres on the border of the two emirates was preventing the construction of a new federal hospital. Neither emirate allowed the federal government to intervene and the dispute had to be referred to an Anglo-French committee.[13] Remarkably, the matter remains unsettled even today.

Dubai was unable to call Sheikh Zayed's bluff, given his important statesmanlike role for the UAE and given Abu Dhabi's

221

enormous commitment to assisting the poorer emirates.[14] Eventually, following a tense four months of negotiations between Zayed and Sheikh Rashid's sons it was finally agreed that federal powers should be increased (including greater presidential control over immigration and the creation of a new federal internal security organisation)[15] and that Dubai would begin to make a modest contribution to the federal budget.[16] In return, Article 23 was to be kept in place and the constitution had to remain in a provisional state. However, within just two years Dubai was again baulking at Zayed's attempts to centralise, as it vigorously resisted Abu Dhabi's claims that collective security was possible only if all of the emirate-level armed forces became integrated under a federal umbrella. Zayed was still hoping to set up a proper Union Defence Force (UDF) that would assume command over the autonomous 1000 man Dubai Defence Force (DDF), in addition to the Sharjah National Guard, and Ra's al-Khaimah's Badr Brigade.[17] In early 1978 he had appointed his second eldest son, Sheikh Sultan bin Zayed Al-Nahyan, as the UDF's first commander-in-chief. Given that Sultan was only in his twenties at the time,[18] given that Sheikh Muhammad bin Rashid Al-Maktum was officially the UAE's Minister of Defence, and given that the DDF was an important symbol of the Al-Maktum family's status,[19] this was interpreted as a gross insult to Dubai. Predictably, Rashid, together with Sheikh Saqr bin Muhammad Al-Qasimi and Sheikh Ahmad bin Rashid Al-Mu'alla—the equally offended rulers of Ra's al-Khaimah and Umm al-Qawain—announced that their three emirates would secede from the UAE unless Zayed reversed his decision.[20] Thus, although the situation was eventually defused following a clearer definition of Sultan's new post,[21] the dispute nevertheless highlighted the continuing reluctance of Dubai to be drawn into a tighter federation in which it would have to play a permanent subordinate role to Abu Dhabi.[22] In a show of defiance, throughout the remainder of his reign Rashid actually tripled expenditure on the DDF, while making no effort to coordinate its procurements with those of the UDF.[23]

Most seriously, in 1979 the UAE again came close to disintegration following the submission to the SCR of a comprehensive memorandum signed by a large number of federalists. The petition called for the removal of all internal borders between the emirates and asked for much greater support for Sheikh Zayed's fresh drive for more rapid centralisation. With the Islamic revolution taking place in nearby Iran and the fear of Shia 'fifth columns' in the Arab Gulf states; with the controversial Camp David meetings having recently been held between Anwar Sadat and Menachem Begin; and with the prospect of a Soviet invasion of Afghanistan increasing the likelihood of a superpower conflict close to the Gulf; many feared serious regional instability and recognised the need for a stronger state with a more effective military and much greater control over its internal security.[24] Other sections of the document called for the SCR to meet more regularly as a formal entity and for it to devolve more of its powers to the Council of Ministers.[25] Moreover, as a portent of the 2006 political reforms and the current debate,[26] it was also requested that the Federal National Council be given greater legislative powers[27] in addition to an 'expanded base of membership' that would be comprised of elected representatives.[28]

Mindful of Dubai's likely misgivings, Sheikh Zayed proceeded cautiously and set up a committee under the chairmanship of his well respected second cousin and the UAE's deputy prime minister, Sheikh Hamdan bin Muhammad Al-Nahyan.[29] Nevertheless, as soon as the contents of the memorandum were made known, Sheikh Rashid and Sheikh Saqr immediately pulled out of the SCR, complaining that all of the recommendations were unconstitutional.[30] With students, businessmen, and many other nationals across the UAE beginning to demonstrate in support of Zayed,[31] the situation seemed hopeless, and it became increasingly likely that Dubai would make its withdrawal permanent.

However, after five months of negotiations, during which Rashid and his sons remained in constant telephone communication with Hamdan, a compromise solution was eventually reached with the help of the visiting Kuwaiti Minister for Foreign Affairs, Sheikh Sabah bin Ahmad Al-Sabah. In return for slightly increasing the level of its pre-arranged 1976 contributions to the federal budget,[32] Dubai would face no further demands from Abu Dhabi to integrate more fully.[33] Furthermore, as discussed earlier in this volume, Rashid was to take over from his eldest son, Sheikh Maktum bin Rashid Al-Maktum, as the UAE's prime minister.[34] Zayed and Hamdan assumed this reshuffle would give Rashid a greater feeling of control over federal matters while also encouraging Dubai to become more enthusiastic about future attempts to centralise.

Federal incoherence

Despite the new spirit of cooperation and its greater control over the premiership, Dubai nevertheless remained something of an unwilling partner throughout the 1980s and much of the 1990s, and in many ways Abu Dhabi and the federalists failed to advance the union any further. Most obviously, even basic infrastructure connecting the emirates was slow to develop, with each government preferring to concentrate on its own transport and communications network. Perhaps the greatest example of such a lack of federal cooperation was the lack of any road between Dubai and Abu Dhabi. In the late 1970s Abu Dhabi had built a four lane dual carriageway connecting the capital city to its second town of Al-Ayn,[35] while the emirate was still separated from Dubai by over 100 miles of sand.[36] It was only in the mid-1990s that the Sheikh Zayed Road was built to link the two largest cities in the UAE.[37] Similarly, smaller roads and street lighting could never be extended effectively from one emirate's territory into another, and in many cases even today one will see beautifully paved sections of road in wealthier emirates petering out into dirt tracks when they reach a neighbour's border. Most notably, on the Indian Ocean coastline of the UAE where Sharjah, Fujairah, and Oman all share the small town of Dibba, foreign visitors will find excellent infrastructure in the Sharjah controlled territory, considerably older roads and lighting in the poorer Fujairah section, and then the well maintained corniche wall and path deteriorating into a pile of rubble when crossing into the Omani enclave. Moreover, up until recently there has been no attempt to create an efficient UAE-wide bus service. Buses and taxis would always go from Dubai to other cities, but then be unable to pick up passengers for the return journey due to a lack of inter-emirate agreements. The drivers would therefore have little option but to come back empty, and their customers would often have to pay a premium to make the return journey with a different transport company.[38]

Similarly lacking has been the implementation of UAE-wide law and order. Notwithstanding the 1976 creation of a federal internal security organisation, in practice Dubai kept control over its own affairs and maintained its own police force.[39] Further-more, although a five judge Federal Supreme Court was set up in the early 1970s along with the Council of Ministers and the Federal National Council,[40] and although in 1994 Sheikh Zayed bin Sultan Al-Nahyan decreed that all sharia courts across the UAE should be answerable to the federal court, both Dubai and Ra's al-Khaimah have kept their own emirate-level court depart-ments and their own special Shia councils to act on matters per-taining to Shia law.[41] Also undermining the federation were the huge number of duplicated projects across the UAE throughout this period, as each emirate tried to compete with its neighbour by building similar factories and facilities, many of which were left empty due to over-capacity.[42] Dubai's efforts to upgrade its airport triggered a spate of developments elsewhere, including expansions to the Sharjah airport and the construction of new 'international' airports in Ra's al-Khaimah, Fujairah, and even in Al-Ayn. Evidently, each ruler considered such an airport to be a symbol of national pride. Given that Dubai's airport was so centrally located, and even closer to most parts of Sharjah than Sharjah's own airport, it was felt that a true federation should have focused on developing its main hubs rather than embarking on unnecessary ventures. Indeed, by the 1990s many of these new airports were struggling, with most airlines preferring to use the facilities in Dubai and Abu Dhabi. Even Sharjah, which had been the lower Gulf's first airport, was being serviced by fewer international airlines,[43] and soon became little more than an air freight terminal.[44] Closely connected to the airports problem was the over-competition between airlines, especially after the debacle between the partly Abu Dhabi-funded Gulf Air and the Dubai International Airport, which eventually led to Dubai setting up Emirates Airlines and unilaterally declaring an 'open skies' policy outside of federal control.[45] Given the small size of the UAE's population and the heavy competition from other regional airlines, many regarded such duplication as a serious blow to the federation. Indeed, there was even a price war between the two rivals in the 1990s, from which Gulf Air came out worse.[46]

The federation's financial infrastructure was also in something of a weakened state. Despite the establishment of a UAE Currency Board and then later a UAE Central Bank,[47] these institutions rarely had sufficient power to intercede in more serious emirate-level banking disputes, as each emirate's government (and at times its ruling family) maintained control over its own sector and, especially in the case of Dubai, sought to create its own regulatory infrastructure. In addition to the serious banking scandals in Abu Dhabi, Sharjah, and Ra's al-Khaimah that are discussed later in this chapter, the Central Bank also repeatedly failed to intervene in merger disputes and other disasters involving the UAE's various commercial banks. The bank mergers that took place in the mid-1980s in Abu Dhabi and Dubai were entirely the work of emirate-level governments, since it was they rather than the Central Bank that put up the necessary funds.[48] In many ways the huge fraud case that crippled seventeen banks across the UAE in 1999 can also be attributed to the Central Bank's lack of oversight,[49] as although its risk bureau was supposed to be producing a quarterly report on the top borrowers across the federation, full information had clearly not been gathered on banking activities in each emirate.[50] Indeed, Madhav Patel's Solo Industries went bankrupt and led to over $400 million of unrecoverable loans for these banks, greatly damaging the UAE's reputation. A number of the victims were branches of foreign banks, whose boards of directors only refrained from suing the Central Bank because they wished to retain good relations with the governments in their host emirates.[51]

On the international stage, the UAE was also failing to act as a federation, despite the original agreement that foreign policy should fall firmly under central control. Throughout the 1980s the seven emirates failed to present a unified front during the Iran-Iraq War. Abu Dhabi, Ajman, Ra's al-Khaimah, and Fujairah immediately backed their Arab brothers in Iraq, given that Saddam Hussein had requested that the UAE sever all ties with Ayatollah Khomeini,[52] while Dubai, Sharjah, and Umm al-Qawain preferred to maintain relations with Iran, which at that time was still their primary trading partner, and in Dubai's case, was the ancestral home of many of its immigrant merchants. For many years Dubai tried to bat for both sides, with its dry docks frequently repairing Iraqi and Kuwaiti ships that had been damaged by Iranian missiles, while Sheikh Rashid bin Said Al-Maktum was also insisting that radio stations in Dubai broadcast both the Baghdad and Tehran versions of the news.[53] As was noted at the time, this confused stance 'subjected the UAE's federal government, which is supposed to have the sole responsibility for conducting foreign political and diplomatic relations, to embarrassment and pressure from Saudi Arabia and other Gulf states.'[54] Similarly, during the creation of the Desert Storm coalition in late 1990 and early 1991, there were mixed signals from the different emirates. Although both Dubai and Abu Dhabi had been keen to ensure that the UAE was the first Arab state to join the US-led liberation force,[55] some of their neighbours were far less enthusiastic, and remained fearful of an Iraqi backlash.[56] Indeed, during the final years of the Iran-Iraq War and during the build up to the invasion of Kuwait, Saddam Hussein had been taking an increasingly aggressive position against the UAE due to its inability to adhere to its OPEC commitments. This problem stemmed directly from both the lack of a unified federal foreign policy and Dubai's continuing desire for Article 23.

In 1967 Abu Dhabi had decided to follow the lead of Saudi Arabia, Kuwait, and Qatar, and applied to join the OPEC cartel.[57] Sheikh Rashid viewed the organisation's activities with suspicion, and preferred to keep Dubai as an independent oil producer. Thus, when the time came to establish a federal ministry for oil in the early 1970s, it soon became apparent that such an institution would have very little control over oil and oil-related foreign policies outside of Abu Dhabi. This lack of federal control became particularly problematic for Abu Dhabi from 1974 and onwards when OPEC began to treat the UAE as a single entity rather than recognising Abu Dhabi's individual membership. Consequently, when the Arab nationalist states pressed OPEC to introduce production quotas in the late 1970s,[58] Abu Dhabi was obliged to take the sole responsibility for ensuring that the federation's overall oil production met these requirements. With Dubai regularly refusing to accept any pro rata share of the necessary cutbacks, Abu Dhabi was often forced to under-produce in order for the UAE to stay within its OPEC quota. By the late 1980s Dubai's unrestrained production was not only leading to tense relations between Abu Dhabi and OPEC, but was also greatly angering Iraq, as the Ba'ath regime desperately needed oil prices to remain high so that it could finance its war effort and eventual post-war reconstruction.[59] Iraq was threatening to punish all fellow OPEC members that were persistently violating their designated quotas. While most assumed these threats were primarily targeted at Kuwait, Iraq's closest neighbour and eventual victim, it has been claimed that the UAE was actually the worst offender.[60] Indeed, although the organisation's secretary general[61] visited Abu Dhabi in 1987 and received assurances from Sheikh Zayed that the UAE 'was at the forefront of preserving the unity and cohesion of OPEC,' it would seem the cartel privately suspected the UAE of producing an estimated 20 per cent above its assigned quota.[62] Thus when Iraqi tanks rolled into Kuwait City in the summer of 1990 and then occupied pockets of territory along the northern coastline of Saudi Arabia, there was a tangible fear in the UAE that the conflict would extend all the way to the lower Gulf: gas masks were purchased and makeshift bunkers were constructed by both nationals and expatriates, as many expected at least a retaliatory missile strike.[63]

Federal integration and disintegration

By the late 1990s, with the government of Dubai beginning to concentrate on its diversification strategies and the launch of its various new sectors, the emirate became more willing to hand over the control of certain costly services and administrative functions to the federal government. At this time Sheikh Rashid bin Said Al-Maktum's sons shared a belief that Dubai should more fully accept its secondary role in the federation, as this would free up resources that could be more effectively channelled into economic development. This is why many UAE nationals consider 1996 to be the real beginning of the union, as Dubai finally accepted the permanency of the original 1971 constitution[64] and agreed to relinquish command of its highly symbolic military. Indeed, in 1997 the DDF was subsumed into the Union Defence Force and then became part of the new UAE Armed Forces, and the old Dubai barracks at 'Defence roundabout' on Sheikh Zayed Road was finally closed. Given the resistance to military amalgamation in the 1970s, it is remarkable that Dubai officials at this time were quoted as saying '...there is no obvious need to maintain an independent force in Dubai because the UAE Armed Forces provides a fully fledged and cost-effective defence capability.'[65]

With perhaps the exception of slightly improved inter-emirate transport (and even then just between Dubai and Abu Dhabi[66]), and improvements to the new trunk road, little more meaningful centralisation or federal advancement has really taken place since this landmark reconciliation. In many ways it would seem that with the success of its new post-oil economy in recent years, Dubai has renewed its quest for autonomy, despite Sheikh Muhammad bin Rashid Al-Maktum's seemingly enthusiastic taking over of the positions of federal Prime Minister and Vice President from his deceased elder brother. Although Muhammad can never realistically aspire to the UAE presidency, and Dubai can never assume hegemony within the federation given Abu Dhabi's much greater capacity for bankrolling the poorer emirates,[67] Dubai is nevertheless now able to position itself as something of a postmodern city state. As the emirate becomes an even greater global entrepôt and free port, a tourism hub, and a centre of international finance, its needs for collective security and meaningful integration with its federal neighbours may diminish as it forges alliances with international partners.

In addition to the federal workarounds that have been necessary for the unilateral establishment of free zones and real estate projects, there remain many other areas in which Dubai has failed to integrate. Little effort has been made to improve infrastructural links with nearby emirates, and only a few roads connect Dubai to Sharjah, despite the latter serving as a dormitory for countless employees in Dubai. When a traffic-easing slip road was constructed in 2002 close to the border, it remained closed for a number of years with its direction signs blacked out due to a financial dispute between the two municipalities. Similarly, only in 2006 was a proper highway finally completed between Dubai and Fujairah on the east coast. Given the somewhat aggressive marketing strategies of the Dubai Ports Authority, Fujairah's deep water container port, which in many ways should be the federation's primary port given its direct access to the Indian Ocean, has grown little since the late 1990s, while Dubai has greatly increased its share of UAE shipping.[68] The Dubai authority used to claim in its advertising literature that Dubai was always going to be the ultimate destination for incoming cargo to the lower Gulf, therefore it made little sense for shipping companies to use any port other than Rashid or Jebel Ali.[69] Also impeding balanced development across the federation, Dubai's tourism industry has done little if anything to help the nascent tourist industries in Ra's al-Khaimah and Fujairah. In many ways these emirates should be the highlights of tourist trips to the UAE given that they have much greater natural beauty than Dubai, but it seems that that most tour operators working from Dubai are reluctant to recommend anything more than day trips and short stays in other parts of the UAE, preferring to keep as much tourist revenue as possible within the emirate.[70] Consequently, over the last few years the disequilibrium between Dubai and the other northern emirates has greatly increased: Dubai's share of contributions to the UAE's GDP has risen, while the combined share of the four poorest emirates has actually fallen.[71] And as most developments continue to take place in Dubai, many young nationals from Sharjah, Ajman, Umm al-Qawain, Ra's al-Khaimah, and Fujairah have little choice but to commute to work in Dubai, or even share apartments there during the week before returning to their family villas in their home emirates at the weekend. Even though UAE nationals, they are effectively internal migrants and have therefore become guest workers in Dubai.[72]

Although oil rich Abu Dhabi has pursued its own distinct strategies and remains somewhat aloof from the lopsided development taking place on the periphery of Dubai, there still exists a lack of basic co-ordination between the two wealthiest members of the federation. There is little sign that the duplicated investments of the 1970s and 1980s have ceased, and in some cases inter-emirate rivalries continue to undermine the reputation of the union. In particular, following the decline of Gulf Air, Abu Dhabi made plans to withdraw from its partnership with Bahrain, Qatar, and Oman, and to launch its own 'national' airline. In 2003, despite the ongoing success of Dubai's Emirates, Abu Dhabi chose to set up its new Etihad Airways. Incredibly, even though Emirates was in its eighteenth year, the Abu Dhabi government dared to designate Etihad as being the 'official national carrier of the United Arab Emirates,' and installed Sheikh Ahmad bin Saif Al-Nahyan as the chairman,[73] with the clear brief of engaging in perfect competition with Dubai.[74] Indeed, over the last few years Ahmad has purchased several billion dollars worth of Airbus aircraft[75] and has entered into a protracted struggle with Emirates. Etihad has frequently undercut its rival, offers some destinations different from Emirates, and provides transport to Abu Dhabi airport for all customers across the UAE, including even those based in Dubai. Although not a full service carrier, and aimed more at the economy market, it is interesting to note that Sharjah has also now launched its own airline, 'Air Arabia' which offers low cost flights to regional destinations and has also managed to cut into Emirates' market share.[76] While many contend that a mixture of regional and transit customers can currently support all of these airlines, there is a fear that a future downswing in the international air industry will hit the highly fragmented UAE air sector very hard.

While foreign policy differences have largely subsided given the amalgamation of the militaries and the declining relevance of OPEC-related policies due to Dubai's post-oil activities and the unilateral creation of an Abu Dhabi-specific Supreme Petroleum Council,[77] federal control over the UAE's financial infrastructure has nevertheless remained limited. The Central Bank still has little influence over Dubai's banks, and has proven itself incapable of setting any controls on the emirate's interest rates. Unsurprisingly, inflation is a constant source of concern in Dubai—although officially only 6 per cent, it is thought that hyperinflation is setting in.[78] Also beyond the Central Bank's control has been the Dubai International Financial Centre which, as a free zone, need not conform to federal legislation and central regulations;[79] and the VAT bands, with Dubai and each individual emirate free to impose their own rate of tax.[80] Similarly, despite the attempts to set up a federal stock exchange in 1999, the Dubai International Financial Exchange and the parallel Abu Dhabi-based UAE Securities Market have both been outside of federal control, despite their potential for synergy.[81] Lastly, it must also be noted that since 2000 there have been a large number of new emirate-level departments, especially in Dubai, most of which fall under the control of the Dubai Executive Council rather than the relevant federal ministry.[82] A good example would be the new Dubai-specific Knowledge and Human Development Authority, which seems to operate autonomously of both the UAE Ministry for Higher Education and Tanmia—the federal body tasked with addressing labour nationalisation issues. While some of these new institutions have been justified on the grounds that their existence will free up ministries and allow federal employees to concentrate on more pressing matters, many have viewed this new layer of local administration as being unnecessary in such a small country and therefore representing a further step away from centralisation. Certainly, there is considerable overlap, with any memoranda of understanding that do exist between the two layers often remaining very vague. Moreover, in those areas for which the UAE has still not developed ministries (including tourism, aviation, and ports), each emirate has sought to create and upgrade independently its own version, thereby reducing the likelihood of a federal ministry ever being set up. In some of the Dubai-specific government departments and authorities only pictures of Sheikh Muhammad appear on the walls, and rarely will one see pictures of the UAE's President, Sheikh Khalifa bin Zayed Al-Nahyan.

Problems in Abu Dhabi

Despite Dubai's apparent autonomy and its indifference to federal powers, the emirate still cannot operate in complete isolation from its immediate surroundings. Although Dubai now relies on the Abu Dhabi-financed military umbrella and has on occasion sought Abu Dhabi's backing for its more ambitious projects,[83] Dubai needs little else from its wealthier counterpart and nothing at all from the five other emirates. However, neither Dubai's development model nor its ruling bargain can be sustained should there be instabilities or other serious problems elsewhere in the UAE. If internal troubles were to erupt among its neighbours it is likely that Dubai's carefully cultivated international reputation would be tarnished, and its foreign investment and tourism related strategies falter, perhaps even more so than if there were to be a major regional conflict.

Given that Abu Dhabi is the backbone of the UAE and is the only other emirate to command worldwide recognition, instability there would impact severely on Dubai's position. There are now two major divides within the ruling family, and should tensions surface either of these could affect the Al-Nahyan's dynastic strength and thereby weaken Abu Dhabi's ruling bargain. The most obvious of these has been the much discussed factionalism among Sheikh Zayed bin Sultan Al-Nahyan's nineteen sons.[84] The eldest of these *Bani Zayed*, Sheikh Khalifa bin Zayed Al-Nahyan, is now almost sixty, and has therefore always held the advantage of seniority over his brothers. This has been particularly important given that he drew most of his power from his long term status as crown prince, a position that was conferred on him in 1971. And being the eldest son also allowed Khalifa to become the deputy ruler of Abu Dhabi, a position that in some emirates and other traditional monarchies is often ceremonial, but in Khalifa's case was a very real portfolio given Zayed's frequent preoccupation with federal and international affairs. Although his only real federal-level title until 2004 was as deputy supreme commander of the UAE Armed Forces (apart from briefly holding the Minister of Finance and Industry and Minister of Defence positions until 1973[85]), Khalifa took this duty very seriously and regularly insisted on his prerogatives.[86] Given that his overstretched father was the honorary supreme commander, and that the UAE Minister of Defence was always a nominal cabinet post for Dubai's Sheikh Muhammad bin Rashid Al-Maktum, Khalifa's position in the UAE Armed Forces thereby always gave him the greatest day-to-day influence over its military.[87] Similarly, because the UAE Minister for Oil and Petroleum Resources position was another meaningless functionary in the federal government (and has now been renamed the Minister of Energy) as a result of Dubai's unwillingness to cooperate over OPEC matters, Khalifa's long-running chairmanship of his father's Supreme Petroleum Council has always placed Abu Dhabi's oil policy, and therefore the vast bulk of UAE-wide oil policy, within his control.[88] Finally, also of importance has been Khalifa's chairmanship over the Abu Dhabi Investments Authority, which has been responsible for most of the emirate's enormous overseas investments,[89] and his influence over Abu Dhabi's Department of Social Services and Commercial Buildings.[90] The latter, and more specifically its constituent 'Khalifa Committee', dispenses most of the government's properties, grants, and loans to Abu Dhabi nationals, hence Khalifa was always the preeminent distributor of allocated wealth in the emirate.

The second eldest of Sheikh Zayed's sons, Sheikh Sultan bin Zayed Al-Nahyan, is now in his late fifties, and is Sheikh Khalifa's half-brother. Often regarded as having the most approachable personality of the Bani Zayed, Sultan has also lived a famously frugal existence and has shown little interest in property ownership or material wealth. He has always been well liked by the local people and the tribal elders, with whom he regularly consults. In 1978 Zayed decided to appoint Sultan as commander-in-chief of the Union Defence Force despite his very young age, as he wished to confer considerable power on his highly popular son. Yet within just four years Sultan suddenly lost this important military post along with all of his accumulated lesser positions. Some sources attribute this reversal of fortunes to Sultan's 'personal problems'[91] and his tumultuous youth,[92] but given that he took a few of his supporters along with him during his temporary exile,[93] it seems plausible that a serious disagreement may have occurred. Indeed, some veteran nationals claim that Sultan had attempted to gain even more powers, perhaps having been badly advised.[94] There have, in fact, been many instances of such an arrangement in the Al-Nahyan's history, where very often a son would assume responsibilities from his aging father and delegate certain tasks to the 'old sheikh'.[95] This would never have worked with Zayed, who, although in his sixties at the time, was still the driving force behind not only the emirate of Abu Dhabi, but also the nascent federal state. Regardless of the real motivations, since his return to the UAE, Sultan has exercised little real power in either Abu Dhabi or the federal government. He has been an essentially ceremonial deputy prime minister in the Council of Ministers, has held the chairmanship of the politically marginal Abu Dhabi Public Works Department,[96] and chaired the now defunct Zayed Centre for Coordination and Follow-Up think tank.[97] Moreover, both of Sultan's other pet projects in Abu Dhabi have had a chequered history up till late 2007, with the enormous Zayed Mosque still incomplete and having run far over schedule, and with the development of the manmade Lulu Island having also proved costly and problematic. As such, apart from a board position on the Supreme Petroleum Council and his continuing unofficial role of visiting bedouin leaders,[98] Sultan has remained firmly outside of the loop for over two decades.

Underneath these two half-brothers has been a powerful bloc of six full brothers whose mother is Sheikha Fatima bint Mubarak Al-Qitbi. As Sheikh Zayed's favoured wife, she continues to be regarded as the UAE's 'First Lady' and events have been recently held to honour her as 'Mother of the Nation'.[99] As something approaching a cohesive political grouping in an otherwise highly fragmented family, the brothers have collectively acquired more power as they have grown older. Partly due to their western education background, they are thought to have much in common with the emerging technocrats in the federal government, and have between them won control of foreign affairs and parts of the military, domestic intelligence, information services, and other institutions closely connected to national security. The eldest of these *Bani Fatima* is the well known Sheikh Muhammad bin Zayed Al-Nahyan, who, now in his late forties, is one of the most powerful figures in both Abu Dhabi and the federation. Although a long-serving member of the Supreme Petroleum Council and, in 2003, occupying the new position of 'deputy crown prince', most of Muhammad's early power came from his position in the UDF and the UAE Armed Forces. Being the recipient of some of Sheikh Sultan's lost powers, Muhammad eventually became chief of staff in 1993[100] and played the leading role in beefing up the UAE's military since its exposed weakness during the Kuwait crisis. Indeed, it was his signature that always appeared on the UAE Armed Forces' massive high-tech arms procurements of the late 1990s. The next-eldest of Fatima's sons is Sheikh Hamdan bin Zayed Al-Nahyan, whose official designation for many years was Minister of State for Foreign Affairs (the supposed number two position in the ministry). Given that the actual minister was a token Ajmani,[101] the real power always resided with Hamdan, who was widely understood to have been second only to his father in formulating federal foreign policy. Sheikh Hazza bin Zayed Al-Nahyan, the third of the Bani Fatima, has for some time been the chief of Abu Dhabi's Security and Intelligence Services; Sheikh Tahnun bin Zayed Al-Nahyan, the fourth son, has served as the chairman of the president's private department, while the fifth, Sheikh Mansur bin Zayed Al-Nahyhan, has occupied the relatively new cabinet position of Minister of the Presidential Office since 2001.[102] Significantly, the youngest of the Bani Fatima, Sheikh Abdullah bin Zayed Al-Nahyan, was placed in charge of the Ministry of Information and Culture, first as its undersecretary,[103] then as the actual minister. Thus he was effectively responsible for all censorship across the federation.[104]

When the eighty-six year old Sheikh Zayed passed away in late 2004 there was understandably some concern among both nationals and expatriates over the succession process given that many assumed that the increasingly powerful Bani Fatima bloc, and in particular the astute and ambitious Sheikh Muhammad, would attempt to bypass Sheikh Khalifa and thereby assume both the rulership of Abu Dhabi and the UAE presidency. The tightly controlled flow of information surrounding Zayed's death did little to assuage people's fears, with many supposedly well-connected medical professionals claiming as early as 11 October that Zayed had either passed away or, at best, was receiving life support. On 12 October stocks in Union National Bank (a national bank guaranteed by the ruling family[105]) plummeted and websites relating to pancreatic cancer (Zayed's supposed condition) were blocked by the Etisalat proxy. For the next three weeks, hearsay gathered pace, speculative travel reservations were being made, ATMs emptied, and, in some cases, food hoarding began. To make matters worse, on 1 November it was announced to the media that Zayed had presided personally over a reshuffle of the Council of Ministers,[106] although tellingly the newspaper reports were unable to provide the usual official presidential photograph or indeed any photographic evidence of the event. Within less than 24 hours of this supposed reshuffle, the formal announcement was finally made that Zayed had died. Abu Dhabi's muezzins called through the night, all businesses were closed immediately, and all shops (apart from those supplying basic necessities) were to close and to switch off their streetlights or risk being fined. Well into the following day, the muezzins continued their lament, and throughout the afternoon a curfew was placed on motor vehicles being driven in the city. Following the state burial at the unfinished Zayed Mosque, prayers at the Sheikh Sultan bin Zayed Mosque, and the respectful visits of various Arab heads of state in addition to France's Jacques Chirac and Britain's Prince Charles, the curfew was finally lifted.[107] All of these events took place at exactly the same time that the rest of the world was glued to their television screens watching the US presidential election night broadcast and its lengthy post-result analyses. Indeed, as would so often seem to be the case with sensitive news relating to the UAE,[108] the news of Zayed's passing was therefore completely buried in the international media, warranting barely a line of scroll-text on CNN and the BBC. As a result, international investors, would-be tourists, and other interested parties were barely aware of the situation. Moreover, on 4 November, a forty day period of official mourning was declared, with the public sector to receive a seven day holiday and with the private sector to have a three day holiday. Although this period was not properly observed in Dubai,[109] the timing was nevertheless most significant for Abu Dhabi and the rest of the UAE, given that these holidays naturally rolled into the upcoming *Eid al-Fitr* vacation and thereby gave the federal and various emirate-level governments a considerable and convenient breathing space of over two full weeks.

Despite the alarming opacity of these circumstances, it soon became apparent that agreements had been reached and a compromise solution found for both the Bani Fatima and Sheikh Khalifa's supporters. The succession was smooth, with Khalifa assuming his father's old positions and Sheikh Muhammad being immediately upgraded from deputy crown prince to crown prince, despite Khalifa having two sons of office-bearing age.[110] Moreover, most other key members of the bloc appeared to have been accommodated. In particular, Sheikh Mansur has maintained his cabinet position while Sheikh Hamdan has become a deputy prime minister in the Council of Ministers alongside Sheikh Sultan. Unlike

Sultan's more nominal position, it would seem that Hamdan's role has been configured to be a powerful assistant to the prime minister. Similarly, with the Ministry of Information and Culture now disbanded, Sheikh Abdullah's status has been considerably strengthened following his appointment as Minister of Foreign Affairs. Perhaps most importantly, given that Muhammad has remained cautious and been careful not to position himself as a direct rival to Khalifa,[111] he has been allowed to emerge as something of an emirate-level prime minister for Abu Dhabi. Indeed, in early 2007 his crown prince position was greatly strengthened as greater executive powers were transferred to his office. While some have interpreted this as an indication of an internal power struggle, it is really more a display of trust, as Muhammad has been given the authority he needs to implement Abu Dhabi's development strategies. Muhammad's Mubadala Corporation, directed by Khaldun bin Khalifa Al-Mubarak and staffed by many of Muhammad's closest advisors from earlier projects,[112] has been given more or less a free reign in determining the direction of the emirate's development. Nevertheless, by installing certain checks and balances on Muhammad and the Bani Fatima, Khalifa has ensured that something of an equilibrium remains between himself and all of his siblings. In particular, in addition to retaining personal control over the Supreme Petroleum Council, Khalifa has indirectly supervised Abu Dhabi's overseas investments by appointing his non-Bani Fatima younger half brother Sheikh Ahmad bin Zayed Al-Nahyan as his replacement for chairing ADIA. And by linking his youngest son, Sheikh Muhammad bin Khalifa Al-Nahyan, with both Ahmad and the non-Bani Fatima director of the Abu Dhabi Department of Economy, Sheikh Hamad bin Zayed Al-Nahyan, Khalifa has effectively created a triumvirate of control over the emirate's finances.[113] It can also be argued that even though Muhammad has now become the deputy supreme commander of the UAE Armed Forces (after Khalifa replaced their father as supreme commander), his real control over the military has actually declined given that he has had to begin sharing power with a newly appointed chief of staff, Hamad bin Muhammad Al-Thai Al-Rumaithi[114]—the UAE Armed Forces' former director of military intelligence[115] and a close ally of Khalifa. It is also noticeable that Khalifa has taken on a function not dissimilar from Sheikh Sultan's, as he has become more actively involved in tribal matters. Indeed, he has sought to maintain a strong base of support in the emirate's hinterland by making frequent trips to meetings of regional majaalis. In the summer of 2005 he toured extensively through western Abu Dhabi and curbed the powers of the region's governor.[116] Crucially, this active role in traditional politics could not easily be undertaken by other, younger members of the family, especially those with western educational and more business-focused backgrounds.

Although less obvious, the second major divide within the Al-Nahyan family is in some ways far more serious, as it involves the steady decline of an entire parallel branch of the family that has strong historical claims to positions of influence, and which today should be on a much more even footing with the Bani Zayed. The roots of this potential discord can only really understood by recalling a series of bloody fratricides in the early twentieth century and by considering the power vacuums that existed following the subsequent successions of Sheikh Shakhbut bin Sultan Al-Nahyan and Sheikh Zayed. In 1909 Abu Dhabi lost its great patriarch, Sheikh Zayed bin Khalifa Al-Nahyan, to natural causes. His eldest son, Sheikh Khalifa bin Zayed Al-Nahyan, was chosen to succeed after having earned sufficient respect from the rest of the family, but given that Khalifa preferred to live a peaceful life, he declined to take his father's place, thereby passing the mantle of rule to his next eldest brother, Sheikh Tahnun bin Zayed Al-Nahyan. Unfortunately, Tahnun was an invalid and lived for just three more years,[117] leaving no male heirs and thereby reopening the question of succession in 1912.[118] Although again offered the position, Khalifa remained disinterested,[119] thereby forcing the tribal elders to skip Zayed's unpopular third son, Sheikh Said bin Zayed Al-Nahyan, and install the more capable and respected fourth son, Sheikh Hamdan bin Zayed Al-Nahyan, as ruler. In many ways, Hamdan's ten-year rule was successful, particularly his instrumental role in settling a serious dispute between the rulers of Umm Al-Qawain and Sharjah that would have likely plunged the lower Gulf into a war that Britain (preoccupied with the First World War in Europe) would not have been able to stop.[120] Hamdan's reign was cut short by an assassination orchestrated by two of his younger brothers, Sheikh Sultan bin Zayed Al-Nahyan and Sheikh Saqr bin Zayed Al-Nahyan.[121] It seems that due to the collapse of the pearling industry at that time and the subsequent economic recession, Hamdan was unable to provide the customary payments to his younger brothers and rivals, and therefore they had chosen to plot against him,[122] perhaps inspired by their avaricious wives.[123] Interestingly, among his family members who fled Abu Dhabi at this time was his daughter, Sheikha Latifa bint Hamdan Al-Nahyan, the future wife of Dubai's Sheikh Rashid bin Said Al-Maktum.[124] Sultan assumed leadership for the next four years,[125] until 1926, when at a dinner party he was shot dead by his former co-conspirator.[126] Saqr had seized his chance because had he waited any longer then Sultan's eldest son, Sheikh Shakhbut bin Sultan Al-Nahyan, would have succeeded.

This was the point when the surviving Sheikh Khalifa, disgusted by the murderous nature of his younger siblings, chose to re-enter Abu Dhabi politics by forming a pact against Sheikh Saqr that included prominent members of the Manasir tribe and even Saqr's disaffected youngest son, Sheikh Muhammad bin Saqr Al-Nahyan. Upon discovery of the plot, Saqr killed Muhammad, prompting one of Muhammad's loyal Baluchi slaves to attempt the assassination of the ruler. Although Saqr managed to escape from the slave, a man from the Manasir hunted him down and finally killed him in 1928.[127] With no obvious successor, Khalifa temporarily installed his only son, Sheikh Muhammad bin Khalifa

Al-Nahyan, in the ruler's fort, and despatched a powerful bedouin contingent to the town to ensure law and order. While two of the deceased Sheikh Sultan's sons had sought exile in Saudi Arabia under the protection of the Sheikh of Al-Ihas,[128] his eldest and youngest sons, Sheikh Shakhbut and Sheikh Zayed bin Sultan respectively, were residing in the Dhahira area of Buraimi[129] as they were being sheltered by the local wali, Sheikh Ahmad bin Muhammad Al-Dhahiri.[130] Khalifa's secretary wrote to Shakhbut and pressed him to return to Abu Dhabi and take over,[131] and Shakhbut duly succeeded. Fortunately for the sheikhdom, the fratricides came to end, with Shakhbut's influential mother, Sheikha Salama bint Buti Al-Qubaysi,[132] publicly condemning any future assassination attempts.[133] Thus, although Shakhbut proved to be an overly cautious and somewhat ineffective ruler,[134] Khalifa's mediating role had nevertheless brought about a much needed period of political stability.

Given that Sheikh Shakhbut's sons were too young to support their father's new administration, Sheikh Khalifa's son, Sheikh Muhammad, was still relied upon heavily, and throughout the 1930s and 1940s was effectively the third most powerful man in Abu Dhabi, after Shakhbut and Sheikh Zayed.[135] Similarly, by the time of Zayed's succession in 1966, the Khalifa branch of the family were again of enormous assistance as Zayed's eldest sons were still only teenagers and the new ruler desperately needed more mature and experienced men whose loyalty he could rely on. Indeed, of Khalifa's six grandsons, the *Bani Muhammad bin Khalifa*, all assumed important positions of power during the early years of Zayed's administration. In particular, the most senior of these, Sheikh Hamdan bin Muhammad Al-Nahyan, was one of Zayed's most vociferous supporters during Shakhbut's deposition, and was at one point even considered as a potential crown prince should anything have happened to Zayed's sons.[136] He was made *wali* of Das island during the late 1960s—a key position given the territory's proximity to Abu Dhabi's offshore oilfields,[137] and then became the first chairman of Abu Dhabi's new Public Works Department,[138] before later serving as the UAE's deputy prime minister for much of the 1970s and the early 1980s. The second eldest grandson, Sheikh Mubarak bin Muhammad Al-Nahyan, was appointed chief of police during the critical first few years of Zayed's rule, and was later rewarded with control of the Ministry of the Interior. Sheikh Tahnun bin Muhammad Al-Nahyan, the third of the Bani Muhammad bin Khalifa, has for some years been a member of the Supreme Petroleum Council and is a former chairman of the Abu Dhabi National Oil Company (ADNOC), in addition to holding the deputy chairmanship of the Abu Dhabi Executive Council. Perhaps most significantly, even today Tahnun remains the *wali* of Abu Dhabi's eastern region, which includes the enormous responsibility of governing the emirate's second largest city, Al-Ayn.[139] Notable among the other grandsons have been Sheikh Saif bin Muhammad Al-Nahyan, who was chairman of the Abu Dhabi Planning Department and the UAE's Minister of Health for much of the 1970s,[140] and Sheikh Surur bin Muhammad Al-Nahyan who was the original chairman of Abu Dhabi's Department of Justice, the chamberlain of the Presidential Court, the chairman of the Abu Dhabi Department of Water and Electricity,[141] and at one point also the chairman of the UAE Central Bank.[142]

Today, many of these grandsons remain influential, and many of their own sons have formed the latest generation of the Bani Muhammad bin Khalifa. In particular, Sheikh Hamdan's eldest son, Sheikh Khalifa bin Hamdan Al-Nahyan, was up until recently the chairman of the Abu Dhabi Department of Economy, while his other sons include Sheikh Hamad bin Hamdan Al-Nahyan, a successful businessman with the nickname 'The Rainbow Sheikh' given his fleet of multicoloured cars, and Sheikh Sultan bin Hamdan Al-Nahyan, the chairman of Protocol and the Presidential Guest House. Sheikh Mubarak's eldest surviving son, Sheikh Nahyan bin Mubarak Al-Nahyan, is the UAE's Minister for

Higher Education and Scientific Research and the president of Zayed University, while his other son, Sheikh Hamdan bin Mubarak Al-Nahyan, was previously the chairman of Abu Dhabi's Civil Aviation Department (and was at one point also the chairman of Gulf Air). Similarly prominent have been Sheikh Tahnun's sons, who between them hold positions on the Abu Dhabi Executive Council, the chairmanship of the powerful General Industry Corporation (essentially a government parastatal), and the chairmanship of Abu Dhabi's Department of Tourism.

While there have been a few major Bani Muhammad bin Khalifa promotions in recent years, including Sheikh Hamdan bin Mubarak's elevation to become Minister of Public Works and Housing,[143] and Sheikh Ahmad bin Saif Al-Nahyan's appointment as chairman of the new Etihad Airways, the family branch has nevertheless now lost most of its former strength, as the Bani Zayed have matured and assumed an increasing number of high profile portfolios. Sheikh Hamdan bin Muhammad's old position of deputy prime minister has gone to Sheikh Hamdan bin Zayed and Sheikh Sultan bin Zayed, while Sheikh Surur's chairmanship of the Central Bank has also been lost (a remarkable turn of events, given that some believed Surur could have become Sheikh Khalifa's new crown prince following Sheikh Zayed's death).[144] Similarly, the branch's members have ceded the directorship of ADNOC, the chamberlainship of the Presidential Court, and indeed almost all of the ministerial portfolios that they had accumulated during the 1970s and 1980s. Most recently, Sheikh Khalifa bin Hamdan has now lost the chairmanship of the Department of Economy to Sheikh Hamad bin Zayed. Rather worryingly, this trend seems set to continue, as the youngest members of the Bani Zayed will soon seek a share of power. Many feel that out of respect for the key historic role played by their great grandfather, the Bani Muhammad bin Khalifa should be more generously compensated, perhaps with some kind of deputy rulership position alongside the crown prince. For most Abu Dhabi nationals,

245

the natural candidate would be Sheikh Nahyan, who, alongside his ailing father, is perhaps the most popular member of the ruling family today. This present balance of power may become a source of instability in future years. While some consider the Bani Muhammad bin Khalifa to be little more than a distaff line of the family and compare it with the 'one-gun Juma' faction in Dubai, there is really little similarity given that the former group's unswerving loyalty was the key to much of Zayed's early success, while the latter bloc never really had a genuine claim on power as Sheikh Juma bin Maktum Al-Maktum was merely Sheikh Said bin Maktum Al-Maktum's younger brother, and frequently sided with Arab nationalist agitators.[145]

Lastly, also a major source of concern has been Abu Dhabi's vulnerability with regard to financial scandals. Although the home of the UAE Central Bank, the emirate has repeatedly failed to eliminate the grey area that often exists in traditional monarchies between the ruling family's wealth and the state's finances. Indeed, on a number of occasions this weakness has been exposed, and in some cases has damaged the UAE's international reputation, and, by association, Dubai's too. Most notably, in 1991 the Al-Nahyan family-backed Bank of Credit Commerce International (BCCI) collapsed spectacularly against a backdrop of corruption, bureaucratic self-interest, and criminal proceedings. The ensuing investigation conducted by US senators Hank Brown and future presidential hopeful John Kerry uncovered 'an elaborate corporate spider-web... which was both an essential component of its spectacular growth and of its eventual collapse.'[146] Moreover, their report claimed that the BCCI was unlike ordinary banks given that from its earliest days it was 'made up of multiplying layers of entities, related to one another through an impenetrable series of holding companies, affiliates, subsidiaries, banks-within-banks, insider dealings and nominee relationships.'[147] Specifically, this impenetrable layering was believed to have facilitated the operation of a number of illegal mechanisms ranging from shell corporations, secrecy havens, kickbacks for front men, and the use of falsified documentation. Most worryingly, the bank's opaqueness and its ability to evade existing controls in the UAE allowed its administrators to engage in a range of activities including money laundering, gun running, the management of prostitution, and even the financing of terrorist organisations.[148]

Significantly, the findings of a British report carried out by Price Waterhouse on behalf of the Bank of England focused on the connection between the ruling family of Abu Dhabi and the bank, and demonstrated that the link between the two entities was 'far beyond the ordinary relationship of a bank to either its shareholders or depositors.'[149] Indeed, it was shown that although members of the Al-Nahyan family held more than $750 million worth of BCCI shares by the time of its collapse, their total contribution to the bank's capitalisation was only $500,000, namely the initial start-up contribution paid to the bank by Sheikh Zayed in the early 1970s. Crucially, Price Waterhouse claimed that the majority of these supposed shares were acquired as a result of fake investments: the sheikhs' representatives (possibly without the knowledge of their employers) would make payments on a risk-free, guaranteed return basis, thereby allowing the bank to project an illusion of substantial royal backing.[150] In addition to these buy-back arrangements, it was also reported that the BCCI's senior managers, most of whom were Pakistani expatriates or Abu Dhabi nationals, had been handling 'almost every financial matter of consequence for Sheikh Zayed and his family, as well as planning, managing, and carrying out trips abroad, and providing a wide range of services limited only by the desires of the Al-Nahyan family itself.'[151] Most notably, the founder of BCCI, Agha Abedi, had for more than twenty years managed personal portfolios for members of the family, while Ghanim Al-Mazrui had served as both Zayed's financial advisor and as a board member of the BCCI.[152] Perhaps most damningly, when the international auditors determined that these and other administrators had received substantial personal financial benefits from the BCCI and had been responsible for bogus loans and other misdemeanours, few were brought to justice.[153] Remarkably, the expatriates involved were not deported to face charges in their home countries and served out their house arrests in Abu Dhabi in relative luxury,[154] while many of the nationals involved were held indefinitely, thereby denying foreign investigators any access to them.[155] Furthermore, requested documents were not made available, with the UAE prosecutor appointed by Zayed ordering that they should remain confidential.[156] Most incredibly, a number of the implicated administrators were actually re-hired, albeit behind the scenes. Regardless of the exact nature of the three dimensional relationship between the ruling family, the emirate-level government, and the BCCI, the conclusions reached by the investigators tarnished greatly the UAE's international image. Indeed, as a result of their observations and experiences in Abu Dhabi, the senators summarised their report by stating that

'Sheikh Zayed, according to his own attorneys in submissions with the Federal Reserve, owns most of Abu Dhabi's resources and land, and the laws themselves are styled as decrees by Sheikh Zayed, in consultation with other bodies and officials who are appointed by Sheikh Zayed... therefore the notion that the UAE's justice system is somehow completely independent from the interests of the ruling family of Abu Dhabi stretches credulity.'[157]

Most damagingly for Dubai, during its high profile hosting of the annual meetings of the WTO, the IMF, and the World Bank more than a decade later in 2003,[158] the BCCI fiasco was resurrected by a disgruntled former Central Bank employee, prompting a large and uncomplimentary article on the UAE to be featured in the *Wall Street Journal* that week.[159]

Although the Al-Nahyan family quickly repaid most BCCI investors in full, being mindful of lawsuits that could be filed by larger deposit holders against the majority shareholder, and although the Union National Bank was created out of the remnants of the BCCI to provide continuity for former customers,[160] remarkably, since then Abu Dhabi's financial infrastructure appears not to have gained any greater transparency, with several further incidents having weakened the emirate's reputation and embarrassed its UAE neighbours.

Problems in Sharjah

Although Sharjah has no real influence in the UAE's federal government or any control over the UAE's military, and although it has far fewer natural resources than Abu Dhabi,[161] its continuing stability is nevertheless of vital importance to Dubai given its close geographic proximity and its emerging role as a low-cost dormitory for many of Dubai's less affluent employees.[162] Indeed, in many ways Sharjah has now become an outlying suburb of Dubai, as the two cities, together with Ajman to Sharjah's east, have now really formed one giant conurbation, with barely no undeveloped land remaining along their shared borders.[163] Tellingly, the early morning traffic jam along the main arterial highway between Sharjah and Dubai is entirely in the direction of Dubai, while in the early evening the flow is reversed. Unfortunately, Sharjah's ruling Al-Qasimi family has never enjoyed the same strong ruling bargain as that of the Al-Maktum family in Dubai, and in many ways Sharjah remains the least politically settled emirate in the UAE. Moreover, much like Abu Dhabi, there have been a series of financial scandals that have brought unwanted attention to Sharjah, and, most worryingly, on occasion these have allowed external non-UAE entities to gain political and economic influence in the emirate.

Certainly, as early as the 1950s Britain had recognised that Sharjah was becoming less likely to play a positive contributing role to any future federation given that its ruler was facing serious internal opposition and was, as previously discussed, openly allowing Arab League agents to visit his sheikhdom.[164] Since Sheikh Saqr bin Sultan Al-Qasimi had ousted his father, Sheikh

Sultan bin Saqr Al-Qasimi, in 1951,[165] visitors to his house were alarmed to see pictures of Nasser hanging on the walls, and perturbed to hear him informally discuss the benefits of the 'great Arab nation' and of the United Arab Republic. Moreover, Saqr indiscreetly visited Cairo and Damascus for long periods, and even allowed Egyptian military officials to stay in his house as honoured guests.[166] These attitudes were believed to be exacerbating the National Front activities that were taking place in Dubai at that time, and Britain's fears were realised in 1958 when Saqr concluded a common market agreement with Fujairah and expressed his intention of inviting Umm al-Qawain and Ajman to join, before then seeking Arab League recognition for this new Sharjah-led union of northern sheikhdoms.[167] Divisions within the family duly emerged, as many of Saqr's relatives understood that such a path would soon lead to their sheikhdom's self-destruction. Saqr had already become paranoid that elements within the Qawasim were plotting his demise, and he confided to the British agent in 1959 that a plot was being hatched against him by his cousin, Sheikh Saqr bin Rashid Al-Qasimi, and the ruler of Ra's al-Khaimah, Sheikh Saqr bin Muhammad Al-Qasimi.[168] Although Saqr bin Sultan doubled his bodyguards accordingly,[169] he almost died in a plane crash in 1960[170] and remained suspicious that assassins had been hired by his rivals.

Although avoiding fratricide, Sheikh Saqr's hosting of the two leading administrators of the Arab League in 1964 and his simultaneous agreements to allow the opening of an Arab League office in Sharjah and the receiving of Arab League seed money[171] were together enough to ensure his demise and to re-open the question of succession. Significantly, the British agent was 'dismayed that Saqr had thrown down the first explicit challenge to Britain's position',[172] and Saqr was promptly summoned to the agent's headquarters where he was shown a document supposedly signed by members of his family (although apparently the only signature was that of his successor), before being escorted out through the back entrance, so as to avoid his armed retainers waiting at the front. After Saqr had then been sent on a plane to Bahrain and then onwards to his exile in Cairo,[173] the agent then invited Saqr's well liked cousin, Sheikh Khalid bin Muhammad Al-Qasimi, to assume the rulership.[174] Given that Khalid was little more than a paint shop owner at the time (running a large store based in Deira),[175] this was a remarkably ambitious example of British political engineering, but was believed to have provided the Qawasim with a much needed compromise solution.

Unfortunately, stability in Sharjah was short lived, with Sheikh Saqr remaining confident that if he should return home then his people would still recognise him as the legitimate ruler. In early 1972, following Sheikh Khalid's inability to prevent Iran seizing Sharjah's Abu Musa island,[176] and a year after his erstwhile British enemies had withdrawn from the lower Gulf, Saqr judged that the time was right to reclaim his position.[177] A band of armed mercenaries, funded by Ahmad Hassan Al-Bakr of Iraq's Ba'ath Party[178] and elements in Ra's al-Khaimah,[179] was placed under Saqr's command, and an assault was launched on Khalid's lightly guarded seaside palace under the cover of darkness. Nearby residents were alerted by the sound of gunfire and Sheikh Muhammad bin Rashid Al-Maktum who was by that time the commander of the Dubai Defence Force,[180] drove to Sharjah with a small force. Unfortunately, by the time Muhammad arrived Saqr's men had already overcome Khalid's bodyguards and had barricaded themselves inside the palace along with thirty hostages. Loudspeaker negotiations began, with Muhammad offering Saqr personal safety if he allowed the DDF to enter the fort. After 16 hours Saqr finally surrendered and the DDF soldiers, joined by a number of Abu Dhabi Defence Force reinforcements who had arrived later, released the hostages. All were uninjured, except for Khalid who was dead. It was unclear to Muhammad if this killing had been an accident or was an act of murder, so Saqr was merely imprisoned.[181]

After a period of deliberation between Sheikh Rashid bin Said Al-Maktum and some other members of the Supreme Council of Rulers, it was decided that one of Sheikh Khalid's younger brothers should be installed as the new ruler of Sharjah, given that Khalid's eldest son, Sheikh Faysal bin Khalid Al-Qasimi, was only eighteen years old at the time. Significantly, the SCR chose Sheikh Sultan bin Muhammad Al-Qasimi who, although in his early thirties, was regarded as one of the most educated men in Sharjah and had already served as the UAE's first Minister for Education.[182] Unfortunately, Sultan was not able to appease all branches of the Qawasim, and was viewed by many as an illegitimate ruler given that he was appointed by an external consensus rather than by a family council. By the 1980s he was increasingly criticised for extravagant and unnecessary 'prestige projects' in the emirate including upgrades to the airport, an unfinished television station, and several empty museums. Convinced that he would enjoy popular support, the ruler's passed over elder brother (who had been serving as Sharjah's deputy ruler), Sheikh Abdul-Aziz bin Muhammad Al-Qasimi, seized an opportunity in the summer of 1987 to launch a coup d'état. The main palaces and government offices were occupied by Abdul-Aziz's supporters,[183] and a radio broadcast was made that claimed Sultan had voluntarily stepped down due to his mismanagement of Sharjah's economy.[184] Crucially, Sultan was in Britain at that time, working on his PhD thesis, and had to be invited to return to the UAE by Sheikh Rashid, who had hastily convened a special session of the SCR to be held in Al-Ayn. Keen to reinstate Sultan and restore stability on their border, the Al-Maktum family pressed the other SCR members to force Abdul-Aziz to step down. Although there was some reluctance to intervene from Abu Dhabi (which may have unofficially supported Abdul-Aziz's cause[185]), the matter was solved after six days of negotiations when Sultan agreed to appoint Abdul-Aziz as his crown prince.[186]

As soon as Sheikh Sultan believed his position to be sufficiently secure, he stripped Sheikh Abdul-Aziz of his crown prince and deputy ruler titles and appointed Sheikh Saqr's youngest brother, Sheikh Ahmad bin Sultan Al-Qasimi, as his new deputy ruler. While some viewed this as a premature move on Sultan's part, the threat from Abdul-Aziz had considerably diminished given that the latter had formed a friendship with Sheikh Zayed bin Sultan Al-Nahyan and had been incorporated into Abu Dhabi's establishment.[187] Indeed, Zayed appointed Abdul-Aziz to be his special envoy on several occasions, and he was allowed to live in Al-Nahyan maintained palaces in both Al-Ayn and Morocco[188] until his death in 2004. Future political stability does, however, seem far from assured as there has not yet emerged a strong candidate to succeed Sultan. Tragically, Sultan's eldest son, Sheikh Muhammad bin Sultan Al-Qasimi, died while on a visit to Britain in 1999.[189] In any event, given that his mother was from Dubai, he would not have been regarded as being a pure Sharjah national, despite his father's position.[190] Although Sultan's second son, Sheikh Khalid bin Sultan Al-Qasimi, does have a mother from Sharjah[191] (who is the granddaughter of a previous Sharjah ruler[192]) at the time of writing he is only thirty years old and has not yet accumulated sufficient popular support or positions of responsibility within the emirate's government. A crown prince has been appointed, but this has been an unusual choice given that the forty-seven year old Sheikh Sultan bin Muhammad bin Sultan Al-Qasimi is the youngest son of another of Saqr's younger brothers (albeit also the ruler's brother in law).[193] Although this new Sultan has been the director of the ruler's office for several years and would perhaps reunite the two diverging branches of the ruling family,[194] he is likely to face strong opposition from Sheikh Faysal, the eldest son of the former ruler (Sheikh Khalid bin Muhammad), who is now believed to be supported by Abu Dhabi. Certainly, Faysal was appointed by Zayed to be the UAE's first Minister for Youth and Sports in 1991,[195] and has since been selected to join the federal government's representations to the United Nations.[196] As such, a third Sharjah coup since the creation of the UAE remains possible.

Further compounding Sharjah's problems have been a series of financial crises, which, although not on the scale of Abu Dhabi's BCCI scandal, have nevertheless exposed the emirate to foreign interference and have on occasion considerably reduced investor confidence in the emirate and its neighbours. Indeed, although by the late 1980s Sheikh Zayed had stepped in and taken care of Sheikh Sultan's debts, this was not enough to prevent the collapse of Sharjah's four commercial banks in 1989 after the Sharjah government had defaulted on loans of over $500 million. Most worryingly, the UAE Central Bank was unable to intervene and the door was left open for a Saudi consortium to step in and provide a rescue package.[197] Significantly for Sharjah, this financial assistance came with a considerable price, as Saudi Arabia gained much greater influence in the emirate, and was eventually able to persuade the ruler to introduce a series of emirate-level laws intended to maintain the outward appearance of Islamic propriety in the city. In particular, alcohol was completely prohibited (even in hotels and private residences), and more recently a number of stringent 'decency laws' have been declared and enforced. These have covered matters such as dress codes, public conduct, gender separation, and promiscuity.[198] At one point Sharjah even attempted to encourage federal immigration officials to deny residence visas to single women under the age of thirty in an effort to curb the influx of prostitutes into the UAE.[199] While it can be argued that such requirements are necessary for maintaining the important religious and cultural legitimacy components of the Qawasim's ruling bargain, most believe that Sultan's actions have been over austere and have prevented Sharjah from attracting foreign investment and tourists of its own, and thereby benefiting from Dubai's nearby successes.[200] Given that Sharjah had been running shopping festivals long before the Dubai Shopping Festival began,[201] and given that Sharjah had been the main tourist destination in the UAE in the 1980s, the laws have been blamed for stalling the emirate's diversification efforts. More recently, Sharjah nationals still remain concerned about external interference as it is feared that Saudi influence is soon likely to be replaced by Iranian influence. It is increasingly likely that Crescent Oil of Iran will supply Sharjah's energy needs in the near future—although there are political delays in Tehran over the matter, the infrastructure would seem to be in place, and it is thought that a close relationship will develop.[202]

Problems in other emirates

As part of the 'greater Dubai' conurbation, Ajman is another important dormitory city as it serves as an even cheaper source of accommodation for Dubai's workers than Sharjah. Fortunately for Dubai, Ajman has enjoyed great stability for many years and seems unlikely to suffer from any major upheavals. Although some members of its ruling family controversially approached Egypt during the 1950s and 1960s to seek financial assistance,[203] the Al-Nu'aymi have generally proved to be a strong and close-knit dynasty. Remarkably, Ajman has had only four different rulers since 1900, and each succession has been a straightforward affair in which the eldest son has succeeded his deceased father. The only exception being the 1981 succession following the death of Sheikh Rashid bin Humayd Al-Nu'aymi, who had outlived his eldest son, Sheikh Ali bin Rashid Al-Nu'aymi. Fortunately, Rashid's second eldest son, Sheikh Humayd bin Rashid Al-Nu'aymi, was well liked and promptly installed, and although Humayd's two eldest sons have since died in car and motorcycle accidents,[204] his third son and crown prince, Sheikh Amr bin Humayd Al-Nu'aymi, seems unchallenged.[205]

Similarly, Umm al-Qawain has remained relatively unproblematic. Despite a series of fratricides in the 1920s that culminated with the murders of the ruler, Sheikh Abdullah bin Rashid Al-

Mu'alla in 1923, and his cousin and immediate successor, Sheikh Hamad bin Ibrahim Al-Mu'alla in 1929, the emirate has since avoided any serious political instability. During the 1960s Sheikh Ahmad bin Rashid Al-Mu'alla shunned all connections with Arab nationalism and the National Front, and was even quoted as stating that 'the British agent was always right and had special gifts from God.'[206] Moreover, from the 1970s onwards almost all positions of power were occupied by the sons and grandsons of Ahmad, whose fifty-two year reign only came to an end in 1981. Ahmad's popular second eldest son, Sheikh Rashid bin Ahmad Al-Mu'alla, succeeded his father unopposed, and in turn his eldest son, Sheikh Saud bin Rashid Al-Mu'alla, is both a strong crown prince and the deputy ruler, as well as being the director of the National Bank of Umm al-Qawain.[207] Saud is also married to one of the daughters of the ruler of Ra's al-Khaimah,[208] thus further strengthening his position within the UAE. Perhaps the only concern in Umm al-Qawain has been the ruling family's somewhat cavalier attitude towards the supply of alcohol. As with Dubai, licences are required for both the sale and consumption of alcohol, but with the emirate's operation of a huge shop at the Barracuda beach resort, many nationals and expatriates from all over the UAE come specifically to Umm al-Qawain to stock up on beer, wine, and spirits. At the weekend even many Saudi nationals drive to the Barracuda before running the gauntlet of spot checks at the border on their journey home. The shop has its own airstrip and jetty, and charges very low prices. The fact that it remains in business may still be enough to tarnish the Al-Mu'alla family's reputation and thereby weaken the religious component of their ruling bargain.

Over on the east coast, the emirate of Fujairah may eventually become an important alternative port for Dubai and the rest of the UAE, if it can overcome its lowly status in the federation's development plans. Much like Ajman and Umm al-Qawain, the emirate enjoys great stability and it is unlikely there will be serious problems in the foreseeable future. Despite some of its tribes-men attacking members of the Trucial Oman Scouts during the 1960s,[209] and despite some of its bedouin clashing with Sharjah bedouin over grazing land near to Dibba in the early 1970s,[210] Fujairah has since enjoyed good relations with all of its neighbours, especially Abu Dhabi, from which it received generous aid during the reign of Sheikh Zayed bin Sultan Al-Nahyan. When Sheikh Muhammad bin Hamad Al-Sharqi, the first independent ruler of Fujairah,[211] died in 1974 the succession process was smooth as the family suffered from no longstanding historical feuds given the emirate's relative infancy. Muhammad's eldest son, Sheikh Hamad bin Muhammad Al-Sharqi, who had already been serving as the UAE's Minister for Agriculture and Fisheries, was well placed to assume power, and his younger brother, Sheikh Saleh bin Muhammad Al-Sharqi, was effectively consoled with the command of the Amiri guard, the chairmanship of the Fujairah Port Authority, and the directorship of the National Bank of Fujairah. Hamad has also sought to accommodate a parallel branch of the family that began to diverge in the early nineteenth century by giving the position of deputy ruler to Sheikh Hamad bin Saif Al-Sharqi—an influential grandson of his great-grandfather's younger brother, Sheikh Surur bin Saif Al-Sharqi.[212] As such, the ruler's eldest son, Sheikh Muhammad bin Hamad Al-Sharqi, who is now in his late twenties, is certain to succeed his father, and in early 2007 was officially named crown prince of Fujairah.[213]

In contrast, the most northerly emirate of Ra's al-Khaimah has suffered great instability over the last few decades and, much like their close relatives in Sharjah, its Qawasim rulers are likely to experience more internal problems in the near future. Although the emirate is neither oil rich nor proximate to Dubai, it nevertheless is an important supplier of local labour to the Dubai workforce given that over 20 per cent of UAE nationals are actually Ra's al-Khaimah nationals,[214] and because it is the only part of the UAE in which the proportion of nationals still outweighs the number of expatriates. As early as the 1960s its rulers had been identified by the British and Sheikh Rashid bin Said Al-Maktum as being potentially uncooperative with Dubai and their other neighbours, while also being the most vulnerable to external influences. Indeed, following the removal of Sheikh Saqr bin Sultan Al-Qasimi from Sharjah in 1964, the British agent immediately began to regard Ra's al-Khaimah as the 'new soft spot through which others, under the cover of the Arab League, are likely to renew their attempts to penetrate the Trucial States.'[215] Much like Saqr and his supporters in Sharjah, it was reported that members of the Qawasim in Ra's al-Khaimah had pictures of Nasser and the recently deceased prime minister of Iraq, Abdul Karim Qasim, mounted on their walls,[216] and that a number of vociferous Palestinian and Egyptian schoolteachers were influential in their *majaalis*.[217]

In late 1971 Sheikh Rashid's suspicions were realised when Ra's al-Khaimah refused to join the new federation,[218] thereby exposing the UAE's northern flank. Much like Bahrain and Qatar, Ra's al-Khaimah feared that if it were to become a part of the UAE then it would soon become locked into a subordinate role to oil-rich Abu Dhabi and the far more prosperous Dubai. It viewed the proposed breakdown of seats in the Federal National Council and the Council of Ministers[219] as being skewed in favour of the two wealthier emirates and thereby a gross insult to the proud history of the Qawasim, which had been the dominant force in the lower Gulf in the nineteenth century,[220] as well as being the most populous of the sheikhdoms.[221] Moreover, Ra's al-Khaimah believed that the recent migration of two of its principal tribes (the Al-Khawatir to Al-Ayn and the Al-Za'ab to Abu Dhabi) had not only been encouraged but also financed by the Al-Nahyan family, which was seeking to boost the number of Abu Dhabi nationals, and was therefore another portent of growing marginalisation under an Abu Dhabi-dominated union.[222] Perhaps most importantly, Ra's al-Khaimah still had strong expectations for oil strikes of its own, and it felt that if the oil companies prospecting in its territories were able to announce major discoveries then the emirate's bargaining position in future federal negotiations would be considerably strengthened.[223] Failing such strikes, its rulers had developed an alternative plan in which Ra's al-Khaimah's port facilities would be offered on an exclusive basis to the United States Navy in exchange for international recognition as an independent sovereign state.[224] Tellingly, at the very end of 1971, just twelve days after the oil companies declared that no commercial quantities of oil existed in the emirate, and just one week after their special envoy to the United States returned to the Gulf with no firm support,[225] Ra's al-Khaimah finally accepted the reality of its situation and agreed to join the UAE—the only conditions being that it would receive generous federal aid to assist with its development projects and that it would always be treated on an equal basis with Sharjah.[226]

Remarkably, in the late 1970s Ra's al-Khaimah was still very much a security liability for the rest of the UAE, as it was once more considering secession. Having come full circle from its overtures to the United States, it attempted to take advantage of mounting Cold War tension in the region by approaching the USSR. Hoping to gain support for a new state that would include Sharjah and would have involved seizing part of Oman, Ra's al-Khaimah was again unsuccessful in acquiring superpower backing,[227] as the USSR eventually chose to construct its deepwater port at Umm Qasr, close to Basra.[228] Nevertheless in the mid-1980s, during the height of the Iran-Iraq War, the emirate once more invited external interference by offering Iraq the opportunity to establish airbases in its territory in exchange for greater independent recognition in the Arab world.[229] This self-interested attitude angered many in Dubai who felt that it would extend the war to the lower Gulf, and there is little doubt that Ra's al-Khaimah's proposed actions exacerbated the UAE's division over Iran-Iraq relations.

The ruling family's dynastic strength has also been a subject of great concern, and it has often been regarded as unrepresentative of the majority of Ra's al-Khaimah nationals. Unlike all of the other emirates, where the ruling families are normally members of the most populous tribe or clan (50 per cent of Dubai nationals are from the Bani Yas, 30 per cent of Abu Dhabi nationals are from the Bani Yas, and 25 per cent of Sharjah nationals are from the Qawasim[230]), the Ra's al-Khaimah branch of the Qawasim are perhaps less then 5 per cent of the emirate's national population.[231] Most worryingly, although the emirate is dominated by the Shihuh—the third largest tribe in the UAE, and something of an anthropological mystery[232]—almost all of its prominent members have been excluded from positions of influence in Ra's al-Khaimah, due to the tribe's disloyalty to the Qawasim during the nineteenth century.[233] Tellingly, the only Shihuh appointments have been a few members of the emirate's Federal National Council contingent and the UAE's ambassador to India—the latter of which was appointed by the federal government rather than by the Ra's al-Khaimah administration. As such, there is some apprehension that the new generation of the Shihuh will become increasingly frustrated with this limited level of participation and in the near future may become a sizeable group of opponents. Indeed, as will be discussed in the following chapter, a young Al-Shehhi so disillusioned with regimes in the Gulf has already been involved in international terrorism—he was the pilot of the second plane to have hit the World Trade Centre on September 11th 2001.[234]

More importantly, there remains something of a question mark over the succession. Sheikh Saqr bin Muhammad Al-Qasimi has ruled unopposed since 1948, after he carefully deposed his uncle, Sheikh Sultan bin Salim Al-Qasimi, by striking a deal in which he would pay both Sultan and Sultan's ambitious sixth eldest son, Sheikh Faysal bin Sultan Al-Qasimi, 16,000 rupees a year in addition to 1 per cent of any future oil royalties.[235] However, Saqr's eight sons and their close relatives have been severely factionalised, thereby preventing any strong crown prince from emerging. When Saqr's eldest son, Sheikh Khalid bin Saqr Al-Qasimi, was nominated by his father to be crown prince in 1961, three of his cousins immediately voiced their disapproval of the appointment. These included Sheikh Abdul-Aziz bin Humayd Al-Qasimi and Sheikh Abdullah bin Humayd Al-Qasimi, the second and third eldest sons of his Saqr's influential eldest brother, Sheikh Humayd bin Muhammad Al-Qasimi.[236] Although they were initially exiled to Saudi Arabia (in a rather civilised fashion, given that Saqr purchased air tickets for them),[237] they promptly returned to Ra's al-Khaimah and quickly gained high profile positions in the emirate-level administration. In many cases they continue to hold these portfolios,[238] and therefore they still represent a potentially divisive force in domestic politics.

Even though Sheikh Khalid added the title of deputy ruler to his crown prince status in the 1980s, he was unable to secure any meaningful appointments for his own sons, as his father maintained a tight personal grip over the emirate's administration.[239] Most damagingly, he had also been unable to develop warm relations with either the federal government in Abu Dhabi or with the distaff branch of the family that his father had ousted and had then sought to compensate. In 1987 there was a concern that Sheikh Faysal had been planning a revolution in Ra's al-Khaimah that would have been simultaneous with the Sharjah coup. Much like Sharjah's Sheikh Abdul-Aziz bin Muhammad Al-Qasimi, it was thought that Faysal also enjoyed a close relationship with Sheikh Zayed. He had been appointed chief of staff of the Union Defence Force (the only non Abu Dhabi national ever to have held the position) following the problems with Sheikh Sultan bin Zayed Al-Nahyan, and shortly afterwards he had married a prominent Al-Nahyan sheikha.[240]

During the 1990s the greatest threat to stability in the emirate came from Sheikh Khalid's younger brothers. With the exception of his fourth brother, Sheikh Muhammad bin Saqr Al-Qasimi,[241] most remained distant from him. Khalid's second brother and the commander of Ra's al-Khaimah's Badr Brigade, Sheikh Sultan bin Saqr Al-Qasimi, hoped to take the deputy ruler position from him, and his ambitious third brother, Sheikh Saud bin Saqr Al-Qasimi, had acquired several powerful positions including the chairmanship of the emirate's municipality, the vice-chairmanship of the Ra's al-Khaimah National Oil Company (RAKNOC), and, perhaps most indicatively, the directorship of his father's court.[242] By the end of 2002 Saud had emerged as an open rival to Khalid and in summer 2003 Saud was strong enough to launch a palace coup, having forced his octogenarian father to strip Khalid of his crown prince position. Violence was expected, given that Khalid had effectively been regent for over twenty years, and Abu Dhabi even sent tanks to Ra's al-Khaimah to protect Saud's palace. In the event, the protests were relatively peaceful, with Khalid's supporters merely chanting 'We will give our blood and souls for you Khalid', although a few policemen were injured and at one point water cannon were deployed.[243]

Sheikh Saud has since been credited with kick-starting Ra's al-Khaimah's economy by improving its manufacturing base,[244] by promoting its tourist industry, and by facilitating the growth of Dubai-style free zones and real estate sectors by introducing the necessary liberalising reforms.[245] In a 2007 statement Saud declared that he had '…put in place a pro-business administrative regime that offered tremendous business opportunities in various sectors.'[246] Nevertheless, Saud does not rule unopposed: many Ra's al-Khaimah nationals question both his ambitions to emulate Dubai's development strategies and his perceived closeness to western businessmen. Although Sheikh Khalid and his family fled Ra's al-Khaimah and sought refuge in Oman following the coup,[247] he is still technically the deputy ruler of the emirate as his father only switched the crown prince title to Saud,[248] and he maintains many loyal supporters across the UAE. Therefore, a return to power cannot be ruled out completely when their father—the world's longest serving head of a government—eventually passes away.

8

SECURITY, CRIME AND TERROR

In addition to concerns over its development model, misgivings among its national and expatriate populations, and its reliance on the stability of its closest neighbours, Dubai's future success is also endangered by a rising level of security threats, both external and internal. Although its wealthier neighbour, Abu Dhabi, has built up the UAE Armed Forces by procuring some of the finest military hardware available, the United Arab Emirates' defensive capabilities are nevertheless insufficient to counter major regional threats from Iran or, to a lesser extent, other Arab states. As such, the UAE has had little option but to remain under a western military umbrella, which not only undermines Dubai's historical preference for neutrality, but also weakens several components of its ruling bargain.[1] Moreover, as an unfortunate but perhaps inescapable hidden cost of its emergence as the region's premier free port, for many years Dubai has also attracted the attention of both international criminal and terrorist organisations, many of which have exploited the emirate's geographic location, *laissez-faire* attitudes, and impressive infrastructure to set up various smuggling, gunrunning, human trafficking, and money laundering operations. Most worryingly, despite Dubai's usefulness to such groups, it has not been able to remain completely in the eye of the storm and has suffered from terrorist attacks on its own soil. Although most of the recent attempts have been foiled, any future escalation of such activity will most likely seriously undermine or even destroy the emirate's increasingly foreign-investment dependent economy.[2]

Military power

The first formal security organisation in the lower Gulf was set up in the late 1950s in order to protect the representatives of prospecting British oil companies. By the late 1960s, these British-officered Trucial Oman Scouts were being funded almost exclusively by Abu Dhabi, as its oil revenues began to accumulate.[3] As part of its efforts to promote collective security, Britain had anticipated that all regional divisions of the scouts would be amalgamated into one unified force following her withdrawal from the lower Gulf, but in practice the different emirates preferred to set up their own security forces. The young Sheikh Muhammad bin Rashid Al-Maktum was placed in charge of the Dubai Defence Force,[4] which by the end of 1971 had 500 men and had purchased a number of patrol boats, fighter aircraft, and tanks.[5] Although by the end of the 1970s the DDF had approximately doubled in size, Muhammad agreed that it was impractical to create a full scale army and thus concentrated on buying high quality equipment so that Dubai would have a lightly armed task force capable of rapid deployment in the event of emergency.[6] Thus, by the time that the DDF was finally absorbed by Abu Dhabi's much larger Union Defence Force in the mid-1990s, it had become a small but well-trained force with a tightly organised structure (including a specific women's unit[7]) and superior hardware. Unfortunately, given that Dubai had been procuring equipment independently of Abu Dhabi for over twenty-five years, this meant that the newly reinforced and genuinely federal UAE Armed Forces was made up of largely incompatible hardware and munitions. For much of the 1980s Dubai had been sourcing its armaments primarily from the USSR, North Korea,[8] and other Warsaw pact suppliers, whereas Abu Dhabi had dealt almost exclusively with Western

European and North American manufacturers. Even more incongruous was the equipment used by the various other emirate-level defence forces which had followed Dubai's lead and had also agreed to integrate. The ruling families of Umm al-Qawain and Ajman offered the UAE Armed Forces the services of their predominantly untrained retainers armed with little more than antiquated rifles.[9]

Given the task of phasing out such mismatched weaponry and upgrading Abu Dhabi's existing stocks, the UAE Armed Forces' two chiefs of staff since this period, Sheikh Muhammad bin Zayed Al-Nahyan and Hamad bin Muhammad Al-Thai Al-Rumaithi, have secured military budgets of between \$2 and \$2.5 billion per annum,[10] expanded their personnel to over 55,000,[11] and managed to persuade western governments to sell them their most sophisticated armaments—most of which are normally restricted to NATO allies.[12] In particular, the UAE Armed Forces has procured \$3 billion worth of Leclerc main battle tanks from France's Nexter corporation.[13] Given that the custom-made UAE versions have additional armour and upgraded guns for desert conditions, they are actually superior to the French Army's own Leclercs. The DDF's old Russian-manufactured BMP-3 armoured personnel carriers have largely been replaced by about 100 Turkish-supplied Savunma Sistemleri carriers. Courtesy of France's Sagem Défense Sécurité, individual soldiers will soon be benefiting from modular infrared units that will allow multimedia navigation between men. Moreover, the UAE Armed Forces' artillery capabilities have been greatly enhanced following the purchase of howitzers from South Africa's Denel corporation and from the Royal Netherlands Army. Similarly, the UAE's air force has taken delivery of much advanced equipment, including French supplied Mirage 2000-9s complete with laser targeting pods and precision guided missiles, British Aerospace Hawk 128s, Sikorsky Black Hawk helicopters, and thirty Apache AH64 gunships.[14] And given the UAE's role in international peacekeeping and humanitarian interventions, the air force has had to improve its long range capabilities and has acquired heavy airlift carriers from the Ukraine.[15] Most notably, the UAE Armed Forces' massive purchase of 80 F16E Desert Falcons in 2004 has made the UAE one of Lockheed Martin's most valued customers.[16] A few dozen of these have already arrived at Abu Dhabi's Al-Dhafrah airbase, and over the next few years the arrival of the remainder should make the UAE's air force the most advanced in the Middle East.[17]

Unlike most other militaries in the developing world, the UAE Armed Forces has committed itself heavily to purchasing custom-made equipment manufactured by joint ventures between western arms companies and domestic enterprises. With the reasoning that such products will be better suited to combat conditions in the Middle Eastern theatre, while also promoting the diversification of the economy and generating employment across the federation, the strategy seems to have found much favour in both government and industry circles. Specifically, in cooperation with a German company, the UAE has begun to manufacture its own military motorcycles and, most impressively, its new Guardian 'stealth jeeps.' Similarly, the air force has commissioned a project to produce the 'Mako' light aircraft to be used for desert reconnaissance,[18] and has consulted with a British company over the development of Al-Hakeem precision guided missiles, and with the European MBDA corporation over the design of UAE-specific Black Shaheen cruise missiles.[19] Although the UAE's navy has historically been small, with only one marine battalion and one naval squadron, and of less immediate concern than the army or air force, it would appear that the same collaborative strategy is about to be applied. As part of the UAE Armed Forces' 'Project Baynunah', in conjunction with a French manufacturer and the new Abu Dhabi Shipbuilding Company, several new frigates and corvettes, in addition to some small amphibious craft and two-person mini submarines, are under construction at Abu Dhabi's Mussafah facility, and should be delivered by 2009.[20]

With the UAE Armed Forces' main priority being improved defence, as it was for the old emirate-level forces of the 1970s and the 1980s, these land, air, and naval procurements will soon be complemented by far more advanced attack warning systems. In particular, a large underground airbase is under construction somewhere in the southern desert of Abu Dhabi that will have a hardened shelter to allow the air force to survive a direct assault,[21] and that will be able to link up with a new integrated electronic warfare system supplied by Northrop Grumman and a number of newly acquired airborne early warning and control aircrafts (AWACs) provided by Boeing. In addition, underwater surveillance systems will be installed at most of the UAE's naval bases, courtesy of the German Konigsberg corporation, and the UAE Armed Forces will be able to benefit from strategic data from the new Space Reconnaissance Centre that is located somewhere in Abu Dhabi and has access to Russian and North Korean satellite feeds.[22]

The Western security umbrella

Nevertheless, despite the absorption of various emirate-level armed forces and several expensive upgrades, the UAE's military strength remains very weak. In particular, there is concern that the UAE Armed Forces has insufficient personnel with the necessary training to operate such sophisticated hardware. Moreover, closely connected to the rentier pathologies discussed earlier in this volume,[23] there is a fear that given their privileged backgrounds and their status as members of an elite group in receipt of distributed wealth, there is little likelihood that UAE nationals employed by the UAE Armed Forces would actually stand their ground in the event of combat. Indeed, given that military salaries are often much lower than other, rent-derived incomes, a career in the armed forces is often looked upon as a source of additional status rather than as a source of livelihood. Thus, for lower and middle-ranking servicemen, military misconduct would not lead

267

to complete socioeconomic destruction. Perhaps most worryingly, however, as with many other public sector professions in the UAE, including the civil service and the police, there are thought to be a growing number of expatriates employed by the UAE Armed Forces. Of the 55,000 military personnel, it has been estimated that over 15,000 are foreigners, most of whom are Yemenis and Egyptians.[24] Understandably this has led to much disquiet over the dependency on mercenaries who can certainly not be relied upon to the same extent as indigenous professional soldiers.

As such, despite the obvious costs to the ideological and religious components of their ruling bargains, in particular their commitment to the Palestinian nation and other Arab and Muslim causes,[25] the UAE's rulers have had little choice but to remain under the security umbrella of western militaries that are predominantly made up of non-Arab, non-Muslim personnel, and which are directed by governments that are in de facto alliance with Israel. Most notably, France, which has been the UAE Armed Forces' greatest arms supplier since the Leclerc deal, has agreed to deploy 75,000 troops to the UAE in the event of an emergency, and it is believed that Britain signed a similar defence pact in the late 1990s, albeit without specifying exact troop numbers.[26] Such arrangements have allowed the UAE Armed Forces to assume a more realistic 'trip wire' role[27]—should UAE territory be invaded, they can serve to delay hostile forces until superpower reinforcements arrive. In exchange for such protection the western powers continue to be rewarded with lucrative oil concessions in Abu Dhabi and Dubai. As previously discussed, in the 1960s the Dubai Petroleum Company negotiated concessions with several American, French, German, and Spanish companies, in order to ensure that Dubai had access to the latest technologies and ensured that such countries would have a vested interest in the emirate's ongoing prosperity.[28] Shortly afterwards, the two main Abu Dhabi oil operators, the Abu Dhabi Company for Onshore Oil Investments (ADCCO) and Abu Dhabi Marine Areas (ADMA), agreed to similar foreign concessions, while the emirate's own nationalised oil company, the Abu Dhabi National Oil Company (ADNOC), accepted a smaller stake. Specifically, ADCO became 10 per cent owned by British Petroleum (BP), 10 per cent owned by Royal Dutch Shell, 10 per cent owned by Campagnie Francaise Petroles (CFP), 5 per cent owned by Exxon (formerly American Standard Oil of New Jersey), 5 per cent owned by Mobil, 2 per cent owned by Partex, and with the remainder controlled by ADNOC. In much the same way ADMA was divided between BP, Total, and the Japan Oil Development Company (JODCO).[29] Many of these concessions were quietly renewed in 2005 and are likely to remain in place for another twenty-five years,[30] while other concessions have since been signed with the Standard Oil Company of Indiana (Amoco), BP, CFG, Mitsu, JODCO, and Bridgeston, to assist the UAE's other major hydrocarbon operators, including Sharjah's Saja,[31] Abu Dhabi's ADGAS, and the Zakum Development Company (ZADCO).[32] While some members of the Federal National Council voiced concern over the ramifications of extending 'conditions of colonial duress and monopoly',[33] especially given that ADNOC and ADGAS now have the ability to deal with secondary oil recovery and sour gas extraction on their own,[34] in most elite circles such concessions continue to be viewed as a cost effective defence solution.[35]

Since the commencement of the 'War on Terror' in September 2001 and the subsequent Anglo-American invasions of Afghanistan and Iraq, the UAE, and more precisely Dubai, with its advanced infrastructure, has also provided western militaries with an important regional base. Although never publicly supporting the United States on the same scale as Qatar and Bahrain, which between them house an entire airwing of the US Air Force and the US Navy's Fifth Fleet, in addition to a CIA base and an array of US special forces living in compounds,[36] the UAE has nevertheless discreetly made many of its facilities available. Quite ironically given the US Congress' hostility to the Dubai

Ports World Company's attempted takeover of US ports in early 2006,[37] Dubai's ports have proved indispensable in the War on Terror. In mid-2006 President George W. Bush stated that '...the UAE is a key partner for our navy in a critical region, and outside of our own country Dubai services more of our own ships than any other country in the world.' Similarly, US Rear Admiral Michael Millar commented on the takeover fiasco by declaring that '...in a sense Dubai Ports World has already been responsible for American security because we dock here in Dubai, and from personal experience I can confirm they are wonderfully efficient.'[38] In particular it is thought that Port Jebel Ali is the US Navy's most highly visited liberty port, with warships such as the *USS John Kennedy* regularly being refuelled or serviced in Dubai's dry docks,[39] which remains one of only two ship repair yards in the Gulf.[40] It has been estimated that around 4,000 US sailors come ashore at Jebel Ali each year, with many claiming in anonymous US Navy surveys that Dubai is their favourite stop-off location due to the availability of alcohol and nightclubs.[41] Moreover, Jebel Ali together with Port Rashid also serve as major transit hubs for US military goods, with most such freight being delivered by three inconspicuous European shipping companies.[42] On a lesser, but still significant, scale, Fujairah's deep water port is also used by the US Navy, with the emirate's major hotels even having a longstanding arrangement to bloc-let many of its rooms for Navy personnel,[43] in much the same way as some of Abu Dhabi's hotels, which have on occasion billeted US soldiers on leave from Iraq.[44]

The use of air infrastructure has also proved to be a key area of cooperation, with Dubai International Airport's Terminal 2 (the original terminal) having probably become the busiest airport involved in the War on Terror, while the aforementioned 1998-built Rashid Terminal 1[45] which is only a kilometre away, has been allowed to concentrate on servicing Dubai's more wholesome tourist, business, and transit flights. Significantly, Terminal 2 is one of the few airports in the world that has regular flights to

Baghdad and Kabul, offered by African Express, Al-Ishtar, Jupi-ter, and other somewhat low-key airlines. While some passengers are Iraqis or Afghans hoping to visit their relatives, most of the $400 seats are reserved for US military personnel or for employ-ees of big contractors such as Halliburton. Also lucrative have been Terminal 2's War on Terror freight facilities, with cargo space on such flights selling for premium rates, and with many well known commercial companies shipping US military goods (including armoured vehicles) via the terminal. On a more formal level, Abu Dhabi has made available its airbase in Al-Dhafrah to the US Air Force and to the CIA, with RQ-4 Global Hawk unmanned reconnaissance aircraft being stationed there and with KC-10 tanker aircraft using the base to support Coalition op-erations in Afghanistan. Most embarrassingly, in the summer of 2005 it was revealed that U2 aircraft were also being serviced in Al-Dhafrah, following the crash landing of one of the spy planes on its return to Abu Dhabi from a mission in Afghanistan. The incident prompted the US Air Force to confirm that its 380th Air Expeditionary Wing had been based there since 2002.[46] In total, it is thought that there are currently over 100 US military person-nel stationed in Al-Dhafrah.[47]

The Iranian threat

Dubai has historically enjoyed fairly warm relations with Iran, given that many of its immigrant merchants are of Persian origin,[48] that Iran has long been the emirate's principal regional trading partner,[49] and that Dubai chose to side with Iran in the Iran-Iraq War.[50] Nevertheless, as a federation, the UAE's greatest external threat since its inception, and therefore the UAE Armed Forces' greatest fear, has always been an attack from Iran, and in many ways the UAE's most recent efforts to solidify its western military umbrella and to improve its War on Terror collaboration have exacerbated this risk as the US continues to challenge Tehran over its domestic energy policies. Spanning over a century and

271

three very different eras of Persian administration, several islands belonging to Sharjah and Ra's al-Khaimah have been claimed and counter-claimed, and remain a source of great contention between the UAE and Iran. The largest of these islands is only about fifty miles from downtown Dubai, and is currently occupied by the Iranian military.

During the mid-1880s, Persian expansion towards the southern coast of Iran and the occupation of the formerly Qawasim-controlled mainland towns of Lingah, Junj, and Luft, had soon extended to various Qawasim-inhabited islands in the lower Gulf, including Qishm and Sirri.[51] However four small but strategically located islands close to the Straits of Hormuz remained in Arab hands following a British warning delivered to Tehran.[52] Even so, by the end of the century Mozzafar Al-Din Shah Qajar had renewed his claims to Henjam, Abu Musa, Tunb al-Kuhbra and Tunb al-Sughra,[53] with Britain finally appearing to acknowledge Persia's new sphere of influence. It was even reported that Persian soldiers had planted a flag on Abu Musa in early 1904 with the assistance of a British officer.[54] Although the First World War and the subsequent overthrow of the Qajar dynasty distracted Tehran from its Gulf ambitions, by the late 1920s Reza Shah Pahlavi had nonetheless resurrected the goal of acquiring the Arab islands in order to bolster the prestige of his new dynasty. In 1928 one of Reza's most senior ministers[55] was despatched to Sharjah with the mission of purchasing or renting the territories, and when that strategy failed a force of Persians then arrived on Henjam and expelled the local ruler, Sheikh Rashid bin Obaid Al-Maktum, whose family had lived there since Sheikh Obaid bin Said Al-Maktum, a cousin of the ruler of Dubai, had left the sheikhdom in the late 1850s.[56]

By the late 1930s, with Persia's name changed to Iran, with nationalist sentiments running high, and with Britain concentrating on developments in Nazi Germany, Reza Shah was encouraged to switch his ambitions to Bahrain—a much greater prize.

Crucially, his son, Muhammad Reza Shah Pahlavi, maintained pressure on Bahrain for many more years following his Anglo-Soviet assisted succession during the Second World War, stating in his own book, *Mission of My Country*, that his divine purpose was to be the saviour of both Iran and the Gulf.[57] By the late 1960s, during the period of federal negotiations preceding British withdrawal, the Iranian Foreign Ministry even claimed that 'Iran has always been opposed to colonialism in all forms, and the so-called federation of the Gulf emirates, by annexing the island of Bahrain to it, is considered a matter which cannot be acceptable to the Iranian government.'[58] However, by the time of Bahrain's declaration of independence in mid-1971 and its concurrent international recognition,[59] Iran had little choice but to return its attention to the lower Gulf, with Abu Musa being regarded as the most attractive consolation prize.[60] Ominously, Tehran informed Britain that it must stop flying over the area, and when Britain uncharacteristically complied[61] there was considerable concern that a secret deal had been struck in which Iran would be allowed to occupy the island when Britain finally left the Gulf.[62] During the month before the formation of the UAE such rumours gathered pace, fuelled by news of Britain's completion of the sale of over $200 million worth of Chieftain tanks to Iran, and confirmed by a British envoy's instruction to the rulers that they should negotiate directly with Iran.[63]

Reportedly rejecting an offer of over $30 million,[64] the Qawasim sheikhs turned down Iran's proposed compensation,[65] and Iran duly invaded Abu Musa along with both of the Tunb islands on the eve of Britain's departure, with Muhammad Reza Shah claiming this was a necessary action to prevent any 'unfriendly power' from gaining control of the Straits.[66] Following a brief struggle involving some fatalities, Sheikh Khalid bin Muhammad Al-Qasimi of Sharjah reluctantly agreed to allow Iran to establish permanent bases on certain parts of Abu Musa in exchange for a financial aid package of nine annual payments of about $2 million.[67] Importantly, the more resolute Sheikh Saqr bin Muhammad of Ra's al-Khaimah refused to come to an agreement, and the UAE duly reported all three islands to the United Nations, requesting international arbitration. Since the formation of the Gulf Cooperation Council (GCC) in 1981 the liberation of these territories has remained a central component of the six members' foreign policy objectives, however in many ways Iran has managed to extend its control even further.[68] Notably, in 1992 Iran reneged on its 1971 deal with Khalid, and Revolutionary Guards encroached further on Abu Musa's towns, requesting all Sharjah nationals to obtain Iranian entry visas.[69] Moreover, in 1995 Iran forcibly required all residents to exit and then return through the island's Iranian port, and has since then prevented teachers and other UAE public sector employees from re-entering.[70] Ominously, Iran has now also opened an airport, has built a town hall, is constructing a university, and conducts naval exercises in nearby waters.[71]

Today, further instability and skirmishes in the vicinity of the islands are still likely should a beleaguered Iranian presidency need to rebuild national pride, and this could hamper both Dubai and Sharjah's oil exports, especially given the close proximity of Sharjah's remaining Mubarak offshore oilfield. Moreover, despite Sheikh Khalifa bin Zayed Al-Nahyan's attempts to balance the United States and Iran by inviting delegations from both countries to the UAE,[72] by declaring to the international media that 'UAE territories will never be used for security, intelligence, or military operations directed against Iran,'[73] and by dispatching groups of sympathetic fact-finding clergy to Qom in Iran;[74] any stray anti-ship missiles or Iranian submarine activity in the event of a US-Iran conflict would nonetheless raise tanker insurance rates and thereby greatly harm the UAE's economy.[75] Lastly, it is also important to note that invasion itself, or missile strikes against targets on UAE soil are not an impossibility. Certainly, there exists a certain arrogance in the UAE that the United States will eventually reach something of a 'grand bargain' with Iran, as the Americans cannot afford to allow the economies of the Gulf states to falter, especially those such as Dubai's that are now so heavily reliant on foreign direct investment, much of which has come from the West. This line of thinking grossly underestimates the UAE's ultimate expendability should the United States need to grapple with a state whose weapons may prevent long term regional stability.

Other regional threats

Although the OPEC disagreements during the 1980s and the invasion of Kuwait in 1990 led to considerable tension between the UAE and Iraq,[76] the Anglo-American enforced regime change in Iraq since 2003 has more or less ensured that the UAE will never need to fear Iraq again. Indeed, over the past three years the UAE Armed Forces has donated much equipment to the new Iraqi military, including several Bell 206 helicopters,[77] and in a further gesture of friendship has provided training for hundreds of Iraqi policemen and other security officials on UAE soil.[78] Similarly, occasional threats from other Arab Gulf states have now all but disappeared, with the last serious dispute with Oman being resolved in 1989 when Sheikh Rashid bin Said Al-Maktum, in one of his final acts of diplomacy, stepped in to mediate a disagreement between Muscat and Ra's al-Khaimah over the sovereignty of the Musandam Peninsula that was on the verge of escalating into armed conflict.[79]

The UAE's long history of tension with Saudi Arabia now also appears to have abated. Notably, throughout the nineteenth and early twentieth centuries the rulers of Abu Dhabi and Dubai had resisted the encroachment attempts of the same Wahhabi-inspired Saudis[80] that had managed to gain influence in Ra's al-Khaimah, Sharjah, and other Qawasim-dominated territories.[81] By the early 1950s, the US concession holder for Saudi oil, ARA-MCO, was urging its host nation to renew these historical claims, especially over the towns surrounding the Buraimi oasis, where it was thought there were large onshore oil deposits. ARAMCO devoted all of its scholarly resources to proving the legitimacy of the Saudi claim, not least by demonstrating that the tribesmen of the area, including those inhabiting the Sheikh Zayed bin Sultan Al-Nahyan-administered town of Al-Ayn, had for centuries paid religious tax to Saudi sheikhs rather than to Bani Yas sheikhs.[82] In late 1952, following a failed peace conference in Dammam, Turki bin Utaishan arrived in Hamasa, another of the Buraimi towns, with an armed Saudi force in addition to money, food, and presents for the local sheikhs. To reinforce further the Saudi position, it was reported that Turki even married the daughter of the sheikh of one of the most powerful Buraimi tribes.[83] Although the Trucial Oman Levies were deployed and the Saudis were expelled, with Turki being shot by a British officer,[84] no real solution was reached between the two parties. Indeed, just three years later Saudi Arabia was accused of bribing a member of the Al-Nahyan family to assassinate Sheikh Shakhbut bin Sultan Al-Nahyan, and in 1959 Saudi Arabia vigorously protested over Abu Dhabi's establishment of a police outpost on the disputed Khor al-Udaid.[85]

When the UAE was formed in 1971 Saudi Arabia refused to acknowledge its existence, and only granted it recognition in 1974 when Abu Dhabi finally agreed to give up Khor al-Udaid in addition to the islands of Khor Duwayham and Huwayat, thereby providing Saudi Arabia with a corridor of land to the Gulf between Qatar and Abu Dhabi. Ironically, while oil has never been discovered in the Buraimi region, this conceded territory is now home to the Shaiba and Zarara oilfields, and is therefore one of Saudi Arabia's most resource rich provinces.[86] This 1974 treaty was never officially registered, and there remains some concern even today that the new generation of Abu Dhabi rulers may challenge Saudi Arabia over the agreement.[87] Since Sheikh Khalifa bin Zayed Al-Nahyan's succession in 2004, most maps produced in Abu

Dhabi, especially by those departments administered by Sheikh Muhammad bin Zayed Al-Nahyan, have depicted the UAE with its pre-1974 Saudi border,[88] perhaps indicating a willingness to re-open the dispute. Nevertheless, since the formation of the GCC and the emergence of greater mutual threats, Saudi Arabia, much like Iraq, is unlikely ever to threaten the UAE again. Indeed, the greatest threat that Saudi Arabia now poses to the UAE is one of internal regime failure—should Saudi Arabia falter, the military bulwark of the GCC would collapse.

Smuggling and contraband

In recent years the level of criminal activity in Dubai has risen appreciably, as a result of what many believe to be a natural and inescapable side effect of economic development and population growth. However, it is important to note that with the exception of delinquent acts performed by thrill-seeking younger members of the rentier elite,[89] most crimes in the emirate are far from petty and are often under the control of large organisations. While it remains relatively safe to walk Dubai's streets at all times of day and night, behind the scenes there are nevertheless massive smuggling, gunrunning, human trafficking, and money launder-ing operations taking place. In many ways such transit-dependent organised crime can be regarded as being the inevitable downside of Dubai's described long history as an attractive free port and a regional entrepôt.[90] However, should the visibility of such activi-ties continue to increase, and should more criminal organisations develop roots in Dubai, then both foreign direct investment and tourism will undoubtedly suffer as the emirate's international rep-utation deteriorates. Moreover, as the remainder of this chapter will demonstrate, as these operations become further intertwined with major terrorist networks, Dubai will become less able to de-fend its crucial *laissez-faire* policies from international criticism.

Since the waves of merchant immigration from Iran and other parts of the Gulf that began in the late nineteenth century,[91]

277

Dubai's re-exporters were often operating in a grey area between legal trade and smuggling. The aforementioned 'informal shipments' of textiles, gold, and other goods out of India and the Far East during the 1950s and early 1960s[92] were only lucrative for Dubai-based merchants if they avoided successfully the taxes, tariffs, and other restrictions imposed by various governments. By the mid-1960s, with Jawaharlal Nehru's administration still in power in New Delhi and with regime change having taken place in Pakistan,[93] even tighter trading legislation was coming into effect in South Asia, and Dubai's once profitable grey area had all but disappeared, with it becoming well known that many merchants, both indigenous and expatriate, were openly engaged in contraband operations. So illicit had their activities become, that very often certain companies would have to wait several weeks before collecting their goods, as they could not risk their dhows being intercepted by patrol boats.[94] Moreover, gold re-exporting became particularly problematic following the opening of Dubai's airport, and improvements to Sharjah's facilities at this time[95]—more frequent inspections began to take place in the former while greater duties on air shipments were imposed by the latter, in an effort to recoup some of the construction costs. In order to keep their overheads low, many of Dubai's gold merchants were forced to hire pilots to land aircraft on Dubai's *sabkha* or salt flats, most often in Deira, and then to transfer the gold from the aircraft to their safes.[96] Similarly, by the late 1960s the British-proposed Dangerous Drugs Regulation that was eventually put into effect by the Trucial States Council also made the shipment of hashish and opium illegal –throughout the previous decade Dubai and Sharjah had been major centres for the re-export (and local consumption) of such substances—and thus the trade was forced underground.[97]

Today, Dubai remains synonymous with smuggling, with many shipping companies continuing to exploit loopholes in other countries' trading regulations or actively evading foreign customs enforcement services, and with such opportunities beginning to attract mafia groups to the emirate from much further afield, including Russia and China. In some widely reported cases, these operations have generated much negative publicity. In 2001 an official report from the World Customs Organisation confirmed that Dubai was one of the main smuggling routes into Europe,[98] and following an investigation by Paul O'Neil, the former US Treasury Secretary General, the United States accused Dubai of serving as a conduit for Taleban gold. As described, the UAE had been slow to distance itself from the Islamic Emirate of Afghanistan,[99] and even in the days following the Anglo-American invasion it had accepted incoming flights from Ariana, the national airline of Afghanistan,[100] and was allowing small airlines based in Dubai and Sharjah to operate flights into Kabul and Kandahar—most of which were thought to be laden on their return with gold bound for re-export to Pakistan and the Sudan.[101] Moreover, Dubai has also recently received much bad international press on those occasions when its smuggling operations have spilled over into violent gang crime. In particular, in 2004 a human carrier for a Russian mafia group smuggling diamonds into Dubai was assassinated along with his entire family,[102] and in a separate incident members of two rival smuggling outfits were involved in a shootout in broad daylight on the premises of a major tourist hotel.[103]

Gunrunning and the Merchant of Death

In much the same way as the blurred distinction between the re-exporting and smuggling of goods, Dubai has also had a long history of involvement in the international arms trade. Importantly, many of the UAE's contemporary arms exhibitions are completely legal, including the aforementioned Dubai Air Show that features not only commercial aircraft but also military aircraft and ordnance,[104] and Abu Dhabi's IDEX which is thought to be one of the largest weapons bazaars in the developing world. As the research department of a US think tank has described, purchasing arms at the latter event is 'as simple and straightforward as buying groceries from a local supermarket.'[105] However, underneath such state-sponsored exhibitions there also exist a large number of gunrunners who use Dubai as a base for massive illegal operations. While this is nothing new, with such activities having been detected and frowned upon in Dubai for over a century, the emirate has if anything become more notorious as an arms trafficking depot in recent years.

As a result of suspicions that Dubai and Ajman were being used by French and other merchants as hubs to ship over 200 rifles per month into India,[106] as early as 1902 the British had introduced specific legislation to tighten up the arms trade in the lower Gulf.[107] Nevertheless, by 1910 the situation had barely improved, with British patrol boats regularly intercepting dhows laden with arms. Most infamously, one of the former trailed a suspicious dhow to Dubai and, when subsequently having received reports of a secret arms cache located in the town, *HMS Hyacinth* laid anchor off the coast[108] and despatched a small force of Royal Marines to conduct a search. Encountering stiff resistance from the gunrunners, several of the soldiers were wounded while nearly 40 Dubai nationals were killed. The battle only came to an end after the ruler, Sheikh Buti bin Suhayl Al-Maktum, emerged from his house and called for a ceasefire.[109] The British Political Resident demanded a huge sum of 50,000 rupees by way of compensation and instructed the British agent in Sharjah to confiscate 400 rifles from Dubai's merchants.[110] By the mid-century little had changed, with major Kuwaiti gunrunners such as Khalf bin Ali Al-Zamami shipping massive consignments of revolvers and cartridges through Dubai during the late 1930s, and with British patrols being stepped up during the Second World War given the concern that German arms shipments were passing through the lower Gulf.[111] Moreover, even though the Trucial States Council responded to British pressure in the late 1950s and introduced new arms regulations, it was estimated that Dubai was still re-exporting over 800 rifles and

300,000 rounds of ammunition each year.[112] Perhaps most worryingly, by the 1960s it was becoming increasingly apparent that various non-Middle Eastern gunrunners were also using Dubai as one of their principal conduits. The British were made aware of a major Belgian arms company that was establishing agents in the sheikhdom,[113] and following independence in 1971 Dubai rapidly emerged as one of the most prominent mercenary supply bases in the world.

Even very recently Dubai and its neighbours, including Sharjah, have faced condemnation for their relaxed attitude towards the many international arms merchants that operate from their territories. Most notable among these has been the infamous arms dealer Victor Bout, dubbed the 'Merchant of Death' by Peter Hain, the British Foreign Office minister. A Tajikstani national and the son-in-law of a former KGB general who in 2005 became the subject of a major Hollywood movie,[114] he operated his own fifty plane airline (the largest Antonov cargo fleet in the world[115]) from Sharjah airport[116] and banked in Dubai.[117] The Merchant of Death was thought to have been the primary supplier of arms to Charles Taylor, the former president of Liberia, in addition to having airdropped weapons into Rwanda, Angola, Sierra Leone, and the Congo, in exchange for 'blood diamonds'.[118] Furthermore, during the late 1990s several United Nations' reports implicated his company in the equipping of the Taleban regime, an allegation Bout has denied.[119] Tellingly, he was only deported from the UAE in late 2001 following intense pressure from the United States as it attempted to cut off the flow of weapons into Afghanistan.[120] While a number of other high profile gunrunners have now also left, with many relocating to the vicinity of the even less regulated Grozny airport in Chechnya,[121] Dubai has nevertheless remained in the headlines over its notorious weapons trade, especially in connection with the supply of centrifuge equipment and other nuclear technologies to Iran. As late as 2004 it was thought that one of the underground nuclear network's chief brokers was operating from a base in Dubai,[122] while the disgraced Pakistani nuclear engineer, Abdul Qadeer Khan, who ran one of the world's largest nuclear proliferation rings, shipped goods to Iran and North Korea with the assistance of a company in Dubai.[123]

Slavery and human trafficking

In parallel to these gunrunning operations, Dubai also has a lengthy and troubled record of association with slave trading and, more recently, international human trafficking, even though there have been concerted attempts to stamp out such activities in the region for over 150 years. As early as the 1840s the British Political Resident was painfully aware of the slaving operations based out of the lower Gulf, most of which were transporting East Africans by land into the Arabian interior.[124] It has been estimated that at one point 12,000 slaves were passing through the region each year.[125] While many British individuals were undoubtedly heavily involved in and prospered from the trade,[126] the growing moral consensus against slavery in the empire that had led to the outlawing of such activities in most British dominions by 1838 had nonetheless also begun to spread to the Gulf,[127] even though these sheikhdoms were merely in treaty relations with Britain, rather than being formal colonies.[128] Consequently, additional slavery-related layers were added to the original 1835 peace treaties. Coming into effect in 1847 these permitted British patrols to detain and search suspected vessels, and required all Somalis (most of whom were British subjects) to be freed from slave labour. Moreover, the export of slaves from Africa on Arab ships was prohibited,[129] and in 1856 the restrictions were further tightened, requiring all of the Trucial rulers to hand over the crews of suspected 'delinquent slaving boats' that entered their ports.[130] Unfortunately these treaties were rarely enforced, with many sheikhs reluctant to terminate what had always been a highly profitable venture. Indeed, it is thought that throughout this period the Qawasim ruler, Sheikh Abdullah bin Sultan Al-Qasimi, was even levying a tax on each slave that was imported successfully through Sharjah or Ra's al-Khaimah.[131]

By the late nineteenth century the situation was little better, with many slaves still being shipped into Dubai and then taken to work on irrigation projects in Oman.[132] Britain's ability to restrain the trade had been compromised by French encroachment into Gulf affairs at that time,[133] specifically the Quai d'Orsay's decision in the early 1890s to allow Arab slave traders to use the French flag and to register their vessels in either the port of Sur in Oman or in Djibouti on the Red Sea coast of Africa.[134] In the 1920s, with such foreign influence having subsided, Britain became more pro-active, and on occasion shelled the forts of rulers that refused to manumit slaves.[135] Moreover, in 1937 the Political Resident publicly re-affirmed Britain's anti-slavery policy in the lower Gulf, stating that the ban on slaving was total and that Britain would organise the repatriation of slaves, thereby easing the financial burden on the rulers and merchants.[136] Nevertheless, as late as the 1950s there were still multiple reports of slave trading in the region, with British documents claiming that in one year alone fifty-nine cases of slave trading were uncovered in Sharjah[137], with British oil companies discovered to be using slaves to assist their exploration teams, and with the renowned traveller, Wilfred Thesiger, recording that hundreds of slaves were travelling through the villages of Buraimi to fuel the increasing demands of the American companies prospecting in Saudi Arabia.[138] Tellingly, even during the Trucial States Council's meetings later in the decade that were attended by Sheikh Rashid bin Said Al-Maktum and his contemporaries, much time was devoted to discussing strategies for curbing the trade.[139]

Although such formal slavery became far less common following the creation of the Trucial Oman Scouts[140] and eventually died out following the formation of the federation, Dubai has until now remained a key shipment hub and in some cases the ultimate destination for a large volume of involuntary or semi-voluntary human cargo. As recently as 2005, the high impact *Annual Trafficking in Persons Report* placed Dubai and the UAE on the very highest rank of countries that are suspected of permitting human trafficking. Rather damningly, this meant that the emirate was considered to be a 'Tier 3' offender: defined as a state that 'does not comply with the minimum standards as laid down by international law and is not making significant efforts to do so.' This placed Dubai on the same level as Burma, North Korea, and Cambodia.[141] Importantly, there are some indications that such pressure has now forced the UAE to tighten up it regulations, in much the same way that ILO pressure required the UAE to permit active workers' associations.[142] Notably, the much maligned use of purchased Pakistani child jockeys and stable workers at camel race tracks[143] has now come to an end, with the federal government finally outlawing the practice and, rather bizarrely, requiring camel trainers to invest in robotic jockeys rather than relying on young boys.[144] More significantly, in mid-2006 a new law was introduced that made the passage and exploitation of humans an imprisonable offence in the UAE.[145] It is thought that the new legislation has already reduced the number of illegally imported domestic servants from South Asia and the Far East, and as a reflection of these improvements the most recent *Annual Trafficking in Persons Report* has downgraded the UAE to the second tier, stating that it is now a country that is merely 'vulnerable to losing ground on its human rights record.'[146]

However, there is little doubt that in 2008 Dubai remains the region's primary centre for modern day slavery. Most of the girls who come to Dubai to fuel the booming prostitution industry[147] are brought across under false pretences. Many are married women with children, and are hired in their home country by visiting agents of lower class Dubai hotels or by the representatives of prominent businessmen. They are invariably promised a minimum salary in return for working as waitress or hostesses, yet upon arrival in the emirate they are normally separated from their passport, are rarely granted a valid employment visa, and are housed along with other many others in substandard conditions. In some extreme cases they are not permitted to leave the hotels they work for, and even if they need medical care they will be escorted to and from the clinic. Normally the only way they can 'buy back' their passport from their sponsor and thereby legally leave the UAE is by participating in prostitution rings. As illegal immigrants they have no recourse and should they report their exploitation to the authorities they fear imprisonment or deportation. Moreover, as an illegal employment conduit to other areas of the Middle East, Dubai continues to serve many companies well, with a large number of Filipinos being issued employment visas in the emirate for dangerous construction work in Iraq and Afghanistan, despite the Manila government's ban on its nationals visiting these countries. Indeed, it is thought that Camp Anaconda, the US base in Balad just north of Baghdad, was built by 8,000 such workers under the constant threat of mortar attacks.[148] Many of these were allegedly hired by a labour recruitment firm in Dubai that flew its employees to Iraq from Dubai's international airport.

Money laundering and terror funding

Equally damaging to Dubai's international reputation, especially since September 11th and the subsequent furore surrounding accusations of terrorist funding, has been the emirate's well known role as one of the world's major money laundering capitals. As with its longstanding relationship with smuggling, gunrunning, and slavery, the emirate's function as an illegal money transfer hub is nothing new, and is in fact rooted far back into the early twentieth century. Most of Dubai's merchants during this period conducted their transactions through a system of trust or *hawala*, in which goods would be shipped to another country and payment would be made without the need for any receipt or documentation. Given personal connections, such transfers were normally quite safe and efficient—if an individual did not complete his side of the bargain then both he and his family would be permanently blacklisted.[149] Even with the arrival of the Imperial Bank of Iran and the British Bank of the Middle East,[150] little changed, with many merchants still preferring to use the *hawala* system to finance the dhows that brought their goods to Dubai's creek.[151] From the 1960s and onwards, with few controls placed on the new banks, most businessmen began to combine *hawala* with the advantages of more sophisticated banking. Significantly, this hybrid system of informal and formal practices made Dubai increasingly attractive to visiting depositors, especially those that had made large sums of money from real estate in India and were unable to channel their profits back into Indian banks given the closed nature of the Indian economy at that time.[152] Many of these property tycoons eventually found themselves unable to return to India due to their association with mafia-run money laundering operations, and many chose to invest their profits in Dubai businesses. Some of these were thought to have been sheltered by sympathetic Dubai nationals who had investments in India, and in some cases were even given UAE passports.[153]

In recent years, international investigations have claimed that Dubai's banks and investment-dependent sectors such as the real estate market are now more involved than ever before in money laundering operations, with the emirate's relatively porous regulatory borders being unable to prevent 'hot money' flowing in from Iran, Pakistan, Afghanistan, and the former USSR. *Terrorism Monitor* has stated that huge amounts of criminal income are regularly transferred from South Asia to the Gulf states, most often through Dubai, and some $20 billion of this is believed to be conducted using the *hawala* system.[154] Similarly, in 1999 the US Secretary of Defence, William Cohen, warned UAE officials that vast quantities of criminal revenues were being laundered through Dubai's banking sector.[155] Worryingly, a later report on crime threat assessment issued by a US intelligence agency declared that 'Dubai has become a significant centre for financing illicit activities, in part because of the preference of many businesses to deal in large amounts of cash makes it difficult for banks to distinguish between legitimate and illicit transactions.'[156] Perhaps most damning, however, was an article published in the *Wall Street Journal* that discussed documents that proved Dubai was a major site for money laundering, and concluded that '...to the United States and other global financial crime investigators, no country in the Middle East is more important than the tiny UAE, the financial hub of the Persian Gulf with a long history of lax regulation and a role as a conduit...'[157]

Faced with such criticism the UAE Central Bank set up a special 'anti-money laundering and suspicious cases unit' in 1999 that was supposedly given access to all relevant powers, and in 2000 a national anti-money laundering committee was established. Furthermore, in late 2001 an anti-money laundering law was passed by the Council of Ministers in an almost immediate response to the widespread rumours that Al-Qaida funding had flowed through Dubai both before and after the September 11th attacks.[158] Early the following year this was strengthened by a further law that allowed the UAE's financial authorities to seize dubious funds while investigations took place, and resolved many earlier legal contradictions regarding the confidentiality of bank accounts.[159] As such, by mid-2002 at a meeting of the Financial Action Task Force held in Hong Kong, the UAE was declared to have finally established a comprehensive anti-money laundering system and to be 'in a very good position to co-operate in the internationally declared fight against money laundering.'[160]

Nevertheless, there are many who doubt that such illegal activities have really been curtailed, with recent whistleblowers revealing that the *hawala* system remains prevalent in the UAE's banking sector and that the Central Bank is powerless to intervene.[161] Indeed, as late as February 2007 the Central Bank was thought still to be trying to freeze accounts belonging to moneylenders—

287

some six years after the legislation came into effect.[162] Amongst
the suspect accounts have been those of drug smugglers in Dubai
that have sought to avoid a team of German investigators,[163] and
a large number of accounts belonging to Indian expatriates that
supposedly have low incomes yet enjoy annual turnovers of millions of dollars.[164] Certainly, in some cases, accounts have been
discovered in major Dubai-based banks that have enormous balances yet have been ostensibly set up by fathers for their sons at
university, or established by tour guides, shopkeepers, used car
salesmen, and perfume vendors, all with official salary statements
of less than $1000 per month.[165] Other incredible examples would
include an airline employee whose salary was $2000 per month,
yet who was receiving transfers from New York banks totalling
over $2 million. When questioned, he stated that he had made
fortunate investments on the New York stock exchange.[166]

The greatest unchecked flow of money has, however, been from
Russia and the Commonwealth of Independent States (CIS).
Ever since the break up of the USSR, it is thought that millions
of dollars were brought to Dubai and the UAE so that Russians
could purchase gold, electronics, and other consumer durables to
then re-export back home.[167] As a natural extension of this trade,
CIS visitors would often establish shell accounts in Dubai banks,
before then seeking to shift their profits to US-based correspond-
ence banks.[168] Incredibly, by 2001 over 300 accounts in just one
Dubai bank were thought to be of CIS origin,[169] and according to
Central Bank auditors over $30 million was being rerouted out of
CIS accounts held in another bank, with no visible connection to
either government contracts or oil transactions.[170] Most disturb-
ingly, later that year a Sharjah national member of the Central
Bank's investigation team had his house attacked by suspected
Russian money launderers, while an Indian member of the team
began to receive death threats.[171]

Incurring the harshest international criticism have been those
Dubai and UAE-based suspect accounts that have been thought

to have links with terrorist organisations. In the summer of 2001 the Saudi Monetary Agency (SAMA) approached the UAE Central Bank with a list of suspects that it believed were receiving substantial incoming funds from sources in Dubai,[172] despite their supposed menial professions as cooks, drivers, and salesmen. The UAE failed to respond to these pre-September 11th warnings and Saudi Arabia blacklisted the Dubai-based banks in question. Only following the personal intervention of members of UAE ruling families was the embargo lifted.[173] Moreover, the US *9/11 Commission Report* estimated that the bulk of the attack's costs, some $500,000, had been wired to the United States via an exchange bureau in the UAE, one of many ill-regulated remittance companies used by South Asian expatriates working in the Gulf to send money home to their families. Specifically, it was claimed that the ringleader, Muhammad Atta, together with the aforementioned young Shihuh man from Ra's al-Khaimah, Marwan Al-Shehhi,[174] who later went on to fly the second plane into the World Trade Centre, had wired money from Dubai to Florida in advance of their arrival.[175] It is thought that the remainder of the attack's funds were also channelled through Dubai's banks. One of Al-Qaida's alleged financial managers, Mustafa Ahmad Al-Hawsawi, was accused of receiving a bank transfer of $15,000 in Dubai on 9 September 2001, before leaving the UAE for Pakistan the following day.[176] Recently, the US government's prosecution's case against the possible twentieth hijacker, Zacarias Moussaoui, also included references to his funding having been channelled through Dubai-based money-launderers.[177]

A history of terror

Notwithstanding the aforementioned anti-British 'Front for the Liberation of Occupied Eastern Arabia' and the later National Front-inspired violence,[178] during the latter half of the twentieth century Dubai and the UAE suffered several spates of serious terrorist attacks and other politically-motivated acts of violence on their own soil. While in most cases Dubai has been a victim of cross-fire due to its unfortunate geographic location and its large expatriate population, it is important to note that a number of these incidents were also purposely intended to discredit the establishment and the ruling family, often by highlighting Dubai's relationship with the West and the religious and cultural shortcomings of the emirate's ruling bargain.[179] The stakes are now much higher, given that Dubai's economy is heavily reliant on free zones, tourism, and other economic activities that are dependent on the international community's confidence. As mentioned in an earlier chapter, it is likely that foreign investment would be cut, tourism would dry up, and the entire developmental model would collapse should there be just one or two terrorist incidents in the emirate today.[180]

Perhaps the first organised series of attacks that were aimed at destabilising Dubai and frightening both the British and the indigenous population were those launched by Omani terrorists in the late 1950s and early 1960s, most of whom supported the Imam Ghalib against the government in Muscat[181] (many of these would later join the more conventional Dhofar Liberation Front later in the decade). Most of the protagonists were actually based in Dubai, as sympathisers provided them with safe houses and in some cases even Trucial States travel documentation, so that they could travel freely without their Omani papers. Land mines were also stored in Dubai, in cars belonging to associates of both Sheikh Saqr bin Sultan Al-Qasimi, the ruler of Sharjah, and Sheikh Ali bin Rashid Al-Nu'aymi,[182] the eldest son of the ruler of Ajman who never became crown prince.[183] Shockingly, in 1959 a three ton lorry transporting Trucial Oman Scouts soldiers was blown up by one of these mines on the road between Dubai and Buraimi,[184] and soon after a Land Rover was blown up in Buraimi itself.[185] As panic spread, all motorists began to place sandbags on the fenders of their cars so as to better absorb such explosions.[186] Throughout 1960 the terror attacks continued, and on one occasion a mine exploded on a private road belonging to Sheikh Abdulla bin Salim Al-Ka'abi, the ruler of the would-be emirate of Mahadha.[187] Most dramatically, in 1961 the Omani rebels struck at sea and became the perpetrators of one of the greatest acts of terrorism there has ever been in the Middle East. The *MV Dara* was the flagship of the British India Steam Navigation Company and was carrying over 800 passengers from Bombay to Basra via Dubai. When she was approaching the coast of Dubai two explosions ripped through many cabins, killing 212 passengers and 24 crew. Although British salvage vessels managed to tow the ship away, its burning hull eventually sank two days later off the coast of Umm al-Qawain.[188] Although the exact method of the attack remains unknown, the British agent surmised that timers had been set so that the bombs would explode upon the Dara's arrival in Muscat and that bad weather had caused them to go off early.[189] Indeed, it later transpired that after planting their explosives the terrorists had left the ship when it berthed in Bahrain before eventually being captured in Oman.[190]

Disturbingly, although the Omani threat soon subsided, during the 1970s and 1980s Dubai and the new federation became something of a proxy battleground for other organised terror groups and freedom fighters that sought international publicity for their causes. In 1973 a Japan Airlines jet en route from Amsterdam to Tokyo was jointly hijacked by members of the Palestinian Liberation Army (PLO) and the Japanese Red Army. After the captain redirected the aircraft to land in Dubai, Sheikh Muhammad bin Rashid Al-Maktum reprised his earlier role as hostage negotiator in Sharjah[191] by communicating to the terrorists from the airport control tower. Having assumed that Muhammad would grant their release given Dubai's pro-Palestinian stance, the hijackers soon realised their miscalculation and demanded to be refuelled. With little or no room for manoeuvre, after three days of threat-laden negotiations Muhammad granted the aircraft safe passage to Libya, where all of the hijackers were allowed to walk free.[192] The following year a British Airways jet was hijacked by the PLO and also forced to land in Dubai, before being refuelled under similar circumstances.[193] In 1977 the UAE faced an even more difficult year with a Gulf Air flight bound for Muscat being hijacked and landed by an unknown team of terrorists, with explosives being detonated in the offices of Egyptian Airlines at Sharjah airport,[194] and a prominent Dubai national and federal Minister of State for Foreign Affairs, Saif Said bin Ghubash, being assassinated by gunmen while escorting the Syrian foreign minister to Abu Dhabi airport.[195] Most dramatically, towards the end of 1977 the Baader-Meinhof Gang chose to fly their hijacked Lufthansa jet with 91 passengers on board to Rome and Bahrain, before finally demanding clearance from Dubai. With an Arabic-speaking ringleader, Muhammad was again able to confront the terrorists, delaying their departure for over 48 hours.[196] This allowed a German commando team to position themselves around Mogadishu airport where they stormed the jet upon its arrival in Somalia, killing all of the hijackers and releasing all of the hostages.[197] Six years later tragedy struck once more, when a Gulf Air flight from Abu Dhabi to Karachi exploded in mid-air somewhere close to Dubai,[198] and in the following year the UAE's ambassador to France, Khalifa bin Ahmad Al-Mubarak,[199] was assassinated upon his arrival in Paris, perhaps in connection with the aforementioned tension over OPEC quotas at that time.[200] The fear that this killing generated was enough to persuade Sheikh Rashid bin Said Al-Maktum finally to hire plain clothes bodyguards to protect him during public appearances.[201] By the mid-1980s little had improved, with bombs being discovered onboard a Jordanian aircraft in Dubai in 1985, and with bombs exploding at the Syrian Airlines office at Abu Dhabi airport in 1986. More recently, in the 1990s several foreign intelligence operatives were assassinated in the UAE, including an Iranian intelligence colonel, and in early 1999 explosives were discovered in one of Dubai's first large-scale shopping malls: Deira City Centre.[202] Infamously on Christmas Eve that year yet another aircraft was diverted to the emirate when Pakistani hijackers seized an Indian Airlines flight en route from Nepal to Delhi. A hostage was murdered and thrown out of the plane when it reached Dubai, before the hijackers then flew to a warmer welcome in Kandahar. Interestingly, the crisis (including the tragedy in Dubai) became the subject of both a National Geographic Channel documentary and a Bollywood action movie.[203]

Since then almost all terror-related incidents in Dubai and the UAE appear to have had at least some connection to Al-Qaida, or rather organisations purporting to be linked to Al-Qaida. In addition to money-laundering and the involvement of UAE nationals in Al-Qaida's international attacks, including the aforementioned Ra's al-Khaimah national Marwan Al-Shehhi, and another of the September 11th hijackers, Fayez Banihammad,[204] there have also been persistent claims that many sympathisers of Al-Qaida live there, and that the UAE is regularly used as a safe haven and a logistical base by various Al-Qaida cells and other associated renegades. Most notably, during the September 11th Commission hearings the former US Secretary of Defence[205] stated that in 1999 agents in Afghanistan had informed the CIA that Osama bin Laden had set up a large hunting camp in the desert of Helmand province complete with marquees, generators, and refrigerators. Hoping to hit the suspected mastermind of the 1998 African embassy bombings, the Pentagon duly drew up plans for a cruise missile strike, but then had to abort the operation when it was learned that a C130 transport aircraft with UAE markings had landed at the camp's airstrip. According to CIA and Department of Defense officials, decision-makers were concerned that such an attack might compromise a UAE sheikh or other senior UAE official.[206] The former CIA director later testified that if the strike had gone ahead '…it might have wiped out half of the UAE royal family in the process', while others claimed that '…the United Arab Emirates was becoming … a persistent counterterrorism problem… as it was one of the Taleban's only travel and financial outlets to the outside world.'[207]

Significantly, although not touching on the widespread rumours that Osama Bin Laden himself had been receiving medical treatment in Dubai during the summer of 2001,[208] the Commission nevertheless also reported that most of the September 11th hijackers had flown to the United States via the UAE. Indeed, it was claimed that 11 Al-Qaida men of Saudi origin, the presumed 'muscle' for the operation, had travelled in groups of two or three from Dubai International Airport between the April and June of that year.[209] And in September 2002 journalists learned that the suspected ringleader of the team that had attacked the US guided missile destroyer *USS Cole* off the coast of the Yemen in 2000 had been captured, but were only informed that the arrest had taken place in an undisclosed location in the Gulf. In a textbook example of carefully timed news management, it was only revealed three months later, on Christmas Eve—traditionally the lowest impact newspaper day in the West—that a 'top ten' Al-Qaida operative had been captured in Dubai. It transpired that the Saudi suspect, Abd Al-Rahim Al-Nashiri, had been apprehended while in the final planning stages of attacks on 'vital economic targets' in the emirate that were aiming to inflict 'the highest possible casualties among nationals and foreigners.'[210] Also in 2002 various international reports were published indicating that hundreds of the 'volunteer soldiers' of the Maktab Al-Khidmat, one of Al-Qaida's original support organisations, that had been captured in Afghanistan were actually UAE nationals.[211] Moreover, the reports claimed that a number of Dubai and Fujairah-based 'welfare associations' had been sending money to radical groups in Afghanistan and South Asia, and had been encouraging young men to join terrorist groups.[212] In 2004 the perceived links between Dubai and Al-Qaida were further strengthened by another round of high profile arrests, leading many to suspect these were merely the tip of the iceberg and that the emirate was still 'playing a key role for Al-Qaida as a through-point' even three years after the September 11th attacks.[213] After alleged pressure from the CIA, the Dubai authorities arrested and extradited Qari Saifullah Akhtar, the leader of the Al-Qaida splinter group Haraktul Jihad Islami, who was believed to be responsible for training thousands of militants in the Rishkor camp close to Kabul, and for carrying money and messages on behalf of Bin Laden. He had disappeared from Afghanistan and Pakistan just days before Anglo-American forces arrived in October 2001.[214] Shortly afterwards, the arrest of Al-Qaida's Ahmad Khalfan Ghailani in Pakistan provided intelligence concerning two of his South African colleagues and 'several other senior men' who were all either travelling from the UAE to Pakistan or were presently based in the UAE.[215]

The present threat of terror

As few would dispute, despite the unrestrained development taking place in Dubai, the necessary socioeconomic reforms, and the consequent and seemingly inescapable erosion of the ruling family's legitimacy,[216] there exists a certain overconfidence that nothing can go wrong and that somehow the emirate will remain aloof from acts of terror on its own doorstep. Along with other Gulf states, there have been accusations that various terrorist organisations have been 'bought off'. Senior Qatari officials were recently alleged to have been paying a multi-million dollar annual ransom to Al-Qaida since 2003 so as to prevent attacks taking place on Qatari territory.[217] Moreover, in 2005 the struggling Iraqi President, Jalal Talabani, made dark references to the sources of the funding for his enemies, most conspicuously the insurgent leader Abu Musab Al-Zaraqawi. Disturbingly, he stated that '…they are getting aid from Al-Qaida and from some financiers among some extremist Muslim organisations abroad… and from countries that I will not name.' Analysts agreed that these mystery countries were most likely to be Bahrain and Qatar.[218] With specific regard to Dubai, it has similarly been claimed that a number of Islamist organisations, in addition to wealthy individuals, are supporting terror organisations financially.[219] However, regardless of whether these payments are in genuine support of the causes or are simply protection money, it would seem unnecessary for the emirate to have to rely on such measures given that at present most groups continue to benefit from Dubai's development successes so long as they can operate in relative freedom and can use the city's infrastructure for their own purposes. Certainly, even if one does subscribe to the belief that there exists some kind of unwritten understanding that the authorities will turn a blind eye to questionable activities, or even if one accepts that Dubai unwittingly permits itself to be used as a logistical terror hub, these steps are unlikely ever to be enough to prevent splinter groups or disaffected individuals from acting unilaterally against an establishment that they undoubtedly perceive to be an ally of the western powers.

Over the last few years there have been many threats made to Dubai and the UAE by such undocumented factions, many of which refer explicitly to the country's close relationship to the United States and its supporting role in the War on Terror. In 2002 a letter signed by the previously unknown 'Al-Qaida Terrorist Organisation in the United Arab Emirates Government' was intercepted by US intelligence services—it warned UAE officials to stop arresting Al-Qaida's 'mujahideen sympathisers'. Interestingly, the letter concluded with a boast that '...you are well aware that we have infiltrated your security, censorship, and monetary agencies along with other agencies that should not be mentioned', and demanded that the UAE '...get the idolaters out.'[220] And in 2003, following the Anglo-American invasion of Iraq, an audio message was recorded by an Al-Qaida operative that sought to incite violence in all of the pro-western Gulf states, including the UAE, by stating '...to the brothers of Qatar, Bahrain, Oman, the Emirates, and to all the lions of jihad in the countries neighbouring Iraq, every one of us has to attack what is available in his country of soldiers, vehicles, and airbases of the crusaders and the oil allocated for them.'[221] Since 2005 the frequency and severity of the threats would seem to have increased even further, with underground Islamist websites publishing chilling warnings that 'Dubai is rapidly changing into a secular state... with the profound use of non-Islamic ways';[222] with Al-Qaida representatives having notified the Dubai authorities that they had discovered both *USS Harry Truman* and *USS John Kennedy* berthed in Port Jebel Ali after they had been used to 'bombard the Muslims in Iraq and Afghanistan';[223] with the US Embassy in Abu Dhabi and the US Consulate in Dubai having had to close temporarily due to bomb threats;[224] and with another new group calling itself 'The Al-Qaida Organisation in the Emirates and Oman' having issued a statement in July 2005 that called for the dismantling of all US military installations in the UAE within ten days, failing which 'the ruling families would endure the first of the mujahideen in their faces.'[225]

NOTES

INTRODUCTION

1   In 2006, Dubai's non-oil GDP contributions were 94%. Personal interviews, Abu Dhabi, UAE Ministry of Economy and Planning, December 2006.

2   Despite a tiny national population, FDI flows into the UAE are thought to be about $3 billion, the bulk of which flows into Dubai. Personal interviews, Dubai, March 2007; and data from the Inter-Arab Investment Guarantee Corporation.

3   For a discussion of model 'global cities' see Saskia Sassen, *Cities in a World Economy* (London: Sage, 2000).

4   Short-term stability ratings are determined by immediate threats to the state's political status quo. In 2004 Dubai was ranked fourth out of 120 global markets. Business Monitor International. *UAE Quarterly Report* (London: 2004), p.3.

5   World Economic Forum. *Arab World Competitiveness Report* (New York: 2005). In this report, global risk consultants Kroll concluded that 'The UAE has also done more to diversify its economic base and its political future looks more secure', and rated the UAE the most secure Gulf state, with Saudi Arabia being the least secure.

6   The notable exceptions being the broader, UAE-focused academic studies conducted by Frauke Heard-Bey, Rosemarie Said Zahlan, and the author. See Frauke Heard-Bey, *From Trucial States to United Arab Emirates* (London: Longman, 1996); Rosemarie Said Zahlan, *The Origins of the United Arab Emirates* (New York: St. Martin's, 1978); and Christopher M. Davidson, *The United Arab Emirates: A Study in Survival* (Boulder: Lynne Rienner, 2005) .

7   For examples of classical dependency theory works on the Gulf, see Jacqueline Ismael, *Kuwait: Dependency and Class in a Rentier State* (Gainesville: University Press of Florida, 1993); Abdulkhaleq 'Abdulla, Political Dependency: The Case of the United Arab Emirates' (unpublished PhD thesis. Georgetown University, 1985).

I.   THE BIRTH OF A SHEIKHDOM

1   As recently as the 1960s there were accounts of locust infestations so great
     in Dubai that Britain had to bring in teams of Indian experts to control
     the problem. Personal interviews, Dubai, December 2006; also see Al-
     Gurg, Easa Saleh, *The Wells of Memory* (London: John Murray, 1998),
     p. 35; and Hawley, Donald, *The Emirates: Witness to a Metamorphosis*
     (Norwich: Michael Russell, 2007), p. 186.

2   These two houses may also have been referred to as 'the two brides'
     which at that time may have translated into Farsi as something similar
     to the word 'Dubai'.

3   Maitra, Jayanti, and Al-Hajji, Afra, *Qasr Al-Hosn: The History and Rulers
     of Abu Dhabi, 1793-1966* (Abu Dhabi: Centre for Documentation and
     Research, 2001), p. 18.

4   The story being that in 1761 a thirsty bedouin hunting party was
     following a trail of dhabi gazelles, and after they set up camp one of their
     party discovered freshwater. Within a few years hundreds of dwellings
     had been constructed. Hence the island became known as the father
     or 'abu' of the dhabi. Personal interviews, Abu Dhabi, January 2005;
     Tammam, Hamdi, *Zayed bin Sultan Al-Nahyan: The Leader on the March*
     (Tokyo: Dai Nippon, 1983), p. 32.

5   Al-Gurg, p. 3.

6   Personal interviews, Sharjah, June 2006.

7   Although now often referred to as the British East India Company,
     its correct name was always the English East India Company. See
     Parshotam, Mehra, *Dictionary of Modern Indian History, 1707–1947*
     (New York: Oxford University Press, 1985).

8   The exception being the French trading post of Pondicherry on the Bay
     of Bengal. Personal interviews, Abu Dhabi, July 2006.

9   See Al-Sagri, Saleh Hamad, 'Britain and the Arab Emirates, 1820-1956'
     (PhD thesis. University of Kent at Canterbury, 1988), p. 3; and Philips,
     C., The East Indian Company 1784-1834 (Manchester: Manchester
     University Press, 1961).

10   Once goods reached Basra, they would follow an overland route to
     Haifa. This route was far more profitable than sailing around the Cape of
     Good Hope. See Buxani, Ram, *Taking the High Road* (Dubai: Motivate,
     2003), p. 70.

11   In many ways the interests of the Company and Persia were compatible,
     as both sought to exclude the Ottoman Empire and other European
     powers from the region. See Al-Sagri, pp. 2-3.

12   Ibid., p. 3.

13   Heard-Bey, Frauke, *From Trucial States to United Arab Emirates*
     (London: Longman, 1996), p. 280.

14   Belgrave, Charles, *The Pirate Coast* (London: G.Bell and Sons, 1966),
     p. 29.

15   Revisionist histories including those of Charles Davies and, most
     notably, Sheikh Sultan bin Muhammad Al-Qasimi, the present day
     ruler of Sharjah, have presented strong cases arguing that the Company's

piracy claims were part of a 'big lie' intended to remove a trading rival. See Davies, Charles E., *The Blood Red Arab Flag: An Investigation into Qasimi Piracy, 1797-1820* (Exeter: Exeter University Press, 1997); and Al-Qasimi, Sultan bin Muhammad, *The Myth of Arab Piracy in the Gulf* (London: Croom Helm, 1986).

16   Belgrave, p. 36.

17   There is considerable evidence that the Wahhabi movement, led by its namesake Muhammad Abdul-Wahhab and then later by the Saudi sheikhs, had gained financial control over a number of Qawasim sheikhs, including the ruler of Rams, a small town just north of Ra's al-Khaimah. See Hawley, Donald, *The Trucial States* (London: George Allen and Unwin, 1970), p. 101.

18   Sultan Said bin Sultan.

19   Personal interviews, Muscat, February 2004; and see Hawley 1970, pp. 96-97.

20   The task force was led by William Grant Keir and comprised of three battleships and nine cruisers. See Belgrave, pp. 135-143; and Wilson, Graeme, *Rashid's Legacy: The Genesis of the Maktoum Family and the History of Dubai* (Dubai: Media Prima, 2006), p. 26.

21   Al-Gurg, p. 15.

22   Buxani, p. 71.

23   See Wilson, p. 29; and Maitra and Al-Hajji, p. 47.

24   As early as the fifteenth century, the Portuguese had used staging points in the lower Gulf in order to provide fresh water for their shipping from the Cape of Good Hope across to colonies in the Far East. Personal interviews, Ra's al-Khaimah, February 2005; Heard-Bey 1996, p. 282; and Abdullah, Muhammad Morsy, *The United Arab Emirates: A Modern History* (London: Croom Helm, 1978), p. 81.

25   In 1816 Sheikh Muhammad bin Shakhbut Al-Nahyan deposed his father, but within just two years he was replaced by the more popular Sheikh Tahnun bin Shakhbut Al-Nahyan. Personal interviews, Dubai, July 2006; and Van Der Meulen, Hendrik, 'The Role of Tribal and Kinship Ties in the Politics of the United Arab Emirates' (PhD thesis, The Fletcher School of Law and Diplomacy, 1997), p. 466.

26   Rush, Alan (ed.), *Ruling Families of Arabia: The United Arab Emirates* (Slough: Archive Editions 1991), p. 38.

27   These full brothers being the previously deposed Sheikh Muhammad and the younger Sheikh Hilal bin Shakhbut Al-Nahyan. Personal interviews, Abu Dhabi, January 2005; and Maitra and Al-Hajji, p. 61.

28   Maitra and Al-Hajji, p. 62.

29   Maktum was the grandson of Suhayl, a prominent eighteenth-century Bani Yas man. Personal interviews, Abu Dhabi, Januuary 2005; and ibid., p. 79.

30   Rush, p. 29.

31   Van Der Meulen, p. 175.

32   Maitra and Al-Hajji, p. 62; and Hopwood, Derek, *The Arabian Peninsula* (London: 1972), p. 225.

33   Heard-Bey 1996, p. 239.

34   Personal interviews, Abu Dhabi, January 2005; and Maitra and Al-Hajji, p. 62.

35   Examples of such towers would include the restored tower at Shindagha, and a tower constructed somewhere close to the present-day Souq Nayaf. Information supplied by Rashad Bukhash of Dubai Municipality.

36   Maitra and Al-Hajji, p. 69; Kelly, John B., *Britain and the Persian Gulf* (Oxford: Oxford University Press, 1968), p. 247.

37   Van Der Meulen, p. 336; Maitra and Al-Hajji, p. 81.

38   Abu Dhabi agreed to pay war indemnities for losses to British shipping if Britain would support their claim. Ibid., pp. 75-6.

39   Although Sheikh Khalifa did manage to seize Dubai's fort in 1838, Qawasim reinforcements expelled his troops after just three days of fighting. Rush, pp. 47-48.

40   Hawley 1970, p. 144.

41   Personal interviews, Abu Dhabi, January 2005.

42   Hawley 1970, p. 144.

43   Personal interviews, Abu Dhabi, January 2005; Van Der Meulen, p. 338.

44   Personal interviews, Dubai, June 2006.

45   Maitra and Al-Hajji, p. 95.

46   Maktum bin Buti's middle brother, Buti bin Buti, was skipped due to Said bin Buti's much greater popularity. Personal interviews, Abu Dhabi, January 2005.

47   It is thought that Sheikh Said killed a man whom he deemed guilty of murder, but who had earlier been acquitted by tribal elders. Outrage at this incident forced Said to flee to the island of Qishm. Rush, p. 81.

48   Maitra and Al-Hajji, pp. 44,133; Lorimer, John G., *Gazetteer of the Persian Gulf, Oman, and Central Arabia* (London: Gregg International Publishers, 1970), p. 768. Sheikh Said was killed during this attempted comeback.

49   Wilson, p. 62.

50   Ibid., p. 33; Personal interviews, Dubai, March 2006.

51   Van Der Meulen, p. 498.

52   Wilson, p. 34.

53   Ibid., p. 63; Personal interviews, Dubai, March 2006.

54   Ibid., p. 63. The two family members being Said's cousins: Said bin Buti and Suhayl bin Buti.

55   Ibid., p. 159; Van Der Meulen, p. 181.

56   Ra's al-Khaimah was the first to sign, and then a general treaty was drawn up for Abu Dhabi, Umm al-Qawain, and Bahrain to sign. See India Office L/P/85/7/195. Another clause in the treaty was that all boats had to be registered and their details passed on to the British. See Al-Sagri, pp. 288-292.

57   The British Political Resident in the Gulf was stationed in Bahrain during this period, while the British Political Agents in Dubai and the other sheikhdoms were often members of pro-British Gulf Arab

families. For a full discussion see Onley, James, 'Britain's Native Agents in Arabia and Persia, 1758-1958', *Comparative Studies of South Asia, Africa, and the Middle East* (no.33, 2003), pp. 129-137; Onley, James, *The Arabian Frontier of the British Raj: Merchants, Rulers, and the British in the Nineteenth Century Gulf* (Oxford: Oxford University Press, 2007), p. 46.

58   See Davidson, Christopher M., *The United Arab Emirates: A Study in Survival* (Boulder: Lynne Rienner, 2005), pp. 30-31; Gause, Gregory F., *Oil Monarchies: Domestic and Security Challenges in the Arab Gulf States* (New York: Council on Foreign Relations Press, 1994), p. 22.

59   In 1890 Britain offered the ruler of Zanzibar, Sultan Ali bin Said Al-Said, a similar set of treaties, thus bringing Zanzibar into Britain's informal network of protectorates.

60   Britain's fear being that inter-sheikhdom disputes over pearling rights might possibly escalate into a regional war. See Heard-Bey, 1996, p. 182; and India Office 1596/64625.

61   See India Office 1596/64625; and Maitra and Al-Hajji, pp. 72-74.

62   See Ibid. pp. 126-127; and Fahim, Muhammad, *From Rags to Riches: A Story of Abu Dhabi* (London: Centre for Arab Studies, 1995), p. 30.

63   Maitra and Al-Hajji, p. 49.

64   Heard-Bey, 1996, p. 182.

65   Lorimer, pp. 1450-1451.

66   Al-Sagri, p. 92.

67   Ibid., p. 51.

68   Lord Landsdowne, a former Viceroy of India.

69   Al-Sagri, p. 64.

70   The position of agent became highly attractive, not so much because of the salary, but because of the placatory gifts one was likely to receive from the rulers. Unsurprisingly, the position was often hereditary, with one family occupying the agency for three generations. See ibid., p. 98.

71   Mostly Khojahs and Sindi Bunnians. Personal interviews, Dubai, June 2006.

72   Al-Sagri, p. 38.

73   India Office R/15/1/267.

74   Al-Gurg, pp. 86-87.

75   Less powerful local rulers received only a three gun salute, and other non-ruling sheikhs received just one gun. Personal interviews, Durham, November, 2006.

76   Maitra and Al-Hajji, p. 126.

77   Lord Curzon.

78   Al-Sagri, p. 70.

79   Most notably the fratricides among the sons of Sheikh Zayed bin Khalifa Al-Nahyan, as discussed in section 7.4.

80   Al-Sagri, p. 97.

81   India Office R/15/1/14/27.

82   Maitra and Al-Hajji, pp. 74-77; Van Der Meulen, pp. 135, 422-423; Lorimer, p. 766.

83 Hawley 1970, p. 145.
84 Hawley 2007, p. 96.
85 By the end of the century, Dubai's boatbuilding industry had begun to rival those of Kuwait and Bahrain. Personal interviews, Dubai, June 2006.
86 John Lorimer.
87 A lakh being 100,000 rupees.
88 Lorimer, p. 2252.
89 Ostensibly for security reasons. See Fahim, pp. 22-24.
90 Ibid., pp. 22, 24.
91 Abdullah 1978, p. 104.
92 Lorimer, p,2248.
93 One such individual being the German merchant, Rosenthal. Foreign Office 371/13712.
94 As will be described later, the main fear being subversive Arab nationalist broadcasts from Cairo and Baghdad. Foreign Office 371/13712.
95 An example being a dispute when the ruler of Abu Dhabi refused to allow the RAF to build a petrol store. See Al-Sagri, p. 86.
96 This statement was made in 1929. Foreign Office 371/13712.
97 Davidson 2005, pp. 19-21.
98 India Office S/18/B/469.
99 Economic rent being the difference between the return made by a factor of production and the return necessary to keep the factor in its current occupation.
100 Personal interviews, Abu Dhabi, March 2001; also see Hitti, P. K., *History of the Arabs* (London: Macmillan, 1964), p. 25; and Ismael, Jacqueline, *Kuwait: Dependency and Class in a Rentier State* (Gainesville: University of Florida Press, 1993), p. 19.
101 Red oxide was mined on the island of Abu Musa. See Heard-Bey 1996, pp. 175-176; and Hawley 1970, p. 203.
102 Imperial Airways needed to have a refuelling base approximately every 200 miles at that time. India Office S/18/B/414; Personal interviews, Dubai, May 2006.
103 By this stage the Shah's influence had spread all the way to the southern coastline of Iran.
104 Buxani, p. 84.
105 Abu-Baker, Albadr, 'Political Economy of State Formation: The United Arab Emirates in Comparative Perspective' (PhD thesis. University of Michigan, 1995), p. 43.
106 Foreign Office 371/18912.
107 India Office R/515/4; and Abdullah 1978. p. 56.
108 Imperial Airways later became BOAC and is now British Airways. Footage of the first British landings in Sharjah can be seen in the ruler's old fort in Al-Hosn place, Rolla.
109 By 1960 this deal had become worth £30,000 annually to the ruler. Abdullah 1978, p. 56; also see India Office R/515/4; and Hawley 2007, p. 196.

110   The Dubai agreements should have been signed in 1931, but members of Sheikh Said's majlis had opposed the deal. In 1933 Said's eldest son, Sheikh Rashid, was able to persuade the majlis members to reverse the decision, allowing his father to sign an agreement that would come into effect within four years. Wilson, p. 72.

111   The flying boats landed on the stretch of the creek near to where Al-Maktum bridge is today. See Buxani, pp. 92-93; and Fenelon, Kevin, *The United Arab Emirates: An Economic and Social Survey* (London: Longman, 1973), p. 86.

112   Wilson, p. 72.

113   India Office S/18/B/414.

114   Wilson, p. 179.

115   Most notably American Standard Oil of New Jersey. Foreign Office 371/19975.

116   The Iraqi Petroleum Company was 51 percent owned by the British Government. Foreign Office 371/19975.

117   Petroleum Concessions Ltd. was dominated by British Petroleum (BP). See Hawley 2007, p. 67; Heard-Bey 1996, p. 295; and, *(in Arabic)* Al-Otaibi, Manna Said, *Petroleum and the Economy of the United Arab Emirates* (Kuwait: Al-Qabas Press, 1977), p. 45.

118   Since the construction of the Sharjah airbase, the agent had been a British national, signifying the region's greater strategic value to the British. Al-Sagri, p. 91.

119   Ibid., p. 155.

120   Peck, Malcolm, *The United Arab Emirates: A Venture in Unity* (Boulder: Westview, 1986), p. 37

121   India Office l/P/S/18/B/458; Abdullah 1978, p. 70; Wilson, p. 68.

122   Wilson, pp. 146-147.

123   IPC took Superior Oil to the International Court of Justice and won. Eventually, however, Continental Oil was able to sign a concession with Dubai. Al-Gurg, p. 168.

124   The base was at Manama in Ajman. Hawley 2007, p. 278; Personal interviews, Dubai, June 2006

125   Personal interviews, Dubai, June 2006.

126   Examples of these can still be viewed in the Fujairah museum. Personal interviews, Fujairah, February 2005.

127   More accurately 'Chelba' or 'Ghallah'. To the author's knowledge, the place name 'Kalba' is in no way linked to the modern Arabic word for 'dog'. The Kalba creek (Khor Kalba) would seem to have a much older origin.

128   Peterson, John E., 'The Arab Gulf States: Steps Towards Political Participation' in *Washington Papers* (no.131, 1988), p. 302.

129   Personal interviews, Dubai, February 2006; Rush, pp. 457-465.

130   Heard-Bey 1996, pp. 75-76.

131   This Sheikh Saqr was the son of the former ruler of Ra's al-Khaimah, Sheikh Sultan bin Salim Al-Qasimi, who had been deposed in 1948. See section 7.6.

132   Rush, p. 528.

133   Hawley 2007, p. 113; Personal interviews, Dubai, February 2006.

134   Rush, p. 133.

135   The uncle being Sheikh Saif bin Abdulrahman Al-Qasimi. Ibid.,
       p. 231.

136   Hawley 2007, p. 86, 280; Personal interviews, Dubai, February 2006.

137   Hawley 2007, p. 182.

138   Heard-Bey 1996, p. 253.

139   Hawley 1970, p. 197; Fenelon 1973, p. 56.

140   Wilson, p. 56.

141   Al-Gurg, p. 11, 32.

142   Ibid., p. 11.

143   Muhammad bin Ahmad bin Dalmuk was 200,000 rupees in debt and
       Muhammad bin Bayat was about 600,000 rupees in debt. See Wilson,
       pp. 74-75.

144   The British agent at this time being Sir Percy Cox. Ibid., p. 59.

145   India Office R/15/1/14/43.

146   Sheikh Buti bin Suhayl Al-Maktum, Dubai's ruler at the turn of the
       twentieth century, had allowed the return to Dubai of his exiled cousins
       Said bin Rashid and Buti bin Rashid, who had been living in Sharjah
       since 1894 after opposing the former ruler, Sheikh Maktum bin Hasher
       Al-Maktum. Personal interviews, Dubai, July 2007.

147   Interestingly by the late 1930s, Saeed had appointed Said bin Buti as the
       governor of the Deira district, a position he took up with great enthusiasm
       as a committed loyalist. Wilson. p. 70, 78; Personal interviews, Dubai,
       February 2006.

148   Personal interviews, Dubai, February 2006; Wilson, p. 71.

149   *HMS Lupin.*

150   Personal interviews, Dubai, Feburary 2006; Wilson, p. 75.

151   Personal interviews, Dubai, February 2006; Wilson, p. 76.

152   Van Der Meulen, p. 338.

153   India Office R/15/4/11.

154   Personal interviews with members of the Al-Tayer family, Dubai, May
       2005 and February 2006.

155   Sheikh Mani, the eldest son of a former ruler of Dubai, Sheikh Rashid
       bin Maktum Al-Maktum, was regarded as the most educated man in
       Dubai at this time. Personal interviews, Dubai, June 2006.

156   Ismael, pp. 152-153; Heard-Bey 1996, p. 255.

157   India Office R/15/4/11; Abdullah 1978, p. 126.

158   'Total revenue' included all income derived from oil concessions and air
       agreements. See Abu-Baker, p. 107.

159   India Office R/15/4/11.

160   India Office S/18/B/469.

161   Abdullah 1978, p. 131; Personal interviews, Dubai, June 2006.

162   Abdullah 1978, p. 131.

163   Ibid., p. 109.

164   Ibid., p. 131; Heard-Bey 1996, p. 256.

165   India Office R/15/4/11.
166   India Office R/15/4/11.
167   Wilson, pp. 84-85.
168   Abdullah 1978, p. 132.
169   Most notably Abdul Kader Abbas' house, which was at that time the
       tallest building in Dubai. Rashid's men were able to fire from its roof
       across the creek. Al-Gurg, p. 17.
170   Heard-Bey 1996, p. 256; Wilson, pp. 84-85.
171   Wilson, pp. 84-85.
172   Foreign Office 371/120571; Al-Sagri, p. 138.
173   Foreign Office 371/23186.
174   The 'fire water' was made using kohl. It is thought that the large fine
       could have been as high as 500 rupees – a huge sum for this time.
       Personal interviews, Dubai, February 2006; Foreign Office 371-120571.
       In the early 1960s the British agent at the time remarked in his diaries
       of seeing a number of one-eyed men walking in the souq. Hawley 2007,
       p. 73.
175   Wilson, p. 88; Personal interviews, Dubai, February 2006.
176   Heard-Bey 1996. pp. 254-5.
177   Al-Gurg, pp. 16-17.
178   Abdullah 1978, pp.132-133; Al-Sagri, p. 137 This was part of a broadcast
       made by the British Political Resident on 28 April 1940 on the BBC.
179   Wilson. pp. 80-81.
180   Al-Sayegh, Fatma. 'Merchants' Role in a Changing Society: The Case
       of Dubai, 1900-1990' in *Middle Eastern Studies* (vol.34, no.1, 1998),
       p. 96.
181   Abdullah 1978. pp. 134-136. The first development plan was
       commissioned in 1960.

2.   FROM ARAB NATIONALISM TO COLLECTIVE SECURITY

1   See section 1.7.
2   Al-Gurg, Easa Saleh, *The Wells of Memory* (London: John Murray,
      1998), p. 18.
3   Al-Sagri, Saleh Hamad, 'Britain and the Arab Emirates, 1820-1956'
      (PhD thesis. University of Kent at Canterbury, 1988), p. 143.
4   Ibid., p. 143.
5   The British agent at this time being Sir Donald Hawley.
6   Hawley, Donald, *The Emirates: Witness to a Metamorphosis* (Norwich:
      Michael Russell, 2007), p. 117.
7   In 1959.
8   Hawley 2007, p. 139.
9   Foreign Office 371/120553.
10   Al-Gurg, p. 96.
11   Abdullah, Muhammad Morsy, *The United Arab Emirates: A Modern
      History* (London: Croom Helm, 1978), p. 112.
12   Al-Nabeh, Najat Abdullah, 'United Arab Emirates: Regional and

Global Dimensions' (PhD thesis. Claremont Graduate School, 1984), pp. 121-123; Al-Nabeh contends that this group had close ties with the Dhofar Liberation Front (DLF) in Oman.

13   Abdullah 1978, p. 144. This incident would seem to have involved a prominent young member of the Sharjah branch of the Qawasim, who in a recent newspaper interview admitted to helping douse a British installation in petrol at about this time. See *Gulf News* 20th January 2005.

14   This was the Iranian school in Dubai. Personal interviews, Dubai, May 2006.

15   Hawley 2007, p. 129.

16   Ibid., p. 116.

17   Ibid., pp. 208-210.

18   Ibid., p. 295.

19   Ibid., p. 200.

20   India Office S/18/B/469.

21   Al-Sagri, p. 160. Al-Sagri is quoting the Political Resident's secret political report of 1956

22   See for example: Al-Sayegh, Fatma, 'Merchants' Role in a Changing Society: The Case of Dubai, 1900-1990' in *Middle Eastern Studies* (vol. 34, no.1, 1998), p. 98; and Abu-Baker, Albadr, 'Political Economy of State Formation: The United Arab Emirates in Comparative Perspective' (PhD thesis. University of Michigan, 1995), pp. 139.

23   Foreign Office 371/120571.

24   Foreign Office 371/120552.

25   Foreign Office 371/120552.

26   Hawley 2007, pp. 77, 103.

27   Foreign Office 371/120552.

28   Al-Sagri, p. 68.

29   Personal Interviews, Dubai, May 2006. Interestingly, in later life it would appear that Bin Sulaim came full circle by eventually supporting Sheikh Rashid and the British.

30   Between 1945 and 1948 a number of tribes engaged in a series of armed conflicts over Khor Ghanadha, a territory close to the present-day Abu Dhabi-Dubai border. Technically, Sheikh Said had been the aggressor, as he permitted a Dubai-based tribe to launch a coastal attack on their enemies, thereby violating the maritime peace treaties. See Al-Gurg, p. 17; Fahim, Muhammad, *From Rags to Riches: A Story of Abu Dhabi* (London: Centre for Arab Studies, 1995), pp. 44,149.

31   Hawley 2007, p. 62.

32   Al-Sagri, pp. 178-180; Personal interviews, Dubai, June 2006.

33   Personal interviews, Dubai, February 2006.

34   Foreign Office 371/120552.

35   Foreign Office 371/120552.

36   Personal interviews, Dubai, February 2006.

37   Buxani, Ram, *Taking the High Road* (Dubai: Motivate, 2003), p. 93.

38   Foreign Office 371/120552.

39   Foreign Office 371/120552.
40   Personal interviews, Abu Dhabi, November 2005; for a full discussion of the Buraimi crisis see section 8.4.
41   Personal interviews, Dubai, February 2006.
42   Foreign Office 371/120552.
43   Hawley 2007. p. 189.
44   Ibid., p. 193; Al-Sagri, p. 176; since 1891 Gray Mackenzie had been licensed shipping agents in Dubai.
45   Al-Sagri, p. 316.
46   Foreign Office 371/120553.
47   Foreign Office 371/120557.
48   Foreign Office 371/120553.
49   Al-Sagri, p. 177.
50   Personal interviews, Dubai, February 2006; Hawley 2007, p. 102.
51   Ibid., p. 76.
52   Ibid., p. 97.
53   Ibid., p. 112.
54   Rush, Alan (ed.), *Ruling Families of Arabia: The United Arab Emirates* (Slough: Archive Editions 1991), p. 300.
55   Hawley 2007, p. 124.
56   Sheikh Rashid refused these men entry to Dubai. Al-Gurg. p. 50.
57   Ibid., p. 90.
58   Al-Sagri. p. 177.
59   Foreign Office 371/120553.
60   Foreign Office 371/120552.
61   Foreign Office 371/120552.
62   Foreign Office 371/120552.
63   Foreign Office 371/120552.
64   Foreign Office 371/120553.
65   Al-Sagri, p. 158.
66   Hawley 2007, p. 94; Wilson, Graeme, *Rashid's Legacy: The Genesis of the Maktoum Family and the History of Dubai* (Dubai: Media Prima, 2006), pp. 154-156.
67   The officer being Peter Lorimer. See Luce, Margaret, *From Aden to the Gulf: Personal Diaries, 1956-1966* (Salisbury, Michael Russell, 1987), p. 130.
68   Personal interviews, Dubai, June 2006.
69   Foreign Office 371/1/120553.
70   Personal interviews with members of the Al-Tayer family, Dubai, September 2005.
71   Hawley 2007, p. 295.
72   Al-Gurg, pp. 89, 121.
73   Foreign Office 371/109805.
74   Foreign Office 371/91326.
75   Hawley 2007, p. 304.
76   Personal interviews, Dubai, June 2006.
77   Most notably Sayed Nofal, deputy secretary general of the League, was

refused landing permission in 1965. See Al-Gurg, pp. 93, 118.

78   The first Kuwaiti oil exports were in 1946.
79   Personal interviews, Abu Dhabi, September 2003. These stamps, dating from 1971, are on display in the Abu Dhabi Cultural Foundation.
80   The attempt was aborted at the last moment. Al-Gurg, p. 94.
81   See section 8.9.
82   Personal interviews, Beirut, June 2005.
83   Fairhall, D., *Russia Looks to the Sea* (London: 1971), p. 234.
84   Al-Sagri, p. 268.
85   In the 1930s a British proposal had called for a ten-member association comprising Bahrain, Qatar, Kuwait, and the Trucial States. Although the Second World War distracted Britain from developing this further, its contents were published in Bahraini magazines and were widely debated by the local populations. See *(in Arabic)* Tabatabai, Adil, *Comparative Studies in the Emirates* (Cairo: 1978), p. 30
86   Foreign Office 371/179916 .
87   Foreign Office 371/179918/31761.
88   Al-Gurg, p. 115; Van Der Meulen, Hendrik. 'The Role of Tribal and Kinship Ties in the Politics of the United Arab Emirates' (PhD thesis. The Fletcher School of Law and Diplomacy, 1997), p. 209
89   Hawley 2007. pp. 178-184; Al-Gurg. p. 113.
90   Heard-Bey, Frauke, *From Trucial States to United Arab Emirates* (London: Longman, 1996), pp. 306-307.
91   Hawley, 2007, p.57.
92   Abu-Baker,, p. 48
93   Hawley, 2007,, p. 177
94   The Continental Oil and Transportation Company of Utah.
95   Wilson, p. 207; see section 1.5.
96   Heard-Bey. 1996., p. 321; Fenelon, Kevin, *The United Arab Emirates: An Economic and Social Survey* (London: Longman, 1973), pp. 46-47, 49-59.
97   Al-Gurg, p.114.
98   The Awamir were still dangerous at this time, frequently raiding villages. Al-Gurg, p. 114; Al-Sagri, p.15.
99   A future federal minister in Sheikh Zayed's first cabinet.
100   Al-Gurg, pp. 117, 122, 125.
101   Ibid., p. 117.
102   Ibid., pp. 128,138; *also see (in Arabic)* Sharabah, Naji Sadiq,'The Federal Experiment of the United Arab Emirates, 1971-1977' (PhD thesis. University of Cairo, 1980).
103   The Foreign Secretary at this time being George Brown.
104   Wilson, p. 258.
105   Anthony, John Duke, *The United Arab Emirates: Dynamics of State Formation* (Abu Dhabi: Emirates Centre for Strategic Studies and Research, 2002), p. 25.
106   Since 1931 Britain had been running a persistent balance of payments deficit, reflecting both her weakening competitive position industrially

and the reduction of her invisible earnings. See Reynolds, David, *Britannia Overruled: British Policy and World Power in the Twentieth Century* (Harlow: Longman, 1991), p .17.

107 By 1967 Britain was spending £317 million on Middle Eastern bases. Wilson, p. 258.

108 Sir William Luce.

109 Personal interviews, Dubai, June 2006.

110 Foreign Office 371/91326.

111 Sultan Jamshid bin Abdulla Al-Said was deposed in 1964. See Yeager, Rodge, *Tanzania: An African Experiment* (Boulder: Westview, 1983).

112 Anthony 2002, p. 19; Al-Gurg, p. 132. Interestingly, Britain had also been experimenting unsuccessfully with federation-building in the Caribbean, East Africa, and Malaya.

113 Sir Edward Heath.

114 Wilson, p. 201.

115 Ibid., pp. 196-198.

116 Ibid., p. 236.

117 Peterson, John E., 'The Nature of Succession in the Gulf', *Middle East Journal* (vol. 55, no. 4, 2001), p. 581.

118 Most notably Jordan, which was relieved to have more monarchies in the Arab League. Personal interviews, Dubai, February 2006; Wilson. p. 265.

119 Ibid., p. 265.

120 Sir William Luce.

121 Wilson, pp.196-198.

122 Heard-Bey, 1996, pp. 343-344.

123 Personal interviews, Dubai, June 2006.

124 Wilson, pp. 296-298.

125 Personal interviews, Dubai, February 2006.

126 Wilson, p. 300.

127 Ibid., p. 313.

128 Rather ominously the site for the proposed new capital was in the *Wadi al-Mawt* or Valley of Death. See Peck, Malcolm, *The United Arab Emirates: A Venture in Unity* (Boulder: Westview, 1986), p. 50; Al-Musfir, Muhammad Salih, 'The United Arab Emirates: An Assessment of Federalism in a Developing Polity' (PhD thesis. State University of New York and Binghamton, 1985), p.74

129 Personal interviews, Dubai, June 2006; Wilson, p. 316.

130 Hawley 2007. pp.12-13.

131 Ibid., pp.84, 174.

132 Overton, J. L., 'Stability and Change: Inter-Arab Politics in the Arabian Peninsula and the Gulf' (PhD thesis. University of Maryland, 1983), p.173.

133 Hawley, 2007, pp.12-13.

134 Personal interviews, Dubai, July 2007; Wilson. p. 322.

135 Ibid., p.321

136 Kelly, John B., *Arabia, the Gulf, and the West: A Critical View of the Arabs*

and their Oil Policy (New York: Basic Books, 1986), p.49. This quote is from Goronwy Roberts' report to the British Cabinet in 1968.

137 Personal interviews with Lord Richard Luce, London, February 2007.

138 The first draft of this federal constitution was drawn up by an Egyptian expert who had also worked on the Kuwaiti constitution, but this was rejected by Dubai. Personal interviews, Abu Dhabi, March 2007. Also see Al-Gurg. p.140.

139 See section 7.6.

140 Wilson, p. 337.

141 Just a few months after the UAE's inception David Holden's article in *Foreign Affairs* expressed grave concerns about the federation's future. Similarly the final Political Resident, Sir Geoffrey Arthur, and the US Undersecretary for Political Affairs, Joseph Sisco, expressed their doubts. See Holden, David, 'The Persian Gulf after the British Raj' , *Foreign Affairs* (vol. 49, no.4, 1971), p.729; Heard-Bey, 1996, p.24; and United States Department of State, 'US policy in the area of the Persian Gulf' (vol. 73, 14 July 1975), p. 74.

142 See section 8.3.

143 Wilson, pp. 268-269.

144 Ra's al-Khaimah formally joined the UAE in February 1972. See section 7.6.

145 Hawley, 2007, pp. 13-14.

146 Al-Sagri, p. 268.

147 See section 5.6.

148 Up until this time the individual emirates had been producing their own postage stamps. Indeed, some rulers generated considerable revenue from this exercise given the high prices that international philatelists were prepared to pay for obscure stamps.

149 This ended the use of the old Qatari-Dubai Riyal in Dubai and the Bahraini Dinar in Abu Dhabi.

3. THE FOUNDATIONS OF A FREE PORT

1 Maitra, Jayanti, and Al-Hajji, Afra, *Qasr Al-Hosn: The History and Rulers of Abu Dhabi, 1793-1966* (Abu Dhabi: Centre for Documentation and Research, 2001), p.129.

2 Ibid., p.129; Personal interviews, Dubai, March 2006.

3 See Abdullah, Muhammad Morsy, *The United Arab Emirates: A Modern History* (London: Croom Helm, 1978), p. 104; Heard-Bey, Frauke, *From Trucial States to United Arab Emirates* (London: Longman, 1996), p. 243.

4 Personal interviews, Dubai, June 2006.

5 Heard-Bey 1996, pp. 189-191.

6 Personal interviews, Dubai, March 2006.

7 Hawley, Donald, *The Emirates: Witness to a Metamorphosis* (Norwich: Michael Russell, 2007), p. 24; Wilson, Graeme, *Rashid's Legacy: The Genesis of the Maktoum Family and the History of Dubai* (Dubai: Media

Prima, 2006), p. 125.

8   The Political Resident being George Middleton at this time.

9   Hawley 2007, p. 207.

10   Wilson, p. 139

11   Ibid., p. 251.

12   See section 8.5.

13   A type of rayon.

14   Buxani, Ram, *Taking the High Road* (Dubai: Motivate, 2003), pp. 109-110, 118; Personal interviews, Dubai, February 2007.

15   Oxford Business Group. 'Emerging Emirates' (London: 2000), p. 45.

16   Personal interviews, Dubai, June 2006.

17   Hawley 2007, p. 18.

18   Personal interviews, Dubai, February 2006.

19   These personal stereos from Dubai were so popular with Keralites that they became known as 'Malbaris'.

20   Buxani, pp. 117-119, 121; Personal interviews, Dubai June 2006.

21   See section 1.1.

22   Al-Gurg, Easa Saleh, *The Wells of Memory* (London: John Murray, 1998), p. 5; Kelly, John B. *Arabia, the Gulf, and the West: A Critical View of the Arabs and their Oil Policy* (New York: Basic Books, 1986), pp. 92-93.

23   Personal interviews, Dubai, December 2005; Fahim, Muhammad. *From Rags to Riches: A Story of Abu Dhabi* (London: Centre for Arab Studies, 1995), pp. 49-50.

24   Personal interviews, Dubai, February 2006.

25   Al-Gurg, p.3.

26   Ibid., p.3.

27   The first Political Residency being Bushire, before Britain transferred her headquarters to Bahrain. Ibid., p.3.

28   Ibid., p.6; Personal interviews, Dubai, June 2006.

29   Personal interviews, Dubai, June 2006.

30   Fahim, p.32.

31   Zahlan, Rosemarie Said, *The Origins of the United Arab Emirates* (New York: St. Martin's, 1978), p.12; Wilson, Graeme *Rashid's Legacy: The Genesis of the Maktoum Family and the History of Dubai* (Dubai: Media Prima, 2006), p. 36.

32   Personal interviews, Dubai, December 2005.

33   Personal interviews, Dubai, September 2005; Al-Gurg. p.5; Van Der Meulen, Hendrik. 'The Role of Tribal and Kinship Ties in the Politics of the United Arab Emirates' (PhD thesis. The Fletcher School of Law and Diplomacy, 1997), p. 204. In some texts this declaration is attributed to Sheikh Muhammad bin Khalifa Al-Qasimi, who nominally ruled Lingah from 1898 onwards.

34   Rush, Alan (ed.), *Ruling Families of Arabia: The United Arab Emirates* (Slough: Archive Editions 1991), p.18.

35   Personal interviews, Dubai, September 2005; Al-Gurg, p.5; Van Der Meulen, p.205.

36   Wilson, p.36.

37   Foreign Office 371/120552.
38   This land had been cleared and made available following a great fire in Dubai in the early 1890s. Buxani, pp. 72-73; Personal interviews, Dubai, September 2005.
39   Personal interviews, Dubai, December 2005.
40   Wilson, p.35.
41   Fahim, pp. 32, 38.
42   The German geographer, Herman Burchardt.
43   Maitra and Al-Hajji, p.201.
44   Fahim, p.31.
45   Ibid., p.38.
46   Al-Gurg, p. 2; Personal interviews, Dubai, February 2006.
47   See section 2.2.
48   Wilson, p. 91; Personal interviews, Dubai, February 2006.
49   Wilson, pp. 66-67; Personal interviews, Dubai February 2006.
50   The agent being Sayyid Abd al-Razzaq Razuqi. Al-Gurg, p.32; Personal correspondence with James Onley, March 2007.
51   The agent refused to endorse job appointments for *ajamis*.
52   Personal interviews, Dubai, December 2005; Wilson, pp. 66-67.
53   Hawley 2007, pp. 204, 206.
54   Personal interviews, Dubai, February 2006.
55   See section 8.3.
56   Wilson, p.333.
57   Van Der Meulen; Author's estimates. There are about 80,000 Dubai nationals, see section 5.4.
58   See section 7.4.
59   Maitra and Al-Hajji, p. 224.
60   Fahim, p.43.
61   Maitra and Al-Hajji, p. 242.
62   Foreign Office 371/109814.
63   Maitra and Al-Hajji, p.243.
64   See section 2.1.
65   Foreign Office 371/120553.
66   Foreign Office 371/120553.
67   Foreign Office 371/120553.
68   Fahim, p.77.
69   Personal interviews, Dubai, June 2006.
70   Maitra and Al-Hajji, pp. 246-247.
71   Hawley 2007, p.90.
72   Fahim, pp. 86-87.
73   This correspondence was intercepted from the Al-Otaibi family of Abu Dhabi. Hopwood, Derek, *The Arabian Peninsula* (London: 1972), p.206.
74   Al-Gurg, p.65.
75   Darwish bin Karem.
76   Personal interviews, Dubai, December 2005; Al-Gurg, pp. 73-75.
77   The aforementioned Easa Saleh Al-Gurg.

78   Al-Gurg, pp. 66-67.
79   Wilson, p.257.
80   Ibid., p. 226; Personal interviews, Dubai, January 2007.
81   Hawley, 2007, p. 114.
82   Wilson, p.196.
83   Hawley, 2007, p.118.
84   Al-Gurg, pp. 134-135.
85   Abu Dhabi opted to use the Bahraini Dinar, replacing its existing Rupees and Maria Theresa Talas. Hawley, 2007, p.34.
86   See section 2.2.
87   Foreign Office 371/120557.
88   Foreign Office 371/120557; Al-Sagri, Saleh Hamad, 'Britain and the Arab Emirates, 1820-1956' (PhD thesis, University of Kent at Canterbury, 1988), p.190.
89   See section 2.4.
90   Personal interviews, Dubai, January 2007.
91   Hawley, 2007, p.221.
92   Al-Gurg, p. 136.
93   Lady Margaret Luce.
94   Luce, Margaret, *From Aden to the Gulf: Personal Diaries, 1956-1966* (Salisbury, Michael Russell, 1987), p.177.
95   Ibid., p.176.
96   Fahim, p.94.
97   Fahim, p.95.
98   Personal interviews, Abu Dhabi, June 2005.
99   Abu-Baker, Albadr, 'Political Economy of State Formation: The United Arab Emirates in Comparative Perspective' (PhD thesis, University of Michigan, 1995), p.129; Joyce, Miriam,'On the Road Towards Unity: The Trucial States from a British Perspective, 1960-1966', *Middle Eastern Studies* (vol. 35, no.2, 1999), p.56; Oxford Business Group. 'Emerging Emirates' (London: 2000), p. 130.
100   In late 1960 Sheikh Said, believed to be an alcoholic at that time, killed his sister Moza with a shotgun and was taken to Al-Ayn to be looked after by Sheikh Zayed, who then later took him to Europe to receive medical treatment. Personal interviews, Exeter, July 2007; Hawley 2007, p. 242, 258. On several occasions following Zayed's deputising for his brother at Trucial States Council meetings, Sheikh Rashid had remarked to the British that in the future he would much prefer to do business with Zayed rather than Sheikh Shakhbut. See Wilson, p. 234. The deposition happened following a meeting in Kuwait at which Zayed met with British officials at a hotel close to the British embassy. Personal interviews, Durham, May 2007.
101   It was reported that Sheikh Shakhbut received a guard of honour as he was escorted to the aircraft, and after four years in exile was permitted to return to Abu Dhabi, where he lived until his death in 1989. Rugh, Andrea B., *The Political Culture of Leadership in the United Arab Emirates* (New York: Palgrave Macmillan, 2007), p.78.

102 See section 2.5.
103 Bloodshed was avoided after Sheikh Hadif challenged the leader of the thieves to a camel race and won.
104 Foreign Office 371/18919.
105 Personal interviews with members of the Al-Shamsi family, Dubai June 2005.
106 Personal interviews, Dubai, June 2006.
107 Foreign Office 371/120552.
108 Wilson, p.179.
109 Buxani, p.85.
110 Wilson, p.111.
111 Ibid., p.125.
112 Ibid., p.96.
113 Ibid., p.129.
114 Buxani, p.91.
115 Ibid., p. 91; Al-Gurg. p.75.
116 Interestingly, Halcrow International are the consultants advising on the dredging of Dubai's new 'Business Bay'. See section 4.7.
117 Buxani, pp. 87-88.
118 See section 7.5.
119 Personal interviews, Dubai, February 2006.
120 Rush, p.133.
121 Hawley 2007, p. 226.
122 Wilson, pp. 96-97.
123 Al-Gurg, p.75.
124 The Bin Lutah family temporarily left Dubai following a quarrel with the Al-Maktum family in 1911. They moved to Ajman and took British subject passports for the purposes of protection. This idea was the suggestion of one of their family members who worked for the British agency. Personal correspondence with members of the Bin Lutah family, Dubai, September 2005.
125 Bedouin used to visit Dubai regularly to sell tins of water they had drawn from wells in Jumeirah or from wells on islands. They would also stretch sails between poles to catch rainwater whenever the weather was cloudy. Buxani, p. 6.
126 Ibid., p. 6; Personal interviews, Dubai, June 2006.
127 Foreign Office 371/120552.
128 Hawley, 2007, p.123.
129 See sections 5.8 and 8.2 for Dubai's involvement in rebuilding the Iraqi and Afghani economies since the outbreak of the War on Terror.
130 Perhaps most notably, after 1991 Dubai's ports became a major staging area for repairing Kuwait's damaged refineries. Many oil-associated Kuwaiti companies relocated to Dubai and the Kuwait Petroleum Company rented a large area of land to help it transfer goods to the port of Shuyabah in Kuwait. Personal interviews, Dubai, September 2005.
131 Buxani, p. 61.
132 Ibid., p.73; Maitra and Al-Hajji, pp. 198-199.

133   Buxani. p.69.
134   Ibid., pp. 106-107.
135   See section 2.3.
136   Personal interviews, Dubai, February 2006.
137   Eventually JVC products were imported by the Al-Shirawi family.
138   Buxani, pp. 119-158.
139   Soon after this influx of Indian merchants, the Indian community in Dubai had split into two factions, represented by the Indian Association and the Indian Welfare Association. By the 1960s this divide had been reconciled following the creation of the Indian National Association. Foreign Office 371/120552.
140   Foreign Office 371/120552.
141   Personal correspondence with James Onley, March 2007.
142   Al-Gurg, p.29; Buxani, pp. 3-4.
143   Ibid., pp. 98-99.
144   Foreign Office 371/120553.
145   Personal interviews, Dubai, June 2006.
146   Personal interviews with members of the Al-Hameli family, Abu Dhabi, June 2006.
147   Buxani, pp. 88-89; Wilson, pp. 173-174.
148   Luce, p.133.
149   Hawley, 2007, p.128.
150   Wilson, p.128; Personal interviews, Dubai, June 2006.
151   Personal interviews, Dubai, February 2006.
152   See section 1.5.
153   Buxani, p. 83.
154   This latter airbase was constructed at Al-Dhafrah in Abu Dhabi. Foreign Office 371/18912
155   Buxani, p.10.
156   Wilson, p.180.
157   Ibid., p.178.
158   See section 1.5.
159   Personal interviews, Dubai, June 2006; Wilson. pp. 178-180.
160   Buxani, pp. 93-94.
161   Al-Gurg, p.104.
162   Ibid., p.105; Buxani, pp. 93-94.
163   Personal interviews, Dubai, June 2006.
164   Hawley 2007, p.114.
165   Al-Gurg, p.106.
166   Ibid., p.103.
167   Buxani, pp. 93-94.
168   See section 1.5.
169   Wilson, pp. 185-186.
170   Buxani, pp. 102-103; Al-Gurg, p.79.
171   Personal interviews, Dubai, September 2005.
172   Buxani, pp. 100-101.
173   Wilson, pp. 207-208.

174   Al-Gurg, p.52. The Imperial Bank of Iran was originally the Imperial Bank of Persia, which had been set up in the late nineteenth century by the Qajar dynasty.
175   Imperial Trading Corporation of Karachi being a good example. See Wilson, pp. 111-112.
176   Hawley, 2007, p.282.
177   Al-Gurg, p.59.
178   Wilson, p.217.
179   Ibid., p. 218.
180   Ibid., p.365; Personal interviews, Dubai, September 2005.
181   Wilson, p. 366.
182   Ibid., p.218; Personal interviews, Dubai, September 2005.
183   Al-Gurg, p.158; Hawley, 2007, p. 300.
184   Al-Gurg, p.158-159.

4.   THE DIVERSIFICATION OF THE ECONOMY

1   See section 1.5.
2   Buxani, Ram, *Taking the High Road* (Dubai: Motivate, 2003), p. 87.
3   Personal interviews, Dubai, January 2007.
4   Wilson, Graeme, *Rashid's Legacy: The Genesis of the Maktoum Family and the History of Dubai* (Dubai: Media Prima, 2006), pp. 240, 247.
5   Ibid., p.240; personal interviews, Dubai, June 2006.
6   Buxani, p. 87.
7   These concessions were held by the Iraqi Petroleum Company's wholly owned subsidiary, Petroleum Concessions Ltd. See section 1.5.
8   Ibid.
9   This information is an updated combination of data gathered from Abdulla, Abdulkhaleq, 'Political Dependency: The Case of the United Arab Emirates' (PhD thesis, Georgetown University, 1985), pp. 107-114; Al-Otaibi, Manna Said, *The Petroleum Concession Agreements of the United Arab Emirates* (London: Croom Helm, 1982); Abu-Baker, Albadr, 'Political Economy of State Formation: The United Arab Emirates in Comparative Perspective' (PhD thesis. University of Michigan, 1995), pp.150-151; Oxford Business Group, 'Emerging Emirates' (London: 2000), p.48; personal interviews, Abu Dhabi, March 2003.
10   Personal interviews, Dubai, January 2007; Van Der Meulen, Hendrik, 'The Role of Tribal and Kinship Ties in the Politics of the United Arab Emirates' (PhD thesis, The Fletcher School of Law and Diplomacy, 1997), p. 268.
11   Wilson, pp. 374-375.
12   *Economist Intelligence Unit,* January 2000.
13   Al-Gurg, Easa Saleh, *The Wells of Memory* (London: John Murray, 1998), pp.186-187.
14   Wilson, p.73.
15   Author's estimates, based on a figure of 55 billion Dirhams for 2006.
16   Personal interviews, Dubai, January 2007.

17   'Dubai International Capital alone intends to acquire assets in excess of
      $25 billion over the next three years', *Gulf Today*, 25 July 2007.
18   A $1 billion investment made in 2005.
19   In the summer of 2007 Dubai International Capital acquired a 31 per
      cent stake in EADS. *Gulf Today*, 25 July 2007.
20   Purchased for around $1.4 billion from the Royal Bank of Scotland in
      2005.
21   The Essex Hotel.
22   The latter of which was acquired in 2006 for $800 million.
23   Personal interviews, Dubai, January 2007.
24   Buxani, p. 87.
25   Personal interviews, Dubai, November 2006; *Gulf News* 24 September
      2004.
26   Van Der Meulen, p. 93.
27   Personal interviews, Dubai, January 2007.
28   Most of this being managed by the Panamanian conduit company,
      Financiera Avenida. Personal interviews, Abu Dhabi, March 2004.
29   Author's estimates. ADIA is currently chaired by the ruler's younger
      brother, Sheikh Ahmad bin Zayed Al-Nahyan.
30   Personal interviews, Abu Dhabi, June 2005.
31   Oxford Business Group, 'Emerging Emirates', p. 43.
32   Personal interviews, Abu Dhabi, June 2005.
33   ADIA is based in the new Samsung building on the Corniche, which was
      completed in 2006 and has now eclipsed the Hilton hotel's Baynunah
      Tower to become the tallest building in Abu Dhabi.
34   Oxford Business Group, 'Emerging Emirates', pp.90-91.
35   *Gulf News*, 2 August 2005; see section 8.1.
36   Personal interviews, Dubai, January 2007.
37   *Gulf Today*, 18 July 2007.
38   Author's estimates and earlier figures from Al-Sharhan International
      Consultancy, 'United Arab Emirates Country Report' (Dubai: 2001),
      pp. 14-15.
39   Personal interviews, Dubai, January 2007.
40   Caused by OPEC-related oversupplying.
41   During this war a stray Iranian missile hit and damaged an Abu Dhabi
      offshore terminal.
42   Al-Gurg, p.162; personal interviews, Dubai, December 2001. In 2001
      a former Egyptian oil minister visited Dubai and stated that 'the real
      benefits of oil as a support for the industry were being gained by the
      West who refused our repeated attempts to sell them refined oil and
      insisted on buying it from us as a crude product. We were not making
      enough profit from oil as far as selling it for a good price as well as
      refining it and manufacturing its products are concerned.'
43   Al-Gurg, p.162.
44   Personal interviews, Dubai, January 2007.
45   By 1995 production had dropped to around 300,000 barrels per day.
46   Personal interviews, Dubai, January 2007.

47   Wilson, p.476.
48   Ibid., pp.368-370.
49   Al-Gurg, p.109.
50   Ibid.
51   Wilson, p. 372.
52   Hawley, Donald, *The Emirates: Witness to a Metamorphosis* (Norwich: Michael Russell, 2007), p.18
53   Personal interviews, Dubai, June 2006.
54   Personal interviews, Dubai, February 2006.
55   Emirates Road, which runs from Abu Dhabi through Dubai and up to Ra's al-Khaimah.
56   *Gulf Today,* 23 June 2007.
57   Personal interviews, Dubai, Feburary 2006; Daily Telegraph, 31 October 2005.
58   See section 3.8.
59   Wilson, p.426.
60   Ibid., pp. 425-427.
61   Personal interviews, Dubai, January 2007.
62   Wilson, pp.478-480.
63   Ibid.
64   Hawley, 2007, p. 285.
65   Wilson, p. 484.
66   Ibid., pp. 482-483.
67   Personal interviews, Dubai, January 2007.
68   Wilson, p. 530.
69   Personal correspondence, March 2007.
70   Built by Emaar properties.
71   Since 2004 construction commenced on a number of new malls in Abu Dhabi, including Khalidya Mall and Al-Wadha Mall.
72   Abu Dhabi Mall, Marina Mall, and Al-Raha Mall.
73   See section 3.8.
74   Dubai Department of Economic Development, 'Statistical Book' (Dubai: 1999), p. 247.
75   See sections 7.4 and 7.5 with reference to banking scandals in Abu Dhabi and Sharjah.
76   Al-Gurg, p.156.
77   Abdulla, p. 250; personal interviews, Dubai, February 2006. EIB is 51 per cent owned by the Abu Dhabi government and 49 per cent by a consortium of local banks.
78   Oxford Business Group, 'Emerging Emirates', p. 88; personal interviews, Dubai, June 2006.
79   Hawley, 2007, p. 34.
80   Davidson, Christopher M., *The United Arab Emirates: A Study in Survival* (Boulder: Lynne Rienner, 2005), p. 123.
81   During the late 1980s the cost of imports was held at around $5.5 billion. See Dubai Department of Economic Development, 'Statistical Book' (Dubai: 2001), p. 110.

82   Personal interviews, Dubai, February 2006.
83   Dubai Department of Economic Development, 2001, p. 75.
84   Crown Prince Court Department of Research and Studies, 'Statistical Book' (Abu Dhabi: 1996), pp. 31, 76.
85   Dubai Department of Economic Development 2001, p.72; personal interviews, Dubai, February 2006.
86   Most notably over 80 per cent in vegetables and dairy products, although only about 25 percent in meat and 20 per cent in poultry. Personal interviews, Dubai, June 2006.
87   Personal correspondence, March 2007.
88   See section 7.3.
89   Personal interviews, Dubai, June 2006.
90   Dubai Department of Economic Development, 1999, p.241.
91   Dubai Department of Economic Development, 'Statistical Book' (Dubai: 2002), p. 245; personal interviews, Dubai February 2006.
92   Personal correspondence, March 2007.
93   Personal interviews, Dubai, February 2006.
94   As described in section 3.5, Hamriyyah was formerly controlled by the Al-Bu Shamis, before being taken over by Sharjah.
95   See *Gulf Today*, 18 July 2007.
96   See articles 15, 16, and 17 of the Dubai Technology, Electronic Commerce, and Media Free Zone Law Number 1 of 2000. Free zone companies are not allowed to hire nationals of 'boycotted countries', most notably Israel.
97   Personal correspondence, March 2007.
98   Wilson, p. 551.
99   Ibid., p. 581.
100   *Gulf News* 22 September 2004; personal interviews, Dubai, June 2006.
101   Personal interviews, Dubai, February 2006.
102   *Khaleej Times*, 2October 2004.
103   Personal interviews, Dubai, February 2006.
104   Buxani, pp. 85, 93.
105   Most notably the Indian Prime Minister, Indira Gandhi, during her 1981 trip to Dubai. Wilson, p.186.
106   Personal interviews, Dubai, January 2007.
107   Wilson, p.486.
108   Personal interviews, Dubai, January 2007.
109   Personal interviews, Dubai, June 2006.
110   Data supplied by the Dubai Department of Tourism and Commerce Marketing.
111   *The Guardian*, 18 June 2007. The QE2 was purchased by Istithmar, the investment arm of the Dubai Ports World Company.
112   Personal interviews, Dubai, January 2007.
113   Data supplied by the Dubai Department of Tourism and Commerce Marketing. In 2006 there were 6.4 million visitors to Dubai.
114   Buxani, p. 160.
115   Personal interviews with members of the Al-Hameli family, Abu Dhabi,

May 2006.
116   See section 7.5.
117   Wilson, p. 532.
118   Personal correspondence, May 2007.
119   The A380 in question was painted in the livery of Emirates Airlines.
120   Wilson, pp. 395-402.
121   *Hatta* being owned by Sheikh Muhammad and winning in 1977; *Shaab* being owned by Sheikh Maktum and winning in 1979.
122   Wilson, pp. 395-402.
123   Darley benefited from the Al-Maktum's great stallion *Northern Dancer*, which was still siring into the late 1980s. Personal interviews, Dubai, January 2007.
124   This course became known locally as the 'Al-Met track'.
125   Wilson, pp. 410-421; personal correspondence, March 2007.
126   This was first sponsored by Sheikh Muhammad in 1982. Wilson, pp. 395-402.
127   Davidson, 2005, p. 230.
128   Personal interviews, Dubai, February 2006. For a journalist's interpretation see *The Daily Telegraph* 15 January 2005.
129   Personal interviews, Dubai, January 2007.
130   The Jumeirah Palm will feature the dolphin islands while the Jebel Ali Palm will feature Arabic lettering.
131   *WAM* (UAE National News Agency) 6 October 2004.
132   Merchant International Group, 'Strategic Research and Corporate Intelligence: Instant Analysis on Dubai' (London: 2005).
133   Personal interviews, Abu Dhabi, 2002.
134   See Law Number 7 of 2006: The Dubai Property Law.
135   Following allegations of insider trading, the Dubai government chose to retain 33 per cent of the shares.
136   Personal interviews, Dubai, June 2006.
137   Personal interviews, Ra's al-Khaimah, November 2006.
138   Most notably Emaar is one of the main developers of the King Abdullah Economic City in Saudi Arabia.
139   Data supplied by the Ministry of Planning.
140   Data supplied by the Ministry of Economy.
141   Ibid.
142   Personal interviews, Dubai, March 2007; and data from the Inter-Arab Investment Guarantee Corporation.
143   Data supplied by the Ministry of Finance and Industry.
144   Personal interviews, Dubai, February 2006.
145   *Gulf News*, 23 September 2004.

5.   POLITICAL STABILITY AND THE RULING BARGAIN

1   In 2005 Saudi Arabia held municipal elections in which males over the age of 21 were eligible to vote. In the next round of elections, to be held in 2009, it is likely that females will be eligible to vote. See *Washington*

Post, 24 April 2007.

2   According to data produced by Freedom House, the United Arab Emirates scores 6 for political rights and 5 for civil liberties (on a scale of 1 to 7, with 7 being the worst). This compares unfavourably with other Gulf states, with Kuwait scoring 4 and Bahrain scoring 5 for both categories. Significantly, the UAE's score places it on a par with many African and Asian dictatorships. See Freedom House, 'The Worst of the Worst: The World's Most Repressive Societies' (Washington, DC: 2007).

3   Strong examples of such modernisation theorists being Daniel Lerner and Karl Deutsch.

4   In 1968 Huntington described a 'king's dilemma' that all modernising monarchs must eventually face. See Huntington, Samuel P., *Political Order in Changing Societies* (New Haven: Yale University Press, 1968).

5   See section 2.3.

6   See sections 1.7 and 2.3.

7   Wilson, Graeme, *Rashid's Legacy: The Genesis of the Maktoum Family and the History of Dubai* (Dubai: Media Prima, 2006), pp. 466-477.

8   Such statements appeared in *The Telegraph* and *The Independent*.

9   Rugh, Andrea B. *The Political Culture of Leadership in the United Arab Emirates* (New York: Palgrave Macmillan, 2007), p.115.

10   Sheikh Maktum attended Gordonstoun school in Scotland.

11   Hawley, Donald, *The Emirates: Witness to a Metamorphosis* (Norwich: Michael Russell, 2007), p.189.

12   Ibid. p.236.

13   See section 7.2.

14   Sheikh Hamdan was educated at the Bell Languages Institute in Cambridge.

15   Personal interviews, Dubai, January 2007. EPPCO is the Emirates Petroleum Products Company.

16   See section 4.1. DUBAL is Dubai Aluminium and DUCAB the Dubai Cabling Company.

17   Personal interviews, Dubai, June 2006.

18   See section 8.9.

19   See section 4.3.

20   Most notably the Lesker Trading Company, which Sheikh Muhammad set up in the 1980s.

21   Personal interviews, Dubai, June 2006. Also see section 7.3.

22   Sheikh Said's first wife was the indomitable Sheikha Hussa bint Murr Al-Huraiz, who eventually became an influential businesswoman. His second wife was taken from Ra's al-Khaimah, after Hussa's death. Lienhardt, Peter, *Sheikhdoms of Eastern Arabia* (Oxford: Palgrave, 2001), pp.171-172.

23   Personal interviews, Dubai, January 2007.

24   See section 4.3.

25   Pope, M. T. G., *Businessman's Guide to the United Arab Emirates* (Sharjah: Dar al-Fatah, 1996), p. 204.

26   Personal interviews, Dubai, January 2007.

27   Van Der Meulen, Hendrik, 'The Role of Tribal and Kinship Ties in the Politics of the United Arab Emirates' (PhD thesis. The Fletcher School of Law and Diplomacy, 1997), p.191.

28   Hawley 2007, pp. 77, 103. Also see section 2.2.

29   Foreign Office 371/120552. Also see section 2.2.

30   Van Der Meulen, p.189.

31   Pope, p.260.

32   Van Der Meulen, p.189.

33   Pope, p. 254.

34   Personal interviews, Dubai, January 2007.

35   Pope, p. 260.

36   Sheikh Muhammad's poetry is often recited at major sporting and cultural events, not just in Dubai but also in other emirates, including at Sheikh Zayed's memorial service and at the opening ceremonies of the Dubai World Cup.

37   Sheikh Rashid engineered this marriage, along with the marriage of his daughter Sheikha Hussa bint Rashid Al-Maktum to Sheikha Hind's brother, Sheikh Ahmad bint Maktum Al-Maktum. Rugh, p.112.

38   Van Der Meulen, p.127.

39   Personal interviews, Dubai, January 2007.

40   During the Kuwaiti succession dispute of early 2006 the nominated crown prince was replaced by the prime minister following a decision by the parliament.

41   Sultan Qabus has no heirs, but has left a sealed envelope containing his nomination for crown prince. If his security council fails to reach a decision within 72 hours of his death, the envelope must be opened.

42   It is believed that Sheikh Said bin Maktum Al-Maktum has married into a family of Baluchi descent.

43   In 2006 Sheikh Rashid won the individual gold medal in the Asian Games endurance horserace.

44   An advert for www.fazza3.com appears on a poster outside the Mall of the Emirates.

45   Sheikh Ahmad, like his father, is a former winner of international endurance races.

46   See section 1.5.

47   Wilson, p.43.

48   Ibid., pp. 43-44.

49   Ibid., p.142.

50   Ibid., p.105.

51   Oxford Business Group, *Emerging Emirates* (London: 2000), p. 70.

52   Personal interviews, Dubai, January 2007.

53   See section 4.3.

54   See section 4.5.

55   It is possible for a Dubai national to walk into a ready made farm, complete with all the necessary equipment and infrastructure to launch an agricultural business.

56 See section 4.4.

57 This continues to happen in some parts of Dubai, where villas that were built specifically for nationals are inhabited by expatriate families. Up until recently the problem was most acute in Abu Dhabi, where it was not uncommon for some of these large villas to be rented out to South Asian families, causing many complaints from disgruntled neighbours.

58 Personal interviews, Dubai, January 2007; Van Der Meulen, p. 202. In 1997 Dubai had only about 40,000 nationals in the mid-1990s.

59 See sections 3.3 – 3.7.

60 See section 6.3.

61 Sharjah's population is c. 120,000; Ra's al-Khaimah's is c. 130,000; Fujairah's is c. 110,000. Based on the author's estimates and data from Van Der Meulen, p. 202.

62 Personal interviews, Dubai, January 2007.

63 CIA World Factbook,'Saudi Arabia' (Langley: 2007).

64 Figures based on the author's estimates and CIA World Factbook, 'United Arab Emirates' (Langley: 2007). In 2005 the official Dubai census recorded 1.2 million, but acknowledged that over 350,000 were excluded from the survey. In 2006 it was estimated that the population had reached 1.6 million. Data supplied by Tedad

65 Author's estimates.

66 In 1930 the 'Native Administration and Authority Decree' made the distinction between Arabs and non-Arabs in Zanzibar and their respective entitlements. Foreign Office 618/47/13.

67 Personal interviews, Abu Dhabi, March 2002.

68 Personal interviews with employees of the Ministry of Labour and Social Affairs, Abu Dhabi, March 2002.

69 As will be discussed in section 6.6, the main internet provider, Etisalat, operates a proxy server that blocks 'culturally incompatible' websites.

70 Most notably the Dhawahir control dozens of top positions in the UAE Armed Forces, the Mazari make up a sizable portion of the Amiri Guard, and the Awamir have held many posts in public works and civil defence. See Davidson, Christopher M., 'After Sheikh Zayed: The Politics of Succession in Abu Dhabi and the United Arab Emirates', *Middle East Policy* (vol.13, no.1, 2006), pp.52-53.

71 Van Der Meulen, pp.192-193; Pope, pp.204, 273, 297.

72 Personal interviews, Dubai, June 2006.

73 Ibid. Also see section 4.3.

74 Van Der Meulen, pp.193-194.

75 In 1833 the Harib family of the Al-Marrar section joined the Al-Bu Falasah in Dubai.

76 Van Der Meulen, p.183.

77 Ibid., pp.194-195.

78 As described in section 4.3, the Al-Ghurair family opened the first shopping mall in Dubai.

79 See section 2.2.

80 Most notably the aforementioned Majid bin Muhammad Al-Futtaim

had secured the lucrative franchise to operate the French Carrefour supermarket chain in Dubai.

81   Van Der Meulen, pp.194-195.
82   Ibid., pp.182-183. Also see section 3.5.
83   Van Der Meulen, p.196.
84   The current Minister for Culture, Youth, and Community Development is Abdul Rahman Muhammad Al-Owais.
85   Van Der Meulen, p.156.
86   Pope, p. 222.
87   See section 3.6.
88   Pope, pp.193, 251, 269.
89   The *ajami* Al-Mulla family of Dubai is not related to the ruling Al-Mu'alla ruling clan of Umm al-Qawain.
90   Personal interviews, Dubai, January 2007.
91   Anwar Muhammad Gargash.
92   For a discussion of the Mubadala Corporation, see section 7.4. Khaldun is from a Saudi-origin family that has provided Abu Dhabi with both judges and ambassadors, including his father who was assassinated while serving as the Ambassador to France. See section 8.9.
93   See section 4.7.
94   See sections 4.1, 4.5.
95   For a discussion of voluntary transformation of the polity as a temporary means of delaying genuine political reform, see Davidson, Christopher M., *The United Arab Emirates: A Study in Survival* (Boulder: Lynne Rienner, 2005), pp. 67-68,
96   The aforementioned brothers Sultan Ahmad bin Sulayman and Khalid Ahmad bin Sulayman, in addition to their nephew Khalifa Muhammad bin Sulayman.
97   Khalfan bin Ahmad Harib.
98   Dhahi bin Khalfan Tamim.
99   In 2003 it was announced that a network of elected regional majaalis would be set up by 2005. *WAM* (UAE National News Agency), 1 January 2003.
100   These include the Dubai Municipality, Dubai Courts, the Department of Civil Aviation, the Lands Department, the Dubai Development Board, the Department of Economic Development, the Department of Tourism and Commerce Marketing, the Knowledge and Human Development Authority, and Dubai Police.
101   Abu Dhabi contributes about 70 per cent of the federal budget, with Dubai only about 15 per cent, and with the remainder coming from various federal parastatals such as Etisalat. Personal interviews, Abu Dhabi, March 2007.
102   See section 2.5. The original constitution was drawn up by an Egyptian expert who had also worked on the Kuwaiti constitution. Personal interviews, Abu Dhabi, March 2007; Al-Gurg, Easa Saleh, *The Wells of Memory* (London: John Murray, 1998), p.140.
103   See Al-Nabeh, Najat Abdullah, 'United Arab Emirates: Regional and

Global Dimensions' (PhD thesis, Claremont Graduate School, 1984).

104   Rashid Abdullah Al-Nu'aymi was the Minister for Foreign Affairs. He is not part of the ruling section of the Al-Nu'aymi family.

105   Hanif Hassan Al-Qassimi is not a member of the ruling Qawasim tribe of Ra's al-Khaimah or Sharjah.

106   Sheikh Khalifa bin Zayed Al-Nahyan is Supreme Commander, Sheikh Muhammad bin Zayed Al-Nahyan is Deputy Supreme Commander, and Hamad bin Muhammad Al-Thai Al-Rumaithi is the Chief of Staff. AFP, 1 January 2005.

107   Rizvi, S. N. Asad, 'From Tents to High Rise: Economic Development of the United Arab Emirates', *Middle Eastern Studies* (vol. 29, no.4, 1993), p. 665.

108   Abdul-Aziz bin Abdullah Al-Ghurair is the FNC's speaker at the time of writing.

109   Muhammad Al-Roken is a Dubai-based lawyer and former professor of law.

110   Al-Nahyan, Shamma bint Muhammad, *Political and Social Security in the United Arab Emirates* (Dubai: 2000), pp.122-123.

111   Ibid., p.121.

112   Ibid., pp.178-179, 188.

113   This has been a common strategy across all traditional monarchies. Most notably, the government of Saudi Arabia had leaked plans to ban satellite dishes and female overseas scholarships, and subsequently dropped the proposals upon discovering the likely scale of the backlash.

114   Sheikh Muhammad's website has existed since the mid-1990s.

115   The World Trade Organisation, which the UAE joined in 1996. Personal interviews with employees of the Dubai Chamber of Commerce and Industry, Dubai, February 2006.

116   *Khaleej Times*, 10 February 2006.

117   Personal interviews, London, December 2006.

118   Personal interviews, London, February 2007.

119   Personal interviews, Dubai, January 2007.

120   *Gulf News*, 21 December 2006.

121   *Gulf News*, 7 May 2007.

122   See sections 1.4, 2.3 -2.5.

123   See section 8.2.

124   See section 1.3.

125   Dubai never joined OPEC, therefore this was effectively a unilateral Abu Dhabi policy. See section 7.3; Brown, Gavin, *OPEC and the World Energy Market* (London: Longman, 1998), p. 361.

126   Dubai, Sharjah, and Umm al-Qawain sided with Iran, perhaps given their large *ajami* populations and their historic trade links with Iran. See Davidson, 2005, p. 206. Also see section 7.3.

127   Personal interviews, Kuwait, November 2005.

128   Personal interviews, Abu Dhabi, March 2007.

129   In late 2005 Sheikh Muhammad bin Zayed Al-Nahyan revealed that Saddam had actually accepted his father's 2003 peace offering.

Personal interviews, Abu Dhabi, March 2007; AFP, 29 October 2005. Muhammad made this announcement during an Al-Arabiyya TV interview.

130   Personal interviews, Ajman, February 2006; *Lebanonwire* 16 October 2005; AFP, 20 October 2005.

131   Personal interviews, Dubai, January 2007.

132   BBC, 13 May 2007.

133   The John C. Stennis.

134   Reuters, 11 May 2007.

135   See section 8.3.

136   The Taleban possessed an embassy in a villa in the Khalidya district of Abu Dhabi, close to the British Embassy.

137   Personal interviews, Abu Dhabi, March 2007.

138   *The Hindu*, 23 September 2001; CNN, 22 October 2001.

139   Wilson, p. 423.

140   Ibid., pp.361-362.

141   Al-Madfai, Madiha Rashid, *Jordan, the United States and the Middle East Peace Process, 1974-1991* (Cambridge University Press, 1993), p. 21.

142   Between 1979 and 1992 Birzeit University was closed 60 per cent of the time due to lack of funding and Israeli harassment. Wilson, pp. 377-378.

143   Ibid., p. 365.

144   This was a gift from Sheikh Zayed to the Palestinian Authority's Ministry of Public Works and Housing in 2004. *Khaleej Times,* 23 October 2004.

145   Hafez Al-Assad almost certainly wished to rebalance Christian and Sunni communities and become the Arab architect of a new Lebanese republic. Personal interviews, Beirut, November 2006.

146   Wilson, p. 424; Personal interviews, Beirut, November 2006.

147   Wilson, p. 457.

148   Personal interviews, Dubai, February 2006.

149   Wilson, p.461.

150   Ibid. p.461; Personal interviews, Dubai, February 2006.

151   Personal interviews, Beirut, November 2006.

152   Personal correspondence, July 2007.

153   Wilson, pp. 505-506.

154   Ibid., pp. 511-513.

155   Personal interviews, Dubai, June 2006.

156   Hawley, 2007, p. 30.

157   Personal interviews, Dubai, February 2006.

158   *Jane's Defense Weekly*, 7 February 2007.

159   Wilson, p. 516.

160   Personal interviews, Dubai, February 2006.

161   Some $2 million was donated by the Muhammad bin Rashid Charitable and Humanitarian Establishment to Thailand in early 2005. *Gulf News,* 12 February 2005.

162   BBC, 19 May 2007.

163 This has grated with many involved in the UAE's domestic education and higher education sectors given that the federal education budget has been frozen since 2003, despite rapidly rising annual enrolments.

164 Personal interviews, Dubai, February 2006.

165 Reuters, 18 October 2002; *India Tribune*,18 October 2002.

166 *Gulf News*, 27 October 2004.

167 See section 4.1.

168 Personal interviews, Abu Dhabi, March 2007.

169 Khalaf, Sulayman, 'Poetics and Politics of Newly Invented Traditions in the Gulf: Camel Racing in the United Arab Emirates', *Ethnology* (vol. 39, no. 3, 2000), pp. 85-106.

170 Ibid.

171 These observations were made by Said Abu Athira—a Jordanian traveller who once famously journeyed by camel from Jordan to the UAE. Personal correspondence, March 2007.

6.   THE DUBAI PARADOX

1   Personal interviews, National Bank of Dubai, Dubai, May 2005.

2   Wilson, Graeme. *Rashid's Legacy: The Genesis of the Maktoum Family and the History of Dubai* (Dubai: Media Prima, 2006), p. 528.

3   Ibid., p.529.

4   *Oxford Analytica*, February 2007.

5   *AME*, 30 May 2007.

6   Al-Gurg, Easa Saleh, *The Wells of Memory* (London: John Murray, 1998), p.219.

7   See section 3.1.

8   Personal interviews, Dubai, January 2007.

9   Personal interviews, Dubai, July 2007.

10 Du is 40 per cent owned by the federal government and 20 per cent owned by the aforementioned Mubadala; the other 40 per cent is owned by private investors.

11 Etisalat telephone calls to India and Pakistan cost about 65 cents per minute compared to about 50 cents per minute to Saudi Arabia and the United States.

12 *Gulf News*, 1 June 2005.

13 *Gulf News*, 3 March 2007.

14 Personal interviews, Dubai, January 2007; Crown Prince Court Department of Research and Studies. 'Statistical Book' (Abu Dhabi: 1996), pp. 32, 76.

15 It is estimated that about 36 per cent of Dubai's non-oil trade is made up of consumer durable imports, 39 per cent from other imports, with 20 per cent from re-exports, and with just 5 per cent being exports. Personal interviews, Dubai, January 2007; Dubai Department of Economic Development, 'Statistical Book' (Dubai: 2002), pp.109-114.

16 Quoting Fatima Al-Shamsi. See Davidson, Christopher M., *The United Arab Emirates: A Study in Survival* (Boulder: Lynne Rienner, 2005),

p.166.
17   See section 4.8.
18   Non-oil contributions are estimated to be 95 per cent of Dubai's GDP. Data supplied by the Ministry of Economy.
19   See section 8.10.
20   The Aqaba free zone was set up in 2000.
21   In 2006 there were 2 million European visitors and 0.4 million North American visitors, out of a total of 6.4 million. Data supplied by the Dubai Department of Tourism and Commerce Marketing.
22   DTCM reports 3.5 million visitors in 2001, compared to 3.4 million in 2000.
23   Personal interviews, Foreign and Commonwealth Office, London, July 2006.
24   In addition to Oman and some other Gulf states, prominent examples would be Cape Verde, which has invested heavily in tourist infrastructure (including a new international airport) and recently launched a real estate sector along much the same lines as Dubai.
25   Personal interviews, Dubai, January 2007.
26   See section 4.8
27   With reference to Palestinian investors see Davidson 2005. pp.258-259
28   See section 4.5
29   Dubai Department of Economic Development. 'Statistical Book' (Dubai: 2001), p.129
30   Ibid. p.130
31   Data supplied by the Dubai Department of Tourism and Commerce Marketing.
32   Personal interviews, Dubai, January 2007
33   See section 5.7
34   Personal interviews with representatives of the World Trade Organisation, Dubai, September 2003
35   *Gulf News* 20th December 2002
36   Most notably Julphar, Globalpharma, and Gulf Inject. See Oxford Business Group, 'Emerging Emirates' (London: 2000), p.91; Business Monitor International, 'United Arab Emirates' (London: 2003); personal interviews, Sharjah, October 2002.
37   *Gulf News,* 5 September 2003.
38   Davidson, 2005, p. 262.
39   These are most commonly 'double taxation' treaties which ensure the mutual reduction or elimination of import and export duties.
40   Oxford Business Group, p. 123.
41   *Khaleej Times,* 2 December 2002. Citing the UAE Minister of Labour and Social Affairs speaking at the Dubai Chamber of Commerce and Industry.
42   The symposium on the 'Declaration of Fundamental Rights and Principles at Work'.
43   Information supplied by the US Department of State.
44   Ibid.

330

45   Information supplied by the Emirates Bankers Association.

46   *Gulf News*, 3November 2002.

47   *Khaleej Times*, 6 February 2004.

48   It was estimated in 1997 for example, that the 300,000 Pakistani workers in Abu Dhabi and Dubai were able to send home an average of $3,000 per capita, for a total remittance of about $1 billion. See Van Der Meulen, Hendrik, 'The Role of Tribal and Kinship Ties in the Politics of the United Arab Emirates' (PhD thesis. The Fletcher School of Law and Diplomacy, 1997), pp.71-72.

49   In September 2005 a peaceful ten day strike was held at a camp in Ajman, with workers complaining that they had not been paid for five months. Personal interviews, Dubai, September 2005. Similarly, in October 2004 over 7,000 workers had demonstrated at the DXB Terminal 3 construction site following the deaths of some of their colleagues. See *Khaleej Times*, 2 October 2004.

50   *Gulf News*, 20 September 2005.

51   *Khaleej Times*, 22 March 2006.

52   Information supplied by the US Bureau of Democracy, Human Rights, and Labor.

53   Personal interviews, Dubai, January 2007.

54   *Khaleej Times*, 1 March 2007.

55   Personal interviews, Dubai, January 2007.

56   *The Daily Telegraph*, 15 January 2005.

57   A prominent example would include Nakheel's decision to squeeze more properties onto Palm Jumeirah, thereby reducing the footprint of each villa. In 2005 a new bypass road was constructed close to Emaar's Meadows project, much to the chagrin of residents.

58   Personal interviews, Dubai, June 2006.

59   *The Daily Telegraph*, 15 January 2005.

60   See sections 3.4-3.7.

61   Personal interviews, Sharjah, December 2003.

62   Personal interviews, Dubai, January 2007.

63   13,.296 were made out to Arabs, 55, 338 to Indians, 30,898 to Pakistanis and 7,160 to Europeans. Data supplied by the Ministry of Labour and Social Affairs.

64   21, 519 were made out to Arabs, 10,205 to Indians, 11,106 to Pakistanis and 2,320 were made out to Europeans. Data supplied by the Ministry of Labour and Social Affairs.

65   17 per cent were nationals, while 9 per cent were other Arabs. Data supplied by Dubai Municipality.

66   Dubai only had about 40,000 nationals in the mid-1990s. Author's estimates; also see Van Der Meulen, p.202.

67   Data supplied by Tedad.

68   Ibid.

69   For example, the aforementioned Sheikh Muhammad bin Rashid Centre for Cultural Understanding has provided tours of mosques for non-Muslims in Dubai. See section 5.8.

70   Dubai Department of Economic Development, 2001, p. 25.

71   According to 2005 census data, 73 per cent of Dubai residents were male. Data supplied by Tedad.

72   If one assumes that the bulk of the 350,000 residents that were not surveyed by the census were males then the figure could be as high as 79 per cent. Data supplied by Tedad.

73   Davidson, 2005, p.150. Reporting the findings of Ali Harjan, a leading Sharjah-based psychologist.

74   Peck, Malcolm, *The United Arab Emirates: A Venture in Unity* (Boulder: Westview, 1986), p.137

75   For some years there has been a threshold salary for family residence visas. This is now about $1,000 per month.

76   While all expatriates are required to take a comprehensive medical exam (including an HIV test) upon application for their residency visa, most prostitutes are living on tourist visas and have therefore not been subjected to such checks.

77   See section 8.7.

78   In 2006 street prostitution was cleared up in the Golden Sands district of Bur Dubai, as part of the Municipality's efforts to gentrify the area.

79   In particular the 'red triangle' of Bur Dubai surrounding the Al Ain Centre and the York International hotel, and Al-Riqqa road in Deira.

80   *Washington Post*, 30 April 2006.

81   Most often, such relocations are to Ra's al-Khaimah or nearby Sharjah, the latter of which (as will be discussed in section 7.5) has promulgated several decency laws aimed at maintaining the former way of life.

82   Sheikh Maktum's first wife was Sheikha Aliya bint Khalifa. See Rugh, Andrea B., *The Political Culture of Leadership in the United Arab Emirates* (New York: Palgrave Macmillan, 2007), p.116.

83   See section 5.2.

84   In summer 2006 Sheikha Bouchra was featured in *Hello*. See *Hello Magazine* June 2006.

85   See *Hello Magazine* March 2004 and March 2006.

86   See sections 5.1, 5.5.

87   Foreign Office 370/109814.

88   *Gulf News,* 1 September 2006.

89   See section 4.1.

90   *Financial Times,* 27 August 2007.

91   For example, the relatively new Ibn Batutta Mall and Mall of the Emirates.

92   Article 177 of the Dubai Penal Code.

93   This took place in a hotel chalet.

94   *Associated Press,* 26 November 2006.

95   See section 5.8.

96   See Hall, Marjorie J., *Business Laws of the United Arab Emirates* (London: Jacobs, 1987).

97   *Boston Globe*, 31 August 2003.

98   *Jewish Week,* 30 May 2003.

99   See section 4.5.
100   *Gulf News*, 7 May 2007.
101   Personal interviews, Dubai, December 2005.
102   Personal interviews, Dubai, January 2007.
103   See section 4.1.
104   *Israel National News*, 26 February 2006.
105   *Gulf News*, 22 December 2002.
106   Ibid.
107   Personal interviews, Dubai, January 2006.
108   *Khaleej Times*, 12 December 2006.
109   See section 4.5.
110   Gulf News 22nd December 2002.
111   See section 5.3.
112   See section 5.4.
113   Personal interviews, Dubai, July 2007.
114   Personal interviews, Dubai, December 2005.
115   Dubai nationals are now working in the Carrefour supermarket chain and as store assistants in Jumbo Electronics.
116   *Gulf News*, 8 December 2006.
117   See section 5.4.
118   *Khaleej Times*, 20 January 2005.
119   Most notably in the Mamalteen district, which is well known as an arena for Eastern European women to meet GCC national men.
120   *International Herald Tribune*, 26 May 2006.
121   *Khaleej Times*, 30 January 2005.
122   See section 5.4.
123   In 2004 there were 52 registered mixed marriages in Dubai. *Khaleej Times*, 30 January 2005.
124   *Gulf News*, 4 December 2006.
125   Personal interviews, Dubai, January 2007.
126   Personal correspondence, May 2007. Information supplied by Women Living Under Muslim Laws.
127   *Oxford Analytica*, February 2007.
128   Personal interviews, Dubai, December 2005.
129   *Oxford Analytica*, February 2007.
130   *Gulf News*, 8 December 2006.
131   Personal interviews, Dubai, February 2006.
132   Thought to be about 12 per cent in the 1990s. See *Gulf News*, 23 September 2004.
133   Personal interviews, Dubai, June 2005.
134   *Gulf News*, 8 December 2006.
135   *Gulf News*, 23 September 2004.
136   *Oxford Analytica*, February 2007.
137   *Economist Intelligence Unit*, January 2001.
138   Personal interviews, Dubai, February 2006.
139   Davidson, 2005, p.151.
140   Data supplied by the Ministry of Higher Education and Scientific

Research.
141 Ibid.
142 Davidson, p.266. Quoting Hisham Sharabi.
143 Ibid., quoting Sheila Carapico.
144 Information supplied by the US Bureau of Democracy, Human Rights, and Labor.
145 Ibid. The member list for this organisation was approved in 2006 but did not feature some of the key members of two earlier attempts to set up a human rights organisation.
146 *Gulf News*, 6 February 2006.
147 See section 5.8.
148 Davidson, 2005, p. 270.
149 Ibid.
150 Ibid.
151 Personal interviews, Dubai, September 2003.
152 Personal interviews, Dubai, February 2006.
153 Personal correspondence with the Press Affairs Directorate of the Sharjah Emiri Court, September 2003.
154 Such organisations would include the UAE Women's Federation, the Abu Dhabi Women's Society, the Association of the Awakening of Abu Dhabian women, and the Women's Committee of the Red Crescent Society.
155 Good examples would include the Goan Cultural Society which stresses in its mission statement that it is a 'social and cultural organisation without any political affiliations' and the Kenya Friendship Society, whose president has stated in speeches that the society is 'absolutely non-political'. Davidson 2005, p. 282.
156 Ibid., p. 267.
157 The author's eye witness account.
158 Personal interviews, Dubai, June 2006.
159 *Gulf News*, 21 October 2004.
160 *Khaleej Times*, 20 November 2004.
161 *Gulf News*, 16 and 17 June 2005.
162 *Gulf News*, 3 May 2006.
163 The 'Dubai Dreams' series was screened in the UK in late 2005.
164 This series was screened during Ramadan in 2005 and featured a Moroccan ladies' *diwan*, in which women would discuss the shortcomings of fictional sheikhs.
165 Information supplied by the US Department of State.
166 Oxford Business Group, p. 95.
167 Personal interviews, Dubai, February 2006.
168 Oxford Business Group, p.95.
169 EMI is chaired by Sheikh Abdullah bin Zayed Al-Nahyan, the former Minister for Information and Culture and the current Minister for Foreign Affairs.
170 Information supplied by the US Department of State.
171 Ibid. This purchase took place in 1999.

172   Wilson, p. 239.
173   Peck, pp. 78-80.
174   Shortly after this disaster, it was reported that about thirty engineers had died, however, it is likely that a large number of unskilled works also perished.
175   Personal interviews, Dubai, June 2006.
176   Personal interviews, Dubai, January 2007.
177   *Gulf News*, 19March 2007.
178   Abdulla, Abdulkhaleq, 'Political Dependency: The Case of the United Arab Emirates' (PhD thesis, Georgetown University, 1985).
179   In late 2001 over 100 employees of EMI were made redundant, and had not been provided with any kind of justification. Information supplied by the US Department of State.
180   Information supplied by the US Department of State.
181   Ibid.
182   *Washington Post*, 30 April 2006.
183   Davidson, 2005.
184   The book is on the shelves of libraries in Zayed University, the American University of Sharjah, and the University of the UAE in Al-Ayn. In most cases the book was ordered through Amazon.
185   See Davidson, Christopher M., 'After Sheikh Zayed: The Politics of Succession in Abu Dhabi and the United Arab Emirates', *Middle East Policy* (vol.13, no.1, 2006).
186   www.uaeprison.com.
187   The 'Secret Dubai' blog is authored by an anonymous Canadian expatriate and was temporarily blocked in July 2005. *Gulf News*, 19 July 2005.
188   See section 5.5.
189   *Gulf News*, 24 April 2006.
190   Personal interviews, Dubai, January 2007.

7.   THE STABILITY OF THE FEDERATION

1   See section 2.4.
2   Al-Sagri, Saleh Hamad. 'Britain and the Arab Emirates, 1820-1956' (PhD thesis. University of Kent at Canterbury, 1988), p. 151.
3   Heard-Bey, Frauke, *From Trucial States to United Arab Emirates* (London: Longman, 1996), pp. 387-393.
4   See section 2.5.
5   Heard-Bey, Frauke, 'The UAE: A Quarter Century of Federation' in Hudson, Michael (ed.), *Middle East Dilemma: The Politics and Economics of Arab Integration* (London: IB Tauris, 1999), p. 135.
6   Rizvi, S. N. Asad, 'From Tents to High Rise: Economic Development of the United Arab Emirates' in *Middle Eastern Studies* (vol.29, no.4, 1993), p. 665.
7   Overton, J. L., 'Stability and Change: Inter-Arab Politics in the Arabian Peninsula and the Gulf' (PhD thesis. University of Maryland, 1983), p. 186.

8   Anthony, John Duke, *The United Arab Emirates: Dynamics of State Formation* (Abu Dhabi: Emirates Centre for Strategic Studies and Research, 2002), p. 115.

9   Heard-Bey in Hudson, pp. 137-138.

10   Al-Musfir, Muhammad Salih,'The United Arab Emirates: An Assessment of Federalism in a Developing Polity' (PhD thesis. State University of New York and Binghamton, 1985), p. 137.

11   Wilson, Graeme, *Rashid's Legacy: The Genesis of the Maktoum Family and the History of Dubai* (Dubai: Media Prima, 2006), pp. 386-387.

12   According to Sheikh Zayed's personal political advisor at that time, Adnan Pachachi, he had offered to stand down as president and had offered to move the federal capital from Abu Dhabi. See Overton, p. 186.

13   Anthony, John Duke, *Arab States of the Lower Gulf: People, Politics, Petroleum* (Washington DC: Middle East Institute, 1975), pp. 214-251; Khalifa, Ali Muhammad, *The United Arab Emirates: Unity in Fragmentation* (Boulder: Westview, 1979), p. 103.

14   Heard-Bey, 1996,. pp. 387-393.

15   Wilson, pp. 386-387.

16   Al-Musfir, p. 137.

17   Al-Nabeh, Najat Abdullah, 'United Arab Emirates: Regional and Global Dimensions' (PhD thesis. Claremont Graduate School, 1984), p. 62.

18   *Middle East Economic Digest,* July 1978.

19   Heard-Bey, 1996, p. 380.

20   *Middle East Economic Digest,* July 1978.

21   Al-Nabeh, p. 62.

22   Ibid.

23   Al-Musfir, p. 161.

24   Davidson, Christopher M, *The United Arab Emirates: A Study in Survival* (Boulder: Lynne Rienner, 2005), p. 203.

25   Peck, Malcolm, *The United Arab Emirates: A Venture in Unity* (Boulder: Westview, 1986), p. 131; Heard-Bey, 1996,. pp. 397-401.

26   See section 5.7.

27   Peck, p. 131; Heard-Bey, 1996. pp. 397-401.

28   Heard-Bey, 1996. pp. 397-401.

29   Wilson, p. 390.

30   Heard-Bey, 1996. pp. 397-401.

31   Personal interviews, Abu Dhabi, September 2003.

32   It has been recorded inaccurately that Dubai was asked to contribute 50 per cent of its oil revenue to the federal budget, when in fact the proposed contribution was much lower. Personal interviews, Dubai, December 2003; Heard-Bey, 1996. pp. 397-401.

33   Wilson, p. 390.

34   See section 5.1.

35   Fenelon, Kevin, The *United Arab Emirates: An Economic and Social Survey* (London: Longman, 1973), p. 18.

36   Peck, p. 51.

37   See section 4.3.
38   For many years it would cost about $5 to travel from Abu Dhabi to Dubai using an Al-Ghazal bus, whereas it would cost $9 to make the return journey using a Dubai Transport bus.
39   Information supplied by the US Department of State.
40   Peck, p. 123.
41   Oxford Business Group, 'Emerging Emirates' (London: 2000), p. 115.
42   Brown, Gavin, *OPEC and the World Energy Market* (London: Longman, 1998), p. 360; Overton, p. 184.
43   Now Lufthansa is the only major international airline servicing Sharjah.
44   Oxford Business Group, p. 111.
45   See section 4.3.
46   Personal interviews, Dubai, February 2006.
47   See section 4.3.
48   Rizvi, p. 669.
49   Al-Sharhan International Consultancy, 'United Arab Emirates Country Report' (Dubai: 2001), p. 41; Oxford Business Group, p. 75.
50   Hakim, Iqbal Ismail. *United Arab Emirates Central Bank and 9.11 Financing* (New York: GAAP, 2005), pp. 2, 187.
51   Ibid., p. 2.
52   Al-Gurg, Easa Saleh, *The Wells of Memory* (London: John Murray, 1998), p. 143.
53   Wilson, p. 437.
54   Peck, p. 133.
55   See section 5.8.
56   Personal interviews, Dubai, February 2006.
57   Saudi Arabia and Kuwait were founding members of OPEC in 1960, while Qatar joined in 1961. Oxford Business Group, p. 49 .
58   Brown, p. 361; section 5.8.
59   Brown, p. 361.
60   Personal interviews, Dubai, January 2007.
61   Dr Roberto Subroto.
62   Brown, p. 724.
63   Personal interviews, Abu Dhabi, September 2003.
64   Personal interviews, Dubai, December 2004; Foley, Sean, 'The United Arab Emirates: Political Issues and Security Dilemmas', *Middle East Review of International Affairs* (vol.3, no.1, 1998).
65   *Middle East Economic Digest*, February 1997.
66   The Emirates Express service was launched in 2005 between Abu Dhabi and Dubai. It is not run by any kind of federal company, but rather represents a bilateral agreement between the two cities' respective municipalities.
67   See section 5.6.
68   Oxford Business Group, p. 113.
69   *Economist Intelligence Unit*, January 2000.
70   Oxford Business Group, p. 105.

71   It is estimated that the four poorest emirates account for only 15 per cent
      of the UAE's GDP. Crown Prince Court Department of Research and
      Studies, 'Statistical Book' (Abu Dhabi: 1996), p. 54; Personal interviews,
      Dubai, January 2007.
72   Personal interviews, Dubai, January 2007.
73   Sheikh Ahmad is also the undersecretary of the Abu Dhabi Civil
      Aviation Department.
74   Personal interviews, Abu Dhabi, February 2006.
75   *Daily Telegraph,* 21 July 2004.
76   Personal interviews, Dubai, June 2006.
77   Brown, p. 361; *Economist Intelligence Unit* , January 2000.
78   Personal interviews, Dubai, June 2006.
79   See section 4.5.
80   See section 6.1.
81   Personal interviews, Dubai, February 2006.
82   See section 5.6.
83   In 2001, Abu Dhabi purportedly provided the Jumeirah group with
      financial assistance as many of its hotels were suffering from low
      occupancies. Moreover, Abu Dhabi is thought to provide Dubai with a
      daily 'gift' of some 100,000 barrels of oil per day. Davidson, Christopher
      M, 'The Emirates of Abu Dhabi and Dubai: Contrasting Roles in the
      International System' , *Asian Affairs* (vol. 38, no.1, 2007), p. 43.
84   For many years, portraits of these sons were depicted along the entire
      height of a residential building in Abu Dhabi's Capital Gardens. Sheikh
      Zayed's 19 sons are Khalifa, Sultan, Muhammad, Hamdan, Hazza, Said,
      Isa, Nahyan, Saif, Nasser, Ahmad, Tahnun, Mansur, Falah, Hamad,
      Dhiyab, Omar, Abdullah, and Khalid.
85   Rugh, Andrea B., *The Political Culture of Leadership in the United Arab
      Emirates* (New York: Palgrave Macmillan, 2007), p. 89.
86   Sheikh Khalifa had held this position since 1976, Van Der Meulen,
      Hendrik, 'The Role of Tribal and Kinship Ties in the Politics of the
      United Arab Emirates' (PhD thesis. The Fletcher School of Law and
      Diplomacy, 1997), p. 97.
87   Personal interviews, Abu Dhabi, May 2005.
88   *Economist Intelligence Unit,* January 2000.
89   See section 4.2.
90   Heard-Bey, 1996. p. 397.
91   Peterson, John E., 'The Arab Gulf States: Steps Towards Political
      Participation' , *Washington Papers* (no.131, 1988), p. 204.
92   Rugh. p. 91.
93   Personal interviews, Abu Dhabi, June 2005.
94   Personal interviews, Dubai, February 2005.
95   A particularly strong example would be Sheikh Shakhbut bin Dhiyab,
      who continued to offer valuable advice and support to his sons for nearly
      twenty years after his initial 'deposition' in the early nineteenth century.
      See Maitra, Jayanti, and Al-Hajji, Afra, *Qasr Al-Hosn: The History and
      Rulers of Abu Dhabi, 1793-1966* (Abu Dhabi: Centre for Documentation

and Research, 2001), p. 44.
96   Pope, M. T. G., *Businessman's Guide to the United Arab Emirates* (Sharjah: Dar al-Fatah, 1996), p. 295.
97   See section 6.4
98   Personal interviews, Dubai, June 2006.
99   A good example being the 'Mother of the Nation' festival held in early 2007 in the Emirates Palace Hotel.
100 *Economist Intelligence Unit,* January 2000.
101 See section 5.6.
102 Davidson, 2005, p. 102.
103 Van Der Meulen, p. 123.
104 See section 6.6.
105 Union National Bank was created from the remnants of the BCCI collapse in 1991.
106 *Gulf News,* 3,November 2004.
107 *Arab News* , 4 November 2004.
108 Another good example being the deliberately delayed announcement of the capture of Al-Qaida's Abd Al-Rahim Al-Nashiri in the UAE in 2002. See section 8.9
109 See section 6.4
110 These being Sheikh Sultan bin Khalifa Al-Nahyan and Sheikh Muhammad bin Khalifa Al-Nahyan. The former is a member of the Abu Dhabi Executive Council and the director of the Crown Prince's Court.
111 Notably, at palace gatherings Sheikh Muhammad will always ensure that he sits at Sheikh Khalifa's feet.
112 Sheikh Muhammad has brought many of his trusted advisors from the UAE Offsets and Dolphin projects to the Mubadala Corporation. For a full discussion of Offsets and Dolphin see Davidson 2005, pp. 127-128.
113 Personal interviews, Abu Dhabi, May 2005.
114 AFP, 1 January 2005.
115 Pope, p. 298.
116 Personal interviews, Abu Dhabi, March 2007.
117 Rush, Alan (ed.), *Ruling Families of Arabia: The United Arab Emirates* (Slough: Archive Editions 1991), p. 92.
118 Maitra and Al-Hajji, pp. 203-204.
119 Ibid., p. 206; Tammam, Hamdi, *Zayed bin Sultan Al-Nahyan: The Leader on the March* (Tokyo: Dai Nippon, 1983), p. 41.
120 Maitra and Al-Hajji, pp. 208-221.
121 Fahim, Muhammad, *From Rags to Riches: A Story of Abu Dhabi* (London: Centre for Arab Studies, 1995), p. 38; Van Der Meulen, p. 29.
122 Van Der Meulen, p. 108.
123 Lienhardt asserts that a strong rivalry existed between the wives of Sheikh Hamdan and Sheikh Sultan. See Lienhardt, Peter, *Sheikhdoms of Eastern Arabia* (Oxford: Palgrave, 2001), p. 180.
124 See section 1.3.

125   Maitra and Al-Hajji, p. 227.
126   India Office R.151.14.27.
127   Mann, Clarence, *Abu Dhabi: Birth of an Oil Sheikhdom* (Beirut: Al-Khayats, 1969), pp. 87-88; Van Der Meulen, p. 110.
128   India Office R.151.14.27.
129   The Dhahira is the area of desert beyond the Hajar mountains, and formerly included five of the Buraimi villages.
130   Zahlan, Rosemarie Said, *The Origins of the United Arab Emirates* (New York: St. Martin's, 1978), pp. 131-132; Maitra and Al-Hajji, p. 180; Van Der Meulen, p. 380.
131   Maitra and Al-Hajji, p. 129.
132   Heard-Bey, 1996,. p. 150.
133   Luce, Margaret, *From Aden to the Gulf: Personal Diaries, 1956-1966* (Salisbury, Michael Russell, 1987), p. 176.
134   See section 3.4.
135   Personal interviews, Abu Dhabi, March 2007.
136   Van Der Meulen, p. 110.
137   Personal interviews, Abu Dhabi, March 2007.
138   Fahim, p. 137.
139   Van Der Meulen, p. 100.
140   Anthony, 1975,, p. 147.
141   Pope, p. 295.
142   Peterson 1988, pp. 204-205.
143   Davidson, Christopher M, 'After Sheikh Zayed: The Politics of Succession in Abu Dhabi and the United Arab Emirates' , *Middle East Policy* (vol.13, no.1, 2006), p. 56.
144   Peterson 1988, pp. 204-205.
145   See section 2.2.
146   See the 'Report to the Committee on Foreign Relations in the United States Senate by Senators John Kerry and Senator Hank Brown', 102nd Congress 2nd Session Senate Print, December 1992, pp. 102-140.
147   Ibid.
148   Ibid.
149   Oxford Business Group, p. 71; Price Waterhouse Report 41 to the Bank of England, June 1991, section 1.33.
150   With regard to Sheikh Zayed's initial share see *Middle East Economic Digest* February 1982; with regard to BCCI's founding and majority shareholders see the Report to the Committee on Foreign Relations in the United States Senate by Senators John Kerry and Senator Hank Brown, pp. 102-104.
151   Report to the Committee on Foreign Relations in the United States Senate by Senators John Kerry and Senator Hank Brown, pp. 102-104.
152   Ibid.
153   Price Waterhouse Report 41 to the Bank of England, June 1991, section 1.33
154   Hakim, pp. 186-187.
155   Report to the Committee on Foreign Relations in the United States

Senate by Senators John Kerry and Senator Hank Brown, pp. 102-104.
156   Ibid.
157   Ibid.
158   See section 6.4.
159   *Wall Street Journal,* 17 September 2003.
160   Personal interviews, Abu Dhabi, March 2001.
161   Sharjah has about $500,000 in oil reserves per national, making the emirate comparable with Saudi Arabia. Personal interviews, Dubai, February 2006.
162   See section 5.3.
163   The border between Dubai and Sharjah, close to Al-Mu'alla Plaza, used to be marshland, but has now been levelled and a great deal of construction has taken place since 2000, with the Sahara Mall and several residential tower blocks extending all the way to Dubai.
164   See section 2.1.
165   Personal interviews, London, February 2007.
166   Foreign Office 371.179916.31761; Hawley, Donald, *The Emirates: Witness to a Metamorphosis* (Norwich: Michael Russell, 2007), pp. 134,141,169,184; Al-Gurg, p. 116; Wilson, pp. 231-232
167   Wilson, p. 234.
168   Hawley, 2007,. p. 170.
169   Ibid., p. 172.
170   Ibid., p. 224.
171   See section 2.1.
172   Foreign Office, 371.179916.31761.
173   Al-Gurg, pp. 119-120.
174   Van Der Meulen, p. 209.
175   Wilson, p. 236.
176   For a full discussion see section 8.3.
177   Peterson, John E., and Sindelar, Richard (eds.), *Crosscurrents in the Gulf* (London: Routledge, 1988), pp. 206-207.
178   Kelly, John B., *Arabia, the Gulf, and the West: A Critical View of the Arabs and their Oil Policy* (New York: Basic Books, 1986), pp. 96-97.
179   Al-Sagri, p. 277.
180   See section 5.1.
181   Wilson, pp. 347-349; Peck, p. 128.
182   Personal interviews, Dubai, June 2006.
183   Peterson and Sindelar, pp. 207-208; Van Der Meulen, p. 211.
184   Brown, p. 359.
185   Personal interviews, Abu Dhabi, June 2006.
186   Peterson and Sindelar, pp. 207-208; Van Der Meulen, p. 211.
187   Personal interviews, London, February 2007.
188   Van Der Meulen, p. 211.
189   *The Independent,* 16 June 2007.
190   Personal interviews, London, February 2007.
191   Sheikha Jawaher bint Muhammad Al-Qasimi, the de facto 'first lady' of Sharjah.

192   Sheikh Sultan bin Saqr Al-Qasimi.

193   Personal interviews, Dubai, February 2006; *Arabic News* 13th May 1999.

194   The two diverging branches being the grandsons of Sheikh Sultan bin Saqr Al-Qasimi and the grandsons of Sheikh Muhammad bin Saqr Al-Qasimi.

195   Peterson and Sindelar; Van Der Meulen, p. 215.

196   Personal interviews, Abu Dhabi, March 2007.

197   Oxford Business Group, pp. 71-72.

198   Sharjah Law Number 1 of 2001.

199   Personal interviews, Dubai, December 2003. Inevitably these attempts were thwarted by Dubai.

200   Personal interviews, Dubai, February 2006.

201   See section 4.6.

202   Personal interviews, Dubai, January 2007.

203   Foreign Office 371.120540.

204   Sheikh Abdul-Aziz bin Humayd Al-Nu'aymi died in 1975 and Sheikh Abdullah bin Humayd Al-Nu'aymi died in 1993. Rugh, p. 176.

205   Personal interviews, Sharjah, June 2006.

206   Foreign office 371.109814.

207   Personal interviews, Dubai, June 2006; Rugh, p. 188.

208   Sheikh Saud is married to Sheikha Somaya bint Saqr Al-Qasimi. Rugh, p. 190.

209   Hawley 2007, p. 221.

210   In 1972 there were clashes close to Khor Fakkan and Dibba. Sheikh Muhammad's Dubai Defence Force arrived and negotiated a peaceful settlement. See Wilson, pp. 350-351.

211   See section 1.5.

212   Personal interviews, Dubai, June 2006; Van Der Meulen, p. 252.

213   *Khaleej Times*, 9 January 2007.

214   As in section 5.4, there are around 130,000 Ra's al-Khaimah nationals compared to only 80,000 Dubai nationals.

215   Al-Gurg, p. 133.

216   Hawley, 2007,. p. 87.

217   Ibid., p. 111.

218   See section 2.5.

219   See section 5.6. Abu Dhabi and Dubai were to have 8 positions each in the FNC whereas Ra's al-Khaimah would only have 6.

220   See section 1.1; as Frauke Heard-Bey describes, '...the branch of the Qawasim family ruling Ra's al-Khaimah even considered themselves to be of nobler descent than their counterparts in the other six sheikhdoms.' See Heard-Bey, 1996,. pp. 369-370.

221   Anthony 2002, p. 74; Van Der Meulen, p. 202.

222   Personal interviews, Ra's al-Khaimah, January 2004. With regard to the Al-Khawatir, see Al-Musfir, p. 76. Around 50 per cent of the Al-Za'ab migrated to Abu Dhabi in 1968 following an invitation extended to them by Sheikh Zayed. See Van Der Meulen, pp. 163-164.

223   Heard-Bey, 1996, pp. 369-370.
224   Anthony, 2002,. p. 74.
225   Ibid., p. 66.
226   Personal interviews, Dubai, June 2006; Heard-Bey, 1996,. pp. 369-370.
227   Personal interviews, Ra's al-Khaimah, September 2002.
228   Personal interviews, Ra's al-Khaimah, December 2004.
229   Personal interviews, Ra's al-Khaimah, September 2002.
230   Author's estimates.
231   Personal interviews, Abu Dhabi, March 2007.
232   Most members of the Shihuh tribe live in Ra's al-Khaimah or on the nearby Omani-controlled Musandam peninsula. They are thought to be of mixed Arabic, Persian, and Baluchi descent, with some contending that they also have traces of Portuguese blood given their fairer skin and coloured eyes. Alternatively, given that they speak a non-Arabic semitic language, another theory is that they are the remnants of the lower Gulf's true indigenous population (Alexander the Great's 'fish eating tribe'), that managed to resist complete displacement by Arab invaders due to their mountainous habitat. A third theory is that the Shihuh are descended from the biblical Shehite tribe, as many have Jewish-sounding names. For further study, anthropologists should visit the northern section of the east coast town of Dibba, which, although technically controlled by Oman, is really more of a Shihuh stronghold that is independent of the Sharjah and Fujairah-controlled southern sections of the town.
233   During the nineteenth century decline of the Qawasim in section 1.1, it is thought that the Shihuh attempted to ally with the Bani Yas. Personal interviews, Ra's al-Khaimah, March 2006.
234   Marawan Al-Shehhi. See section 8.9.
235   Hawley, pp. 207, 282. This deal was struck in 1953, after Sheikh Sultan accepted the futility of any further opposition to Sheikh Saqr. See Rush, pp. 81-82.
236   Ibid., p. 279.
237   Ibid., pp. 283-284.
238   In particular, Sheikh Abdul-Aziz became head of Federation Affairs in the emirate's government in addition to being appointed chairman of the local Department for Tourism.
239   Van Der Meulen, pp. 241-242.
240   Personal interviews, Abu Dhabi, March 2007.
241   Sheikh Muhammad represented Ra's al-Khaimah in the federal government as the Minister of State for Supreme Council Affairs for much of the 1990s.
242   Personal interviews, London, February 2007.
243   Author's eyewitness account; Reuters 14 June 2003.
244   Most notably by investing in a large concrete production plant.
245   See section 4.5.
246   See *Gulf Today*, 18 July 2007.
247   Sheikh Khalid was offered protection in exile by Sultan Qabus bin Said

Al-Said.

248 UAE-based newspapers often erroneously describe Sheikh Saud as both the crown prince and the deputy ruler.

8. SECURITY, CRIME, AND TERROR

1 See sections 5.3-5.8.
2 See section 6.2.
3 See section 2.4.
4 See section 5.1.
5 Wilson, Graeme, *Rashid's Legacy: The Genesis of the Maktoum Family and the History of Dubai* (Dubai: Media Prima, 2006), p. 307.
6 Personal interviews, Dubai, January 2007.
7 Wilson, p. 523. This unit was created by Sheikh Muhammad at the time of the Kuwaiti crisis.
8 Van Der Meulen, Hendrik, 'The Role of Tribal and Kinship Ties in the Politics of the United Arab Emirates' (PhD thesis. The Fletcher School of Law and Diplomacy, 1997), p. 44.
9 Personal interviews, Dubai, January 2007; Wilson, pp. 343-344.
10 *Jane's Defence Weekly*, 7 February 2007.
11 Personal interviews, Dubai, January 2007; Van Der Meulen, p. 95. Prior to amalgamation, in 1995 the Union Defence Force had about 45,000 personnel.
12 In contrast, many non-NATO states are not eligible to purchase the most sophisticated equipment unless they receive governmental oversight from the supplier countries. Personal interviews, Abu Dhabi, December 2004; Abdulla, Abdulkhaleq, 'Political Dependency: The Case of the United Arab Emirates' (PhD thesis, Georgetown University, 1985), p. 208.
13 Oxford Business Group, 'Emerging Emirates' (London: 2000), pp. 58-59.
14 Personal interviews, Abu Dhabi, March 2007.
15 Personal interviews, Dubai, June 2006.
16 Personal interviews, Dubai, January 2007; *Counterpunch*, 4 December 2004.
17 *Jane's Defence Weekly*, 7 February 2007.
18 Personal interviews, Abu Dhabi, June 2005.
19 Personal interviews, Dubai, January 2007.
20 Personal interviews, Dubai, June 2006.
21 *Janes Defence Weekly*, 7 February 2007.
22 Personal interviews, Dubai, January 2007.
23 See section 6.1.
24 Personal interviews, Dubai, January 2007.
25 See section 5.8.
26 Oxford Business Group, pp. 58-59.
27 Foley, Sean, 'The United Arab Emirates: Political Issues and Security Dilemmas', *Middle East Review of International Affairs* (vol. 3, no.1,

1998).

28   See section 4.1.
29   Al-Otaibi, Manna Said, *The Petroleum Concession Agreements of the United Arab Emirates* (London: Croom Helm, 1982), pp. 15-151; Abdulla., pp. 107-114; Oxford Business Group,. p. 48; Personal interviews, Abu Dhabi, September 2003.
30   Personal interviews, Abu Dhabi, March 2007.
31   Abdulla, pp. 134-135; Al-Otaibi, pp. 188-204.
32   Abdulla, pp. 107-114; Al-Otaibi, pp. 15-151; Oxford Business Group, p. 48; Personal interviews, Abu Dhabi, September 2003.
33   Abu-Baker, Albadr, 'Political Economy of State Formation: The United Arab Emirates in Comparative Perspective' (PhD thesis, University of Michigan, 1995), pp. 147-148; *(in Arabic)* Al-Otaibi, Manna Said, *Petroleum and the Economy of the United Arab Emirates* (Kuwait: Al-Qabas Press, 1977), pp. 39-40.
34   Personal interviews, Abu Dhabi, March 2007.
35   Personal interviews, Abu Dhabi, September 2003.
36   Personal interviews, London, July 2006.
37   See section 4.3.
38   *Emirates Today,* 26 April 2006.
39   Personal interviews, London, July 2006.
40   The other dry docks being in Bahrain. See section 4.3.
41   Personal interviews, London, December 2006.
42   One company being British, one Danish, and the other Norwegian. Personal interviews, Dubai, January 2007.
43   Personal interviews, Fujairah, June 2006.
44   Personal interviews, Abu Dhabi, December 2004.
45   See section 4.3.
46   *International Herald Tribune,* 22 June 2005.
47   *Jane's Defence Weekly,* 7 February 2007; Personal interviews, London, July 2006.
48   See section 3.3.
49   See section 6.2.
50   See section 7.3.
51   See section 3.3.
52   Kelly, John B., *Britain and the Persian Gulf* (Oxford: Oxford University Press, 1968), pp. 92-93; Al-Gurg, Easa Saleh, *The Wells of Memory* (London: John Murray, 1998), p. 5.
53   Al-Gurg, p. 5.
54   Personal interviews, Dubai, June 2006.
55   Abdul Hussein Taimurtash.
56   Following a quarrel with the ruler of Dubai (Sheikh Hasher bin Maktum Al-Maktum), Sheikh Obaid bin Said Al-Maktum had left Dubai along with fourteen other families. They first moved to Tunb al-Kuhbra, but then following water shortages later relocated to Henjam. After the Persian invasion they were welcomed back to Dubai, perhaps given that one of Obaid's daughters had married the ruler of Dubai in 1887.

Personal interviews, Dubai, June 2006; Wilson, p. 64; Rush, Alan (ed.), *Ruling Families of Arabia: The United Arab Emirates* (Slough: Archive Editions 1991), pp. 309-310.

57   Wilson, p. 260.

58   Ibid., p. 295.

59   See section 2.5.

60   Wilson, pp. 90, 295, 332.

61   Ibid., pp. 325-326.

62   Such rumours had begun in Ra's al-Khaimah earlier in the 1960s. See Hawley, Donald, *The Emirates: Witness to a Metamorphosis* (Norwich: Michael Russell, 2007), pp. 188-190.

63   Britain's special envoy was the former British Political Resident in the Gulf, Sir William Luce. It was reported that Luce even brought an Iranian military official with him on his visits to the rulers of Sharjah and Ra's al-Khaimah. Mobley, Richard A, 'The Tunbs and Abu Musa Islands: Britain's Perspective' in *Middle East Journal* (vol. 57, no. 4, 2003), pp. 628-644; Wilson, pp. 325-236.

64   Mobley, pp. 628-644.

65   Kelly, 1986, pp. 92-93.

66   See Laquer, Walter, *The Struggle for the Middle East* (London: Routledge, 1969).

67   Niblock, Tim (ed.), *Social and Economic Development in the Arab Gulf* (London: Croom Helm, 1980), pp. 205-215; Van Der Meulen, p. 238.

68   Peck, Malcolm, *The United Arab Emirates: A Venture in Unity* (Boulder: Westview, 1986), p. 120

69   Van Der Meulen, p. 238.

70   Oxford Business Group, pp. 98-99.

71   Personal interviews, Dubai, January 2007.

72   See section 5.8.

73   *Gulf News*, 29 March 2007 .

74   Personal interviews, Dubai, February 2007.

75   Van Der Meulen, p. 279.

76   See section 7.3.

77   Worryingly, they continue to be a flashpoint for naval skirmishes, and in the near future could again become a means of rebuilding national pride for a beleaguered Iranian presidency.

78   The training has been provided by German security companies operating in the UAE. *Islamic Republic News Agency*, 16 January 2004.

79   Wilson, pp. 496-497.

80   For example Sheikh Said bin Tahnun Al-Nahyan's assault on the Wahhabis in Buraimi in 1848, and Sheikh Zayed bin Khalifa Al-Nahyan's spirited defence of Buraimi against the Omani-Wahhabi renegade, Said Turki in 1870. Maitra, Jayanti, and Al-Hajji, Afra, *Qasr Al-Hosn: The History and Rulers of Abu Dhabi, 1793-1966* (Abu Dhabi: Centre for Documentation and Research, 2001), pp. 102-103,177.

81   See section 1.1; Hawley, Donald, *The Trucial States* (London: Geo Allen and Unwin, 1970), p. 101.

82   Hawley, 1970,. p. 188.
83   He married the daughter of an Al-Bu Shamis sheikh – a different sub-
        section of the aforementioned Al-Bu Shamis tribe of Hamriyyah. See
        Hawley 2007, p. 160; section 3.5.
84   Hawley, 2007,. p. 160.
85   Ibid., p. 104; section 1.4.
86   Fahim, Muhammad, *From Rags to Riches: A Story of Abu Dhabi* (London:
        Centre for Arab Studies, 1995), p. 159; Anthony, John Duke., *Arab
        States of the Lower Gulf: People, Politics, Petroleum* (Washington DC:
        Middle East Institute, 1975), pp. 148-149; Al-Nabeh, Najat Abdullah,
        'United Arab Emirates: Regional and Global Dimensions' (PhD thesis,
        Claremont Graduate School, 1984), p. 91
87   Van Der Meulen, p. 23.
88   Oxford Business Group, p. 20; personal interviews, Dubai, June 2006.
89   Personal interviews, Dubai, February 2006.
90   See section 3.1.
91   See sections 3.3-3.7.
92   See section 3.2.
93   Buxani, Ram, *Taking the High Road* (Dubai: Motivate, 2003), p. 101;
        Hawley, 2007,. p. 102. In 1958 General Ayub Khan seized power in
        Pakistan, ushering in a new dictatorship.
94   Buxani, p. 101.
95   See section 3.8.
96   Al-Gurg, p. 103.
97   Foreign Office 371/120553; also see section 2.2 for the discussion of
        narcotics seizures in Dubai in the 1950s.
98   *The Guardian*, 17 December 2001.
99   See section 5.8.
100   Hakim, Iqbal Ismail, *United Arab Emirates Central Bank and 9/11
        Financing* (New York: GAAP, 2005), pp. 145-146.
101   Daly, John, 'Viktor Bout: From International Outlaw to Valued Partner'
        in *Terrorism Monitor* (vol.2, no. 20, 2004).
102   Hakim,, p. 5; personal interviews, Dubai, January 2007.
103   Hakim, p. 5.
104   See section 4.6.
105   Hakim, p. 88. Referring to a report issued by the Combat Films and
        Research Department of the Kennedy Center.
106   In particular, the British were concerned that Anotonin Goguyer was
        active in the arms trade in the lower Gulf. See Slot, B. J., *Mubarak
        Al-Sabah: Founder of Modern Kuwait, 1896-1915* (London: Arabian
        Publishing, 2005), p. 46.
107   Al-Sagri, Saleh Hamad, 'Britain and the Arab Emirates, 1820-1956'
        (PhD thesis, University of Kent at Canterbury, 1988), p. 305; Wilson,
        p. 39.
108   Wilson, p. 39.
109   Ibid., p. 40.
110   *The Times*, 30 December 1910.

111 Wilson, p. 78.

112 Foreign Office 371/120553.

113 Hawley, 2007, p. 202.

114 The movie *Lord of War*, starring Nicholas Cage, was loosely based on the 'Merchant of Death'.

115 Kuzio, Taras, 'Loose Nukes and Al-Qaida', *Terrorism Monitor* (vol. 2, no.6, 2004).

116 Hakim, pp. 88-89,,92.

117 Ibid., p. 17.

118 Ibid., pp. 88-89,,92.

119 Ibid., p. 17.

120 Ibid., pp. 88-89,,92.

121 Yassman, Victor, 'The Russian Criminal World Played a Key Role in Chechnya and Continues to Do So', *Terrorism Monitor* (vol. 1, no. 8, 1995).

122 Hakim, pp. 92-93.

123 Personal interviews, Dubai, January 2007.

124 Lorimer, John G., *Gazetteer of the Persian Gulf, Oman, and Central Arabia* (London: Gregg International Publishers, 1970), p. 2475.

125 Hawley, 1970, p. 200.

126 Ibid.,

127 Al-Sagri, p. 41; Heard-Bey, Frauke, *From Trucial States to United Arab Emirates* (London: Longman, 1996), pp. 288-289.

128 See section 1.4.

129 Heard-Bey, 1996, pp. 289-290.

130 India Office SB/159; Lorimer, p. 725.

131 Lorimer, p. 725; personal interviews, Dubai, June 2006.

132 India Office,SB/159.

133 See section 1.4.

134 Abdullah, Muhammad Morsy, *The United Arab Emirates: A Modern History* (London: Croom Helm, 1978), p. 25; Hawley, 1970,. p. 136.

135 Most notably in 1925 the fort of the headman of Fujairah, Sheikh Hamad bin Abdullah Al-Sharqi, was shelled. Hawley, 2007,. p. 72.

136 Personal interviews, Dubai, June 2006; Wilson, p. 78.

137 , These reports are from 1954. Foreign Office 371/120553.

138 Thesiger, Wilfred, *Arabian Sands* (London: Penguin, 1991), pp. 272, 284; Hawley 1970, p. 173.

139 Personal interviews, Dubai, June 2006.

140 See section 2.4.

141 *Reuters,* 8 July 2006; *Gulf News,* 15 July 2006.

142 See section 6.2.

143 Buxani, pp. 80-81.

144 The robot jockeys were developed by a Swiss firm and cost about $5500 each. See *New Scientist,* 21 August 2005.

145 *Gulf News,* 15 July 2006.

146 Personal interviews, Dubai, January 2007.

147 See section 6.4.

148 Camp Anaconda is considered so dangerous that its moniker amongst US personnel is 'Mortaritaville'.

149 Hakim, p. 3.

150 See section 3.8.

151 Hakim, p. 36.

152 See section 3.2.

153 Personal interviews, Dubai, January 2007.

154 Vassiliev, Alexei, 'Financing Terror: From Bogus Banks to Honey Bees', *Terrorism Monitor* (vol.1, no. 4, 2003).

155 Personal interviews, Dubai, June 2006.

156 Personal correspondence, March 2007.

157 *Wall Street Journal,* 17 September 2003.

158 *Khaleej Times,* 6 February 2002.

159 *Gulf News,* 18 February 2004.

160 *Khaleej Times,* 6 February 2002.

161 Hakim, p. 1.

162 Personal interviews, Dubai, January 2007.

163 Hakim, pp. 3-4.

164 Ibid., pp. 42-47 for examples.

165 Ibid., pp. 57-59.

166 Ibid., pp. 123-124.

167 Ibid., p. 34.

168 Ibid., p. 34.

169 Personal interviews, Dubai, January 2007; Hakim, pp. 14, 22, 24.

170 Hakim, pp. 164-167.

171 Ibid., p. 6.

172 Personal interviews, Dubai, January 2007.

173 Hakim, pp. 199-200.

174 See section 7.6.

175 *Daily Telegraph,* 1 December 2001; Hakim, pp. 151-152.

176 *USA Today,* 2 September 2004.

177 Personal interviews, Dubai, January 2007

178 See section 2.1.

179 See section 6.4.

180 See section 6.2.

181 Most of the terrorists were thought to be drawn from the Bani Harth and the Bani Riyam. See Luce, Margaret, *From Aden to the Gulf: Personal Diaries, 1956-1966* (Salisbury, Michael Russell, 1987), p. 164; Hawley 2007, p. 62.

182 Personal interviews, Dubai, June 2006; Hawley, 2007,. p. 289.

183 See section 7.6.

184 Hawley, 2007,. p. 173.

185 Ibid., p. 177.

186 Personal interviews, Durham, February 2007.

187 Hawley, 2007,. p. 220; section 1.5.

188 Buxani, pp. 11-12; Wilson, pp. 191-194.

189 Hawley, 2007,. p. 288.

190   Personal interviews, Dubai, June 2006; Luce, p. 165.
191   See section 7.5.
192   Wilson, pp. 358-360.
193   *Merchant International Group Strategic Research and Corporate Intelligence,* 25August 2005.
194   Ibid.
195   Wilson, p. 431.
196   Ibid., pp. 429-431.
197   Personal interviews, Dubai, June 2006.
198   *Merchant International Group Strategic Research and Corporate Intelligence,* 25 August 2005.
199   Khalifa was the father of the aforementioned Khaldun bin Khalifa Al-Mubarak. See section 5.5.
200   See section 7.3.
201   Fahim, p. 159; Wilson, p. 355.
202   Personal interviews, Dubai, June 2006; *Merchant International Group Strategic Research and Corporate Intelligence,* 25 August 2005.
203   The 2003 movie *Zameen* starred Abhishek Bachchan.
204   *USA Today,* 2 September 2004. The UAE provided the second largest contingent of 9/11 hijackers after Saudi Arabia.
205   William Cohen.
206   Personal correspondence, March 2007.
207   Hakim, p. 1; personal correspondence, March 2007.
208   It was widely rumoured in Dubai that Bin Laden was receiving treatment for his kidney ailments in a Dubai-based hospital during the summer of 2001.
209   *USA Today,* 2 September 2004.
210   Personal interviews, Dubai, December 2003; *The Times,* 24 December 2002.
211   Robinson, Adam, *Bin Laden: Behind the Mask of the Terrorist* (New York: Arcade, 2002), pp. 91-93.
212   Wilston, John, 'The Roots of Extremism in Bangladesh', *Terrorism Monitor* (vol. 3, no. 1, 2005).
213   Quotes from Evan F. Kohlmann, a Washington-based terrorism researcher.
214   Personal interviews, Dubai, June 2006; *Financial Times,* 10 August 2004.
215   *China Daily,* 9 August 2004.
216   See section 6.4.
217   *Khaleej Times,* 4 May 2005.
218   Personal interviews, Dubai, June 2006; Reuters, 9 May 2005.
219   Personal interviews, Beirut, November 2006.
220   Paraphrased from unclassified document AFGP/2002/603856 located at the Combating Terrorism centre at the US Military Academy at West Point. Also see *Scripps Howard News Service,* 28 February 2006.
221   Personal correspondence, March 2007.
222   This statement appeared on a website in 2005.

223   This statement was made in March 2005.
224   These closures took place in late March 2005.
225   Personal correspondence, March 2007.

BIBLIOGRAPHY

Abdekarim, Abbas (ed.), *Change and Development in the Gulf* (London: Macmillan, 1999).

Abdulghani, Abdulhamid Muhammad, 'Culture and Interest in Arab Foreign Aid: Kuwait and the United Arab Emirates as Case Studies' (PhD thesis, University of California at Santa Barbara, 1986).

Abdulla, Abdulkhaleq, 'Political Dependency: The Case of the United Arab Emirates' (PhD thesis, Georgetown University, 1985).

Abdullah, Muhammad Morsy, *The United Arab Emirates: A Modern History* (London: Croom Helm, 1978).

(*in Arabic*) Abdullah, Muhammad Morsy, *Between Yesterday and Today* (Abu Dhabi, 1969).

Al-Abed, Ibrahim, and Hellyer, Peter (eds), *The United Arab Emirates: A New Perspective* (London: Trident, 2001).

(*in Arabic*) Al-Abid, Saleh, *The Qawasim's Role in the Arabian Gulf, 1747-1820* (Baghdad, 1976).

Abir, Mordechai, *Oil, Power, and Politics: Conflict in Arabia, the Red Sea, and the Gulf* (London: Frank Cass, 1974).

Abu-Baker, Albadr, 'Political Economy of State Formation: The United Arab Emirates in Comparative Perspective' (PhD thesis, University of Michigan, 1995).

Agwani, M., *Politics in the Gulf* (New Delhi: Vikas, 1969).

Al-Akim, Hassan Hamdan, *The Foreign Policy of the United Arab Emirates* (London: Saqi, 1989).

Amin, Abdul Amir, 'British Interests in the Persian Gulf' (PhD thesis, University of Leiden, 1965).

Anthony, John Duke, *The United Arab Emirates: Dynamics of State Formation* (Abu Dhabi: Emirates Centre for Strategic Studies and Research, 2002).

—, *Arab States of the Lower Gulf: People, Politics, Petroleum* (Washington DC: Middle East Institute, 1975).

(*in Arabic*) Al-Ayderus, Muhammad Hassan, *The State of the United Arab Emirates* (Kuwait: Zat Al-Salasil, 1989).

(*in Arabic*) —, *Political Developments in the United Arab Emirates* (Kuwait: Zat Al-Salasil, 1983).

(*in Arabic*) Badawi, Jamal, *Supporting the Federal System* (Abu Dhabi: Al-Ittihad Press, 1975).

(*in Arabic*) Bashir, Iskander, *The United Arab Emirates* (Beirut: Al-Khayats, 1982).

(*in Arabic*) Batikh, Ramadban Muhammad, 'The Development of Political and Constitutional Thought in the United Arab Emirates' (PhD thesis, University of the UAE, 1997).

Beck, Nelson R., 'Britain's Withdrawal from the Gulf and the Formation of the United Arab Emirates' in *Towson State Journal of International Affairs* (vol. 12, no. 2, 1978).

Belgrave, Charles, *The Pirate Coast* (London: G. Bell and Sons, 1966).

Bhargava, Pradeep, *A Political Economy of the Gulf States* (New Delhi: South Asian Publishers, 1989).

Bhutani, Surendra, The *Contemporary Gulf* (New Delhi: Academic Press, 1980).

(*in Arabic*) Bilal, Muhammad, *Changes in Population and Power Among Immigrants and Citizens of the United Arab Emirates, 1976-1980* (Sharjah: Sociologist Society, 1990).

Bowen, Richard LeBaron, 'The Pearl Fisheries of the Persian Gulf', *Middle East Journal* (vol. 5, no. 1, 1951).

Brown, Gavin, *OPEC and the World Energy Market* (London: Longman, 1998).

Bulloch, John, *The Gulf* (London: Century, 1984).

Busch, Briton, *Britain and the Persian Gulf, 1894-1914* (Los Angeles: University of California Press, 1967).

Buxani, Ram, *Taking the High Road* (Dubai: Motivate, 2003).

354

Chubin, Sharam (ed.), *Security in the Persian Gulf: Domestic Political Factors* (Montclair: Allenheld Osman, 1981).

Clements, Frank A., *United Arab Emirates: World Bibliographical Series Volume 43* (Oxford, Clio, 1998).

Codrai, Ronald, *The Seven Sheikhdoms: Life in the Trucial States Before the Federation of the United Arab Emirates* (London: Stacey International, 1990).

Collard, Elizabeth, 'Economic Prospects for the United Arab Emirates' *Middle East International* (no. 21, 1973).

Cordesman, Anthony H., *Bahrain, Oman, Qatar, and the United Arab Emirates: Challenges of Security* (Boulder: Westview, 1997).

Cotrell, Alvin (ed.), *The Persian Gulf States* (Baltimore: John Hopkins University Press, 1980).

Crystal, Jill, *Oil and Politics in the Gulf: Rulers and Merchants in Kuwait and Qatar* (New York: Cambridge University Press, 1995).

Daly, John, 'Viktor Bout: From International Outlaw to Valued Partner', *Terrorism Monitor* (vol. 2, no. 20, 2004).

Davidson, Christopher M., 'The Full Extent of Arab Nationalism and British Opposition in Dubai, 1920-1966', *Middle Eastern Studies* (vol. 43, no. 6, 2007).

—, 'The Emirates of Abu Dhabi and Dubai: Contrasting Roles in the International System' in *Asian Affairs* (vol. 38, no. 1, 2007).

—, 'After Sheikh Zayed: The Politics of Succession in Abu Dhabi and the United Arab Emirates' in *Middle East Policy* (vol. 13, no. 1, 2006).

—, *The United Arab Emirates: A Study in Survival* (Boulder: Lynne Rienner, 2005).

—, 'The United Arab Emirates: A Study in Survival' (PhD thesis, University of St, Andrews, 2003).

Davies, Charles E., *The Blood Red Arab Flag: An Investigation into Qasimi Piracy, 1797-1820* (Exeter: Exeter University Press, 1997).

Ehteshami, Anoushivaran, 'Reform From Above: The Politics of Participation in the Oil Monarchies' , *International Affairs* (vol. 79, no. 1, 2003) .

El-Din, Amin Badr, 'The Offsets Program in the United Arab Emirates', *Middle East Policy* (vol. 5, no. 1, 1997).

Fahim, Muhammad, *From Rags to Riches: A Story of Abu Dhabi* (London: Centre for Arab Studies, 1995).

Fairhall, D., *Russia Looks to the Sea* (London: 1971), p. 234.

Fenelon, Kevin, The *United Arab Emirates: An Economic and Social Survey* (London: Longman, 1973).

—, *The Trucial States: A Brief Economic Survey* (Beirut: Al-Khayats, 1969).

Field, Michael, *The Merchants: The Big Business Families of Arabia* (London: John Murray, 1984).

Findlow, Sally, 'The United Arab Emirates: Nationalism and Arab-Islamic Identity' in *Emirates Centre for Strategic Studies and Research Occasional Papers* (no. 39, 2000).

Foley, Sean, 'The United Arab Emirates: Political Issues and Security Dilemmas', *Middle East Review of International Affairs* (vol. 3, no. 1, 1998).

Gallagher, John, and Robinson, Ronald, 'The Imperialism of Free Trade', *Economic History Review* (vol. 6, no. 1, 1953).

Gause, F. Gregory, *Oil Monarchies: Domestic and Security Challenges in the Arab Gulf States* (New York: Council on Foreign Relations Press, 1994).

Ghanem, Shihab, Industrialisation in the United Arab Emirates (London: Avebury, 1992).

(*in Arabic*) Ghubash, Moza, *Human Development in the United Arab Emirates* (Abu Dhabi: Cultural Foundation, 1996).

Graham, G. S., *Great Britain in the Indian Ocean, 1810–1850* (Oxford: Stevenson, 1967).

Green, Timothy, *The World of Gold* (London: Michael Joseph, 1968).

Al-Gurg, Easa Saleh, *The Wells of Memory* (London: John Murray, 1998).

Hall, Marjorie J., *Business Laws of the United Arab Emirates* (London: Jacobs, 1987).

Hakim, Iqbal Ismail, *United Arab Emirates Central Bank and 9/11 Financing* (New York: GAAP, 2005).

(*in Arabic*) Al-Hamid, Muhammad Ahmad, 'Gulf Security and its Impact on the Gulf Cooperation Council' in *Emirates Centre for Strategic Studies and Research Occasional Papers* (no. 16, 1997).

Hawley, Donald, *The Emirates: Witness to a Metamorphosis* (Norwich: Michael Russell, 2007).

—, *The Trucial States* (London: George Allen and Unwin, 1970).

Hay, Rupert, 'The Impact of the Oil Industry on the Persian Gulf Sheikhdoms', *Middle East Journal* (vol. 9, no. 4, 1955).

Heard-Bey, Frauke, 'The United Arab Emirates: Statehood and Nation-Building in a Traditional Society', *Middle East Journal* (vol. 59, no. 3, 2005).

—, *From Trucial States to United Arab Emirates* (London: Longman, 1996).

—, 'The Gulf States and Oman in Transition', *Asian Affairs* (vol. 3, no. 1, 1972)

Henderson, Edward, *This Strange Eventful History: Memoirs of Earlier Days in the United Arab Emirates* (London: Quartet, 1988).

Herb, Michael, *All in the Family: Absolutism, Revolution, and Democracy in the Middle Eastern Monarchies* (New York: State University of New York Press, 1999).

Hitti P. K., *History of the Arabs* (London: Macmillan, 1964).

Holden, David, 'The Persian Gulf after the British Raj', *Foreign Affairs* (vol. 49, no. 4, 1971).

Holden, David, *Farewell to Arabia* (New York: Faber and Faber, 1966).

Hopwood, Derek, The *Arabian Peninsula* (London: 1972).

Hudson, Michael (ed.) *Middle East Dilemma: The Politics and Economics of Arab Integration* (London: IB Tauris, 1999).

Huntington, Samuel P., *Political Order in Changing Societies* (New Haven: Yale University Press, 1968).

Hvidt, Martin, 'Public-Private Ties and their Contribution to Development: The Case of Dubai', *Middle Eastern Studies* (vol. 43, no. 4, 2007).

Hyam, Ronald, *Britain's Imperial Century, 1815-1914: A Study of Empire and Expansion* (London: Macmillan, 1976).

(*in Arabic*) Ibrahim, Abdul-Aziz, *Britain and the Emirates of the Omani Coast* (Baghdad: Matba'at al-Irshad, 1978).

(*in Arabic*) Ibrahim, Muhammad, *Foundations of the Political and Constitutional Organisation of the United Arab Emirates* (Abu Dhabi: 1975).

(*in Arabic*) Isa, Shakir Musa, *The Experience of the United Arab Emirates* (Beirut: Al-Khayats, 1981).

Ismael, Jacqueline, *Kuwait: Dependency and Class in a Rentier State* (Gainesville: University of Florida Press, 1993).

Johns, Richard, 'The Emergence of the United Arab Emirates', *Middle East International* (vol. 21, 1973).

Joyce, Miriam, 'On the Road Towards Unity: The Trucial States from a British Perspective, 1960-1966', *Middle Eastern Studies* (vol. 35, no. 2, 1999).

(*in Arabic*) Kawari, Ali Khalifa, and Al-Sadun, Jasim, The *Gulf Cooperation Council Countries: A Futuristic View* (Kuwait: Girttas, 1996).

Kazim, Aqil, *The United Arab Emirates: A Socio-Discursive Transformation in the Arabian Gulf* (Dubai: Gulf Book Centre, 2000).

Kelly, John B., *Arabia, the Gulf, and the West: A Critical View of the Arabs and their Oil Policy* (New York: Basic Books, 1986).

—, *Britain and the Persian Gulf* (Oxford: Oxford University Press, 1968).

—, *Eastern Arabia Frontier* (New York: Prager, 1964).

Khalaf, Sulayman, 'Poetics and Politics of Newly Invented Traditions in the Gulf: Camel Racing in the United Arab Emirates', *Ethnology* (vol. 39, no. 3, 2000).

—, 'Gulf Societies and the Image of Unlimited Good', *Dialectical Anthropology* (vol. 17, no. 1, 1992).

Khalifa, Ali Muhammad, *The United Arab Emirates: Unity in Fragmentation* (Boulder: Westview, 1979).

Khoury, Enver M., *The United Arab Emirates: Its Political System and Politics* (Maryland: Institute for Middle Eastern and North African Affairs, 1980).

Kostiner, Joseph (ed.), *Middle East Monarchies: The Challenge of Modernity* (Boulder: Lynne Rienner, 2000).

Al-Kuwari, Ali Khalifa, *Oil Revenues in the Gulf Emirates: Patterns of Allocation and Impact on Economic Development* (Essex: Bowker, 1978).

Kuzio, Taras, 'Loose Nukes and Al-Qaida', *Terrorism Monitor* (vol. 2, no. 6, 2004),

Laquer, Walter, *The Struggle for the Middle East* (London: Routledge, 1969).

Lienhardt, Peter, *Sheikhdoms of Eastern Arabia* (Oxford: Palgrave, 2001).

—, 'The Authority of Sheikhs in the Gulf: An Essay in Nineteenth Century History' in *Arabian Studies* (vol. 2, no. 1, 1975).

Long, David, *The Persian Gulf* (Boulder: Westview, 1978).

Lorimer, John G., *Gazetteer of the Persian Gulf, Oman, and Central Arabia* (London: Gregg International Publishers, 1970).

Luce, Margaret, *From Aden to the Gulf: Personal Diaries, 1956-1966* (Salisbury, Michael Russell, 1987).

Al-Madfai, Madiha Rashid, *Jordan, the United States and the Middle East Peace Process, 1974-1991* (Cambridge: Cambridge University Press, 1993).

Maitra, Jayanti, and Al-Hajji, Afra, *Qasr Al-Hosn: The History and Rulers of Abu Dhabi, 1793-1966* (Abu Dhabi: Centre for Documentation and Research, 2001).

(*in Arabic*) Al-Majd, Kamal Abu, *The Constitutional System of the United Arab Emirates* (Cairo: 1978).

El-Mallakh, Ragi, Economic *Development in the United Arab Emirates* (New York: St, Martin's, 1981).

Mann, Clarence, *Abu Dhabi: Birth of an Oil Sheikhdom* (Beirut: Al-Khayats, 1969).

Mellamid, Alexander, 'The Buraimi Oasis Dispute', *Middle Eastern Affairs* (vol. 7, no. 2, 1956).

Mobley, Richard A., 'The Tunbs and Abu Musa Islands: Britain's Perspective' in *Middle East Journal* (vol. 57, no. 4, 2003).

Moyse-Bartlett, Hubert, *The Pirates of Trucial Oman* (London: Macdonald, 1966).

Al-Musfir, Muhammad Salih, 'The United Arab Emirates: An Assessment of Federalism in a Developing Polity' (PhD thesis, State University of New York and Binghamton, 1985).

(*in Arabic*) Mutawa, Muhammad A, *Development ad Social Change in the Emirates* (Beirut: Al-Farabi, 1991).

Al-Nabeh, Najat Abdullah, 'United Arab Emirates: Regional and Global Dimensions' (PhD thesis, Claremont Graduate School, 1984).

Al-Nahyan, Shamma bint Muhammad, *Political and Social Security in the United Arab Emirates* (Dubai: 2000).

Al-Nahyan, Sultan bin Khalifa, *National Security of the United Arab Emirates: A Perspective in Light of Global Changes to the New World Order* (London: Rivermill, 2003).

(*in Arabic*) Al-Naqib, Khaldun H., *The Authoritarian State in the Contemporary Arab Mashriq: A Comparative Structural Study* (Beirut: Al-Khayats, 1991).

Niblock, Tim (ed.), *Social and Economic Development in the Arab Gulf* (London: Croom Helm, 1980).

Nonneman, Gerd, 'Rentiers and Autocrats, Monarchs and Democrats, State and Society: The Middle East between Globalisation, Human Agency, and Europe' *International Affairs* (vol. 77, no. 1, 2001).

Onley, James, *The Arabian Frontier of the British Raj: Merchants, Rulers, and the British in the Nineteenth-Century Gulf* (Oxford: Oxford University Press, 2007).

—, 'Britain's Native Agents in Arabia and Persia, 1758-1958', *Comparative Studies of South Asia, Africa, and the Middle East* (no. 33, 2003).

Al-Otaibi, Manna Said, *The Petroleum Concession Agreements of the United Arab Emirates* (London: Croom Helm, 1982).

(*in Arabic*) Al-Otaibi, Manna Said, *Petroleum and the Economy of the United Arab Emirates* (Kuwait: Al-Qabas Press, 1977).

Overton, J. L., 'Stability and Change: Inter-Arab Politics in the Arabian Peninsula and the Gulf' (PhD thesis, University of Maryland, 1983) .

Pal, Dharm, 'British Policy Towards the Arabian Tribes on the Shores of the Persian Gulf, 1964-1868', *Journal of Indian History* (vol. 24, no. 1, 1945).

Parshotam, Mehra, *Dictionary of Modern Indian History, 1707–1947* (New York: Oxford University Press, 1985).

Peck, Malcolm, *The United Arab Emirates: A Venture in Unity* (Boulder: Westview, 1986).

Peterson, John E., 'The United Arab Emirates: Economic Vibrancy and US Interests', *Asian Affairs* (vol. 34, no. 2, 2003).

—, 'The Nature of Succession in the Gulf', *Middle East Journal* (vol. 55, no. 4, 2001),

—, 'The Arab Gulf States: Steps Towards Political Participation' in *Washington Papers* (no. 131, 1988),

—, and Sindelar, Richard (eds) *Crosscurrents in the Gulf* (London: Routledge, 1988).

Philips, C., *The East Indian Company 1784-1834* (Manchester: Manchester University Press, 1961).

Pope, M. T. G., *Businessman's Guide to the United Arab Emirates* (Sharjah: Dar al-Fatah, 1996).

Pridham, B. (ed.), *The Arab Gulf and the West* (London: Croom Helm, 1975).

(*in Arabic*) Al-Qadir, Mustafa, *Contemporary Studies on the History of the Arabian Gulf* (Cairo: 1978).

(*in Arabic*) Qasim, Jamal Zakariyya, *Old Emirates and New State* (Cairo: 1978).

(*in Arabic*) Al-Qasimi, Nora Muhammad, *The Indian Existence in the Arabian Gulf, 1820-1947* (Sharjah: Department of Education, 2000).

Al-Qasimi, Sultan bin Muhammad, *The Myth of Arab Piracy in the Gulf* (London: Croom Helm, 1986).

Ramahi, Saif, and El-Wady, A., *Economic and Political Evolution in the Arabian Gulf States* (New York: Carlton, 1973).

(*in Arabic*) Al-Rahman, Abdullah Abd, *The Emirates in the Memory of its Children* (Dubai: Dubai Printing Press, 1990).

(*in Arabic*) Rashid, Ali Muhammad, *Political and Economic Agreements Made Between the Oman Coast Emirates and Britain, 1806-1971* (Sharjah: UAE Writer's Union Publications, 1989).

Reynolds, David, *Britannia Overruled: British Policy and World Power in the Twentieth Century* (Harlow: Longman, 1991).

Rizvi, S.N. Asad, 'From Tents to High Rise: Economic Development of the United Arab Emirates', *Middle Eastern Studies* (vol. 29, no. 4, 1993).

Robinson, Adam, *Bin Laden: Behind the Mask of the Terrorist* (New York: Arcade, 2002), pp. 91-93.

Rugh, Andrea B., *The Political Culture of Leadership in the United Arab Emirates* (New York: Palgrave Macmillan, 2007).

Rugh, William A., 'The United Arab Emirates: What are the Sources of its Stability?' in *Middle East Policy* (vol. 5, no. 3, 1997).

(*in Arabic*) Al-Rumaithi, Muhammad G., *The Impediments to Development in the Contemporary Arab Societies of the Gulf* (Kuwait: Matabi Dar al-Siyasah, 1977).

(*in Arabic*) Al-Rumaithi, Muhammad G., *Petroleum and Social Change in the Arabian Gulf* (Cairo: Dar al-Shab, 1975).

Rush, Alan (ed.), *Ruling Families of Arabia: The United Arab Emirates* (Slough: Archive Editions 1991).

Sadiq, Muhammad, and Snavely, William, *Bahrain, Qatar, and the United Arab Emirates: Colonial Past, Present Problems, and Future Prospects* (Lexington: Heath, 1972).

Al-Sagri, Saleh Hamad, 'Britain and the Arab Emirates, 1820-1956' (PhD thesis, University of Kent at Canterbury, 1988).

Sassen, Saskia, *Cities in a World Economy* (London: Sage, 2000).

Al-Sayegh, Fatma, 'Merchants' Role in a Changing Society: The Case of Dubai, 1900-1990', *Middle Eastern Studies* (vol. 34, no. 1, 1998).

(*in Arabic*) —, *The United Arab Emirates: From Tribe to State* (Dubai: Al-Khaleej Books, 1997).

(*in Arabic*) Al-Shamlan, Saif Marzuq, *History of Pearl Diving in Kuwait and the Arabian Gulf* (Kuwait: Zat al-Salasil, 1989).

Al-Shamsi, Said Muhammad, 'The Buraimi Dispute: A Case Study in Inter-Arab Politics' (PhD thesis, American University, 1986).

(*in Arabic*) Sharabah, Naji Sadiq, *The United Arab Emirates: Politics and Rulership* (Abu Dhabi: Al-Kitab al-Jamiy, 1995).

(*in Arabic*) —, 'The Federal Experiment of the United Arab Emirates, 1971-1977' (PhD thesis, University of Cairo, 1980).

(*in Arabic*) Sharaf, Muhammad Yasir, *United Arab Emirates Society* (Abu Dhabi: Al-Mutanabi Books, 1997).

Slot, B, J, *Mubarak Al-Sabah: Founder of Modern Kuwait, 1896-1915* (London: Arabian Publishing, 2005).

Suwaidi, Jamal S. (ed.), *The Gulf: Challenges of the Future* (Abu Dhabi: Emirates Centre for Strategic Studies and Research, 2005).

(*in Arabic*) Tabatabai, Adil, *Comparative Studies in the Emirates* (Cairo: 1978).

Tammam, Hamdi, *Zayed bin Sultan Al-Nahyan: The Leader on the March* (Tokyo: Dai Nippon, 1983).

Taryam, Abdullah, *The Establishment of the United Arab Emirates, 1950-1985* (London: Croom Helm, 1987).

Thesiger, Wilfred, *Arabian Sands* (London: Penguin, 1991).

Tomkinson, Michael, *The United Arab Emirates* (London: Jarrold and Sons, 1975).

Van Der Meulen, Hendrik, 'The Role of Tribal and Kinship Ties in the Politics of the United Arab Emirates' (PhD thesis, The Fletcher School of Law and Diplomacy, 1997).

Vassiliev, Alexei, 'Financing Terror: From Bogus Banks to Honey Bees', *Terrorism Monitor* (vol. 1, no. 4, 2003).

Wheatcroft, Andrew, *With United Strength: Sheikh Zayed bin Sultan Al-Nahyan, the Leader and the Nation* (Abu Dhabi, Emirates Centre for Strategic Studies and Research, 2005).

Wilson, Graeme, *Rashid's Legacy: The Genesis of the Maktoum Family and the History of Dubai* (Dubai: Media Prima, 2006).

Wilston, John, 'The Roots of Extremism in Bangladesh', *Terrorism Monitor* (vol. 3, no. 1, 2005).

Wriggins, Howard (ed.), *The Dynamics of Regional Politics: Four Systems on the Indian Ocean Rim* (New York: Columbia University Press, 1992).

Yassman, Victor, 'The Russian Criminal World Played a Key Role in Chechnya and Continues to Do So', *Terrorism Monitor* (vol. 1, no. 8, 1995).

Yeager, Rodger, *Tanzania: An African Experiment* (Boulder: Westview, 1983).

Yorke, Valerie, *The Gulf in the 1980s* (London: Royal Institute of International Affairs, 1980).

363

Zahlan, Rosemarie Said, *The Making of the Modern Gulf States* (London: Unwin Hyman, 1989).

—, *The Origins of the United Arab Emirates* (New York: St, Martin's, 1978).

INDEX